MW01245158

ened critic. Dr. Channing, moreover, was a Unitarian, a sect which is not powerful in the United States, and which is much vilified by the orthodox in Britain; and yet he dared to encounter the prejudices of his countrymen when the orthodox in general took counsel of discretion.

The extent of this merit cannot be appreciated by those who have not lived in the United States. The New York Evangelist says, "The truth is, that ministers are so dependent upon the money-making part, and so easily influenced by the fashionable part of their congregations, that, however forcibly they may preach against sin in general, there is a great want of that moral courage which will point out particular and popular sins, and say to their audiences, ' Ye are the men.' " Dr. Channing has not only said to his countrymen, " Ye are the men," but has represented to them in the boldest manner the principles which they, as Christians, are bound to follow; regardless equally of " the money-making" and " fashionable" portions of his congregation and the community at large.

If the Edinburgh Review had come forward in a spirit worthy of its own principles and of its former fame, and added its influence to give effect to these generous efforts, it would not indeed have raised Dr. Channing's reputation on either side of the Atlantic, for happily this is beyond its control, but would have done credit to itself and the country which gives it birth. The course which it has actually followed, has gratified the enemies of Dr. Channing in America, encouraged them in their depreciation of his talents and usefulness, and made the friends of moral, religious, and political freedom lament the decay of what once was the vigorous champion of the great and the good.

CHAPTER V.

Cape Cottage—Portland—Jeremy Bentham—Phrenology—Hartford in Connecticut—Phrenology—Advertisements—The Banks—Miss Martineau and the Ladies of Boston—The Amistad Africans—The Militia—The Late War—The New England Voice—Phrenology—Sunday—Education and Phrenology—Phrenology—The People of Connecticut—Religious Denominations in Connecticut—The Politicians—Fires—Mrs. Sigourney—Bank Suspension—The Deaf and Dumb—Phrenology—Natural Language—The Temperaments—Taxes—Sunday—Effects of the Institutions of England and America—The Eglinton Tournament—Education in the State of New York.

1839.

SEPT. 12. Ther. 55°. *Cape Cottage.*—We have now resided eight weeks in this delightful retreat, and I borrow the description of it from C——'s letter to a friend. " Here you may picture us quietly seated in our summer retreat, a handsome, rather large cottage, built of wood, clap-boarded, and painted white, with those green outside window-shutters which give such an air of coolness and neatness to New England cottages in general. Cape Cottage stands upon Cape Elizabeth, a projecting point, jutting out into Casco Bay, and forming one of its extremities. It lies three miles and a half from Portland, whether by a good road or by the sea. Casco Bay is full of islands beautifully grouped; common report states them to amount to 300, but the fisherman whose boat we hire to carry us among them, limits their number to 43. Portland Harbor, which is formed by an indentation in the land, is protected from the Atlantic on all sides by these islands, through which, however, several channels allow ships to approach it from various points. Nothing can exceed the picturesque beauty of the vessels when appearing and disappearing through these openings. The harbor is defended by two forts, named after natives of Portland, Fort Preble, on the main land, and opposite to it on an island, Fort Scammel. The Americans have improved the name of the cape, by changing the Indian ' Pooduc' into ' Cape Elizabeth;' but they have been less successful with the islands, to three of which they have given the unpoetical appellations of ' Hog,' ' House,' and ' Bang.' The main channel to the harbor lies in front of our windows, at the distance of a hundred yards. It is about one mile broad, and is bounded on the opposite side by Hog Island. We enjoy a view of the vessels bound to and from Portland, and certainly no craft can look better under a soft southern breeze and a bright sun; for their sprightly elegant forms glide like nautilus shells on a ground of lapis lazuli, with their white sails unsullied by dirt or coal-smoke.

" The coast is rocky, and not unlike that of Cullercoats on our own northeastern shores. The rocks are of mica-slate, which is not always a very picturesque formation; but here they contain iron, which, by rusting, has subjected them to disintegration, and the waves have torn them into manifold forms, and strewed them about in a thousand fantastic groups. They seem as if fashioned for the very purpose of delighting the idler; you may scramble over them for miles, and every pinnacle will afford you a varied view; or you may sit under their shade, screened from all winds and from the sun at every hour of the day. Here you may ruminate on ocean, earth, and heaven, and, if fond of adventure, you may, by indulging in a little absence of mind, be surrounded by the tide, and become a living statue ornamenting a craggy point of rock, till the falling waters set you free. From this grandeur of devastation and disorder, you are brought by a sweep of the coast into a sweet, placid, little bay, where you would think the miniature wavelets could never swell into fury, and yet we have seen the Atlantic, when roused by a northeasterly gale, pour terrific masses of water into those seemingly peaceful retreats.

" The place is essentially scenic: every white sail that starts out from behind a jutting rock makes you think that an adventure ought to belong to it, and every man who takes up a fishing-rod, and places himself on an eminence, however common-looking before, is immediately transformed into a picturesque object, and is invested with interest. Although Nature has not endowed me with those strong perceptive faculties that constitute enthusiasts in scenery, yet a fine prospect appeals also to the moral part of our nature, and leads us, by a process too rapid for analysis, from physical to mental beauty, and to its Author, Infinite Goodness. I can seldom recall to my mind's eye, as some persons can, any scene, however lovely or however dear, but, through my mind's affections, it may be long remembered. I sit on these rocks and recall the songs of the sea that I used to hear in my dear native land, and among them comes oftenest back that sweet ode of Mrs. Hemans, " The Treasures of the Deep," in the tones of my own fascinating cousin Mrs. A——.

" The land that skirts the coast is like our English downs, grassy and gently undulating, with here a projecting rock and there a little pool. It affords pasture to cattle, sheep, and horses, and is all open to the footsteps of the wanderer. Beyond this, the country is divided into small farms, the possessors of which are also many of them fishermen, whose neat white cottages gleam forth from amidst brushwood, tall Indian corn, and rather stunted trees. As we range along the shore, one ear drinks in the murmur of the waves and the splashing of oars, whilst the other feeds on the notes of American robins, the sharpening of scythes, and the lowing of herds.

"These rural sounds, I am sorry to say, are not always pleasant. In a ramble I took a few days ago, I was distressed by the peculiarly plaintive tone in which a cow, standing alone by a barn, was lowing. 'What's the matter with her?' I asked of a man who leaned over the wall. 'Calf killed,' was his abrupt reply; and as he spoke he spread a fresh skin on the wall. The poor mother recognised it, ran up to it, began licking it, and smelling to the little hoofs that hung down, she then looked into the man's face and lowed most piteously; and again caressed the remains of her lost darling! 'She'll go on that way for four or five days', said her master; and sure enough it was so, for I never passed that way, for more days than four, that I did not hear her plaintive tones.

"A profusion of wild flowers, some of which are cultivated in gardens at home, may be gathered on the downs and in the fields. Our parlor is generally adorned with bouquets of them, including fragrant dog-roses that grow even in the clefts of the rocks quite down to the margin of the tide. Wild raspberries, of excellent quality, wild strawberries, and the whortleberry, or Scotch "blaeberry," abound everywhere. They, an excellent sea-fishing, attract numerous parties of pleasure from Portland, who arrive, some in handsome barges by the bay, others in equipages of all varieties of form by the road: they spend a few hours rambling singly or in groups, give liveliness to the scene, and return home in the evening. The fields also are alive with grasshoppers, large and small, which hop into your face without ceremony, and are often brought home and hung up in one's closet in some fold of dress, from which they skip forth next morning much to their own gratification and to our surprise. Besides the shrill chirping, which is the only sound uttered by our English grasshoppers, some of these emit a noise like that of castanets in action, or the tapping with an iron-shod walking-stick on a hard stone. Nobody can tell me whether this sound proceeds from the Cicadæ; but, from watching them, I perceive that the individuals which make it are larger than their chirping brothers. As you walk along, you encounter also whole clouds of primrose-colored butterflies, and pale blue diagon-flies. These are harmless, I wish we could say as much of those blood-thirsty mosquitoes, which infest us everywhere, and seem as if sent to remind us, amidst all these sweets, that we are still in a world of mingled good and evil. My poor husband has lain on the sofa for three weeks, lame with their bites on his ankles, and is only now again able to walk. My own eyes have often been closed up for days by the mountainous swellings with which they have been encircled, but, thanks to Providence, the mosquitoes have generally taken them in turns, and left me one at a time fit for use. We have learned, however, to exclude them from our rooms. We have nailed catgut muslin over every window, through which they find it difficult to squeeze even their slender bodies; and this, with ablutions of camphorated spirits, nearly frees us from their in-door intrusion.

" We have hired a horse and gig from Captain ——, (a respectable butcher in Portland), and had delightful drives into the country. The ground in general, within 10 or 12 miles of our cottage, is pleasing and rural, without being either rich or highly cultivated, and in this dry season most of the roads are good. Every drive brings us within sight of the ocean or the bay, at one point or another; and three tall snow-white towers, crowned with lanterns, and used as lighthouses, are pretty objects in the scene. The condition of the country and people is obviously behind that of the rural population in Connecticut and Massachusetts; but the abundance of spruce firs, generally grouped in small masses, the undulating and verdant surface, and the detached farm-houses and offices, constantly remind me of England. and, in many points of view, of the "Park" of some great earl. Here you seldom see a cottage, however small, that is not brilliant with white paint, and verdant with green shutters, and without something like a garden about it, producing a pleasing impression of cleanliness and comfort.

" A few days ago some one brought up to the house a portion of common sea-weed, which, by a freak of nature, had grown into the exact similitude of a lady's mantelet or cloak, such as have been lately worn in the world of fashion. It was double, and trimmed round with what was doubtless intended for an embroidered flouncing, since it had regular holes in it like what our grandmothers called punching. It was of a very becoming form, I assure you: they are not uncommon here, both of green and brown colors, so we may suit our complexions in the article, which, perhaps, some mermaid mantua-maker has sent up, in hopes to decoy the poor thoughtless lovers of finery to her emporium below the waves!

" But it is time that I should introduce you to the interior of our cottage. It would never do for an American rural retreat; for, although a 'public house,' as they name a hotel, it is of such moderate dimensions, that the family of one of the ministers of Portland, that of a senator from Maine to Congress, and ourselves, with the landlord and his family, fill it. This is exactly to our taste, but would be very humdrum to those who rejoice in the crowds of Saratoga, or the White Sulphur Springs of Virginia. At breakfast, dinner, and tea, we form a very agreeable family party, and, as we have our separate parlors, we have retirement at command when desired. We find our fellow-·boarders,' as we are called here, excellent and agreeable society. The senator has been in England, and, when in Edinburgh, visited Sir Walter Scott, to whom he carried letters of introduction. Sir Walter played off a little hoax on him, which he never discovered till we told him of it. The 'Great Unknown' took him, as his friend, to a public entertainment, given on the occasion of the coronation of William IV, and placed him near Mr. Blackwood, the celebrated bookseller, who was then a bailie, and wore a massive gold chain round his neck, as an insignium of office. Sir Walter introduced the American to Mr. Blackwood, and whispered into his ear, 'You must always call him *my lord;* he is a bailie!' The senator did as he was directed, and it was only on my husband telling him that a bailie is not styled 'my lord' in Edinburgh that he became aware of the trick. 'Oh, then,' said he, laughing, 'the humorous baronet has been playing off the Yankee against the bailie, and enjoying the joke all the while in his sleeve.' Add to this society visits from various friends in Portland, and from one of the best of Boston's accomplished sons—one engaged in kindred pursuits with my husband, who has come hither and spent several days with us, and you have a picture of our social parties.

"We boast of no finery in our cottage, but it will vie with a palace for order and cleanliness; our fare is not such as would suit a London alderman, but it is abundant, savory, and well-cooked. Air, exercise, and minds agreeably occupied, yet void of care, give an exquisite relish to our dinners of fresh fish, (cunners and polloks caught by the rod on the rocks, by the master of the inn, his son, or their boys), our 'chowder,' or fish-soup, our young Indian corn, and our squash—the last a very delicate vegetable, I assure you, notwithstanding its frightfully vulgar name. Fowls, turkeys, beef, veal, and mutton, make up our fare, and we are in no danger of suffering want either of substance or variety in our meals.

"You hear much of the want of respect and other faults in the manners of the people here, and, perhaps, if you had seen our hostess quietly keep the seat in our room in which I found her this morning, and heard her tell me, while I was standing before her, that she was trying my air-cushion, and continue to ask various questions about it, without rising, you would have imagined that this was a confirmation of the fact: But in incidents of this kind the *manner* is every thing. Our hostess is a naturally genteel woman, and had not the slightest idea of intruding; her curiosity to understand the nature of the air-cushion bespoke an active intelligence, of which we enjoy the advantage in her management of the general affairs of her household. Besides, in this country, such freedoms do not constitute marks of disrespect, and every land should be tried by its own laws of politeness. Those stiff-necked persons who cannot turn to the right or the left as the road bends, had better stay at home, and enjoy their rigid postures in their own chimney-corners. At the same time, I must remark that in this country, where equality is the birth-right of all, *manners* should form a much more important branch of education than they do. There are many persons who, through thoughtlessness, or selfishness, or mere ignorance, are in the habit of committing offences against delicacy, refinement, and common sense. These certainly should be taught, with all possible celerity and assiduity, that in a state of society where all ranks may mingle together, and where the lowest may be found in juxtaposition with the highest, *all* are bound to conduct themselves so that they shall not be an annoyance to any. My husband tells them pithily that if they be all sovereigns, as they claim to be, they are bound to be all gentlemen. I go so far with this idea that I maintain that this not only should, but, by proper training in childhood, *might* be the case in all societies. Look at the manners of the poorest children who have been well trained in one of Wilderspin's infant schools; they are inoffensive and well bred, and the sum of their own enjoyment is not diminished by this accomplishment: Nay, it is increased; for good breeding is the consequence of the education of the moral sentiments, which leads to refinement as well as to virtue. We often hear of an aristocracy of intellect. I wish that all over the world we saw an aristocracy of good breeding: If such existed, political equality would not be far distant.

" But I am writing a dissertation, when I meant only to give you a description. I must introduce you, then, to mine host's eldest daughter Tabby. She is an excellent, sensible, and obliging young woman, and between her and me there have been amicable interchanges of books and other civilities. Her collection of books comprises Byron, Moore, Mrs. Hemans, &c. in poetry; a full and well written history of the North American Indian tribes; a description of Herculaneum and Pompeii; a

History of all Religions, and many other works. Well, Tabby has just come in to borrow a dress for a pattern, to which I made her most welcome. I mention this incident only to assure you that it may be done, and has been done, without the least shadow of that offensive familiarity which has been attributed to such a request by some of our English historians of American manners. I am quite sure that Tabby would have had pleasure in lending me any of her patterns, and thinks that in borrowing mine she but increases the sum of general enjoyment without in the least deducting from particular advantage. It was a pleasure to me to oblige her; and I can testify besides, that there was no domestic duty which could add to my comfort, which Tabby did not as cheerfully perform as if she had never either owned a work on poetry or borrowed the pattern of a piece of dress.

" The youngest daughter of this family might sit for a picture of Laura or Beatrice. Her face is lovely, with the real golden hair parted from her smooth white brow, and the very peculiarly rich chesnut colored eyes, which are so rare and so beautiful. This girl, if her form were equal to her face, would be one of the fairest creatures I have seen in this land of fair ones. These girls, and the fishermen, and the boys who attend to the horses and carriages that come here, may be seen strolling together among the wild raspberries, or conversing familiarly under the large portico (with which all American inns are furnished), a perfect specimen of equality; but if you imagine by this that the girls permit, or the men offer, rude jesting, romping, or other improprieties of behavior, you commit the error of supposing them to be, in manners and feelings, the exact counterparts of our own people of the same station, which is not the case. Their 'sovereignty' has at least taught them self-respect, and this is a great means of insuring respect from others.

" It is a great comfort to us to be served by the landlord's daughters, and by his wife as cook; for the want of ' help' is as great an evil here as in other parts of the Union A lady of note, in speaking to me of the flourishing state of the cotton factories at Saco, fifteen miles from Portland, said, ' If you want to know the real aristocracy of this country, look at the factory girls;—they will not come to us as servants—they make us work much harder in our kitchens than they do at their spinning-jennies. It would be all fair if we and they could ride and tie; but absolutely it is we who are the domestic drudges.' This you will think is a sad picture of life in a democracy, but, as you are a benevolent lady, perhaps the cause of it may lessen your regrets. These factory girls are the daughters of small proprietors who farm their own lands, or of respectable tradesmen; they engage in labor to make up a little purse for marriage, or to help an old father and mother, and they naturally prefer that kind of work which yields them the best return. The factory owners pay them two, or two and a half dollars a week of wages, and, in domestic service, they could not obtain much above one-half of this sum.

" If you are not tired of my descriptions, I will introduce you to two more of our friends and companions—fine young New-foundland Dash, with an ingenuous earnest countenance, ever watching for our casting sticks into the bay that he may swim and bring them back; and little stuffy Yorick, with eyes so clear that I think they must be made of Labrador pebbles, and whose bark is the most perfect expression of self-importance, seemingly uttered to warn the meaner crowd to preserve their proper distance.

"How do we spend our time? In reading, writing, walking, driving, talking, scrambling, and sitting amidst those delicious rocks, in balmy air! The hours fly like minutes, and the days like hours. One amusement of my husband's amuses me. You must know that Portland is a great port for ' the lumber trade'—Anglicè, the log and deal trade; and the coast of the bay is literally strewed with deal-ends and fragments of wood of all shapes and sizes. He gathers those that suit his purpose, fashions them with his knife into the form of ships, fits rudders and masts to them, uses the outer surface of birch bark for sails, and sends them forth into the bay or the Atlantic, as the wind answers. We see them scudding joyously before the gentle southwest wind out into the ocean. If any of them reach your coast, capture them and condemn them as lawful prizes. Another of our amusements is watching the great ' sea sarpent.' I think that we have found out what perhaps has given rise to some of the stories you may have read about it. One night there was a brisk gale from the southwest, and the appearance of stormy weather. In the morning the porpoises came rolling in to this harbor in great numbers, and some of them of enormous size. They followed each other in a long straight line, and as the backs of a dozen of them in different parts of this line shot up, at the same moment, a small stretch of imagination could supply solid substance to the watery spaces between them, and thus picture them as one continuous creature. Our host, who is a sensible man, gravely asked if we had seen the ' sea sarpent,' ' who,' said he, ' with his family, is reported to be somewhere off this coast.' I heard him put the same question to a chance fisherman, who answered as gravely, ' Oh yes, we've run along side of him for ten miles!' The only drawback, besides the mosquitoes, to our enjoyment, is periodical visitations of dense fogs. They come so regularly every Monday, that we at last reckon them as due on that day.

They blot out by their leaden vapor all our lovely islands, bays, roses, cliffs, and even the foaming surge, as if they had never been. One day, as I stood under the portico, the mist opened for a few seconds, just sufficient to show the steamboat from Boston, like a dim ghost, dripping with the heavy fog, and laboring most disconsolately into port; having, as we afterwards heard, been obliged twice to take refuge on her voyage. She gave us one melancholy glance and groan, and was again shrouded from our view.

"1'th September. This afternoon, dear ———, we must bid adieu to our pretty cottage and all its *agrémens*. I have taken my last look of those rocks and waves, and grassy seats, and sunny islands, and I am sad to part with them! It is strange to find one's affections taken captive by a place which one could see only for a few weeks, and which we must leave without the remotest prospect of ever revisiting it: but so it is—our affections answer to the calls of their objects, and leave reason to decide in its own way on the wisdom of their doing so. I have stored my memory with images of goodness, peace, and beauty, and so, my dear Casco Bay, I will not repent of knowing you, though I must leave you behind. You are lying in a glorious sunshine on our last interview, and I carry off your last smile of loveliness as that by which you shall hereafter live in my memory and affections—adieu. I am," &c.   C. C.

September 12. Ther. 55°. *Portland.*—This afternoon we left Cape Cottage. and came in a fine barge with two sails to Portland. The evening was delightful, the sea smooth, and the wind fair. The town looked beautiful as we approached it by water. It stands on the slope of a ridge, and from the manner in which it is built, looks very large for its population, which is only 16.000 inhabitants. We remained six days in the town, and enjoyed the hospitality of many friends, who had formed our acquaintance at the Cottage. The society of Portland appeared to us to be very agreeable, and free from form and ceremony. We were entertained at dinner, tea, and evening parties, every day that we remained, and felt new regrets in leaving so many kind and interesting friends.

Phrenology.—Among other gentlemen in Portland who take an interest in Phrenology we became acquainted with Mr. John Neal, a lawyer and a distinguished author in the United States. He gave me "The New England Galaxy for January and February 1835," to read, on account of the report which it contains of a trial of a boy, in whose defence he had pleaded and led evidence, avowedly on phrenological principles. The case was the following.—

In the month of July 1834, a boy of nine years of age, named

Major Mitchell, the natural son of a poor woman living at Durham, 23 miles from Portland, actuated by some provocation offered to him by David F. Crawford, a boy of eight years of age, induced this boy, by threats and promises. to go with him into a wood to get some flags. When there, Mitchell beat Crawford with his fists, then stript off his clothes, bound him to a tree with the suspenders of his breeches, and flogged him with twigs from head to foot to the effusion of his blood, castrated him with a piece of tin, and then attempted to drown him in a pool. Crawford at last escaped from his hands, and arrived at home lacerated and naked. Mr. Neal finding the boy Mitchell prosecuted criminally by the Commonwealth, and friendless, undertook his defence. He learned from his mother that. "when about a week old, he fell off a high chest on the floor, and was taken up for dead. He struck on the top of his head, and when lifted his hands were clenched and his head swollen." He had been at school, but had never advanced beyond spelling words of one syllable. His head presented a very large development of Destructiveness, also large Acquisitiveness and Secretiveness, deficient moral organs, but a fair development of the anterior lobe. Mr. Neal considered that his brain had been injured, and that he was partially idiotic.

The defence was 1st, The deficiency of evidence of the facts; 2dly, The great improbability of the alleged mutilation having been perpetrated by the accused; and 3dly, That his conduct, if according to the accusation, proceeded from injuries sustained by his brain in his infancy. The second defence rested on the trifling nature of the wound, as observed when the boy came home, and the fact that one of Crawford's brothers was deficient naturally in this respect, whence it was probable that this boy was so too. The third defence was supported by medical authorities and testimony.

Mr. Neal proposed to put in as evidence, "Spurzheim on Insanity," voce Fatuity, p. 104 of the first American edition: "Combe's System of Phrenology, case of E. S." &c.; but he was met by the objection, that in the case of *Ware* v. *Ware*, 8 Grem. 1. 56, the supreme court had decided, that "medical books of the highest authority" were not competent evidence. He called Dr. Jesse W. Mighles as a witness, who testified as follows: "I am a believer in Phrenology as a science. Great changes have taken place in the treatment of insanity, as well as in the mode of dissecting the brain, since that work (Dr. Spurzheim's) appeared. I have examined the prisoner's head; there *is* something remarkable in it—a very unnatural *depression*. I presume it is congenital. All heads are more or less deficient in symmetry, but the *want* of symmetry *here* is quite remarkable. I have examined it repeatedly before, and had come to the conclusion long ago, before I was called, that some injury had probably happened to it. The right ear is lower than the left, and there is a considerable protuberance on that side. An injury to the muscle of that ear, caused by a fall or blow on the head, might naturally produce these appearances. Certain functions of the brain may cease in consequence of a blow—the functional power (of a part) may be destroyed, while the rest continue undisturbed. Such is the doctrine of the books, and I believe it.''

Cross examined—''I do not speak of this destruction of the functional power of the brain in part, while other parts continue uninjured, from experience. Change of moral or intellectual character might appear a twelvemonth after the injury, from irritation or inflammation.''

Mr. Neal proceeded to ask certain questions at the witness as a phrenologist. The Attorney-General objected, and Mr. Neal maintained his right. ''At this moment the court interfered and asked a question, which resulted in a declaration by the witness, that he could not, of his *own knowledge*, say that such and such enlargements of a given organ would produce a correspondent change of character. He *believed*, although he did not *know* of his own knowledge, that a blow on the head might change the character of the individual in some particulars, though it left him unaltered, undisturbed in others.''

Justice Emery charged the jury. ''He commented in a clear and lucid manner on the whole testimony.'' ''But it is said'' (he continued) ''that the head has a large peculiar formation called the organ of Destructiveness. There is no disposition to keep out of courts of justice *true* science, but, on the contrary, to pay it marked deference. If a question were raised here as to a fact committed in the East Indies, and by two persons it should be said to have been full moon at the time, and *astronomers* should be called who should demonstrate from calculations, that there could not have been a full moon at that time, it would be proper evidence for a jury. So, if *dyers* be called as to the effect of chemical combinations upon colors; or if *physicians* be called to show the effects of poison upon the human frame, such is competent testimony. But when it shall have been demonstrated by proof like this, that a bump here, or a bump there, shall affect the mind, either to destroy the powers of mind, or decidedly to alter its character, then, and not till then, will such become proper evidence to be submitted to a jury. Where people do not speak from *knowledge*, we cannot suffer *a mere theory* to go as evidence to a jury; especially where one says he is a believer in the system, and has no personal knowledge upon the subject. Our decisions are made in the day-light, and the jury are judges of the law as well as of facts."

The jury found the prisoner guilty on both counts, and sentenced him to nine years' confinement at hard labor in the State Prison at Thomaston. " The boy showed no emotion. The same downcast look—the same unalterable countenance—the same dull and sleepy eye—the same stoop, and the same half-open mouth characterised him from the first to the last moment of his trial." Mr. Neal concludes—" I am sure that he understood little or nothing of what he saw, though he told me he did, appeared grateful, and promised to be a good boy when he got to Thomaston."—" · They give you enough to eat there, don't they" was his only remark, when told that he should be in prison as long as all his life previous to his sentence."

To Mr. Neal is due the merit of being the first barrister, so far as my information extends, who has had the courage to bring Phrenology directly into a court of law, and to plead upon its principles. The case was very unfavorable for him—first, from the want of direct evidence of the boy's head having been injured; and, secondly, from Dr. Mighles not having had a practical knowledge of the science. Judge Emery's charge was obviously correct, in the circumstances of the case: but the principles which he lays down convey an instructive lesson to phrenological physicians to obtain practical knowledge by observation, and not to rest satisfied with conviction founded on mere testimony or philosophical adaptation. If Dr. Mighles had observed nature, he would have been able to describe the peculiarities of the head more accurately and intelligently, and to say positively whether the head was necessarily that of an idiot, or imbecile boy, or not. He would also have been better able to distinguish between a swelling caused by a blow on a muscle, and one arising from the prominence of a part of the skull caused by the development of brain beneath; and, in this latter case, he would have been better able to bear *direct* evidence to the connection subsisting between this fact and the boy's vicious dispositions. If he had possessed practical knowledge, he would have been better able also to distinguish a congenital deformity of head from one caused by an external injury, and to point out the bearing of each of them upon the case before him; and, lastly, he would have spoken with the weight of an observer *interpreting nature*, or narrating facts of which extensive and scientific observation had put him in possession, instead of appearing before the jury as a reader merely, resting his conviction and testimony on statements and arguments contained in books, which books other men of respectable reputation are pleased to treat with ridicule or disrespect. The phrenologists who have observed nature know that, most probably, he was in the right; but they have no direct guarantee that he was so in this individual case (which *they* have not seen), and, consequently, even they must hold the judge fully justified in refusing to place any reliance on such evidence.

In making these remarks, I have in view solely the application of Phrenology to future cases, and do not at all blame Dr. Mighles. He probably never contemplated that he would be called on to make such a solemn use of his phrenological knowledge, and he deserves credit for having had the courage to avow his conviction and state his impressions, when judicially summoned to do so, undismayed by that terror of public opinion which makes cowards of so many able men, when the merits of Phrenology are in question.

Jeremy Bentham.—Mr. Neal, when a young man, lived for some time in the house of the late Jeremy Bentham in London, and he mentioned the following anecdote of him. "Mr. Bentham," said he, " had no objection to be known to the world *precisely as he was.* I frequently amused him for a moment or two by imitating some of his peculiarities of speech, walk, and gesture, and he actually invited Matthews to dine with him, because I thought that a true Bentham on the stage by Matthews would be well received by the public. He regarded it as sitting for a picture, a live-picture, and was tickled with the idea. What the result of the negotiation between him and Matthews was, I do not know, farther than this, that Matthews never saw him to my knowledge." This occurred in December 1826, and is mentioned in a Memoir of Bentham published by Mr. Neal. I told Mr. Neal that the cast of Mr. Bentham's head, taken after death, shows an excessive development of the organ of Love of Approbation. Mr. Neal remarked that Mr. B. "would not bear contradiction from any one except Mr. Doane the barrister, one of his secretaries, and myself. Every body also flattered him to his face—if not by downright eulogy, by submissiveness or unquestioning acquiescence." There is proof of this in every page of the Memoir above referred to. When he understood that Mr. Neal was keeping notes of his conversations, he desired him to write them out every night, and made him read them to him in the morning!

Sept. 18. Ther. 42°. *Phrenology.*—To-day I assisted at the dissection of a brain in presence of Dr. Rea, Dr. Mighles, Mr. Neal, and a number of other gentlemen, who take an interest in Phrenology. Dr. Rea mentioned to me that he had attended a woman who became insane on account of the death of her son, and attempted to drown herself. The head was hotter at the organ of Philoprogenitiveness than in any other part. He cupped her at that part, put on a blister and an issue a little below, and cured her. She is now well.

In the evening, at 7 P. M., we left Portland in the steamboat for Boston, and sailed past Cape Cottage and the scenes which we had so abundantly enjoyed. We took our last look of them with regret, and breathed forth our best wishes for the success and happiness of our late excellent host and his amiable family. Next morning at seven o'clock, after a prosperous voyage, we entered Boston bay and harbor, and found them bathed in sunshine, and beauty, and alive, in every direction, with white sails and gliding forms.

Sept. 23. Ther. 59°. *Hartford in Connecticut.*—We travelled by the railroad from Boston to Worcester, and by the stage from Worcester to Springfield, and thence to Hartford by the Connecticut river, and arrived here after a very pleasant journey. We met with interesting companions in the public vehicles, and were overwhelmed with kindness at Springfield during our brief stay. The country appeared as picturesque and beautiful as it did last year on our first arrival. New England bears well a repeated inspection, nay, a scrutiny.

Phrenology.—It had been my intention, when I came to the United States, to lecture in Baltimore in October of this year, and then to proceed to Cincinnati and Louisville, and deliver courses in these cities during the winters of 1839—40, but, as already mentioned, no class could be mustered in Baltimore, and the same obstacle has presented itself in Cincinnati. Before I left New York in May, Dr. Gross, from that city, called for me, and was authorised to announce that I should lecture in Cincinnati, if wanted. He gave public notice on his return, but apparently met with so little success that I never heard from him, or from any one else on the subject. I therefore accepted an invitation to deliver a course of twelve lectures on Phrenology in Hartford, one of the two capitals of the state of Connecticut. Its population is about 10,000 persons, who are employed chiefly in trade. I am now preparing for my course.

Advertisements.—The " Courier and Enquirer" of New York states, that, between the 14th September, 1838, and the 14th September, 1839, it published 143,428 *new* advertisements, or 464 a day'

The Banks.—The signs of coming adversity are thickening. The United States Bank continued selling bills of exchange on London at par (9¼ per cent.,) when the banks in New York demanded and obtained 10 and 10½, or from 10s. to 20s. per cent. of premium. This excited much speculation, and a new occurrence has raised this into astonishment. The United States

Bank has lately sold its own post notes, payable at long dates, in Boston, to the extent of $800,000, at a discount equal to 16 and 18 per cent. per annum. The sales were readily effected, as the credit of the bank was undoubted; but the seller proceeded to the Boston banks, in whose notes the purchases were paid for, and immediately drew specie from them for the whole amount! This, it is said, has been shipped to England to enable the bank's agent there to retire its drafts sold to the public at par! The effect has been to paralyse trade in Boston. The banks, drained of their specie, are contracting their issues, and fearing farther disasters. The shares of the United States Bank, which were lately sold at $118 for the share of $100, have now fallen to par.

Miss Martineau and the Ladies of Boston.—Miss Martineau has excited great indignation in New England by certain expressions in her book, which are here interpreted to amount to an accusation of drinking against the ladies of Boston. We have never seen any thing that could lead us to suspect the existence of such a vice; and have inquired what could give rise to the statement. One of our chance fellow-passengers, who is extensively acquainted in that city and New York, said that she knew some' American ladies who indulge in as many as three glasses of wine after dinner, and then, by means of lavender and cordials, support a state of artificial excitement during the remainder of the evening. " This," she said, " I call drinking." I must leave the ladies to settle this delicate point among themselves; I can only testify that it was not my fortune to meet with any of these excited fair ones, in any part of New England.

Sept. 24. Ther. 46°. *The Amistad Africans.*—The case of the Africans, captured in the "long, low, black schooner" in Long Island Sound, is exciting an extraordinary degree of interest. The advocates of abolition represent them as heroes who have nobly risen against their oppressors, and recovered their freedom at the hazard of their lives; while the patrons of slavery designate them as pirates, murderers, and banditti, and call for their trial and execution. We visited them this day in the jail of Hartford, in which they have been placed, waiting the disposal of the courts of law. They are all young, and three of them are children. Several seemed to be in bad health, but the rest were robust and cheerful. They are genuine Africans, and little more than three months have elapsed since they left their native shores. Their heads present great varieties of form as well as of size. Several have small heads, even for Africans; some short and broad heads, with high foreheads, but with very little longitudinal extent in the anterior lobe. Their leader Cinquez or Jinquez, who killed the captain of the schooner, is a well-made man of 24 or 25 years of age. His head is long from the front to the back, and rises high above the ear, particularly in the regions of Self-Esteem, and Firmness. The breadth is moderate, and Destructiveness is large, but not excessive. Benevolence and Veneration are well marked, and rise above the lateral organs; but the coronal region altogether is narrow. The anterior lobe also is narrow; but it is long from front to back. The middle perpendicular portion, including Comparison and Eventuality, is decidedly large. Individuality is full. The temperament seems to be nervous-bilious. This size and form of brain indicate considerable mental power, decision, self-reliance, prompt perception, and readiness of action.

The Supreme Court of Connecticut has just decided that it has no jurisdiction over these Africans, and that it lies within the district court to dispose of them. They are well treated, and defended by able counsel, who are paid by public subscriptions.

It is impossible to look without horror and indignation on these young and unoffending men and children deprived of their liberty, reduced to slavery, and converted into mere "property," by *Christians;* I say by Christians, because I have no doubt that if any one were to deny that their reputed owner, who also is here, or his advocates in the American press, were Christians, he would be prosecuted for a libel on their religious character!

Sept. 25. Ther. 52°. *The Militia.*—There was a grand muster of militia here to-day. Some of the companies looked quite military, while others certainly were only citizen-soldiers in appearance. The mounted officers, dressed in blue coats and white breeches, with abundance of lace, large cocked hats and white feathers, by dint of galloping and prancing supported their military pretensions extremely well. I feel a respect for citizen-soldiers, notwithstanding their awkwardness, because they are powerless for evil and aggression, and become always the more formidable the more real occasion there is for their services.

The Late War.—These soldiers remind me of a "history of the late war (that of 1812) between the United States and Great Britain, by H. M. Brackenridge,"* which I have read. It is ably and temperately written. I heard a distinguished American citizen remark as follows in reference to this war: "We had abundance of provocation to justify it, but I never could help regretting the time we took to declare it. We had suffered great injuries both from the French and the British, which we

---

* It has gone through six large editions, and is now stereotyped.

had long submitted to; and there was something ungenerous to
my feelings in our selecting that moment (the 19th of June,
1812) to commence it. Napoleon was then at the summit of
his power, and was marching, as every one believed, to the sub-
jugation of Russia, while England alone maintained the cause
of humanity and freedom. We chose that moment to join the
side of the conqueror, and throw our weight into the scale
against Britain." This observation appeared to me to express
admirably the real merits of the question which party was to
blame for the commencement of that contest. The war itself
was conducted by us in the worst spirit. The battles on the
lakes, the bombarding and ravaging of the towns on the Atlantic
coast, the burning of the Capitol at Washington, and the conflicts between single ships, chiefly frigates, had, every one of
them, the tendency to inflict misery on individuals, and to kindle
the most rancorous feelings between the nations, but to decide
nothing. After having been on the field of some of these battles,
and read the narratives of all of them, and having contrasted the
small numbers of men engaged in them (from 500 to 3000),
with the enormous extent of territory and resources of the
United States and of Britain, they reminded me of nothing but
two furious women scratching each other's cheeks and tearing
each other's hair. They bore no reasonable relation to the
only conceivable object of war, that of compelling either nation
to yield. The attack by the British on New Orleans appears
to me to have been the only part of their operations that was
worthy of their fame; I mean the object aimed at in that enterprise, and not the manner in which it was conducted. If the
British had captured New Orleans and closed the Mississippi,
they might have occasioned serious embarrassment to the Americans; but, as far as I can discover, no other of their projects,
although successful, would have carried any important consequences in its train. The command of the Canada lakes would
have enabled them to defend that province, which, however,
was in no danger from the Americans, for their force never was
capable of making conquests. Victory on the lakes might have
enabled the British to retard the settlement of some of the American Western States, but only in a small degree, for these were
accessible by the Ohio, the Mississippi, and the Wabash, independently of the lake navigation.

The British of those days seem to have been actuated by an
unbecoming hatred and contempt of the Americans. This last
feeling led to most of the defeats which they sustained, both by
land and sea; and the same sentiment still lingers among many of
the British aristocracy, who exercise a great influence over the
destinies of England. I have already explained, vol. i, p. 284-5,

that the Americans are really a war-loving, if not a warlike nation, and it would be well that the British understood their real character. It may appear to be an unpatriotic opinion, but my impression is, that, in a fair combat, either by sea or land, of man to man, and gun to gun, the Americans, after acquiring discipline and experience, would beat the British; and the reasons of my opinion are these.—The two nations belong to the same stock, and are equal in physical organisation The instinct of self-preservation is the motive which induces men to shun danger and to run from a fight, and bravery is in proportion to the motives which can be thrown into the opposite scale. The masses which compose fleets and armies are drawn from the humbler classes of society. In Britain, these have little education, no sphere of political action, no influential compatriots to sound their praises or to cover them with shame on their return as conquerors or cowards. They have no field of ambition to excite their individual energies before they become soldiers or sailors, and when they have embraced these professions the road to high preferment is closed against them. Their motives to fight, therefore, are derived from their native force of character and discipline. In native qualities the Americans are their equals, and in all other motives, except discipline, their superiors. There is more mental activity, a greater range of interests and ideas, a more influential public opinion, and a far wider field of ambition, operating in the case of the American seaman, militia-man, and volunteer, than in that of the British sailor or soldier. The discipline on shore will at first be inferior in the Americans: because the British constitution renders discipline almost natural to British soldiers, while that of America trains her population to an aversion to subordination. At the commencement of a war, therefore, the British, with equal numbers, will be more than a match for the Americans; but every day will diminish the disparity. The singular feature, in the case of the Americans, is, that victory or defeat equally tends to increase their belligerent efficiency. A large and influential portion of the people was at first opposed to the war of 1812 against England, and some of the New England states actually refused to march their militia towards Canada on the requisition of the general government; but first the triumphs of the American frigates, and finally the burning of the Capitol at Washington, and the ravaging of their coasts, rendered them not only unanimous but enthusiastically devoted to the war; and if it had continued longer, their energy and efficiency would have rapidly increased.

The Americans are engaged in avocations which prosper most in peace; they are devoted to gain, and averse to subjection to authority. As formerly observed, therefore, although they are full of warlike predilections, these circumstances present strong practical checks on their indulging in the gratifications of war. Add to these impediments the fact, that, after one of the political parties has identified itself with a war, its opponents will make "political capital" out of every thing connected with it; in other words, however just or necessary hostilities may be, they will operate on the feelings of the people against the war, for the sake of destroying their political adversaries. Thus, immediately after the commencement of a contest, and while it is yet known to the people chiefly in the form of burdensome taxes, interruption to trade, and destruction of credit, there will always be a powerful opposition to it, and great distraction in the national councils. At this stage of hostilities the United States Government will appear powerless, and the Union seem to be on the eve of dissolution; but only let the contest fairly begin, and let either victory or defeat visit the American arms, and in the exact ratio of the pressure from without will be the condensation of public sentiment within. In short, the American nation, like a steel spring, seems to have no energy when it is fully expanded, but it gathers strength with every ounce of pressure that is applied to it. Its territory is so vast, and its climates so various, that it forms a world within itself; and although a European maritime war would cause great loss and misery to the Atlantic cities, it could not materially affect, far less permanently destroy the general prosperity of the Union.

I sincerely trust that the days of war between the United States and Britain are gone by, never to return; but if the mad passions of either should provoke hostilities, Britain seems to me to have only one course to pursue that will effectually lead to peace. She should act not only justly but generously in the conduct of the war, so as to enlist the sympathies of the good in America in her favor; she should avoid all petty attacks that would serve to irritate public sentiment without the possibility of producing any great results; never engage the Americans without a force sufficient to insure victory: block up their ports, and leave them without petty injuries to excite resentment, without victories to gratify national vanity, and without the pressure of external danger to alarm them for their national safety: in short, let the war be conducted as one of blockading on the sea coast, and self-defence in Canada, and not as one of attack and aggression, and the Americans will sooner come to reason under this administration than under any other. They will suffer loss and annoyance, and yet have no strong passion excited to counterbalance the irritation which these will produce. They are a people impatient of small evils, but capable of meeting great ones with a heroic spirit. They cannot aggressively injure Britain; for their whole institutions render them feeble for conquest; and their attempts on Canada, unless aided by the native population, would be easily repelled. Even should they conquer that province, it is more than probable that they would render as essential a service to the British nation as they did when they achieved their own independence. I repeat, however, that a war between these two nations would be a disgrace to the civilisation of the nineteenth century, and an event which every enlightened American and Briton must deprecate and deplore.

The New England Voice.—It has frequently been remarked, that the people of the New England States have a peculiar intonation of voice, which distinguishes them from Europeans and other Americans; but I have rarely found any of themselves who recognised the difference. They have occasionally asked me to define it, which it was not easy to do; but I found this method the shortest and most successful with them on this point. I said, "Do you discover that I am Scotch?" "Yes, very easily." "How?" "By your tone, accent, and manner." "Then, by the same means, I discover that you are Yankee; and your peculiarities are as strongly marked as mine." They comprehended this illustration at once. Their voice is nasal, hard, and unmusical, except when corrected by a refined education.

Sept. 27. Ther. 38°. *Phrenology.*—Dr. Brigham kindly undertook the arrangement of the course of lectures in Hartford. The number of lectures has been reduced from sixteen to twelve, of two hours each, and the fee from five to three dollars. I delivered the first lecture this evening, and the attendance was fifty subscribers, twenty visiters, and twelve complimentary hearers. At 6 P. M. the thermometer stood at 65°, a rise of 27° since the morning.

Sept. 29. Ther. 40°. *Sunday.*—We heard the Rev. Mr. Gallaudet preach a sound but moderate orthodox discourse in the Rev. Dr. Hawes' church. Dr. Hawes is a Presbyterian congregationalist, and has a large church, well filled, and a most respectable congregation. Connecticut has retained her Calvinism more unbroken than perhaps any other State in the Union. There are now, however, both Unitarian and Universalist congregations within her boundaries. She is celebrated also for the severity of her ancient moral and religious code, known under the name of "the Blue Laws;" and although there has been a great relaxation in modern times, a trace of the olden spirit is still discernible. The 250th hymn, used in the church which we attended to-day, contains these lines:—

> "Awake and mourn, ye heirs of hell,
> Let stubborn sinners fear,

> Ye must be driven from earth, and dwell,
>   A long for-ever, there.
> See how the pit gapes wide for you,
>   And flashes in your face;
> And thou, my soul, look downward too,
>   And sing recovering grace."

These lines embody the very soul of Destructiveness and Self-Esteem.

Education and Phrenology.—This State possesses a large school-fund, the produce of western lands claimed by Connecticut under an old title, and allowed by Congress; but she has yet made small progress in applying it systematically and with effect. The legislature, however, has appointed a superintendent of public schools; and Mr. Barnard, the gentleman who now holds the office, entertains enlightened views on the subject of education, and is anxious to improve not only the mode of teaching, but the things taught in the common schools of the State. He had heard of the value attached to my lectures on Phrenology in relation to education, in the three great cities of Boston, New York, and Philadelphia, and regretted that so small a number of the inhabitants of Hartford had taken an interest in them.

Several causes are mentioned as accounting for this circumstance. Two itinerant phrenologists have commenced lectures in Hartford since my course was announced; one of them lectures free, as an inducement to the people to pay him fees for examining their heads, and another admits the public at a very low price. The free lectures are crowded, and those for which a fee is demanded are slenderly attended. Besides these two, there have been other phrenological lecturers here during the summer, who have fleeced the people of their money, and left little knowledge in its stead. Farther, the people are accustomed to hear lectures free, and have no idea of paying any serious sum for instruction. They are treated to a new topic, if not a new lecturer, every night, and do not comprehend the advantage of following out any subject in a scientific form, through a series of lectures. Besides, they are all able to read and write, and between scraps of information picked up from these desultory lectures, from newspapers, and from the speeches of politicians, and the absence of any class possessing high literary or philosophical attainments, they believe themselves to be exceedingly well informed. Finally, the propagation of opinion, except on political subjects, is difficult and slow in the United States. Every state presents a focus of interests that engage the chief attention of its own citizens; while every town and hamlet has a set of particular interests that excite contests and discussions, and fill the local newspapers with small details. Hence, the great body of the people of Hartford, although readers of news-papers, seem to know little of the interest excited among the friends of education by my lectures in the large cities, although two of them, Boston and New York, are little more than a hun-dred miles distant from Hartford; or if they know, they pay little deference to the opinions expressed in these cities. I men-tion these facts, not from feelings of individual vanity or disap-pointment, but because they are illustrative of the condition of the public mind, and are not confined to Hartford, but are gene-ral over the Union. I have found by experience, that moral opinion travels more rapidly and certainly in Great Britain and Ireland. So little progress has yet been made by the people of the United States in regard to a correct appreciation of what constitutes a good education, and of its value to them, that an opposition is at this moment hatching in Massachusetts against the Board of Education of that State, which is described in vol. i. p. 52-3. Some Democratic politicians hope to catch a few votes by persuading the ignorant that that system of State-educa-tion is an infringement of private rights; they maintain that a free people have a right to educate their children in their own way, without superintendence; for they cannot say that the Board of Education exercises any control over them; it has no power except that of moral suasion. The Board may recom-mend, but cannot enforce any thing. Some divines also, I am told, in that state, are sounding the alarm among their flocks, that the Board of Education is the harbinger of infidelity.

Oct. 1. Ther. 32°. *Phrenology.*—Having been requested by Mr. Barnard to repeat my first and second lectures to the members of the Young Men's Institute, and to admit them to the course on reduced terms, I agreed to do so, and gave him *carte blanche* as to terms. This evening I delivered the first lecture to them free, and was honored with an attendance of 360 ladies and gentlemen. Mr. Barnard addressed them after the lecture, told them that arrangements had been made, by which they might be admitted to the whole course on their paying one dollar, and the lecture-fund of the Institute would pay fifty cents additional for each who should attend; and he recom-mended to them to avail themselves of the opportunity of hear-ing the philosophy of phrenology and its application to educa-tion explained.

Oct. 2. Ther. 40°. This evening I repeated my second lecture to the members of the Young Men's Institute, and thirty-five individuals attended.

The People of Connecticut.—In conversing with a gentleman from a neighboring state about the population of Connecticut, I was told that their Calvinistic education, and external circumstances, had rendered them moral, industrious, and frugal; so much so that they are distinguished for the absence of serious crimes, for general propriety of deportment, and for the comfort and respectability of their outward circumstances; but that they are accused by their neighbors of some degree of narrow-mindedness.* Like the Americans in general, however, although they are keen in the pursuit of wealth, and economical in its application, they are generous when an object which excites their sympathies is presented to them. They contribute handsomely to charitable institutions. Dr. Howe mentioned that he raised $1200 here very easily for the Institution for the Blind in Boston; and this year $2200 were raised by a "ladies' fair" for charitable purposes. Twenty hearers of a favorite minister subscribed $300, purchased a pianoforte, and presented it to his daughter. There is a "sewing society" also in this town, consisting of young ladies, who meet once a-week at each other's houses, at 2 P. M., and sew and gossip till 7 o'clock, when a number of young gentlemen drop in and close the evening with music and a dance. They have adopted an orphan child, which is boarded, clothed, and educated at their expense; their needlework providing the necessary funds. I was told that they avoid waltzing, and even playing waltzes, these being regarded as sinful.

Religious Denominations in Connecticut.—The population of this state is estimated at upwards of 300,000. Its sects are the following.—" The Congregationalists have 232 churches, 277 ministers, including 49 who have no pastoral charge, and about 40,000 communicants. The Calvinistic Baptists have 98 churches, 77 ordained ministers, 20 licentiates, and upwards of 10,000 communicants. The Episcopalians have 63 ministers, and about 7000 members. The Methodists had, in 1833, 40 ministers, and 7000 members. There is a considerable number of Universalist Societies, two Unitarian, two or three Roman Catholic, several Free-will Baptist, a few Friends, a few Sandemanians, and one Society of Shakers."—*Chronicle of the Church, Newhaven, 18th Oct.* 1839.

Oct. 4. Therm. 54°. *The Politicians.*—The Whigs and Democrats are equally dishonest as politicians; that is to say, they flatter, coax, and mislead the people to get into power; but they pass better laws, and act on purer principles, when assembled in the legislature, than any one could expect, judging from

* I see no reason to question that these effects may be produced by Calvinism in a certain state of society, when acting on favorably constituted minds, but I doubt whether they will be its general results, especially when operating on an enlightened people in an advanced state of civilisation.

their conduct while candidates for office. The explanation is, that all profess the love of virtue and the people; and, when in power, they feel that any flagrant dishonesty, or unprincipled selfishness, would instantly be exposed by their opponents, and made use of as a lever to turn them out of place. The corruption, moreover, is chiefly in the towns. The farmers and country voters are deceived or misled, but not bribed. They look at the conduct of their rulers without bias or blind partiality; and even the most unprincipled politicians are afraid to commit too glaring iniquities before their eyes. In all the states this class is composed, to a great extent, of proprietors of the soil; and it forms a large proportion of the constituency of the whole United States. If it were better educated, it would serve as a sheet-anchor to their institutions; and, even in its present condition of imperfect enlightenment, it arrests the politicians of either party when their measures have obviously deviated too far from the line of common sense, and especially from that which leads to public prosperity.

Oct. 9. Ther. 48°. *Fires.*—There have been two enormous fires in New York and Philadelphia. The loss in New York is stated at $1,000,000, and that in Philadelphia at $1,400,000.

Mrs. Sigourney.—I borrow the following remarks from C——'s journal:—" We have several times seen Mrs. Sigourney, the American Hemans, and spent an evening at her house. Her history is very interesting, and would prepossess one in her favor, even although disjoined from the talents she has shown. She was s pattern of filial piety, and in the other relations of life has been not less exemplary. One evidence of her excellent qualities is presented by the many warm and sincere friends whom she has attached. Her appearance is pleasing, and her manners entirely natural and unassuming. Her talent for poetry was manifested at a very early age, and was promising even from the first, though a comparison of her juvenile productions with those of her matured intellect shows a considerable improvement. She resembles Mrs. Hemans in being eminently the poetess of the affections; every object and incident creative of human sentiment, or ministering to attachment, finds a responsive note on her truly sweet and feminine lyre. Her prose works, on education and other kindred topics, deserve, and have obtained, a conspicuous place in the literature of her country; and, whatever the merits of her writings may be comparatively with those of other authors, she may justly claim the praise of never having published a line which morality or gentle womanhood need blush to own. She conducts a periodical (an annual) named the 'Religious Souvenir,' of which I have not had an opportunity of judging, but it is popular, and, I believe, has a wide circulation."

Oct. 10. Ther. 51°. *The Bank Suspensions.*—News has arrived that the United States Bank, and most of the banks of Pennsylvania and Maryland, have suspended cash payments. The United States Bank stock has fallen to $97 in New York, and they utmost consternation prevails. In Hartford the public mind is quiet, and they have confidence in their own banks, but a deep anxiety is visible on the countenances of the men of property. The banks are prohibited by law from paying dividends during their suspension, and as the losses of the fire insurance companies will suspend their dividends, many persons whose capital is invested in the stocks of these institutions, will suffer great privation through the want of their incomes. Besides, the commercial transactions of the whole Union are deeply affected by the derangement of the exchange. The arrival of every post and steamboat from New York is watched with intense anxiety, to learn whether the banks in that city mean to suspend.

It may be proper to mention, for the information of readers who are not old enough to recollect the suspension of specie payments by the Bank of England, that a bank-suspension does no necessarily imply a bankruptcy. The Pennsylvania banks proceed with their business as usual, only they decline to pay specie for their obligations. The consequence is, that their bank-notes are at eleven per cent. discount in New York, where the banks continue to redeem their obligations in specie.

The Deaf and Dumb.—I conversed with the Rev. Mr. Gallaudet, who for many years was the principal of the American Asylum for the Education of the Deaf and Dumb, about the mental condition of these individuals, and he dissented from Miss Martineau's views regarding them, expressed in one of her works on America. He considers that the knowledge which they possess, if they be well educated, is both extensive and precise; and that, if they be well trained, they are in general amiable and happy in their dispositions.

Phrenology: Natural Language.—Every propensity and sentiment of the mind, when *predominantly* active, produces a peculiar tone in the voice, expression in the eye and countenance, and also a peculiar attitude and gait. This is the natural language by which its activity is made known, and, when strongly marked, it is recognised and understood in all ages and countries. Lavater's system of physiognomy was founded on this fact in nature; but it was imperfect, because he did not know the primitive faculties which the various expressions noted by him indicated, and he also introduced, as signs of mental character, the hard parts of the face, which do not owe their forms to the state of the brain. Phrenology reveals the functions of the primitive faculties, and enables us to connect peculiar expressions of voice, countenance, and gait, with the active condition of particular powers, and also of particular groups of them, and thus renders physiognomy, or natural language, a branch of the philosophy of mind. The Rev. Mr, Gallaudet, without the aid of phrenology, but from extensive practical observation and experience, has been led to the conclusion that these natural signs may be taught with manifest advantage to children in general, as a branch of education. In the Literary and Theological Review, No. II, for June 1834, he published an article entitled "On the Language of Signs" as "auxiliary to the Christian Missionary." "It is quite practicable," says he, "to convey by the countenance, sings, and gestures, the import not only of all the terms employed to denote the various objects of nature and art, and the multifarious business and concerns of common life, but also those relating to the process of abstraction and generalisation, to the passions and emotions of the heart, and to the powers and faculties of the understanding; or, in other words, the language of the countenance, signs, and gestures, is an accurate, significant, and copious medium of thought. Instances have occurred in the instruction of the deaf and dumb, in which, in the space of two years, 5000 words have been taught to several intelligent pupils, who were previously entirely ignorant of them and *of all language*, excepting that of their own natural signs, together with a command of written language, which would place them on an equality, with regard to the expression of their ideas, with the most intelligent persons among those heathen nations who have nothing but an oral language."

These views are not, in his case, purely theoretical, but founded on experience. He adduces some examples in support of them. "In the summer of 1818, a Chinese young man passed through Hartford, Connecticut. He was so ignorant of the English language that he could not express in it his most common wants. As principal of the deaf and dumb asylum of that place, I invited the stranger to spend an evening within its walls, and introduced him to Mr. Laurent Clerc, the celebrated deaf and dumb pupil of the Abbé Sicard, and at that time an assistant-teacher in the asylum. The object of this introduction was to ascertain to what extent Mr. Clerc, who was entirely ignorant of the Chinese language, could conduct an intelligent conversation with the foreigner by signs and gestures merely. The result of the experiment surprised all who were present. Mr. Clerc learned from the Chinese many interesting facts respecting the place of his nativity, his parents and their family, his former pursuits in his own country, his residence in the United States, and his notions regarding God and a future state.

By the aid of appropriate signs also, Mr. Clerc ascertained the
meaning of about twenty Chinese words." P. 201. I asked Mr.
Gallaudet how he knew that Mr. Clerc's inferences were correct, and he told me that in this and all the other instances mentioned in the article in question, he had ascertained either from
interpreters or dictionaries that they were so.

"About a year afterwards," he adds, "I visited Cornwall, in
Connecticut, where upwards of twenty heathen youths were at
that time receiving education under the patronage of the American Board of Commissioners for Foreign Missions." He propounded questions to them by signs. "For example: Thomas
Hoopoo, a native of Owhyhee, was asked if his parents were
living; how many brothers and sisters he had; when he left his
native shores; whether his countrymen worshipped idols and
sacrificed human victims; how the women were treated by the
men; what was the climate of his country; what its productions;
with many inquiries of a similar nature, all of which he well
comprehended, and to many of which he replied by signs.
The meaning, too, of a number of Owhyhean words was ascertained by signs merely, and found to correspond with the import
which had been previously assigned to them in a dictionary
which had been for some time preparing in the school; and,
indeed, in a variety of instances, the most correct meaning of
such words was established, by the medium of signs, in a more
satisfactory way than had been previously attempted."

"Opportunities have occurred of intercourse by signs between
the native Indians of our country, who have visited the institution for the deaf and dumb, and the instructors (of the pupils),
the results of which, in a greater or less degree, have corresponded with those mentioned above."

"May not this curious language of signs and gestures be
made subservient to the speedy acquisition of the oral language
of people, who have no written or printed language, by the
Christian missionary, or to the communication to them of his
own language, or to their mutual intercourse with each other,
not only on ordinary, but on the most momentous topics, even
while they are entirely ignorant of each other's spoken language?"

To many persons these representations may appear almost
incredible, but I obtained some explanations which render them
more comprehensible. Mr. Gallaudet conversed by signs with
the Africans of the Amistad, and learned many particulars of
their history and opinions, and afterwards ascertained from an
interpreter of their language that his inferences were correct.
For example, to discover whether they recognised a God, he
assumed the natural language of veneration, looked up as if
beseeching and adoring, and pointed to the sky. "Goolly!"

said the Africans, " Goolly, Goolly!" then looking grave, they imitated thunder, uttering the words " Goolly—Bung! Bung!" There could be no doubt that they gave their name for God.

The exposition of the natural language of the faculties given in my lectures, led to these remarks. Mr. Gallaudet considers that it would essentially benefit children to teach them the natural language of the faculties at the time when they learn to read. The meaning of many words, particularly those which signify emotions could be conveyed to them more effectually by this medium than by any other. In exhibiting the natural language of any faculty, the faculty itself is called into action, and teaching the natural language will thus become an important auxiliary in training children to virtue. He has the testimony of his own experience in favor of this view. In showing to his deaf and dumb pupils the natural language of Benevolence, Veneration, and the other higher sentiments, he was conscious that these faculties became more active and were cultivated in himself. In his pupils the effect was equally decisive. When they were out of humor, the bland look of Benevolence, and the resigned expression of Veneration, if perseveringly exhibited to them, rarely failed to restore their equanimity and cheerfulness.

I owe to Mr. Gallaudet the first clear view of the importance of natural language in common education.

A great part of his natural language is the same with that taught by phrenologists, both being drawn from nature.*

Many years ago Mr. Gallaudet went to Edinburgh to study under Mr. Kinniburgh, the teacher of the deaf and dumb in that city; but Mr. Braidwood had placed him under a bond, with a large penalty, not to instruct teachers for eight years. He and the directors threw open the institution to Mr. Gallaudet, and allowed him to see everything, including the lessons that were given to the pupils, but they observed the terms of the bond, and gave him no direct instruction. He then went to Paris and studied under the Abbé Sicard. His system of signs is described in the Encyclopædia Americana. Mr. G. prefers the single-hand alphabet. It is as precise and expressive as the double-hand alphabet, and can be used when one hand is disabled or otherwise employed.

---

* In visiting the institution for the deaf and dumb, I mentioned to Mr. Gallaudet that, when a boy attending the High School of Edinburgh, I had learned the finger-alphabet, and could use it readily, but that my mother had told me that speaking with the fingers was forbidden in Scripture, and I had given it up and forgotten it. He was surprised to hear of this prohibition; but he subsequently found the verse to which I alluded in Proverbs, ch. vi, v. 12—" A naughty person, a wicked man, walketh with a froward mouth. He winketh with his eyes, he speaketh with his feet, *he teacheth with his fingers.*"

Oct. 12. Ther. 48°. *The Temperaments.*—To-day I gave an exercise on the temperaments, which was well attended. The predominating temperaments were the sanguine-bilious and the nervous-bilious· There were a few instances of nervous-bilious-lymphatic.

Taxes.—The revenue of the general government of the United States is almost all derived from custom-house duties, the post-office, and sales of public lands. The taxes paid by the particular states, and also by the counties and townships, are raised in a very simple manner. Select men, or assessors, are appointed in different districts by the citizens. They estimate the whole property, real and personal, of each individual. In Connecticut the annual revenue of the property thus estimated is assumed to be six per cent., and the taxes are imposed in the form of an income-tax on it. The sum total of *all* the taxes payable in Connecticut, exclusive of the duties to the United States' government, amounts to about four per cent. on this estimated revenue. The select men are changed from time to time, and the circum stances of each citizen are so well known that the assessments on the whole are fairly imposed. The rule generally followed is to assume a pretty large amount of property to belong to each individual, and to leave him to prove by his books and affidavit that the estimate is too high. Assuming the whole free property of a citizen to amount to $20,000, or 4000*l.* sterling, the revenue of this sum at six per cent would be $1200, four per cent. on which would amount to $48, or nearly 10*l.* sterling, being the aggregate amount of all the taxes on an income of 240*l.* sterling per annum.

Oct. 13. Ther. 54°. *Sunday.*—We heard a sound orthodox discourse in Dr. Hawes' Church from a young clergyman, but were disappointed in not hearing Dr. Hawes himself. An American gentleman, who had travelled much on the Continent of Europe, and to whom I remarked the similarity which exists between a Sunday in Scotland and in Connecticut, observed, that he had been much struck at first with the difference of a Continental Sabbath from both. If a French family, said he, of the most respectable character, should come from Paris to Connecticut, and follow here the practices which they had been accustomed to observe from their infancy at home on Sundays, they would, by our laws, be liable to fine and imprisonment, and if they did not take warning in time, they might, by an accidental outburst of popular feelings, be chased out of the state, or lynched! The kingdom of heaven, we may hope, will ultimately receive at least all the Christian nations, if not the whole family of mankind, and it appears strange that they should find it so difficult to tolerate each other's habits on earth!

Oct. 15. Ther. 51°. *Effects of the Institutions of England and America.*—I lately conversed with an American gentleman, the father of a family and the owner of a princely estate, all cleared and improved, on the different effects which the institutions of England and those of the United States produce on men placed in circumstances like his. We were led to the conversation by reading the remarks of Baron Perignon, in his " Vingt Jours a Londres," at the coronation of Queen Victoria, in which he says—" Here I make an observation which relates to the manners of this country of aristocracy and liberty, and which establish̓ an immense difference between them and the French. In France, the two cries of the Revolution were, no privileges (*point de privilèges*), equality for all (*pour tous l' égalité*). In England, on the contrary, all is privilege, and one may almost say that there is no equality. In this country, each has his rank, each his caste,—he looks above and below him, that he may not step too high, nor descend too low, and there is no condition, however bad it may be, in which he does not find something to satisfy his pride in being able to class himself above some other person." The " Court Journal" of 11th May 1839, after quoting this passage, adds—" These remarks are certainly well founded. England is essentially an aristocratic country;—every class is an is aristocracy of itself, forming, as it were, an '*imperium in imperio*,' preserving its own importance, and affecting an exclusiveness as respects those of lower station. It is the extensive prevalence of this principle that precludes the possibility of equality, and which is a bar to that familiarity which exists in France, and prevails, indeed, even between domestics and those they serve."

I asked my friend, who had been in Britain, what, if his princely domain had been situated in England, the great object of his ambition would have been? "Tell me your opinion first," said he. " Well, then," said I, "in all probability you would have been intriguing at court, or throwing your whole influence into the scale of one or other of the political parties, and bargaining for a peerage, to gratify your vanity. You would have executed an entail to transmit your property to your eldest son and his heirs;—and, in short, you would have been occupied chiefly with projects of private or family ambition." He replied, that " he could well understand the powerful influence of the English institutions in giving a selfish direction to the ambition of an individual placed in circumstances like his, and in inducing him to attempt to secure high rank to himself, and permanent wealth to his remote posterity; but that in the United States all such projects would be visionary dreams. Our institutions," he continued, "produce a higher aim. I know perfectly that, under

them, my property must be divided. It will make all my own
children rich; but it will be again subdivided among their children, and in less than a century it will, in all probability, have
passed entirely into other hands, and no trace of it as a domain,
or of us as a family, in the English sense, will be left. This
makes me feel that I can best serve my posterity by employing
my present influence in improving the institutions and general
condition of my country. If the United States shall preserve
their freedom, and increase in intelligence and virtue, as it is my
earnest desire that they should do, then I know that my posterity
will enjoy the best field for the exercise of their own talents and
virtues, and that every one of them will command that extent of
fortune, consideration, and happiness, which his qualities will
deserve; and I desire for them no better inheritance."

In point of fact, the effect is precisely what is here described.
This gentleman exercises a generous and refined hospitality,
without pretension or parade, and devotes his time and fortune
to the improvement of the public institutions of the state in which
he resides. Among other objects, he has aided very efficiently
the friends of education, in obtaining a law passed which provides for the establishment of a library in connection with every
common school district. He appeared to me to be a nobler
character than an Englishman scrambling for a peerage, as the
reward of political subserviency, to gratify his individual ambition.

The Eglinton Tournament.—At the time when the preceding
conversation occurred, the New York newspapers contained
pretty extensive reports of the Eglinton Tournament. The ordinary Americans, who have no distinct notion of the state of
society in Britain, cannot comprehend it. How any men, not
insane, could expend such large sums of money in such pure
Tom foolery, appears to them very mysterious. The intelligent
Americans express their gratitude to Providence that they have
no titled and wealthy aristocracy to play such childish and fantastic tricks, and ask me whether there are not numerous poor
and ignorant persons in Scotland for whose instruction 40,000*l.*
or 50,000*l.* might have been better employed than in getting up
this pageant. "The tyranny of public opinion" would prevent
any similar waste of resources in the United States, although individuals could be found willing to indulge in it.

Education in the State of New York.—One of the most common errors, in my opinion, committed by foreigners who write
about America, as well as by the Americans themselves, is
greatly to over-estimate the educational attainments of the people. The provision in money made by the law for the instruction of all classes is large compared with such countries as

Britain or Austria, but, contrasted with what is necessary to bestow a really good education on the people, it is still very deficient. The farmers, for example, are indisposed to dispense with the services of their older children, during the busy season of agricultural labor, nor are they generally in circumstances to admit of it. It is extremely difficult, therefore, to keep open district schools (except for very young children, taught by females for a small compensation) for more than four or five months in the year. A school district in the rural parts of New York state contains only from ten to twenty families. Allowing $350 or $400 per annum to be a moderate remuneration for a qualified teacher (and this is less than a carpenter or blacksmith would earn,) it is nearly impossible to raise this amount from so small a number of persons, most of whom are in moderate circumstances. At present, the sum raised for the salaries of common school teachers is only $12 50 cents (or 2l. 13s.) per month for each teacher, this being, according to the report of the superintendent of common schools, the average compensation given in the state of New York in 1836 to male teachers. If the people would have properly qualified teachers, the sum that would need to be raised is from $70 to $100 per month, for each of them, as the school term might be longer or shorter. This the people will not pay, and the consequence is, that the education received by probably nineteen-twentieths of the children, in the agricultural districts, owing to the condition of most of the common schools, is defective in the extreme; nor can there be any decided improvement in the condition of the schools without an improvement in salary, and in the literary attainments and professional skill of the teachers.

To supply, in some degree, this great defect, a law was passed in the State of New York, about four years ago, empowering such school-district in the state to tax itself to the amount of $20 for the first year, and $10 for each subsequent year, for the purchase of books for a district library. There are 10,207 districts in the whole state, and the work of forming these libraries is begun by the friends of education, and is a popular measure. Some of the clergy, however, object to it, because it appears to assume that "the mere intellectual instruction of a community will necessarily tend to reform that community," a principle which they do not admit.*

Phrenology enables us to perceive that intellectual instruction will not cultivate the moral and religious sentiments, and that only sedulous training, added to intellectual instruction, will lead to virtuous conduct. The Americans need proper normal schools

* See the American Annals of Education, vol. vii, p. 441.

in which their teachers may be instructed in the philosophy of mind, and in the art of training and teaching, and they must also pay them handsomely before they will command good education. If the Americans were animated by an enlightened patriotism, they would submit to a large taxation to accomplish this object, because on its fulfilment will depend the future peace and prosperity of their country.

A few years ago Mr. Robert Cunningham, formerly Principal of the Edinburgh Institution for Languages, Mathematics, &c., a full account of which is given in President Bache's interesting Report on Education in Europe, was compelled by the state of his health to relinquish his situation. Having spent his two months' vacation in 1835 in visiting the principal schools of Prussia, and the same period of the subsequent year in an educational tour in France and Switzerland, he had become deeply interested in the subject of Normal Schools, and on the failure of his health, partly with a view to its recovery, and partly in the hope of being instrumental in introducing Normal Schools into America, he visited the United States. After travelling over the Eastern and Middle States, and visiting the principal schools, he was induced, by the hope of carrying out his ulterior object, to accept an appointment as Professor of Ancient Languages in Lafayette College, Pennsylvania. Here he labored for nearly two years, endeavoring by every means in his power to arouse public attention to the subject of Normal Schools, and to obtain support in carrying out his views. Disappointed in his expectation, he received in the interim an invitation to return to Scotland, and to become Rector of the Normal Seminary in Glasgow, at a salary of £300 ($1500) per annum, which situation he now fills with great credit to himself and advantage to his country. As similar institutions are much wanted in the United States, he has, at my request, kindly prepared for this work an interesting description of the one over which he presides. It is printed in the Appendix, No. VI.

CHAPTER VI.

The Banks—Schools—Ridicule of Public Characters—Salaries of the Judges
—Slavery—Washington College—State Prison at Weathersfield—Moral
Responsibility—The Bearing of Phrenology on Scripture—The Hart-
ford Retreat—Phrenology—The Deaf and Dumb Institution—Hartford—
To Worcester and Boston—Boston—The Pulpit—Phrenology—Educa-
tion—The Negroes of the Amistad—Phrenology—The Sub-Treasury
Law—The Colonisation Society—Orestes Augustus Brownson—Insanity
—The Law—The Election in New York—The Fifteen Gallon License
Law—Taxation—The Swedenborgians—Whig Caucus Meeting—New
York Election—Boston Election—The License Law—Ventilation of
Schools.

1839.

OCT. 17. Ther. 48°. *The Banks.*—The arrival of every
mail continues to be watched with unabated interest to ascertain
the progress of suspension. The banks of New York, Massachusetts, and Connecticut have all declared their resolution to
continue to pay specie; those of Rhode Island, and the banks to
the south and west of Philadelphia, with few exceptions, have
suspended. The stock of the United States Bank has been down
to $70 in New York. The consequences to trade are ruinous.
The difference of exchange between Philadelphia and New York
was at one time 13 per cent. If a merchant had $1000 in his
banker's hands in Philadelphia, and owed that sum, payable in
New York, he must have added to it $130 of exchange, before
he could have retired his note in New York. If, previous to the
suspension, a merchant in New York had sold $1000 worth of
goods to a merchant in Philadelphia, and taken the purchaser's
promissory-note for the amount payable in the latter city, he
would have received payment, after the suspension, in a depre-
ciated currency consisting of suspended bank notes, and he would
have lost 13 per cent. in exchange before he could have converted it into the currency of his own domicile. On the other
hand, if a merchant in New York had owed $1000 payable in
Philadelphia, he would have gained 13 per cent.; for he could
have bought up Philadelphia bank notes from the brokers in New
York at that rate of discount, which, when sent to Philadelphia,
would have discharged his debt to the extent of their nominal
amount. The exchange against Baltimore rose to 13 per cent.,

against Mississippi to 30 per cent., and against Cincinnati to 18 and 20 per cent. The citizens of the specie-paying states, who owed debts in these districts, bought up the irredeemable currency at these rates of discount, and discharged their obligations with it, making an enormous gain, while the merchants of the suspended territories either ceased to retire their obligations payable in the specie-paying cities, or submitted to the same extensive loss of exchange, to maintain their credit. By far the greater number ceased to pay altogether.

The law afforded no remedy for these evils. If a merchant sent a bill for $1000, payable at his own counting-house in New York by a Philadelphia merchant, to the latter city, under protest, and commenced a prosecution for payment, the law's delay enabled the debtor to stave off judgment until the meeting of the legislature, when they legalised the suspension, and made all the debts due by the citizens of the state payable in their own currency, thus throwing the loss of exchange on their distant creditors. During the bank-suspension in 1837, the state of New York paid the interest of its debt, not in its own depreciated bank notes, but in specie; that is to say, it paid the difference of exchange in addition to the interest; but the state of Pennsylvania paid the interest of her debt in her own depreciated bank notes, and made her foreign creditors sustain the loss of the exchange.(a)

Great as these evils are in a mere pecuniary point of view, their moral consequences are still more deplorable. They exhibit extensive mismanagement and speculation on the part of the most wealthy and influential institutions of the Union, accompanied by a disregard of their legal obligations; and this conduct appears to sanction every individual departure from the dictates of honesty and prudence. They also defraud industry of its natural rewards; for no profits can compensate the loss occasioned by these disturbances in the value of the currency. In short, the unjust loss and dishonest gain, the relaxation of every principle of honor and punctuality, and the utter derangement of commercial transactions, which attend bank-suspensions, render them national calamities of the most formidable description; and only the amazing vigor, industry, economy, and youthful enterprise of this people, could enable them to endure, and recover from these shocks. In the meantime, however, individual suffering is great and extensive. Innumerable families are compelled to give up housekeeping, to sell their houses and furniture, and go with their children into hotels or boarding-

---

(a) This injustice was speedily corrected by the state, and has not been repeated since.

houses. Others are forced to sell their horses and carriages, and dismiss their servants; and nearly all to stint and economise, amidst fear and trembling, never certain what evils a day may bring forth. The number of bankrupts has become so great, and so many men of unquestionable character are irresistibly involved in ruin, that the feelings of all have become hardened, and insolvency ceases to be regarded as a disgrace. It is vain to descant upon these evils, and vainer still to lament over them, unless a remedy be applied that will strike at their root. This can be done only by a thorough reformation of the currency of the whole Union. Since General Jackson destroyed the United States Bank as a national institution, the different states have encouraged banking within their own territories, and the legislatures of many of them have become partners in the banks. Each bank has issued its own paper as extensively as possible; and in prosperous times, when there was no demand for specie for Europe, there was literally no check on these emissions. The two measures of the Democratic party, requiring the public lands and the government duties to be paid in specie, are both recent; yet they supplied the first checks that have operated since the destruction of the United States Bank, and their tendency is most salutary, although they have been condemned by the Whigs.

Oct. 17. Ther. 58°. *Schools.*—The secretary of the American Common School Society "estimates the total number of children in the United States between the ages of four and sixteen years at 3,500,000; and of this number 600,000 do not enjoy the benefits of a common school education." (*Chronicle of the Church.*)

Oct. 21. Ther. 38°. We attended the Episcopalian church and heard Mr. Burgess preach. The church is well appointed and well filled, and the music was excellent. They use an improved prayer book.

Ridicule of Public Characters.—The Americans indulge extensively in ridicule of the governors and other men set in authority over them. The judges and clergy appear to be the only public characters who escape from this outrage. The practice exerts an evil influence on the minds of the people themselves. It diminishes their Veneration and fosters their Self-Esteem, and is without a shadow of apology. The subjects of despots are often forced, by an irresistible and irresponsible power, to groan under the administration of weak or wicked men, and have no means of escaping from their inflictions, or even of solacing themselves amidst their sufferings, except by venting their displeasure in satire and wit. In America the people choose their own magistrates of all grades; and in Connecti-

cut the judges for a long series of years were nominated every
six months, and even now they are elected annually. It seems
a reasonable expectation that the electors should reverence the
objects of their own choice, at least while they permit them to
retain power; but the minority, who do not concur in the appointment, take revenge for their disappointment by lampooning
the individuals who have obtained the suffrages of the majority.
They plead the example of England in extenuation of this conduct. In England, the person and character of the sovereign
are sacred by law, but the ministers are delivered over to the
public as objects of unbounded invective and derision. In the
United States, the people themselves are the sovereigns, and
they are as sacred as the Queen in England. No newspapers,
or orators, dare to proclaim their ignorance, their fickleness,
their love of money, or any of their other imperfections. The
president of the Union and the governors of the states are
merely their executive magistrates or ministers, and, like their
prototypes in Britain, they are abandoned to the abuse and ridicule of all.

Salaries of the Judges.—The judges of Connecticut, as before
mentioned, were for many years elected by the people half-year-
ly, and now they are elected annually. So forcibly, however,
does habit, and the tendency to acquiescence in established arrangements operate, that the judges are regularly re-elected, and
are allowed to serve till they reach seventy years of age, when
they are no longer eligible. In fact, an annual appointment is
very nearly as secure a tenure of office as one for life, unless the
incumbent be guilty of glaring incapacity or misconduct. The
salaries, however, in this state are so small that they present no
temptation to a lawyer, in even moderate practice, to leave the
bar and ascend the bench. The chief justice receives only
$1100 per annum of salary, and the four associate justices $1050
each. The salary of the governor of the state is $1100. An
instance occurred, not many years ago, of a chief justice, a
man of talent and high legal accomplishments, whose family increased to such an extent, that he could not maintain and educate
them on his salary. He resigned his office, returned to the bar,
and speedily doubled or tripled his income. The Americans
respect men of wealth; and as there are now many persons in
Connecticut, in no very exalted station, whose incomes are
double or triple those of the judges, the latter are liable to be
looked down on by vulgar minds on account of their poverty.
They are also unquestionably open to strong influences from
popular opinion. Nevertheless, the testimony of good and able
men here is strong in favor of their intelligence, uprightness, and
independence.

Slavery.—I conversed with a gentleman who passed a winter in Bermuda, when there were many Negro slaves on the island. None, however, had been imported for more than fifty years before the time of his visit, and during that interval they had been educated, well treated, and employed as pilots, and in other offices of trust. He said that they were finely-formed men, their features had improved, and their countenances had lost the heavy African expression. They not only looked but actually were intelligent. This shows the capability of the Negro race of improvement by cultivation.

Washington College.—This is the name of the college in Hartford. In 1840 the number of students was—resident graduates, 13; seniors, 14; juniors, 13; Sophomores, 29; freshmen, 14. Total, 83.

Oct. 22. Ther. 22°. *State Prison at Weathersfield.*—To-day I visited this state prison, situated a few miles from Hartford, with six or seven gentlemen who have attended my lectures. Among them were the Rev. Principal Totten of Washington College, the Rev. Mr. Gallaudet, Dr. A. Brigham, and others. It is conducted on the principles adopted in the state prisons at Boston and Auburn already described. There are nearly 200 prisoners at present on the books. They sleep in separate cells, but labor in large workshops, back to back, and in presence of keepers, who prevent speech or communication. The prison yields about $7000 per annum of profit to the state, a satisfactory proof that it is managed with vigor and economy. I here learned a curious fact illustrative of the Connecticut character. By the existing statutes, adultery is a crime punishable by three years' imprisonment and hard labor in the state prison. The law is rarely executed against ladies and gentlemen who go astray; but when an idle pauper becomes a burden on the city's funds, it is not uncommon to permit a few facilities for the commission of this crime to encompass him;—if he err he is tried, condemned, and sent to the state prison, where his morals are corrected, and he is forced to maintain himself.

Moral Responsibility.—In the course of my lectures in Hartford, I had stated and illustrated the difference between the heads of men who are habitual criminals, and those who are virtuously disposed, and impressed on the minds of my audience the peculiar forms and proportions of the animal, moral, and intellectual regions of the brain which distinguish these two classes, and also those which are found in the intermediate class in whom the three regions are nearly in equilibrium. Mr. Pillsbury, the superintendent of the prison, brought a criminal into his office, without speaking one word concerning his crime or history. I declined to examine his head myself, but requested the gentle-

men who accompanied me to do so, engaging to correct their
observations, if they erred. They proceeded with the examination, and stated the inferences which they drew respecting the
natural dispositions of the individual.   Mr. Pillsbury then read
from a manuscript paper, which he had prepared before we
came, the character as known to him.   The coincidence between
the two was complete. The prisoner was withdrawn, another was
introduced, and the same process was gone through, with the same
result in regard to him. So with a third, and a fourth.   Among
the criminals, there were striking differences in intellect, and in
some of the feelings, which were correctly stated by the observers.

These experiments, I repeat, were made by the gentlemen
who accompanied me, some of whom were evangelical clergymen, of the highest reputation.   They inferred the dispositions
from their own perceptions of the forms of the heads.   They
recognised the great deficiencies in the moral organs, and the
predominance of the animal organs, in those individuals whom
Mr. Pillsbury pronounced to be, in his opinion, incorrigible; for
the question was solemnly put to him by Dr Brigham, whether
he found any of the prisoners to be irreclaimable under the existing system of treatment, and he acknowledged that he did.
One of the individuals who was examined had been thirty years
in the state prison, under four different sentences, and in him the
moral region of the brain was exceedingly deficient.   I respectfully pressed upon the attention of the reverend gentlemen, that
the facts which they had observed were institutions of the Creator, and that it was in vain for man to be angry with them, to
deny them, or to esteem them of light importance

Mr. Pillsbury added that he could not trace above one in fifty
criminals who was thoroughly corrected, and the reformed were
young offenders committed for not less than five years for the
first time.   A shorter confinement led them directly back to
crime   More offenders against the person than against property
are reformed.

In treating of the difference between the functions of Individuality, which observes things that exist, and those of Eventuality, which observes motion, or active phenomena, I had mentioned in my lectures that a spectator of a military review, who
has large Individuality and small Eventuality, will observe and
remember the details of the uniforms, and other physical appearances of the men, but overlook and forget the evolutions;
while another spectator with large Eventuality and deficient Individuality will observe and recollect the evolutions, but overlook and forget all the minute particulars in dress and appearance. It having been observed that Mr. Pillsbury's head presented
this last combination, Mr. Gallaudet, without giving any expla-

nation of his object, asked him whether in seeing a review, he would observe and recollect best the appearance of the men or the evolutions.   He replied instantly, " The evolutions."

Oct. 23. Ther. 3*l*°. *The Bearing of Phrenology on Scripture.*—The facts before mentioned have led several members of my class to serious reflections on the relation between Phrenology and the prevalent interpretations of Scripture.   I have repeated to them what I have said to all others, that Nature will not bend, nor will she cease to operate, and that if they discover any discrepancies between her truths and their own interpretations of the Bible, these interpretations must be corrected and brought into harmony with nature.

I afterwards learned that a relaxation of the principles of Calvinism has already taken place in the theology of Connecticut, which renders the views of the human mind presented by Phrenology less formidable to the divines of that state than to those of the Church of Scotland.   Dr. Taylor, Professor of Divinity in Yale College, celebrated as one of the most orthodox institutions in the Union, has for some years abandoned the doctrine of the total corruption of human nature, and been supported by a large majority of the clergy of the state.   Dr. Tyler now leads the orthodox, or total-corruption party, and has been enabled to found a new theological seminary at Windsor, on the Connecticut, which numbers seventeen or eighteen students.   I have looked into the controversy on this subject, and find the following statement of Dr. Taylor's views given by himself in a letter addressed to Dr. Hawes, of Hartford, dated the 1st of February, 1832:—

"I do *not* believe," says he, " that the posterity of Adam are, in the proper sense of the language, guilty of his sin; or that the ill-desert of that sin is truly theirs; or that they are punished for that sin.   But I do believe, that, by the wise and holy constitution of God, all mankind, in consequence of Adam's sin, become sinners by their own act.

"I do *not* believe that the nature of the human mind, which God creates, is itself sinful; or that God punishes men for the nature which he creates; or that sin pertains to any thing in the mind which precedes all conscious mental action, and which is neither a matter of consciousness nor of knowledge.   But I do believe that sin, universally, is no other than selfishness, or a *preference* of one's self to all others—of some inferior good to God; that this free voluntary preference is a permanent principle of action in all the unconverted, and that this is sin, and all that in the Scriptures is meant by sin.   I also believe, that such is the *nature* of the human mind, that it becomes the occasion of universal sin in men in all the appropriate circumstances of their existence; and that, therefore, they are truly and properly said to be sinners by *nature.*"*

The phrenological doctrine, that every faculty is manifested by a distinct organ; that the Creator constituted the organ, and ordained its functions; that therefore each is good in itself, and has a legitimate sphere of action; but that each is also liable to be abused, and that abuses constitute sin, approaches closely to Dr. Taylor's views, as expressed in the preceding letter. There is a general opinion abroad that Dr. Taylor is still progressive in his opinions, and that he will announce farther modifications of Calvinism. Those who embrace liberal opinions in theology say, that they expect him still farther to purify the faith of Connecticut; while those who adhere to the ancient creed express their fears that the extent of his *backslidings* is not yet fully developed.

Oct. 24. Ther. 51°. *The Hartford Retreat.*—This is a lunatic asylum beautifully situated, and having 17 acres of ground attached to it. The patients perform no labor, and the classification is very imperfect; nevertheless Dr. Fuller the physician mentioned that the cures amount to 90 per cent. of the recent cases. He told me that a part of the head which he had pointed out (Concentrativeness) is always small in the incurably insane, or that it becomes small if the disease be continued; and that, when that part is large, he expects recovery. This was new to me, and I record it, to call the attention of phrenologists to the subject. Dr. Brigham, who accompanied me, pointed out a case of mania proceeding from disease of the cerebellum, which he had successfully treated by local depletion in that region.

Oct. 25. Ther. 48°. *Phrenology.*—I delivered the last

---

* The controversy on this point extends to a volume of above 400 pages. Those parts of it which I consulted were the following —" Two discourses on the nature of Sin delivered before the students of Yale College, July 30, 1826, by Eleazar F. Fitch, Professor of Theology." "*Concio ad clerum,* a Sermon delivered in the chapel of Yale College, September 10, 1828, by Nathaniel W. Taylor." "A Review of the above Sermon by Joseph Harvey, 1829." "An examination of the said Review, Hartford, 1829." "An Inquiry into the nature of Sin, as exhibited in Dr. Dwight's Theology. By *Clericus,* 1829." "Strictures on the Review of Dr. Spring's Dissertation on the means of Regeneration. By Bennet Tyler, D. D., Portland, 1829." "A Vindication of said Strictures, by the same author, Portland, 1830." "Letters to Rev. Nathaniel W. Taylor, D. D., by Leonard Woods, D. D., Andover, 1830." "Correspondence between Rev. Dr. Taylor and Rev. Dr. Hawes, Hartford, January, 1832." "Remarks on Rev. Dr. Taylor's Letters to Dr. Hawes. By Bennet Tyler, D. D., Boston, 1832." "Letters on the present state and probable results of Theological Speculations in Connecticut, 1832." "A Dissertation on Native Depravity. By Gardiner Spring, New York, 1833." These productions show at once the importance attached to the question under discussion, and the thorough investigation which it received.

lecture of my course, and a committee was appointed to present resolutions.

Oct. 26. Ther. 47°. The committee waited upon me, and presented the resolutions, which are printed in the Appendix, No. VI. Tickets were, at my request, presented to the editors of all the periodicals published in Hartford, who, as I was informed, attended the lectures. They did not, so far as I observed, notice them during their progress, and I was told that the cause of their silence was the fear of giving offence by either approving or disapproving. After the close of the course, " The Congregationalist" printed a favorable notice, but avoided offering any opinion on the merits of Phrenology.

The Deaf and Dumb Institution.—We visited this institution along with Mr. Gallaudet. The United States' government gave a donation in its favor of a township of land in Alabama, which has been sold, and the proceeds invested; and it is thereby enabled to provide food, lodging, and tuition, for its pupils, for the annual payment by each of $100, or 20*l.* sterling. Mr. Gallaudet called our attention to the happy expression of the countenances of the pupils, and again differed from Miss Martineau in his opinion of the mental condition of the deaf and dumb. He regards it quite possible, when their natural talents and dispositions are good, to educate them, and to train their dispositions thoroughly. We saw them perform a variety of exercises, indicating great intelligence and mental resources.

I gave Mr. Gallaudet the proposition, that, "many years ago, Columbus discovered America," to be communicated by signs merely, without finger-spelling or the use of any language except that of the countenance and gestures, to his former pupil David. In our presence he made a variety of signs, and David wrote, " A long time ago Columbus sailed west and discovered America." The communication made to David was, that, "a long time ago a great man sailed west," &c.; he supplied the name from his general reading. Mr. G. next mentioned to us, that he would communicate by signs also, without words, that " the American leaders signed the Declaration of Independence." He made a variety of gesticulations, and David wrote, "John Hancock advised them to make war with England and be independent." David has a large anterior lobe of the brain and very large organ of Imitation, with an excellent development of the moral organs, and a sanguine and nervous temperament. He is now one of the assistant teachers of the Institution, and supports his aged mother out of his salary. When he was a child, she lamented over his deafness, and regarded him as her greatest burden. He is now her only stay.

We saw also Julia Brace, who is blind, deaf, and dumb. The

anterior lobe of her brain is well developed, indicating natural
intellectual talent, but the coronal region is rather deficient. She
has great acuteness in smell and touch; and delivered our hand-
kerchiefs to us by smell, after they had been mixed, and we had
changed places. She examined C——'s dress from her bonnet
to her shoes, most carefully, by touch. She dresses herself,
makes her own bed, and does up her own hair; but she has received very little instruction, and seems unhappy. She has
neither occupation nor amusement. As she has large organs of
Time, I recommended that she should be taught to beat time for
her entertainment. The deaf and dumb pupils here dance with
pleasure and success.

Oct. 27. Ther. 53°. *The Pulpit.*—To-day we heard the
Rev. Dr. Hawes preach. His text was in Matthew, vi, 19.
" Lay not up for yourselves treasures upon earth," &c. He is
the eminent Congregationalist minister to whom Dr. Taylor's
letter before quoted was addressed. He agrees with Dr. Taylor
in his opinions about original sin. He preached a bold, liberal,
and practical sermon, in relation to the commercial crisis which
has just occurred. He told his congregation that a character
made up of deep anxieties about dollars and cents could not be
pleasing to God, that the wealth of many of them was about to
be swept away; and that, from their natural reluctance to part
with it, strong temptations to act dishonestly would arise; but
he entreated them to part with all freely except their integrity.
God required them to pay all they owed, to the last cent, and if
they did so, so far as they had the means, and preserved their
honor, they would be more worthy than if they parted with conscience, and had the whole world as their own. He said that
there is something fundamentally wrong in the " credit system"
of this country. Only one young man in twelve who begins
business in New York succeeds and becomes rich: the rest
pass through speculation and various fortunes to bankruptcy and
ultimate ruin. " The crash which is now heard at a distance
will soon reach you, and the laboring poor will be thrown out of
employment, and they must rely on you for subsistence. The
missionaries whom you have sent abroad will look to you for a
continuation of your supplies; you must not abandon them in the
wilderness. You can answer these calls only by retrenchment.
Calculate the sums you spend on sumptuous clothing, elegant
furniture, and costly entertainments, and lop off part in time,
and prepare the saving for these calls. Do not despond. When
all your accumulations are gone, you will have your fertile land,
your bright sun, your strong arms; and if you preserve also a
pure conscience, you will still have the best blessings of life, and
you know that God will never cease to be gracious." This is

merely a faint outline of the discourse, written down from memory after my return home from the church. In tone, matter, and manner, it was bold, searching, honest, yet sympathetic and encouraging—such, in short, as sermons should generally be. It bore the directest reference to real life, and applied Christianity to practical duties. Instead of being forgotten as soon as uttered,* as many sermons are, my impression is that it will be distinctly remembered in Hartford long after the present day.

Hartford.—The situation of Hartford is very beautiful, and many of the citizens live in detached villas surrounded by grass plots and shrubberies, situated on gentle eminences commanding extensive views of the valley of the Connecticut and the hills by which it is bounded. The custom of being over-housed is said to prevail here extensively. I was told that the annual expenditure in many of these large and handsome villas will not exceed $1500 (£300 sterling) per annum. In England, they would suffice for the accommodation of families possessing £1500 or $7500 a-year.

Oct. 28. Ther. 48°. We left Hartford with sincere respect for the kind friends whose society we had enjoyed, and, at 2 P. M., sailed up the river for Springfield. The water in the Connecticut is now very low, and, although the steamboat is small and draws little water, we could not pass the rapids, but entered and passed through a canal six miles long. We rose by three locks of ten feet in height each, and again entered the river. The steamboat has its wheel and paddles in the stern. In the canal we moved at the rate of six miles an hour, and the surge was not greater than I have seen raised by a tow-boat going at the same rate. For ten days past the weather has been, and still continues to be, clear, calm, and mild. The rich tints of autumn render the woods gorgeously beautiful, and the whole scenery is exceedingly picturesque. We arrived at Springfield at half-past six.

Oct. 29. Ther. 40°. *To Worcester and Boston.*—This day, at half-past eleven, we started for Worcester by the rail-

---

* The Edinburgh Review for October 1840 expresses " our wonder that there should be so small a proportion of sermons destined to live; that, out of the *million* and upwards preached annually throughout the Empire, there should be a very few that are remembered *three whole days after they are delivered,*—fewer still that are committed to the press, scarcely one that is not in a few years absolutely forgotten." P 66. There is only one answer that can be given to this statement. As the sermons are preached by the best educated men in the country, and by men of at least average abilities, the subjects of them must be such that they do not stand in a natural relation to the human faculties, and therefore do not interest or edify their hearers. In no other department of industry would such a waste of labor be permitted.

road, which has been opened since we travelled to Springfield a
month ago.   Yesterday a stray horse had its legs and head cut
off on this railroad by the engine, and the night before a carter
had left a cart with stones standing on the track, against which
a train loaded with merchandise had run in the dark and been
smashed to pieces.   We hoped to be more fortunate, and were
so; but, although we encountered no danger, our patience was
sufficiently tried.   About ten miles from Springfield we came to
a dead " fix," and the whole train stood motionless for three
long hours, enlivened only by occasional walks in the sunshine,
and visits to a cake-store, the whole stock of eatables in which
was in time consumed, the price of them having risen from
hour to hour in proportion to the demand.   The advance was
equal to at least 250 per cent. between the first sales and the
last.   The cause of our detention was the non-arrival of the
train from Worcester, which, from there being only a single
track of rails, could pass our train here and nowhere else.   We
heard nothing of its fate, and expected it to arrive every minute
till four o'clock, when at last an express on horseback came up,
and announced that it had broken down, but that it was now
cleared off the rails, and that we might advance.   Again I admired the patience and good humor of the American passengers,
which never forsook them in all this tedious detention.   A
clergyman, of some pretty liberal sect, but whose name I did
not learn, knew me, and spent two hours of this time in discussing the attributes, power, and foreknowledge of the Deity—the
laws of nature and Phrenology—often in language to which I
could attach no definite ideas.   When he raised his hat, I saw
that he possessed very moderate organs of Causality; yet he
was acute in all the perceptions that related to Individuality and
Eventuality: he seemed also to be sincere and amiable; and,
having a high nervous temperament. he delighted in metaphysical discussions, although he was not fitted by nature to excel in
this field of philosophy.   At 6 P. M. we arrived at Worcester;
but here we found ourselves in another " fix."   The afternoon
train from Boston does not arrive till 7 P. M., and we could not
proceed to that city until it appeared.   It was now dark, and
for another hour and a half the passengers sat with exemplary
patience in the cars.   At half-past seven P. M. we started again,
and arrived in Boston, without farther impediment, about ten
o'clock, with pretty good appetites, as we had breakfasted at
half-past seven in the morning, and been allowed no meal since
that hour.   The car was seated for fifty-six passengers, and
contained at least thirty.   There was no aperture for ventilation, and, when night came, the company insisted on shutting
every window to keep out the cold.   A few who, like us, pre-

ferred cool air to suffocation, congregated at one end, where we opened two windows for our relief.

Oct. 30. 1840. Ther. 40°. *Boston.—Phrenology.*—Some weeks ago the friends of education in Boston sent me an invitation to return and deliver a second course of lectures on Phrenology, in this city; and they have secured an audience, hired a chapel, in Philip's Place, Tremont street, and made all other necessary arrangements for my accommodation.

Education.—A course of weekly lectures is now in the progress of being delivered gratis by the educated gentlemen of Boston to the assistant-teachers of the common schools. To-day, we heard Mr. Mann deliver an excellent address on "corporal punishment." The hall in Tremont Row was crowded. He drew a striking picture of the different mental conditions of the children who are assembled in the common schools. They not only differ in their natural dispositions, but at home some may have been spoiled and indulged in their every whim; others may have been taught by example to swear, to lie, and to steal; others may have been beaten unmercifully and capriciously, and have known no law except that of force. The schoolmaster is called on to reduce this mass of discordant elements to order, and to infuse into it the spirit of obedience, attention, exertion, self-command, and mutual respect. He did not think that in the present state of the civilisation of Boston, corporal punishment could be entirely dispensed with in common schools. He, however, deprecated its excessive use. There were teachers, he said, who, if consulted about the situation of a school-house, would plant it at the side of a birch-grove, "not for the sake of the shade, but of the substance." In his view, the minimum of infliction would indicate the maximum of qualification in the teacher for his duties. He recommended that corporal punishment should always be inflicted in private, because the imagination exaggerates its terrors, while familiarity lessens them: that the rod should be used in solemnity and sorrow, and never in passion; and that the quantity of punishment should be such as to render it a real chastisement, but never cruel. He entered into a philosophical exposition of the objects of punishment, and of its effects on children of different natural dispositions. His discourse contained, also, admirable illustrations of his principles, in which wit and logic were gracefully combined, and the whole was interspersed with passages of touching eloquence. Altogether the lecture was a moral and intellectual treat.

Oct. 31. Ther. 48°. *The Negroes of the Amistad.*—By the American law one foreigner may prosecute another in the courts for assault and battery, although committed on the high seas, if both are found within the American jurisdiction. Availing themselves of this law, the negroes captured in the Amistad have, by their counsel, applied to the court for a warrant of imprisonment against Ruiz and Montez, the Spaniards who claim them as their slaves, which has been granted; and these two gentlemen are now in prison through default of bail. This is done at the instance of the abolitionists, and is resorted to in order to force the court to decide whether the Africans are slaves or free. The assault and battery charged, is the fact of forcing them on board of the schooner and carrying them captive out to sea. If they were free men, this is an indictable offence, for which their pretended owners are answerable: If they are slaves, the act was justifiable. Meantime many of the New York newspapers are abusing the abolitionists for resorting to this form of law, as if they were felons themselves. They have an unbounded sympathy for Ruiz and Montez, " the Spanish gentlemen," who, they say, having escaped from the murderer's knife, have been cast for protection on the American shores; but none for the Africans who were stolen from their homes by " Spanish gentlemen," and sold as slaves in Cuba, in defiance. if not of the laws of Spain and America, at least of the dictates of mercy and justice.

The annual election for the officers of state and the members of the legislature of Massachusetts is approaching, and the voters are addressing letters to the candidates to learn their sentiments on the abolition of slavery in the District of Columbia, the prohibition of the slave-trade between the different states of the Union, and other points connected with slavery. Most of those who have been appealed to have answered in favor of abolition.

The Sub-Treasury Law.—I have repeatedly expressed my humble opinion that the Democratic party is in the right with regard to instituting a national treasury, with sub-treasurers, in various parts of the Union, who shall receive the revenue of the United States in specie, and lock it up in strong boxes until needed, and who shall be punished as felons if they embezzle any part of it. They are laboring hard, through the newspapers, in the speeches of their orators, and by lectures specially devoted to the subject, to unfold to the public the principles which regulate the currency, the evils of excessive bank issues, and irredeemable paper; and, altogether, they afford on this subject an example of sound sense, real patriotism, and respect for the understandings of the people, which cannot be sufficiently commended. The Whigs meet their arguments by declamations about the evils into which the Democrats have brought the country; they ascribe the present universal derangement of the currency, the stagnation of trade, and the general bankruptcy which prevails, to the " hard cash" principles of Van Buren and his party; and promise them "credit," wealth, and plenty, if they will turn the Democrats out of office and put *them* in. The imperfectly educated people understand little of abstract reasoning; they are rarely capable of tracing a principle in political economy through present evil to distant good, while they are captivated by promises of future prosperity, and readily believe in what they wish to be true, viz., that Whig rule will restore banks, credit, wealth, and general happiness. They are going rapidly round to the Whig side.

Nov. 3. Ther. 38°. *The Colonisation Society.*—Several years ago a society was instituted in the United States, called "the American Colonisation Society," to provide means for transporting free negroes to the settlement of Liberia, on the coast of Africa, where they might form a separate and independent colony; thus ridding the Union of the black population, and spreading civilisation into the interior of the African continent. Mr. Elliott Cresson came to England, and was warmly received by many philanthropists as a missionary from this society. The abolitionists now declaim against this society in unmeasured terms, and I have endeavored to discover their objections to it. Some of these are as follows: 1st, It is physically impossible that the society's operations can put an end to negro slavery in the United States; because the annual increase of slaves by birth alone is so great that the whole American navy would not suffice to transport the blacks to Africa. The society, by pretending to do something, endeavors to divert the public mind both from its own inadequacy to accomplish any important good, and from the crying evil of slavery itself. 2dly, It serves also to support the marketable value of slaves and slave-labor, by removing free negroes who might compete with them. 3dly, It is converted by the slave-owners, who are its warm supporters, into a powerful prop to slavery. The free blacks form the only conductors of discontent between the philanthropic whites and the slaves. Where there are no free negroes in a district, the blacks born in it are reared with the conviction that slavery in the negro and liberty in the white, are institutions of nature, with which they never think of interfering. Intercourse with free negroes destroys this illusion, and engenders a desire in the slaves to improve their condition. The legislatures of some of the slave states observing this fact, have passed laws prohibiting the return of free negroes who leave their territories. There is a clause, however, in the articles of union, which provides that every American citizen shall enjoy the privileges of citizenship in all the states, and, as these acts of the slave-holding legislatures deprive the free negro citizens of this general right, which the union guarantees, it is thought that the supreme court of the United States would annul

THE COLONISATION SOCIETY.

them as unconstitutional. To avoid the agitation of this question, the planters patronise Liberia as a place to which, by annoyance, by terror, or by bribes, they may force the free negroes to fly, and thus indirectly obtain the advantages which they contemplated by their laws enacting banishment against them. (a)

I believe that there is force in these objections; yet the evils on which they rest appear to me to arise from abuses of the colony of Liberia, and not to be necessarily inherent in the scheme. In the United States the free negroes suffer many evils from the climate and from their degraded social condition, and they also encounter great obstacles to their advancement, from being forced to compete in all branches of industry with a race superior to themselves in native energy of mind, in education, and in social power and respectability. To many of them a home in a climate congenial to their constitutions, and amidst a society of their equals, at the same time carrying with them the benefits of American civilisation, would be advantageous: and such Liberia, if honestly administered, might unquestionably become. I cannot, therefore, join in the condemnation of this scheme as necessarily fraught with evil, however much it may have been abused; and it appears to me, that, although universal emancipation were actually accomplished, Liberia might still be useful as an asylum for such of the American negroes as could find no satisfactory resting-place in the Union.

In vol. i, p. 264, I inserted several advertisements by slave-merchants in Washington, the capital of the Union. A friend in Boston informed me to-day, that the "jails" mentioned in them are licensed, directly or indirectly, by the United States government, as sovereigns of the district of Columbia, and that they, or the city of Washington, draw $400 a-year from each as the price of the license! This may be meant to operate as a check on their increase, and to give an opportunity for laying them under regulations; but the whole transactions of these slave-dealers are sadly in discord with the principles of humanity and justice consecrated by the American Union.

We went to Dr. Channing's church in Federal street to-day, Sunday, but he did not preach. A stranger officiated in his stead. As soon as the sun sets, we hear the pianofortes, and the ladies' voices singing in full activity. Dr. Tuckerman, well known for his highly philanthropic exertions in consoling and reclaiming the vicious poor of Boston, is extremely ill of con-

(a) The simple and conclusive answer to this accusation, is the fact, that the larger number of the emigrants in Liberia were slaves manumitted at a great pecuniary sacrifice to their owners, for the express purpose of their enjoying the rights and privileges of freemen in Africa, whither they went of their own free will.

sumption, and we were not allowed to see him when we called. He is much esteemed, and his illness is deeply regretted.

Nov. 5. Ther. 27°. *Orestes Augustus Brownson.*—This gentleman was originally a preacher, and afterwards became a politician; and his mental fertility and originality are so great that, two years ago, he established " The Boston Quarterly Review" to afford a vent for his thoughts. He has not only conducted, but essentially written it since. In his eighth number for October 1839, an article appeared on the " Education of the People." " Religion and politics," says he, " do in fact embrace all the interests and concernments of human beings, in all their multiplied relations." * * " If, then, we are to have in the commonwealth a system of populur education, which shall answer the legitimate purposes of education, we must have a system which shall embrace both religion and politics." (p. 402.) Mr. Brownson is a warm Democrat, and his object is avowedly to undermine the Board of Education. He objects to the Board because it recommends the teaching of Christianity "so far, and only so far, as it is common to all sects." " This," says he, ",if it mean any thing, means nothing at all." " There is, in fact, no common ground between all the various religious denominations in this country, on which an educationalist may plant himself. The difference between a Unitarian and a Calvinist is fundamental. They start from different premises." " The gospel of Jesus Christ is ' another gospel,' as expounded by the one, from what it is as expounded by the other." " If we come into politics, we encounter the same difficulty. What doctrines can the destiny of society will these normal schools inculcate? If any in this commonwealth at present, they must be Whig doctrines, for none but Whigs can be professors in these schools. Now the Whig doctrines on society are directly hostile to the Democratic doctrines. Whigism is but another name for Hobbism. It is based on materialism, and is atheistical in its logical tendencies!"

These latter words would serve admirably well for a motto to a pamphlet by the Bishop of Exeter against national education, but my object in noticing Mr. Brownson's article is to make a few remarks on the insidious course of argument by which he (the friend and advocate of "equal rights and social equality," as he calls himself) labors to destroy the most beneficial institution for the welfare of the people which his country can boast of. His argument, reduced to a logical form, appears to me to be the following:—" All education," says he, " that is worth any thing, is either religious or political." But there is no common ground in Christianity in which all sects can meet, and as our " equal rights" prohibit any one sect from enforcing its doctrines on all, therefore there can be *no religious* education by the state. Again: This commonwealth is nearly equally divided between the Whig and Democratic opinions. "Equal rights" prohibit either party from forcing its peculiar principles on *all* the children of the state: therefore there can be no "political" education. As, however, all good education must be either re-ligious or political, and as neither of these can possibly be ac-complished in Massachusetts, there can be no education by the state at all.

Such, accordingly, is Mr. Brownson's avowed conclusion; and there is a remarkable harmony between the results reached by the ultra-Democratic and by the ultra-Tory party in Eng-land, when arguing on the subject of the education of the people. It is explained by the unity of their objects; both desire to keep the people in ignorance that they may use them—the Tories as docile laborers and administrators to the comfort and luxury of genteel life, and the ultra-Democratic politicians as stepping-stones to power. One aim of this article was obviously to fo-ment the opposition to the Board of Education, which I have already mentioned as being secretly hatching; but I am told that it is so completely ultra in its propositions, that Mr. Brownson has defeated his own object.

The only public education which he advocates is that of grown people by means of the pulpit and lyceum. He has some good remarks on the necessity of the pulpit extending the range of its interests, and embracing the affairs of this world in a far more direct manner than it has hitherto done; and I have heard the same idea frequently thrown out by men of various religious opinions in the United States. He urges also the advantage of making the lectures in the lyceums embrace man's moral and social nature, or politics. He ministers to the Self-Esteem of the uneducated mass; for he tells them that they are wiser than the government, and says that it is the duty of the rulers to re-ceive instruction from the people, and not to pretend to give it. "Democracy," says he, "is based on the fundamental truth, that there is an element of the supernatural in every man placing him in relation with universal and absolute truth; that there is a true light which enlighteneth every man that cometh into the world, that a portion of the spirit of God is given unto every man to profit withal. Democracy rests, therefore, on spiritual-ism, and is of necessity a believer in God and in Christ. No-thing but spiritualism has the requisite unity and universality to meet the wants of the masses." p. 406.

This paragraph shows what Mr. Brownson means by his charges of irreligion against the Whigs. They regard the human faculties as standing in need of education. This, in his opinion, is atheism and materialism. He maintains that " there is an element of the supernatural in every man, placing him in relation with universal and absolute truth," which is spiritualism and true religion. In other words, this "element of the supernatural" means the unenlightened and untrained impulses of the human faculties, ever ready to take on whatever impressions, and to move in whatever directions, men of bold and ardent minds choose to communicate to them. It was this " element of the supernatural" which enabled the maniac Thom to persuade the people of Kent that he was Jesus Christ, and to induce them to die in testimony of their belief. So far from its being true that " there is no common ground between all the various religious denominations in this country," the contrary may with more reason be maintained; namely, that here, where no men are bribed by privileges and endowments to profess opinions which they do not believe to be true, but where the mind is left in free-dom to deal with Scripture according to its own perceptions of truth, those views in which all sects of intelligent and well-in-formed men are agreed must really constitute Christianity, and those in regard to which there "is no common ground between them" must be non-essentials. The " Christian Examiner" for July, 1839, observes that, " ever since the apostolic days, the tendency has been to make the metaphysical view of Christ the essential and only important one. However a few may have felt, the mass of Christians have held the moral view of Christ wholly subordinate. Men have never been martyred because they held too low notions of the Saviour's character. His cha-racter has formed no subject for creeds. But creeds have almost always been filled with speculations as to his nature. To sustain particular views on this point, no efforts, no penalties, have been thought too great. For this churches have hurled denunciations against heretics; for this the Inquisition has dug dungeons, and armies have been arrayed with hostile banners, and the sky of Christendom been red with the flames of martyrdom. Christians often have not merely ceased to imitate, but have ceased to think of the character of Christ, in contentions about his nature." Do not these remarks forcibly embody the proposition, that Chris-tian sects have never disputed concerning the excellence of the precepts and the practical conduct of Jesus Christ? and do these form no " common ground" between them, on which to base a religious education? These precepts and that example also, be it observed, relate, to a great extent, to *human conduct in this world*, with which alone states and governments are entitled to interfere. The metaphysical and abstract opinions about which the great differences exist, have reference chiefly to man's destiny in a future state, and regarding them every individual is entitled, by the principles consecrated at the reformation, to judge exclusively for himself.

If the people of the United States fairly understood Phrenology, these attempts to perpetuate their ignorance, in order to render them the enthralled slaves of selfish and ambitious politicians, would rouse their warmest indignation. Phrenology represents our various faculties as general powers or capacities merely, each having at once an extensive sphere of legitimate action, and a still wider field of abuse. Education is the process of communicating to these faculties instruction how they may best accomplish their own gratifications, or how they may avoid evil and pursue good. The faculties have all innate activity, and in acting they will infallibly produce either good or evil; evil, if left blind and unguided; good, if enlightened and trained to virtue. In a busy life, education must begin early, otherwise it can never be accomplished well. Every individual in a civilised community, to borrow from a friend a forcible illustration, is a copartner for life with all the other members of that community: the social body having thus a direct interest in the ability and inclination of every member to discharge his duty, and to observe the laws of the copartnery, is entitled to insist on every one of them submitting to that degree of instruction which is necessary to render him fit for his situation. In other words, every state has the right to instruct and train its members so as to accomplish them for their secular duties, while it has no title to interfere with their private judgments concerning the best means of ensuring their safety in a future life.

The " London Morning Advertiser" of 10th Oct. 1839, mentions, that " At a public meeting held in the Tower Hamlets, it was stated by Mr. H. Althans, the advocate of education, that, when the new Lancasterian school was opened in Bethnal Green, a few weeks ago, out of 300 boys above the age of ten years, who presented themselves for admittance, no fower than **173** were found to be utterly ignorant of every letter of the English alphabet." This is trusting to the inward light on the great scale, and may probably satisfy Mr. Brownson; but if, by the law of England, these 300 boys had had the prospect of voting in the election of the queen, the judges, and the clergy, as well as of the members of the two Houses of Parliament, and of all the civic functionaries, it is highly probable that the bishops would have done more for their instruction, and that the House of Peers would not have thrown out the bill for granting 30,000*l*. for normal schools.

Nov. 17. Ther. 33°. *Insanity.*—In my lectures, after describing the healthy states of the mental faculties, I have added remarks on the effects of disease in the organs on their manifestations, and by this means endeavored to convey to my audiences rational ideas of the causes and nature of insanity. A gentleman, whom I met with in society this evening, told me that this part of my course is particularly interesting and consolatory to him. A near relative of his is insane, and he finds that the lectures are clearing up to his understanding the phenomena of the deranged mind which he had observed, but which he could not previously comprehend; and he now understands also how a cure may be effected in insanity as well as in any other disease. He expressed his conviction, also, that the diffusion of these views among the people will have a great effect in dispelling the ideas of horror and mystery which are so generally connected with insanity, and which, in his own case, he feels to constitute no small portion of the evil. In my last lecture, I remarked that there is no raving or violence in a well conducted lunatic asylum, except when particular patients are laboring under diseased excitement of Combativeness and Destructiveness, and that such cases are rare, and the excitement generally of short duration. He recognised the correctness of this description from his own visits to the Asylum, and wished that the public could comprehend it, that their sympathies for the insane might be divested of terror. There is more proper feeling about insanity in the United States, so far as my observations extend, than in Britain; the relatives of persons affected generally view it as a disease, and are more rarely ashamed of it as a disgrace.

The Law.—In Massachusetts conveyancing is reduced to its simplest elements, and the records of deeds, with the exception of two volumes, are complete, from the foundation of the colony to the present day. Nevertheless, vexatious questions about titles occur here, as in other countries, only not in such great numbers. By the law of this state, an administrator must obtain a license from the proper court to sell the real estate of a person deceased, and it is effectual for only one year; but it may be renewed if necessary on application. Some years ago, an administrator, in strict conformity with the law, sold some valuable property by auction, within the year, and received the price, but, by some oversight, omitted to subscribe the deed of conveyance till three days after its expiration. The heir of the deceased now claims the property, which has risen much in value, and declines to refund the price. The chancery powers of the Supreme Court of Massachusetts are not complete, and, if the title should be set aside, it will require some dexterity so to shape the claim for indemnification against the heir as to reach him effectually. If the case should be brought into the chancery department of the Supreme Court of the United States,

there would be no difficulty, for its powers are universal to redress all wrongs.

The Election in New York.—The election of the governor
and other officers of state in New York is exciting great interest.   The question of the currency is brought to the polls, and
the newspapers teem with the sentiments of the candidates for
or against the banks, as the qualifications or disqualifications for
office.   The Whigs are in favor of a paper currency, regulated
by a national bank; the Democrats advocate specie as the basis
of the medium of exchange.

The Fifteen-Gallon License-Law.—The last and most formidable step in opposition to this law has now been taken.   The
counsel for the rum-dealers have pleaded before the juries that
the law itself is *unconstitutional;* that is to say—that the legislature, in enacting it, exceeded the powers conferred on them
by the constitution of the state; that, therefore, the law is not
binding; and that, as the juries are judges of the law as well as
of the facts submitted to their cognisance, they are entitled to
reject the law; and accordingly acquittals have been boldly demanded on this ground.   The judges have strenuously resisted
this argument, and instructed the juries that they are judges not
of the *validity* of the law, but of its *applicability* to the case
before them, and that if they shall assume to themselves the
power of deciding on the *validity* of the statutes, there will be
an end to all law and justice in the commonwealth.   The men
of judgment and principle among the jurors have recognised the
force of this argument, and perceived that, if juries were rendered masters of the law, they might subvert the whole institutions of the state, and resolve society into its first elements; and
they have, therefore, stoutly resisted the doctrine, which, on
the other hand, has been as eagerly caught at and embraced by
the reckless and unprincipled, who desire only to augment the
power of the people, be the consequences what they will.   Several juries have been dismissed without returning verdicts, in
consequence of irreconcilable differences among the members on
this point.   The proper mode of trying this question is to appeal to the Supreme Court, which has power to determine
whether any act of the legislature be constitutional or not.

Taxation.—In Boston, the middle class of citizens pays most
taxes, and contributes most liberally to charitable institutions.
The city-taxation is much higher than that for state purposes,
and, like the state-taxes, is levied on the whole estimated property, real and personal, of each citizen.   Some rich men, to
avoid this, live beyond the limits of the city, where they display
the symbols of their wealth, and come to town to transact business in humble stores or counting-houses.   By this means they

withdraw much of their property from taxation for civic purposes. There are other very rich men who continually migrate from state to state, and live in hotels and boarding-houses, to avoid taxation. At the same time, other rich men make a munificent use of their wealth. Mr. Dwight has presented $10,000 to the state, to be expended in instituting normal schools, as an inducement to the legislature to grant an equal sum. Before this gift, no normal school existed in Massachusetts.

Nov. 10. Ther. 27°. *The Swedenborgians.*—To-day we attended divine worship in the Swedenborgian chapel. It accommodates five or six hundred persons, is commodious and neatly fitted up, and generally well filled. There is something extremely amiable and spiritual in the mental condition of this class of Christians, and their service was refined and soothing. They have a spiritual interpretation for every incident and doctrine in Scripture. Wonder, Individuality, and Comparison. seemed to be predominant organs in most of the congregations.

Whig Caucus Meeting.—This is Sunday, and in the evening I attended a great Caucus meeting of the Whig party held in Faneuil Hall. It was called by public advertisements and placards, to-morrow being election-day for the great officers of state. No one could give me any reasonable explanation of the origin of the word *Caucus*, which is applied to political meetings. It is an unmeaning-looking vocable to a stranger, and, as used, it seems to imply a general in contra-distinction to a ward meeting of a political party. I was tempted to invent an etymology for it, and to suppose it to be derived from the Latin *cæcus*, blind, because the people have at some period been viewed as giving themselves up at these meetings blindly to the guidance of their political leaders. The Sunday terminates at sunset, and the Caucus met at 7 P. M. The hall was densely crowded, and probably between two and three thousand persons were present. The youthfulness of the assembly was very striking. Without pretending to accuracy, I guessed the ages as follows. Five per cent. of the whole appeared to be boys under fourteen years of age; sixty per cent. young men between fourteen and twenty-eight; fifteen per cent. between twenty-eight and forty; fifteen per cent between forty and fifty; and five per cent. above fifty. In size of brain and combination of organs, the speakers were inferior to the men whom I daily meet with in society. Their ideas were few; their words and figures many; and nearly all was assertion and declamation. Their speeches were addressed to Acquisitiveness, Self-Esteem, and Love of Approbation, much more than to Benevolence, Veneration, and Conscientiousness. The staple of their orations was praise of *"old* Massachusetts;"

of "our *ancient* and beloved Commonwealth;" of prayers that
she might be preserved from bowing the knee to Martin Van
Buren, of denunciations against the Democrats, termed also the
Locofocos; against specie, and the Treasury and Sub-Treasury
bills; and of praises of paper currency, the "credit system," the
Whigs, and Whiggery. The appeals which produced the loudest
acclamations were those which embodied a warlike figure, or a
witty and degrading representation of the Democrats. "To-
morrow," said one speaker, " old Massachusetts will go the poll
like old Ironsides (the pet name of one of their frigates) to battle.
She moved so calmly onward, and so silent were her crew, that
the enemy expected her to strike without a contest, but when old
Ironsides came up, yard-arm to yard-arm, every spirit flashed
with energy and ardor, she sent from all her decks and tops
such a storm of hail and thunder that no sound could be heard
except that of her own mighty voice, when she held her arm,
universal silence reigned, her prostrate enemy floated beside her
sailless, mastless, and helmless, a pitiable wreck at the mercy of
the waves. So shall old Massachusetts make the Locofocos
float on the waters of the state to-morrow at sun-down." This
burst of eloquence called forth loud, long, and unanimous
thunders of applause.

There was no discussion of principle in the speeches; no
statement of facts; in short, very little intellectual substance of
any kind. The object of them clearly was, not to operate on
the understanding, for the whole audience was of one mind, but
to produce *excitement*, with a view to rouse up the voters to go
to the poll next day. Contemplated in this light, and seeing
that the speeches were addressed to a young and essentially an
unintellectual audience, they certainly had the merit of being
well adapted to accomplish the end for which they were
delivered.

I was much struck with the circumstance that the people
must have remarkably few real grievances in any degree chargeable against the Government, when the opposition orators are
able to muster only such slender materials for assailing them.
The statement by one of them that the Sub-Treasury Bill would
lead to a monarchy, was loudly applauded! One of the speakers compared the Democratic candidates to Milton's devils, and
introduced Milton's verses descriptive of them, which he and
his audience applied to particular "Locofocos;" but, from my not
knowing the persons alluded to, the effect was lost on me. The
personal appearance of the individuals who composed the assembly was highly respectable, and their conduct completely orderly.

Our own political meetings are often meagre enough in their
array of facts, principles, and solid arguments; but most of them

are superior to this display—probably owing to the circumstance that we have more real grievances to complain of. When mere excitement is the object with us, we are not inferior to the Americans in the powers of declamation and abuse; and to satisfy my American readers on this point, as well as to maintain my own character for impartiality between the two nations, I shall treat them with the report of a speech delivered just about the same time with the foregoing addresses, by Mr. Bradshaw, the Conservative M.P. for the city of Canterbury. It is as follows:—

"'The Queen thinks that *if the monarchy lasts her time it is enough;* but the people of England will never consent that the crown should be degraded and debased for the inglorious ease of any created being. (Tremendous cheers.) We have not forgotten the *forced abdication of the second James,* nor are we ignorant that the title to the throne of these realms is that derived from a Protestant princess. Look at the appointments that these men and women have lately made. There is not one of them that is not a direct insult to the nation. (Loud cries of hear, hear.) See the *Irish Papists* preferred to place, to power, and to patronage. I shall take leave, on thus referring to them, to contrast the solemn oath sworn by her Majesty at her coronation with her subsequent acquiescence in these acts. (Cheers.) This oath is the compact made between the Sovereign and the people; its obligations are mutual. (Hear.) I will now read it to you, and be you judges whether or no they have been truly fulfilled. Here are the late appointments of Papist councillors, I take them together, and thus I cast them from me with disgust and indignation. (Cheers.) The Prime Minister tells us with rare effrontery that it is his duty to get support wherever he can. Nothing is too low or too foul for his purpose. The *stews of the Tower Hamlets and the bogs of Ireland* are ransacked for recruits (loud laughter); and thus he crawls on, having cast behind him every feeling of honor and high principle. (Loud cheers.) But his ministry, his sheet anchor, is the body of Irish Papists and Rapparees whom the priests return to the House of Commons. (Great applause.) These are the men who represent the bigoted savages, hardly more civilised than the natives of New Zealand, but animated with a fierce undying hatred of England. (Hear.) I repeat, then, deliberately, that *the Papists of Ireland, priests and laymen, peer and peasant, are alike our enemies*—aliens are they in blood, language, and religion. (Loud cheers.) Their hatred of this country is as undisguised as it is inextinguishable, and they have become only more rampant and hostile by the concessions so unwisely made to them. Yet on these men are bestowed the countenance and support of the Queen of Protestant England. But, alas! her Majesty *is Queen only of a faction*, and is as much of a partisan as the Lord Chancellor himself. But shall we quail at this impending danger, and meanly submit without a struggle? No, we will present the same bold front as our fathers did of old (great applause), and God defend the right. (Reiterated applause.) *We will resist to the death ill government*, and unjustly usurped authority. (Loud cheers.) *We will no longer submit to be governed by a profligate court.* (Applause.) It is in your hands, my friends, it is in the hands of the people of England, that her destinies are placed for good or for evil. Upon you, then, be the responsibility. You have the power, see that you make a worthy use of it; but if you will not be true to yourselves, dare not ever again to invoke the sacred name of liberty, and renounce the proud name of freemen of England." (Applause.)

When England can boast of such eloquence from an aristocratic conservative, the political orators of the American democracy must not suppose that they have improved upon the parent nation in the flowers of vituperation and incendiarism.

Nov. 11. Ther. 22°. *New York Election.*—The democratic party have triumphed in the election of the members of the legislature for the *city* of New York, by a majority of fifteen hundred. The newspapers of that city belonging to both parties acknowledge that it has been conducted with order and decorum, and that the result fairly expresses the opinion of the majority. This election took place under the amended law, mentioned in vol. ii, p. 20, and it affords a striking example of the power of a democracy to rectify its own errors; for the civic election last April was marked by disgraceful and wholesale bribery and perjury by both parties.

In the *state* of New York, the Whigs have elected the governor and the majority of both Houses of the Legislature, so that the Democrats have the ascendency in the city alone.

Boston Election. The License-Law.—This is the election day in the city of Boston for the governor and other officers of the state and the members of the legislature; and I went to a polling station to observe the proceedings. All was order and good humor, but opinion is sadly distracted about the license-law, and these differences are now about to operate on the legislature through the medium of the ballot-box. I have already mentioned that, by moral agitation alone, the cause of temperance had made so great a progress in Massachusetts, that, in 1838, the legislature had passed an act, in which both Whigs and Democrats concurred, prohibiting the sale of any liquors containing alcohol in less quantities than fifteen gallons except by special license; that the law was opposed from the first by several friends of temperance as going too far, and as being erroneous in principle; and that it was subsequently evaded by devices, opposed by the rum-dealers by passive resistance, and finally assailed by appeals to juries to disregard it as unconstitutional. The Attorney-General of the state struggled hard against all these forms of hostility to the law, and obtained many convictions against offenders in spite of them; but now the question comes to be decided by the people of the whole state. This is done by their voting for candidates pledged to their various opinions, and even political differences have given way, in a slight degree, to zeal for or against the license-law. At the poll to-day, I found a "regular Whig ticket," containing a list of candidates all Whigs, and a "regular Democratic ticket" all Democrats, both made up without reference to the temperance question, a "*Union* Liberal ticket," containing candidates all Whigs, but the one-half temperance and the other half anti-temperance men, or, as a friend wittily said, a "ticket composed of a glass of rum and a glass of water" alternately. There is a "Whig temperance ticket," the candidates in which are all both Whigs and temperance advocates, a "Democratic temperance ticket" in which they are all Democrats and friends of temperance. Besides these, there was a "Liberal Whig" ticket, an "Independent Democratic" ticket, a "Union Temperance" ticket, and an "Abolition" ticket, the precise meaning of some of which I did not learn. I may here anticipate events subsequent in time, in order to complete this subject at this its most interesting crisis. The result of this day's election all over the state was, that the Whig governor Edward Everett was removed, and Mr. Marcus Morton, a Democratic judge, was chosen governor by a majority of *one;* the Whigs maintained their ascendency in the Senate and House of Assembly, but by a diminished majority; and when the houses met, one of their first acts was to repeal the license-law by nearly a unanimous vote.

Mr. Everett retired from office on 1st January, 1840, and I was told by some of his friends that, within a few days after the loss of his election was announced, he received nearly a hundred and fifty letters from political adherents, expressing their deep regret that they had not gone to the poll on the day of election, because they had considered his return *so certain* that *one* vote could be of no importance to his cause! The path of duty in such cases is plain. Every citizen who wishes well to a public man is bound to vote for him. It is a strange perversion of morals to argue that because *other* men will discharge *their duty*, I may safely neglect mine. In answer to my inquiries, what causes had led to Mr. Everett's exclusion from office, three were mentioned: *First*, He had studied so assiduously to please all, and offend none, that he had taken no decided part on the question of the license-law, and had not allowed himself to be clearly ranked either with its supporters or opponents. If he had taken either side, he would have been more decidedly supported: *Secondly*, The circumstance of his being a Unitarian always carried some orthodox votes against him; and, *thirdly*, he had been four years in office, and some part of the people become impatient of the continued supremacy of one individual, and like to practise " rotation in office."

The first of these reasons, I believe, was the one which chiefly operated against Mr. Everett; yet, according to sound constitutional principles, his conduct was right. He held the situation of chief magistrate, and possessed a veto on the acts of the legislature: To have declared himself the ally of a particular side of a question that would certainly come before the legislature in its next session, would have been tantamount to intimating that the members of the legislature might save themselves the trouble of discussing it; for his negative could extinguish all enactments inconsistent with his declared opinions.

Mr. Marcus Morton, it is said, has stood on the Democratic ticket for governor of this state for fourteen years, and is now elected for the first time, and by a majority of one! He is described to be an able lawyer and an honest man.

Nov. 13. Ther. 33°. *Ventilation of Schools.*—When Mr. Elliot, the present mayor of Boston, entered on his office on the 1st January last, he delivered a public address, in which, among other improvements, he strongly advocated the necessity of ventilating the common school houses. Effect has been given to his recommendation in a new school-house which I this day visited. The ceilings of the rooms are high. In winter a large supply of air, heated by a brick furnace to a moderate temperature, is introduced, and it is let off by five or six separate flues in different parts of the room, which can be opened and shut at pleasure. In each of the rooms the temperature, regulated by a thermometer, was 67° F., the external air being 35°. The garret which used to be lost, has, at Dr. Howe's suggestion, been floored and plastered, and furnished with swinging ropes; and in bad weather the children play in it during the intervals of teaching. All the seats have backs. The teachers told me, that since they have occupied this school-house, the vivacity and capacity of the scholars have obviously been raised, and their own health and energy increased.*

* The following statement occurs in " Reasons for establishing a society for improving the dwellings of the laboring classes in Edinburgh," issued in December, 1840. " A metal tube, opening from the upper part of the

The advantage of not separating the sexes in their hours of recreation, is forcibly illustrated by the following statement extracted from Mr. Stow's excellent work on the "Training System."*—" In a large Foundling Hospital, in the south of Ireland, the boys and girls, from infancy, are permitted (not compelled) to play together, and the result has been, to the knowledge of the superintendents and directors, that only three girls had gone astray in sixteen years; many had given proofs of decided piety; and a large proportion of the females had gone out into service, and otherwise settled in life. Whereas, in Dublin and elsewhere, where the females in hospitals and charity schools are strictly excluded from the other sex during the whole course of their residence in these institutions, the number that had almost immediately gone astray on their leaving the hospitals was lamentable in the extreme."—p. 82. Mr. Stow's work, and that of Wilderspin, are worthy of the attention of every person interested in education.

wall of the room, and joining a general tube which terminates in the furnace of some neighboring factory, is all that is required to ensure a constant supply of fresh air to the inmates of that chamber, though, as often happens, they should be upwards of a dozen in number. A few years ago, a large building in Glasgow, each room of which contained a family, and the tenants of which were in all five hundred, was ventilated in this way, and the result was most satisfactory. Previously to the ventilation, diseases, and particularly typhus fever, had been very fatal to the inmates; five persons had been ill of the latter disease in one room, and in two months, at the end of 1831, fifty-seven had been attacked by it. After the apparatus was applied, four and a half years elapsed, during which there were only three cases of fever, and two of these in a room where the tube had been destroyed." I earnestly recommend these facts to the attention of the Americans of all classes; for they are little sensible of the extent to which they injure themselves by living in bad air.

* " The Training System established in the Glasgow Normal Seminary and its Model Schools, by David Stow, Esq." &c. 1840.

CHAPTER VII.

Nov. 14. Ther. 41°. *Mr. Lalor's Prize Essay on Education* has arrived in Boston, and I hear it very highly commended. It recognises the benefits which phrenologists have
conferred on the cause, and I am told that, coming to America
backed by the approval of the Central Society of Education in
London, it will give additional weight to the views which this
science unfolds in regard to teaching and training the young.

The Chartists.—A friend brought to me "The Western
Messenger," vol. vii, No. VI, published in Cincinnati in October 1839, and requested me to read the first article, on "The
Chartists," and to give him my opinion whether it fairly represented their case. I have read it, and, while it shows a want of
correct information on some important points, it contains a great
deal of truth, and truth which, read here at a distance from the
prejudices which obscure one's judgment at home, makes me
blush for my country. It points out forcibly the unjust taxation
of Britain, by which property is exempted and consumable
articles loaded with duties, throwing the chief burden on the poor,
who by their numbers are the great consumers. It describes
the ill-regulated condition of the jails, and the tyranny of the
magistrates, who all belong to the aristocratic class, in committing
the poor to these prisons for the most trifling offences, and also
in exacting heavy bail from James Lovett and Joseph Collins
the chartist leaders. It exposes the sufferings of the manufac-

turing population, quoting the reports of the commissioners on the Factory System, and Bulwer's England and the English. It represents the poor-law improvement act as an additional oppression on the poor, but this is a mistake; it accuses the Whigs, as a party, of being as averse to further reform as the Tories, another error; it regards the Chartists as in the right, and as justified in taking up arms; the latter, a view from which the wisest philanthropists who know the whole circumstances, will dissent.

I mentioned to my friend that, in June 1838, I had visited Warwick jail, and could confirm the charges made against it. I saw untried prisoners confined in society of convicted felons, and subjected to the same severity of prison discipline. They were ranked up in the court-yard with the condemned, to be gazed on and recognised by visiters, and I had observed one young man of respectable dress and gentlemanly appearance, said to be a clerk in a shop in Birmingham, and still untried, who looked as if he wished the ground to open and swallow him up, so ashamed was he of his condition, yet in the eye of the law he was still innocent! In the society of thieves and prostitutes condemned to transportation to New South Wales, I saw a girl of eight or nine years of age sentenced to imprisonment for having stolen a flower from a flower-pot in a low window in the town, the owner of the flower-pot being a relative of the magistrate who committed the child.* Such facts, I say, made me ashamed of my country, and showed how callously the rich rule when the poor have no legitimate means of making their grievances felt by their masters. If these magistrates had been elected by the people by ballot, such outrages to humanity and justice could not have long existed.

The grand obstacle to the remedy of these evils is the ignorance of the people. In those few instances in which the elective franchise has been preserved to them, they have sold themselves shamefully for sums of money to the highest bidder, and, in the late commotions, they talked of obtaining their rights by physical force. This alarms the middle classes, and affords the aristocracy decent pretences for coercing them by law, and opposing

---

* I mention these cases from memory, and have no note of the names, but similar facts are not rare. In the "Globe" of 21st September 1840, a case is referred to in which the Rev. James Barker, clerk, prosecuted a boy named Thomas Bridge for damaging his fence to the value of one halfpenny. Robert Webb, aged twelve years, testified that the accused pulled some hazel-nuts from the hedge of the prosecutor, but it was not proved that he had damaged the fence. The prosecution, therefore, failed, but the penalty, if the boy had been found guilty, might have been confinement in the county jail for two months, including the tread-mill.—" *Newmarket Petty Sessions.*"

their instruction. The middle classes of society, in whose hands the supreme political power is now lodged, are also so imperfectly educated, that they fear the people and worship their superiors in rank, wealth, and titles. "The greatest enemy of the political conduct of the House of Lords," says a recent critic, "submits to their superiority of rank as he would do to the ordinances of nature; and often thinks any amount of toil and watching repaid by a nod of recognition from one of their number."* This spirit must be changed before justice will be done to the people in Britain; and the middle classes must open their sympathies to the wrongs of the poor, and insist on justice for all.

Nov. 16. Ther. 42°. *Domestic Servants.*—A lady told us that her mother, seeing the annoyances suffered from bad servants, had, on her first entering on housekeeping, resolved that her luxury should consist in good servants; that she lived in a humbler house than many of her neighbors of the same income, but sought out first-rate "helps" and paid them high wages. She has been uniformly well served, and one servant has been in her family for twenty-five years. A few other ladies testified to a similar experience.

Endowments for Education.—A Mr. Smithson of London has left $500,000 to the Government of the United States, to be employed in extending the limits of knowledge among men, or for some similar purpose: and a Mr. Lowel has lately left a larg sum to the city of Boston for providing gratuitous lectures to the people. It is questionable how far legacies for these purposes do good. It is in vain to expect that the general education of the people can be accomplished by means of legacies. They need instruction from competent lecturers, and they will never obtain these, until they consent to pay them. Legacies induce the people to think that they should not compensate lecturers by themselves paying for instruction; and while this idea prevails, a body of professional lecturers can never be found. Gifts of money to provide lecture-rooms and apparatus may be extreemly useful, because these will furnish the physical accomodations for lecturing, and enable the lecturers to lower their terms; but the remuneration for the instruction given should be contributed by the people themselves. Legacies to endow lecturers on education, whose business it should be to act as missionaries to rouse the people to do their own duty, may also, in the present state of human knowledge, be beneficial. No part of the Smithson Fund is to be applied to ordinary teaching, but all is to be dedicated to institutions of a scientific character, calculated to extend the boundaries of knowledge.

* Edinburgh Review, vol. lxxii, p. 10.

Infant Schools.—I find several attempts are in progress in Boston to work out the system of teaching and training which is adapted to infant schools, and to a certain extent they are successful, but nearly the whole processes are invented by the sagacity of a few individuals. Wilderspin's work, and the other manuals for infant-school teaching, are not reprinted in this country, and the originals are not in general circulation. I have advised some of the friends of education to invite Wilderspin to come to the United States and show them these schools in really efficient operation; but they fear public opinion, which will not sanction such a step. Public opinion exerts a troublesome influence in many respects in this country. It will not favor infant-schools, until they shall be *seen* in successful action; yet it will not countenance the best means of accomplishing this demonstration. It frowns and opposes, and insists on being convinced, and leaves to philanthropic individuals the expense, toil, and risk of achieving the public good. If they be successful, it will then deign to smile, if not, it will visit them with obloquy. It is so powerful, also, that individuals find it extremely difficult to act without its support. Owing to the want of its sanction children cannot be easily collected into these infant schools. The parents are afraid of ridicule from their neighbors, or of something wrong, or at least unusual, being taught to their offspring, and decline to send them.

Nov. 17. Ther. 33°. We heard a discourse in the church in Chauncey Place, preached by the Rev. Mr. Dewey of New York, on the character of Job. Mr. Dewey is here on the invitation of the Society for diffusing useful knowledge, and has delivered several lectures to large audiences.

In society this evening I heard a great deal of sensible discussion about the present condition of public affairs. The recent increase of the democratic party in Massachusetts is variously accounted for. The hostility to the license-law is regarded as its chief cause. Both Whigs and Democrats concurred in enacting this law, because it was at first extremely popular, but no sooner did its stringency begin to give offence than the Democrats made "political capital" out of it; that is to say, they ascribed the law to the Whigs, and constituted themselves its vigorous opponents; and they have turned that capital to good account. It is true that the Whigs had a majority in the Legislature which passed it, and could have stifled it, but it is equally certain that the Democrats as a party did not oppose it, while they believed that the people were in its favor. I perceive, however that some of the profounder men of the Whig party descry in the event other influences. They acknowledge that the true democratic principle is advancing, and has much in-

fluenced this election, and that the days when the wealth and
education of Massachusetts were permitted 'to govern it are fast
passing away. This appears to me to be a natural result of the
present condition of American society. No adequate foundation
for an aristocracy of birth or wealth is afforded by the institutions
of this country, and the intelligence of the people has reached
that point at which they are capable of combination, and have
become aware of their own power. The Whigs, therefore,
should throw themselves cordially into the arms of the people,
and, by advancing their improvement in every way, become
their leaders on higher principles than those of mere wealth and
station.

I hear some sagacious persons also remarking that the present
extreme embarrassments of commerce will do good, because
nothing but the want of physical means will prevent this people
from going too far a-head in pursuit of gain. They are deficient
in self-control; and things so often " right themselves," that much
is taken away from the effect of the lessons of experience. This
last observation is correct. The natural sources of prosperity in
this country, in abundance of fertile land, great ingenuity, ceaseless activity, and economy, are so great, that all classes recover
from the prostrations caused by their errors in an incredibly short
space of time.

Nov. 18. Ther 37°. *The Planet Venus.*—To-day, at half-
past eleven o'clock A. M. we saw the planet Venus shining
brightly in a clear sky, the sun shining at the same time. She
was a little west of south. Multitudes of people were standing
in the streets gazing at the spectacle. Some said that they had
seen stars in sunlight before, but to most of them the spectacle
seemed to be new.

Nov. 20. Ther. 27°. *Phrenology.*—The friends of education have requested me to deliver one lecture to the assistant-
teachers, and three lectures in the Odeon Theatre, at the end of
my present course, to which I have with great pleasure acceded.

Portrait of Sir Walter Scott.—In visiting Mr. Ticknor, in
Park street, we saw an original portrait of Sir Walter Scott
painted at Abbotsford in 1824, by Leslie, the celebrated American artist. It is a most truthful representation of the original
man, and the head appeared to me to be perfect. As a work of
art, also, it will stand investigation, although in this respect it is
surpassed by one or two portraits of him by other artists. Taking it for all in all, however, those who look on this picture
have all but seen Sir Walter Scott himself. It represents him
in his short green coat, his usual dress in the country. Having
seen Sir Walter frequently in the Court of Session for more than
five and twenty years, and having minutely studied his head, I

was much gratified to see such a faithful representation of it as this picture presents.

Nov. 21. Ther. 21°. *Phrenology and Animal Magnetism.* —A brother lecturer introduced himself to me to-day, and gave me his own history as follows: Originally he kept a store, and while in this employment became a little acquainted with Phrenology. He examined the heads of his customers; his interest increased; and then began to study it in books. He afterwards gave up the store, and commenced lecturer, head-examiner, and magnetizer. He gives three lectures; the first free, at which he examines heads to excite interest. He charges 12¼ cents (6⅓d.) to every person who attends each of the subsequent lectures, and he examines heads privately for fees. In all his lectures he gives his audience *facts.* "If," said he, "you were to address them with reason, you would never see them after the first lecture." Out of a village of 1500 inhabitants he generally drew from two to three hundred dollars in a week. He was a pure specimen of a Yankee. His temperament was sanguine, bilious, and nervous, indicating great activity; his head was of moderate size, the organs of the observing faculties were large, and those of reflection moderate. I expressed my fears that his mode of proceeding did injury to Phrenology in public estimation as a science. He said that he believed it did so with the better educated classes, but that the people would not receive it in any other way. These facts indicate the condition of the public mind in the rural districts of the United States.

Jeffreys' Respirator.—Last year I exhibited one of these respirators at the end of my lecture on Physical Education in Boston, and described its structure and use. I did the same in New York and Philadelphia. They were previously unknown. I perceive that they are now coming into use in Boston.

Evidences of Christianity.—In conversing with an American clergyman to-day, he remarked that the men who affirmed that they felt no difficulty about the evidences of Christianity, were either incapable of thinking, or hypocrites. In his opinion, the evidence was attended with many difficulties, and they were great either way. There was too much evidence to enable a reflecting mind to reject Christianity, and too little fully to satisfy the understanding when independently applied to its investigation. I remarked that it appeared to me that all the practical portions of Christianity were daily gaining strength from the development of science and the progress of civilisation. Free trade and free institutions are examples of the maxim, "Love your neighbor as yourself" carried into effect on the large scale. The importance attached to doctrinal points will probably diminish in proportion as men become sufficiently civilised to practise the precepts. The doctrines also will one day undergo a new investigation when they come to be considered in relation to the functions of the brain. One point is certain, that all that is true will gain ground; and only error is in danger of suffering from free discussion. My esteem for both the intellect and honesty of this divine was increased by his candor.

Nov. 23. Ther. 12¼°. *The Winter*.—The weather continues brilliantly clear. In the forenoon, the wind from the northwest is high and cutting, but it lulls in the evening and during night. The sun rises at ten minutes past seven, and shines directly into our windows. At 8 P. M. we have a large anthracite coal fire made up; it burns bright all night; it keeps the temperature in our bed-room at 58°; and is still a good fire in the morning when we rise. We leave a portion of the window open all night to supply the room with fresh air; and altogether suffer less from cold than in Scotland.

Africans and Indians.—Some time ago I communicated to a scientific friend, whose opportunities of observation have been ample, and whose powers of analysis are profound, the ideas which I entertained of the African and native American Indian races, such, nearly, as I have described them in vol. i, p. 259-69. He has expressed his opinions by letter to the following effect:—
"Your views respecting the intellectual capacity and general character of the African race do not, I think, differ very materially from my own. Your estimate of them is certainly higher than mine, though not perhaps very strikingly so. And had you had as free access to masses of them, especially of those fresh from their native country,* as I have had, I feel persuaded that the difference in our opinions respecting them would have been less. That they are superior to the North American Indians in their moral and social qualities, and therefore in their *tameableness*, cannot be doubted. But that they are superior in intellect I am not yet prepared very positively to affirm. Nor would I affirm the opposite. That our Indians are in all the attributes of mind greatly above *some* of the African varieties is certain. This is especially true as relates to the Boschesemen and other tribes of the Hottentot race. They and the Papuans are such miserable representatives of humanity, that it would puzzle a jury of naturalists to decide to which they are most nearly allied, the genus *Homo*, or the genus *Simia*. All that I have ever very strenuously contended for on this subject is, that the Caucasian race is constitutionally, greatly, and irreversibly

---

* My friend is correct in this remark. The Africans of the Amistad, who were only a few months from their native shores, presented heads, on the whole, inferior to the negroes whom I had previously seen in the United States.

superior to the other races of man. And of this I am as fully
satisfied as I am that the *Caballus equus* is superior to the
Caballus, asinus, zebra, or quagga. And the superiority is
explained and substantiated by Phrenology."(a)

(a) In connection with this subject, the following, which is a portion of
Mr. Combe's Journal in a former year, is here introduced It was omitted
in its proper place, in order to prevent any injury to the institution in
which the observations were made, caused by the prejudices of its inmates
or others against the *post mortem* examinations.

A native of the Sandwich Islands had died, and we examined his skull
and brain. The skull presented the form which usually characterises the
Caucasian variety of mankind, and resembled, in dimensions and form,
those of the natives of the Sandwich Islands in the Phrenological Society's
Museum in Edinburgh. The brain corresponded with the skull. We
examined also the skull and brain of an American Indian.

At my request the following account of these skulls and brains was drawn
up by one of our company —

The Sandwich Islander was born in Maouvi. At eight years of age,
he left his native island in a foreign ship. He passed his life as a sailor.
He spoke a little English He was a good looking man, and a favorable
specimen of his tribe. Age, twenty-four years. His brain, denuded of the
membranes, weighed exactly 3lb. troy weight.

The North American Indian's parents were of the Gay Head tribe. He
lived principally among the whites; served on shipboard, and could read a
little. He was a well-made man, and his organisation superior to that of
the generality of his tribe. He died at the age of twenty nine years. His
brain weighed 2lb. 12½oz.

Both brains showed a proportionately large development in the animal
region that of the Sandwich islander the largest.

The organs of the moral sentiments were clearly the largest in the brain
of the latter· the anterior lobe was also longest, but they were of equal
height.

His skull was higher and broader in the coronal region; it resembled
more closely the Caucasian skull The brain presented a corresponding
development.

Mr. Combe pointed out the greater development of the region of Cautiousness in this skull; and on examining the corresponding convolutions of
the brain, they appeared decidedly fuller than those in the brain of the
Indian.

The skull of the Indian was fuller in the region of Veneration than that
of the Sandwich islander; and the corresponding convolutions in the brain
were also clearly larger.

The skull of the latter was more protuberant in the region of Benevolence than the Indian's, and the corresponding convolutions of the brain
were also fuller.

The skulls of both were equally developed in the region of the organ of
Hope, and a corresponding fulness was observable in both, in the convolutions which constitute this organ. In general, the convolutions were
rounder and plumper in the brain of the Sandwich islander than in that of
the Indian; but the latter was the firmer and harder of the two

The natives of the Sandwich Islands appear, from the skulls which we
have in Edinburgh, as well as from this instance, to possess a higher development of the moral and intellectual organs, in proportion to those of the

Teachers.—I delivered a lecture to the assistant school·
teachers, and other persons interested in education, and had a
large audience. The subject of the lecture was the question,
Does the mind manifest a plurality of faculties differing from
each other in functions and relative strength, or is there only one
general power equally susceptible of all emotions, and equally
applicable to all pursuits? I pointed out the great difference that
would ensue in practical teaching, according as the one or other
theory was embraced. After the lecture, the teacher of a distinguished private seminary mentioned to me that, in consequence of the views which he had derived from my lectures on
Phrenology last year, he had ventilated his school, alternated the
studies, and increased the intervals of relaxation, and had found
the health of himself and his scholars improved, their powers of

animal propensities, than the North American Indians, and they have exhibited corresponding qualities of mind. They are more easily civilised
and christianised.

In March 1838, an eminent philosophical divine wrote to me that he had
remarked " the simplicity of the sutures in *brutes*, and in the savage compared with the more civilised man;" " and that, on the inspection of one-
quarter or less of a skull, he could decide whether it were that of a Carib,
for instance, or a European The complexity of the sutures in the latter
attracts the notice of the most inexperienced eye." We examined the following skulls with a view to the determination of this point, and the same
gentleman who prepared the former report also kindly drew up the following remarks —

" Observations on the Sutures of the Crania, exhibited to Mr. George
Combe.

" The first was the skull of an Indian of the Gay Head tribe, aged fifty-six.
The sutures were but faintly marked by a continuous line, the serrations
had disappeared. The sagittal suture had disappeared entirely.

" 2 A Penobscot Indian's skull presented regular and distinct sutures.
The serrations in the coronal suture were short, and not so minute as in the
Caucasian crania. The serrations in the sagittal and lambdoidal sutures
were distinct, and rather long, but not minute.

" 3 A native of Celebes. The coronal suture presented no serrations;
the bones seemed merely in juxtaposition, and the dividing line was straight
and distinct. The sagittal suture presented in the front part only a continuous straight line; in the back part a waving line, but no distinct serrations. The lambdoidal suture presented no regular serrations shooting
distinctly across and into each other, but an irregular line.

" 4 A negro's skull presented a coronal suture with minute and distinct
serrations; a sagittal and lambdoidal suture with distinct and coarse serrations projecting across and far into each other.

" 5 A Sandwich Islander aged twenty-four. The sutures were hardly
discernible; the serrations not at all.

" 6. The skull of a North American Indian, aged twenty-nine, presented
very faintly marked sutures with short serrations. The sutures not discernible on the inside of the skull."

These cases support the observation that the sutures are simple in savage
skulls.

application increased, and greater enjoyment imparted to them all. I mention these little incidents to encourage others.

The Rights of Women.—It is currently reported that at the late election of the state officers of Massachusetts, about one hundred votes were given in favor of Mrs. Maria Ann Chapman as governor, or rather "governess," of the state. This is a lady of superior talent and amiable qualities, who has distinguished herself as an abolitionist. I have never been able to learn in an authentic form to what extent votes were really given for her; or whether they were bestowed in earnest, in recognition of the rights of women, or as a hoax: but from the way in which the fact is mentioned, I am inclined to believe that some votes have been given for Mrs. Chapman. As Victoria governs England with great eclat, there are persons who think that there is no good reason why Mrs. Chapman should not govern Massachusetts; more especially as her people could remove her at the end of the first, or any subsequent year, if she did not give them satisfaction, which Victoria's subjects cannot do.

Nov. 24. Ther. 31°. *The Rev. Mr. Pierpont.*—Mr. Pierpont is distinguished in America and in Europe for his poetical talent. He is the author, among other excellent pieces, of the celebrated song "The Pilgrim Fathers." A majority of the pew-holders of his church lately decided that his reply to some charges brought against him by certain of his hearers is satisfactory, and he continues his ministrations. The charges were in fact ridiculous, his real offence having been his ardor in the temperance cause. In his "Reply," he gives some amusing illustrations of these accusations. "I adverted," says he, "to the fact that casks of rum bearing the Boston brand might be seen lying on the wharves of Smyrna, and was led to inquire whether, if one of our merchant vessels carries missionaries to Asia in the cabin, and New England rum in the hold, the influence of the new world is, on the whole, a blessing to the old, if with our religion she takes our rum?" * * "I proposed to them from the pulpit the question, Whether is nearer the kingdom of God the sober believer in Mahomet, or the drunken believer in Jesus?" His congregation consisted to a great extent of distillers, one of whom led the opposition against him. Speaking of this individual, he says, "He heeded not the hail from Hollis' Street pulpit that rattled upon the copper of his still—his still. 'whose worm dieth not, and whose fire is not quenched,' even on the Christian Sabbath!"

Another of the charges against him was that he followed "an imported mountebank," which was understood by him to mean condemnation of his attachment to Dr. Spurzheim and Phrenology. In a beautiful apostrophe to the "Shade of the lamented

Spurzheim," he answers this accusation. "Thou wast honored in thy life as few in this land have been. Thou wast honored in thy death and in thy funeral obsequies as, in this generation, no other man has been. The munificent merchant of Boston who gave thy bones a resting-place in the sacred shades of Mount Auburn, and placed over them that beautiful copy of the tomb of Scipio, was content to cut thy name upon its front as thine only epitaph, feeling, that wherever science was honored, or philosophy loved, no other could be needed. It was left for the chairman of a committee of Hollis' street society to express his own views of this philosophy, and thy worth, and under the name of 'Spurzheim' he writes, 'THE IMPORTED MOUNTEBANK.'

"Yes, gentlemen, I *have* entered somewhat into the 'exciting topic' of Phrenology. I was a hearer of Dr. Spurzheim, and have been since, and mean to be again, a hearer of the lectures of George Combe. To these two 'imported mountebanks' I feel myself more indebted for instruction in the philosophy of mind, and upon the conditions of the healthy manifestation of the mental powers, than to all other men, living or dead."*

It was subsequently stated in the Boston newspapers that it was not Dr. Spurzheim, but Mr. George Thompson the anti-slavery lecturer, who was meant by the "imported mountebank" in the publication of Mr. Pierpont's opponents. Mr. Pierpont had repeatedly offered to his congregation to submit his conduct to an "ecclesiastical council," but the discontented members declined this appeal. This is the ordinary way of settling differences between pastors and their people. The accusers and the accused name a number of clergymen of the same persuasion with themselves, as umpires; they subscribe a regular bond of arbitration to them, and the courts of law enforce the decision given upon it.

We heard Mr. Pierpont preach to-day from the text, "Try

---

* I was surprised at the observation that Dr. Spurzheim's monument was reared by "a munificent merchant in Boston." I learned, on inquiry, that at the time of Dr. Spurzheim's death, when the sympathy was strong, a good many small sums were subscribed by the citizens of Boston for this purpose, but, that when the money came to be demanded two years afterwards to pay the artist, the feeling had died away, and some difficulty was experienced in making the collection   Mr William Sturgis, a merchant, a man of large fortune and generous spirit, no Phrenologist, but a great admirer of moral worth, and who had taken a deep interest in Dr Spurzheim as a man, requested that these efforts should cease, and paid the requisite sum, $1000, out of his own pocket. The Phrenological Society of Boston presented him with a copy of all Dr Spurzheim's works, with a handsome letter expressive of their esteem and gratitude, which was published in the Boston newspapers at the time, but the notice of it had not reached me. The name of Mr William Sturgis will descend honorably to posterity associated with that of Dr. Spurzheim.

all things, hold fast that which is good." The sermon contained a regular and very able discussion of the nature, aim, and modes of action, of the two spirits of "Reform" and "Conservatism," which are so active in the world. Both are implied in the text. "Try *all* things" is the maxim of the determined reformer. "Hold fast by that which *is good*" should satisfy the most timid Conservative. The error committed by many reformers consists, not in "trying all things," but in not "holding fast by that which is good," while the error of Conservatism lies in holding fast by that which is only *comparatively* good, and refusing to try *any* thing with a view to making it better. Conservatism resisted printing as a substitute for writing in the manufacture of books; it resisted the substitution of mechanical power for human and animal labor, it resisted Christianity as superseding Heathenism; it resisted the Reformation and clung to Popery. Both spirits are necessary for the welfare of the world, and our object should be to prevent either from becoming the sole motive of action. The text is unlimited in its application; we are commanded to "try *all* things." There is no truth so thoroughly established, and no custom so sanctioned by time, as to have any legitimate claim to exemption from trial. The world is progressive, and new generations are constantly appearing on the stage: if we wish to strengthen the minds of the young, we should permit, nay encourage them to "try," by the tests of reason and Scripture, all the doctrines and observances which we teach them. If these be "good," they will stand only the faster by being "tried" again and again, and if they cannot undergo this scrutiny, they are not "good," and we should not ask the young to receive them as true.

Nov. 25. Ther. 57°. *Mr. Abbott Lawrence.*—This gentleman was lately chosen as one of the representatives from Massachusetts to Congress. We visited him this evening, before his departure for Washington. He is a man in whom the moral and intellectual qualities are happily blended; he is much esteemed, and full of patriotism in the best sense of the word. He labors assiduously to raise the moral and intellectual condition of his countrymen, in the belief that if they excel in these qualities all other things will be added unto them. In my journal of this date, I find these words written: "He is in horror at the prospect of the bad air in the chambers at Washington. I urged him to make a motion to have them ventilated." When this was written, he appeared to be in good health, and in a green old age, apparently under or about sixty. He went to Washington; engaged warmly in his duties; and within three months was taken seriously ill. His life was despaired of; and after long and protracted suffering, he escaped by only a hair's-breadth from the grave. Before we left America he was under the necessity of resigning his seat on account of his health, and retiring into private life! Perhaps the bad ventilation had some influence in producing this deplorable result.

The Weather.—In the early part of the day the thermometer rose to 70° F. The wind was in the south, and much rain fell; but before sunset the wind changed, and the sky became clear. At 10 P. M. it was freezing. Next morning the thermometer stood at 11°.

Nov. 27. Ther. 24°. This evening I concluded my second course of lectures. The attendance is stated in the Appendix, No. VII.

Nov. 28. Ther. 23°. *Thanksgiving Day.*—I heard Mr. Gannet, Dr. Channing's colleague, preach to-day in his church in Federal street. His text was, " Do all to the glory of God." He said, that " Thanksgiving Day" presented one of the few occasions on which politics could legitimately be introduced into the pulpit. As religious principle should regulate every action of life, political action formed no exception. He strongly condemned the practice of voting with one's party in opposition to the conscientious dictates of individual judgment. He insisted on the necessity of every man in this country bringing his conscience and his understanding to the study of political questions before deciding on them, as he would do in any other matter of serious import, that he may do justice to himself and to society, by exercising an enlightened and salutary influence on public affairs. He denounced all political frauds, lying, slandering of opponents, and unconscientious arguments, as forbidden by Christianity. The sermon was sound, bold, and forcible. In the other services, there was presiding good taste and Christian sentiment towards all nations on the earth.

Nov. 29. *Phrenology and Education.*—The remark was occasionally made to me by persons who had heard my lectures on Education, without having attended those on Phrenology, that the views presented were so sound and luminous that I should have done much more good if I had omitted Phrenology, and delivered them simply as founded on common sense. This, said they, would have saved the lectures from the prejudices which exist in so many minds against Phrenology, and which render them suspicious of every doctrine and practice springing out of it. My answers were, first, That a knowledge of the influence of the organs on the power of manifesting the mental faculties, is a fundamental requisite to the right understanding of the subject of education. Secondly, That to have withheld this important knowledge, because it was unpopular, would have been improper and uncandid. By following such a course I

should also have been extending the impression already produced by too many disingenuous phrenologists, that the science
is worthless, and that the soundest views of education may be
obtained without its aid, which I know not to be the case.
Thirdly, That such conduct would have been unjust and injurious towards the founders and defenders of Phrenology. It would
have been appropriating to myself the fruits, and leaving to them
not only the toil but the obloquy of having raised them.
Fourthly, That lectures on education, founded on Phrenology,
make a deeper and more permanent impression on the understanding than if based on mere common sense, and can be more
certainly and successfully carried into practice. Every man's
common sense differs from that of his neighbor. In New England, I had visited a common school, the head master of which
told me, that he devoted one-half of his whole hours of teaching
to arithmetic and mathematics, because he had discovered that
pupils who excelled in those branches soon became proficients
in every other, such as grammar, geography, and repetitions.
No phrenologist could have held such views, because he must
have known that arithmetic and mathematics depend on different
organs from those which take cognisance of language, grammar,
and general reasoning. I observed that the organs on which
arithmetic and mathematics depend predominated over the other
intellectual organs in this person's own head, in consequence of
which he could teach these branches with most ease and success,
and his common sense led him to conclude that all his pupils
were similarly constituted to himself. When teachers rely
solely on common sense and their own experience, they act
merely on the suggestions of their strongest propensities, sentiments, and intellectual faculties, whatever these may be, without
reference to the differences which exist between their minds
and those of their pupils. Phrenology presents a scientific guide
to all.

Nov. 30. *St. Andrew's Day.*—By invitation from the office-
bearers, I attended the celebration of the hundred and eighty-
second anniversary of the Scots Charitable Society of Boston,
held in the Pavilion Hotel. Mr. W. H. Wilson was in the
chair, and Mr. John L. Millar acted as Vice-President. The
room was ornamented with transparencies of St. Andrew, St.
George, and St. Patrick; and other emblems and memorials of
the "Father Land." Mr. Everett the governor of the state, Mr.
Elliot the Mayor of the city, Thomas Colley Grattan, Esq.,
the British Consul (author of "High-ways and By-ways"), and
a number of other distinguished guests, were present. The
history of this society is interesting. On the 6th of January
1657, a few Scotchmen of the town of Boston associated them-

selves together for the purpose of raising funds for the relief of
their poor and distressed countrymen, and the records of their
proceedings have been preserved for nearly the whole interven-
ing period between that date and the present time.   The resolution founding the association is expressed in singularly solemn
and forcible religious phraseology.   "We look for the assistance
of the Great God, who can bring small beginnings to greater perfection than we, for the present, can think of or expect; and we
likewise hope that God, who hath the hearts of all men in his
hand, and can turn them which way soever he pleases, will double
our spirits upon them (that shall come after us), and make them
more zealous for his glory, and the mutual good one of another
than we."   In 1684 their numbers being considerably increased,
they assumed the form of a regular society.   "The society thus
constituted, continued in existence until the breaking out of the
troubles of the Revolution, when, on account of the loyalty of
its members, who, desiring to fight neither against their native
or adopted country, all retired either to the Provinces or to Great
Britain.   After the declaration of Independence was acknowledged by Great Britain, many of the former members of the
society returned to their old homes, and in the year 1784" they
obtained a charter re-establishing the society.   The society continued to flourish until the war of 1812–13–14, when it suffered
severely, and it afterwards "continued a languishing existence
for fifteen years."   It again, however, revived, and is now in a
flourishing condition.   It has been the means of alleviating much
misery; and it forms a striking and cheering example of the inherent vitality of a good principle   Almost every other institution of this state, religious, civil, and judicial, has been destroyed
and reconstructed again and again since this society was founded,
but it has lived through all vicissitudes, and risen from its ashes
even when it seemed to have been finally extinguished by adversity.

  Besides Scotchmen, the company consisted of Englishmen,
Irishmen, and Americans; and nothing could be more pleasing
than to observe the tact and good sense with which, in the expression of their national feelings, each of these sections avoided
all extravagance and matter of offence to their neighbors.   The
only jar which struck on my mind was in hearing the Governor
of Massachusetts, with great good nature, join in singing the
Queen's anthem, and, in allusion to her enemies, giving utterance
to the sentiment "confound their politics," "frustrate their
knavish tricks;" more especially as he was lately in great
danger himself of being forced to become one of her enemies
when the "Maine troubles" wore a threatening aspect.   Victoria,
or rather her counsellors, are not so infallible as to render it cer-

tain that she is always in the right in her quarrels; and even, independently of this consideration, good taste would dictate that, to render the anthem perfect, it should be purified of the manifestations of Self-Esteem and Destructiveness which are implied in these words.

The health of Governor Everett was given by the chairman, and received with great cordiality. In returning thanks, he delivered an appropriate, classical, and eloquent address. The delivery was graceful, animated, and fluent. He describes the Scottish character in the chastest language, and with nice discrimination, he adverts felicitously to the leading incidents in the history of the country, and enumerates her distinguished writers with a just critical acumen, shewing altogether a highly cultivated, well-stored, and accomplished mind. It is so characteristic of his mental attainments, that I insert it in the Appendix No. VIII.

Mr. Grattan also delivered a speech full of fervid eloquence and generous sentiment, and the proceedings of the whole evening constituted a highly intellectual treat. Champagne was constantly administered by the servants after the cloth was drawn, but the company used it, and all the other wines and liquors, in most exemplary moderation.

Dec. 1. Ther. 40°. *A Scottish Sacrament.*—Burns, in his "Holy Fair." has rendered a Scottish sacrament in the *country* famous in all parts of the world where his dialect is understood; but I was struck with the description of the same solemnity in a city, given by an American gentleman of serious habits and a cultivated mind, who had visited Edinburgh about thirty years ago. The subject was introduced by his asking me whether the same state of things continued to exist which he witnessed at that time. I asked him what he particularly alluded to, when he gave me the following picture of his impressions: He happened to be in Edinburgh in the week of the sacrament, and was introduced to the Rev. Dr. Campbell, long since deceased. The solemnity of the Thursday's fast day; the long and serious discourse delivered on the Saturday; the extreme solemnity of the Sunday's dispensation of the bread and wine, and the deep impressiveness of the Monday's prayers and preaching, appeared to him more than reverential; they were awful. His mind was depressed by the terrible images and sentiments which had been constantly brought before it during these days. The clergymen also who officiated, as well as the congregation who listened, seemed to him to be broken down under a sense of guilt and apprehension of punishment. He was invited to dine on the Monday, after the close of the exercises, with Dr. Campbell and his brother clergymen who had assisted him on the occasion. He

at first shrunk from accepting the invitation. He conceived that
the evening would be passed in practically carrying out the awful
admonitions of the previous days, and that every man would be
found searching deeper and deeper into his own heart, drawing
forth another and yet another sin, and casting it from him. As,
however, he had received so much kindness from the reverend
doctor who gave the invitation, he considered it his duty to accept it. He entered the house with the most solemn feelings,
and prepared his mind to meet his friends in harmony with the
spirit which he believed to pervade them. He was surprised to
see a bright and benignant smile on Dr. Campbell's countenance,
and was speedily introduced to the late Rev. Dr. Ireland, and a
whole circle of other doctors in divinity. They all looked dif-
ferently from what he had expected. They seemed to be happy,
smiling, and good natured. Dinner was served, the cloth withdrawn, and the servants left the room, when forthwith there broke
forth bursts of merriment, droll stories, an universal hilarity that
appeared to him like the opening of the clouds and the sudden
gleam of sunbeams after the awful darkness of a thunder tem-
pest. The bottles circulated freely, first port and sherry, and
by-and-by a call was made for the " mountain dew." This was
compounded into " toddy," and the mirth grew more vivacious;
the stories deepened in a certain kind of interest; the confines of
good and evil seemed constantly threatening to intermingle, and
only at a pretty advanced hour in the evening did this joyous
and jovial party separate. He was then young, and unused to
the ways of the world, but he had often reflected on the subject
since. He had come to the conclusion that in the one scene the
ministers were acting in their professional, and in the other in
their natural capacities; and he did not think the less of the Scottish clergy from his having been permitted by this incident to see
them in their natural condition. He had been brought up in different views of Christianity himself, but he rejoiced to see that
the austere doctrines of their church had left their social qualities
unblighted and unimpaired; and that they were amiable, cheerful, kind-hearted, and sensible men. I told my friend, that no
very marked change has taken place in these particulars in modern times. The Scottish clergy regard the " Monday's dinner"
after the sacrament as the only remnant of the " carnival" that is
left to them, and they think it no sin to enjoy it as such.*

---

* Since my return to Scotland, I have been assured by a friend who has
frequently attended these " Monday dinners" in Edinburgh, that within the
last ten or fifteen years a most decided improvement has, in some quarters,
taken place. The description in the text *was* accurate at its own date, and
my Scottish readers will judge how far it continues generally to be so.

Dec. 2. *Quackery.*—In conversing with a gentleman on the great extent to which this evil appears to prevail in the United States, so far as one can judge from the advertisements in the newspapers, he said that quackery extends through all departments of business; even in lecturing, said he, " it abounds so extensively, that prudent people pay no attention to certificates, none to resolutions, and none to newspaper reports, because all these can be obtained by impudence and money; often they are forged; and the only mode of treating them according to their deserts is to regard them with utter neglect. This operates against the man of talents and sound acquirements, until, by extensive and persevering efforts, he has reared a personal reputation. This is the real cause," said he, " of the people of Baltimore, Cincinnati, and latterly Providence, having declined to pledge themselves to attend your lectures, until you appeared among them and showed what you could do." I remarked that the names appended to the resolutions of my classes were a guarantee against imposition. " Few names," said he, " except those of politicians, are much known beyond their own district in our wide extended country; and besides, even our respectable citizens are so often drawn by their good nature into commending persons whom they wish to advance, that it is at all times difficult to tell whether any encomium proceeds from the merits of the party praised, or the kindness of the individual who utters it."

Mobs.—To-day I heard Judge Thatcher deliver a clear and sensible address to the grand jury of the county of Suffolk, from which I learned that, during the last session, the legislature of Massachusetts has rendered any city or county in the state liable for three-fourths of all damages done by mobs, if the owner have used reasonable care to protect his property. This law will form a good check on mobs, but it is difficult to discover why the compensation does not reach the entire loss.

" *The Perkins Institution and Massachusetts Asylum for the Blind.*"—This institution is now removed from Pearl street in the heart of the city, to Mount Washington, on Dorchester Heights, looking down on the bay. It was built in the days of speculation for a hotel, and is a splendid establishment. It is now admirably fitted up for the purpose of educating and instructing the blind in trades. The pupils were removed to it last summer; and during the first three months after their removal, the boys and girls consumed 25 per cent. additional of provisions. They enjoy here purer air, more extended exercise, and seabathing. Dr. Howe cultivates the sense of propriety in the children as assiduously as if they could see. They are taught to keep their own bed-rooms in order, and to lay every object in its proper place. In bathing they are clothed, and they are prohibited from ever appearing undressed even before each other. They have the same delicacy of feeling in this respect which is found in well-trained children who see. We entered into the school about sunset, and commenced an examination of the boys in geography, natural philosophy, and arithmetic. Dr. Howe and Mr. Mann, who accompanied us, carried the questions into a wide range of topics by conversation, and we found the pupils possessed not only of great acquirements in knowledge. but of well cultivated powers of reasoning. It became quite dark, and no lights were brought, but our examinations proceeded uninterruptedly. Nothing before ever enabled me so completely to realise the condition in which the blind habitually live as this scene did. For the time, we participated with them in being in unbroken night, and by no other means can one so fully appreciate the value of their attainments. In the dark we were helpless; but they read, cyphered, demonstrated mathematical propositions, traced the courses of rivers, seas, and mountains, on their maps, fetched and carried whatever object they wanted, knew where everything lay, and were as full of vivacity as if they had enjoyed the benefits of light.

I have already adverted to the great improvement in printing for the blind accomplished in this institution. In the type used by Dr. Howe, a chapter of the Bible is printed in less than half the space occupied by the type in use in Scotland, and is as easily read. It may be true that a page of the Scotch print may be cheaper, estimated by the square foot; but as it contains only half the quantity of matter, the expense of printing any given book is greater.*

Dr. Howe openly acknowledges that he owes whatever success has attended his exertions in improving the education of the blind (and it is great) entirely to the light derived from phrenological vews of mental philosophy:—" Before I knew Phrenology," said he, " I was groping my way in the dark as blind as my pupils; I derived very little satisfaction from my labors. and fear that I gave but little to others. Our upper classes are all instructed in the general principles of intellectual philosophy, and we explain to them both the old and the new systems; but I never knew one of them who did not prefer the latter, while I have known many who have taken a deep interest in the philo-

---

* Since my return to Great Britain, I have shown specimens of Dr. Howe's type to several persons who take an interest in printing for the blind. The superior legibility and economy of the Boston printing are generaly admitted, but one gentleman, highly educated and accomplished, who is himself blind, thinks that if there were two lines less in the page it would be still more distinct.

sophy of Phrenology, and heard them avow that they were made happier and better by understanding its principles. Some of our teachers are persons of considerable intellectual attainments, and all of them have adopted the new philosophy since they joined the institution, not because they were induced to do so by any request of mine, or on any consideration of extrinsic advantage to themselves, but solely because their duties led them to examine all the theories of mental philosophy, and the new system recommended itself most forcibly to their understandings, and appeared most susceptible of practical application."*

Much as we found to interest us in this institution, the most attractive of all the pupils is the girl Laura Bridgman, now about nine or ten years of age. She has from infancy been deaf, dumb, and blind; and is also destitute of the sense of smell. She has grown considerably in stature since last year, and I observed a distinct increase in the size of her brain. The coronal, or moral region, in particular, has become larger, not only absolutely, but also in proportion to the animal region. Her temperament is nervous, with a little sanguine. The head altogether is of full size and well formed. The organs of the domestic affections are amply developed, and in the best feminine proportions. Self-Esteem, Love of Approbation, Cautiousness, Firmness, and Conscientiousness, are all large. The anterior lobe of the brain also is large, and both the knowing and reflecting departments are well developed. The organs of Order are large, and she shows great tidiness in all her arrangements.

Phrenology leads us to understand that in this child the moral and intellectual powers exist in great vigor and activity, and that all that is wanting to her successful education is the means of conveying knowledge to them. Dr. Howe and his assistants, guided by this science, have succeeded wonderfully in the work of educating her. I perceive a manifest and important improvement since last year. She manifests the most sensitive delicacy in regard to sex. When I placed my hand on her head she was troubled, and removed it; but she did not interest herself to remove a female hand. The natural language of her countenance expresses intelligence and happiness; and we were told that she is very happy. She has been taught the finger-alphabet, and converses readily with the masters and scholars. She has been instructed in writing also; and when informed of our names, she felt C.'s dress and mine, recognised us as old acquaintances, recollected our visit of last year, and wrote in pencil the words—

* Dr. Howe, at my request, put this testimony into writing, and authorized me to use it.

·· Laura glad see Combe,'' and presented them to us. The following is a fac-simile of them·—

Two of the pupils named Baker, to whom she was much attached, were absent on a .visit to their friends, and she had worked a bag which she wished to send to them. She had just finished a letter to them in the same character as the above, which she kindly allowed me to carry with me, as a specimen of her chirography, and said she would write another. It was in the following terms. "Louisa and Elizabeth Baker.——Laura is well. Laura will give Baker bag. Man will carry bag to Baker. Laura will cry, Baker will come to see Laura. Drew," another pupil, "is well. Drew give love to Baker. Laura Bridgman.''

I asked Dr. Howe by what means he succeeded in teaching her the connection between the letters "delivered," and the act of delivering, and so forth. He said that the meaning of all such words was communicated only by very frequent repetition of the act, and by writing the letters each time. He took a bag, for instance, and time after time made Laura deliver it to him, and write the letters, and thus he succeeded in connecting the mental conception with the words. She has large organs of Philoprogenitiveness, and has a little doll which she caresses and dresses very neatly. She has a great admiration of ornaments, and was delighted with C.'s bracelets and brooch. She has a separate box for her own bonnet, and another for the other parts of her dress, and preserves them all in the greatest order. She has at present no ideas of religion. Dr. Howe waits for the farther maturity of her organisation, and the greater development of her faculties, before he attempts to convey to her this species of knowledge; and in the mean time every one is enjoined not to allude to the subject, lest they should convey impressions that might render her unhappy, and which it might be impossible to eradicate.

I add the following particulars from the " Annual Report of the Trustees" of the Institution for 1840.

" There is one whose situation is so peculiar, and whose case is so interesting in a philosophical point of view, that we cannot forbear making particular mention of it; we allude to Laura Bridgman, the deaf, dumb, and blind girl mentioned in the two last reports.

"The intellectual improvement of this interesting being, and the progress she has made in expressing her ideas, is truly gratifying.

"She uses the manual alphabet of the deaf mutes with great facility and great rapidity; she has increased her vocabulary so as to comprehend the names of all common objects; she uses adjectives expressive of positive qualities, such as hard, soft, sweet, sour, &c.; verbs expressive of action, as give, take, ride, run, &c., in the present, past, and future tense; she connects adjectives with nouns to express their qualities; she introduces verbs into sentences, and connects them by conjunctions; for instance, a gentleman having given her an apple, she said, *man give Laura sweet apple.*

"She can count to high numbers, she can add and subtract small numbers.

"But the most gratifying acquirement which she has made, and the one which has given her the most delight, in the power of *writing a legible hand*, and expressing her thoughts upon paper: she writes with a pencil in a grooved line, and makes her letters clear and distinct.

"She was sadly puzzled at first to know the meaning of the process to which she was subjected; but when the idea dawned upon her mind that by means of it she could convey intelligence to her mother, her delight was unbounded. She applied herself with great diligence, and in a few months actually wrote a legible letter to her mother, in which she conveyed information of her being well, and of her coming home in ten weeks. It was indeed only the skeleton of a letter, but still it expressed in legible characters a vague outline of the ideas which were passing in her mind. She was very impatient to have *the man* carry this letter, for she supposed that the utmost limit of the Post-office Department was to employ a man to run backward and forward between our Institution and the different towns where the pupils live to fetch and carry letters. We subjoin to this Report a correct *fac-simile* of Laura's writing, observing that she was not prompted to the matter, and that her hand was not held in the execution; the matter is quite original, and the chirography is entirely her own.

"She has improved very much in personal appearance as well as in intellect, her countenance beams with intelligence; she is always active at study, work, or play; she never repines, and most of the time is gay and frolicsome.

"She is now very expert with her needle, she knits **very**

easily, and can make twine bags, and various fancy articles very
prettily.   She is very docile, has a quick sense of propriety,
dresses herself with great neatness, and is always correct in her
deportment.   In short, it would be difficult to find a child in the
possession of all her senses, and the enjoyment of the advantages
that wealth and parental love can bestow, who is more contented
and cheerful, or to whom existence seems a greater blessing than
it does to this bereaved creature, for whom the sun has no light,
the air no sound, and the flowers no colour or smell.

" For the method of teaching her, and for further particulars
of her case, we refer you to Appendix B."*

The United States and Cuba.—It is calculated that about
fifty Americans of the better class settle annually in Cuba, and
there is a great trade between this island and the United States.
The Spaniards are becoming acquainted with the American Institutions, and it said that they would not be averse to join the
Union.   The slave states it is said would gladly consent to their
admission, because this would add powerfully to their strength;
and the other states, through motives of interest, might not be
averse to the compact.   The realisation of this idea may be very
distant, but circumstances might arise to accelerate it.

Dec. 7. Ther. 38°.   *The Law of Scotland.*—At a party
to-day at the hospitable residence of Mr. Grattan the British
Consul (whose urbanity. generous sentiments, and high literary
talents, have already endeared him to the Americans), we met
Judge Story of the Supreme Court of the United States.   He
expressed his admiration of the Commentaries on Bankrupt and
Commercial Law by Mr. George Joseph Bell of Edinburgh;
and mentioned that Mr. Bell had lately sent him his " Principles
of the Law of Scotland," with a kind letter, which had gratified
him much.   He said that the freedom with which the Scotch
lawyers have investigated first principles, renders their pleadings
and writings particularly interesting in the United States, where
the law is in the progress of constant change and improvement.
He had also studied Mr. Fergusson's Reports of the Cases decided by the Scotch Judges, annulling, for offences committed
in Scotland, marriages contracted in England; and he acknowledged that he had derived many valuable lights from them in
preparing his own Treatise on the Conflict of Jurisdictions.
There is, said he, great depth of reasoning and soundness of
conclusion in the opinions of the Scoth Judges.   In the United
States, their doctrine has long been adopted in the practice of
the supreme court.   He was glad to see that the English Judges

* The Appendix B is so interesting that I have transferred it entire to
the Appendix to this volume, No. IX.

had at length given effect to the cogent reasoning and luminous exposition of principle adopted by their Scotch brethren; and he admired the unswerving firmness with which the latter had adhered to their own views, opposed as they long were by the great weight and authority of the English Judges. He added, "·These remarks are not confidential; you may if you please communicate them to the Scotch Judges with an expression of my high esteem."*

Dec. 8. Ther. 38°. *The Judges in the State of New Hampshire.*—One of the Boston lawyers mentioned to me that the Judges in the State of New Hampshire are appointed only for three years; that he has pleaded before them and found them to be very able and upright men. They are changed occasionally, but they resume their places at the bar without any feeling of degradation. Their elevation to the bench is found to have invested them with additional reputation and respect, and their practice is increased. I met ex-Chancellor Kent in New York, and was told that after descending from that high office, at sixty years of age, beyond which the law of the state did not admit of his being re-elected, he continued to exercise almost chancery powers in his private chambers, and sustained no loss of income, but the reverse. He was applied to for opinions in important cases, and practised extensively as arbitrator in references. He never appeared again at the bar in any court. In Rhode Island the Judges are elected annually; but it is said that anarchy has threatened to make more serious inroads on social order in that than in any other of the old states.

Conventional Hypocrisy.—In the twentieth volume of the Boston "Christian Examiner" there is a review of a religious work, published anonymously, but reputed to have been written by a member of the Church of Scotland. The reviewer observes, that "the author who has called forth these remarks is kept in countenance, to at least a great degree, in thus solemnly professing what he does not believe, either in letter or spirit, by such men as his countrymen Robertson, Blair, and the great body of the liberal party of the clergy of Scotland, whose opinions, it is well known, lean strongly towards Arminianism. He is kept in countenance, too, in this, by great numbers in England, on the continent, in our own country, including professors of our theological institutions, and in all other places, where these creeds and confessions are imposed. But the commonness of the sin only renders it a more fitting subject of reprobation."

---

* The conflict between the Law of Scotland and that of England, in these cases of divorce, is not yet terminated, and a legislative enactment will probably be necessary to bring it to an end.

Dec. 12. Ther. 12°. *Sir Walter Scott and the Ballantynes.*
—Mr Lockhart's " Ballantyne humbug handled" is attracting
attention in the literary circles here. It is known that the Ballantynes have answered it (it is said effectually and conclusively
in Edinburgh), but their reply has not reached the United
States.*

The Patroon Troubles.—The head of the Van Rensselaer
family is styled the Patroon of Albany, a title corresponding to
the English Lord of the Manor.   Many years ago a large tract
of land, lying on both sides of the Hudson, was let out on leases
for long terms by one of the ancient patroons, for certain rents,
payable in grain, poultry, and services with carriages and teams.
The late Mr. Van Rensselaer, who died in the present year,
was indulgent in commuting these rents, and he even allowed
many of them to stand over unexacted.   His son is now insist-
ing on the tenants paying up arrears, and he demands the
modern market price for both the produce and services.   The
tenants consider their situation as at once anomalous and grievous.
They are substantially proprietors of their farms; but their
tenures are only lease-hold.   They conceive themselves also to
suffer hardship in regard to the rates at which the produce is
commuted.   They have thought that the accession of the new
patroon afforded a fitting opportunity to rid themselves of their
grievances; and, after offering him terms which he declined to
accept, they unanimously resolved not to comply with his demands.   He appealed to the law, but they resisted the sheriff
in serving legal writs upon them.   The *posse comitatus* of
Albany was called out, and they resisted them.   The sheriff
reported this resistance, as rebellion, to the governor of the
state, and he issued a spirited proclamation denouncing it as an
outrage on the law, and called out the militia of the cities of
Albany, Troy, and New York.   The Albany and Troy militia
marched into the disaffected territory.   The insurgents seized
the artillery and powder magazines belonging to their own
militia regiments, obstructed the roads, and prepared for battle.
The militia, however, pressed on, and showed a firm determination to support the law, on which the tenants surrendered at
discretion, without any bloodshed.   This occurrence excited
great interest all over the Union, and in Boston I heard it discussed by both Whigs and Democrats, and the conduct of the
tenants was unanimously and strongly condemned by both parties.   M. De Tocqueville justly remarks, that, in the United
States, the ascendency of the law is maintained by directing

* I have read it since my return to Scotland, and regard it as completely
supporting the observations made in vol. i, p 118.

civil processes and executions only against *individuals*, whose
reasons or desires for resisting it are never participated in by so
large a portion of the community as to give them the power to
set it at defiance.   These tenants were so numerous that they
conceived that they could successfully resist the law; but the
state authorities soon convinced them of their mistake; and the
press every where condemned them.   The legislature in its
subsequent session passed an act for the equitable commutation
of their grain-rents and services, and otherwise redressed their
grievances.

This occurrence enables one to understand how social order
and safety to property should essentially prevail, while mobs
and outrages, in which the people seem to set all law and justice at defiance, may occasionally occur.   I have heard Americans themselves, in moments of disappointment, remark that
there is a steady movement by the people all over the Union,
towards placing themselves above the law; that mobs resist it,
juries trample on it, and the people, through their legislatures,
continually change it.   There is no force which can give effect
to the law when the people choose to oppose it.   If the *posse
comitatus* is called out, it consists of the mob.   If the constables
and militia are summoned, they are themselves the law breakers.
In short, the officers of the law are left powerless against the
people.   This representation is correct when violent feelings
pervade the people *generally;* when, for instance, they are
pleased to burn halls, or maltreat editors, on account of abolition
proceedings; but the feeling must be wide-spread and vividly
excited before these evils can be produced; and, in point of fact,
they are comparatively rare.   In civil suits, and criminal prosecutions against individuals for ordinary offences, the people
support the officers of justice; and hence arise order and security
as the general rule, to which occasional outrages are only the
exceptions.

The Presidency of the United States.—Mr. Van Buren's first
term of office (four years) will expire in March, 1841, and a
new election of president will take place in the latter part of
1840.   Since we arrived in the United States, most of the Whig
newspapers have announced Mr. Clay as the candidate for the
presidency on the Whig side against Mr. Van Buren, who is
nominated by the Democrats for re-election.   The Whigs have
held a general convention of delegates from all the states of the
Union, at Harrisburgh, in Pennsylvania, at which they have set
aside Mr. Clay, and nominated General William Henry Harrison, residing at North Bend, in the state of Ohio, as their candidate, and John Tyler, of Virginia, for the vice-presidency.   Mr.
Clay has written a handsome letter waiving his claims, and

urging unanimity in the Whig ranks in favor of General Harrison
and Mr. Tyler. The delegates, on returning to their respective
states, summon the members of their party to a general meeting,
and explain to them the reasons that guided the convention in
their choice Town and county meetings are next held, to which
these explanations are communicated, and by this machinery the
Whigs of the whole of this vast country are induced to commence operations in one spirit, to ensure success to the object
of their choice. The Democrats follow similar measures, but as
they possess power, theirs is a defensive rather than an aggressive
contest.

Honor and Honesty.—Some time ago I became acquainted
with a teacher of the higher branches of education, who now
successfully conducts a private seminary in this state, and whose
history is instructive. He pursued the same vocation in England, and told me that there he had a fair attendance of scholars,
but that many of the parents, even in respectable circumstances,
did not pay the school-fees for their children, and when he urged
for payment, they resented his urgency, and in the circles in
which they visited, accused him of imputed offences, concealing
the real one, till his reputation was injured, and his school seriously thinned. As he did not move in the same rank with them,
he had no means of defence, and left the country and came to
the United States. I asked him, whether he did not experience
the same grievance here? He said no; that the Americans considered school-fees as debts of honor, and paid them in almost
all circumstances. I am sorry to say that in Scotland teachers
are no better treated in this respect than this gentleman was in
England. I have repeatedly been informed by teachers in my
own country, that their fees are ill-paid by the fashionable portion of the middle-classes, and that they have the mortification
to know that, while they are teaching two or three children
without recompense, the parents are sumptuously entertaining
fashionable society, at an expense which would have cleared off
the school-arrears in one week. They have assured me, also,
that urgency on their part is resented in the same way, and with
the same effects, as in the case before described. It is difficult
to conceive a greater dereliction of all feelings of honor and
honesty than such conduct implies.

Dec. 13. Ther. 31°. *Smallpox.*—There has been a serious
alarm in Boston caused by the re-appearance of the smallpox,
attended by a considerable number of deaths. In calling on
Dr. Smith, the health officer, I have seen crowds of persons
from one year old to fifty, undergoing vaccination. The British
Parliament has rendered it penal to inoculate for the smallpox;
but this has not yet been done in Massachusetts.

Dec. 14. Ther. 25°. *Railroad Stock.*—I find that some bankers and men of property in the United States entertain doubts concerning the stability of railway stocks as investments for capital, and the following have been stated as some of the reasons for the distrust:—1*st*, The uncertainty of American legislation. When an incorporated company is reaping a great profit by any public undertaking, it excites envy, and some patriots discover that the public interests require a rival road, or a rival bridge, to be erected, and the Legislature, which answers to the popular call, gives effect to their designs. The first company's rights are not violated in direct terms, but a rival is established which ruins it. 2*dly*, The railroads are constructed slightly, and many soon wear out. 3*dly*, There are such rapid changes in the great currents of trade and travelling, that nobody can be certain that any particular line of railway will be as extensively used ten years hence as at present: and lastly, these roads are new, and the timid have not confidence in them. In Massachusetts, the state has reserved to itself power to purchase up the railroads at the end of twenty years, on paying the prime cost, and ten per cent per annum of interest from the commencement, deducting all dividends and bonuses on the stock previously paid out of the profits. The majority of the legislators in most of the states are farmers; that is, proprietors who farm their own lands;* many of whom are changed every year. There is no efficient public officer in the legislatures for revising private bills (such as Lord Shaftesbury in the British House of Peers), and the law is in constant fluctuation. The lawyers are ever beginning and never ending their studies, and decisions have less weight in establishing the law than in England, because new statutes frequently interfere with them.

This representation is strongly drawn, but contains substantial truth. I heard the stock of the Philadelphia, Wilmington, and Baltimore Railroad strongly recommended by some sagacious persons, and the reasons assigned for their opinion were these:— 1*st*, It connects the two great cities of Philadelphia and Baltimore, and lies in the direct line of communication between the east and the southwest. 2*dly*, In part of its course it is bounded by the sea on the one side and high ground on the other, and its proprietors have united with the Steam-boat and Railway

---

* In 1810 the House of Assembly of the state of New York, numbering 128 members, presented the following professions: 59 farmers, 23 lawyers, 18 merchants, 7 physicians, 2 cabinet-makers, 2 lumbermen, 1 furrier, 1 gardener, 1 mariner, 1 joiner, 1 blacksmith, 1 post-master, 1 mechanic, 1 grocer, 1 yeoman, 1 agriculturist, 1 teacher, 3 with blank occupations, and 1 with none. Of the whole number 74 were born in the state of New York, 22 in Connecticut, 13 in Massachusetts, 10 in Vermont, 3 in New Hampshire, 2 in Rhode Island, 2 in New Jersey, and 1 in Prague, Germany.

Company already existing on the side next the sea, so that
rivalry is nearly impossible. *3dly*, The railroad traverses portions of three states, Pennsylvania, Delaware, and Maryland,
and the Company enjoys charters from them all. It would be
extremely difficult to induce all the three legislatures to unite at
the same time, and on the same terms, in establishing a rival
company. *4thly*, The charters are perpetual, and are not liable
to come under the discretionary action of the legislatures in being renewed. *5thly*, The railroad, after defraying all current
expenses, including tear and wear, yields a surplus revenue
applicable to the redemption of its debt. This statement of
advantages confirms, to some extent, the previous views; but
there are other railroads, particularly those between Albany and
Buffalo, that seem nearly as safe, except that they are all liable
to be acted on by the Legislature of the single state of New
York.

Dec. 16. Ther. 31°. *Observance of the Sunday.*—This
day we have a very severe snow storm, the first unequivocal
symptom of winter. In visiting Lowell I made inquiries about
the observance of Sunday by the manufacturing population,
about 20,000 in number, and was assured that it is kept sacred
in the most exemplary manner. The only exception mentioned
is, that occasionally the mills and dams are repaired on Sundays,
to avoid throwing large numbers of people idle on week-days.
The interests of the owners and of the workmen concur in this
arrangement, and the clergy, who are dependent on both, do not
object. These operations are viewed as works of necessity. If
the Scottish clergy were equally dependent on their flocks, they
would not prohibit (as they actually do in some cities) the laboring poor from burying their dead relations on Sundays, under
pretence that this is a desecration of the day; causing, by this
sanctimoniousness, the loss of a day's labor to these suffering
people, at the very time when sickness and death increases their
necessary expenses.

Dec. 19. Ther. 8°. Our English thermometer now ceases
to be serviceable. It is graduated only to 10° above zero, and
to-day the mercury has fairly disappeared in the bulb. An
optician in Washington street, Boston gave me 8° as the temperature in the morning, and mentioned that occasionally the
English opticians, when sending scales for thermometers to the
United States, forget the difference of the climate, and send them
graduated only to zero, or to 10° above it. They should range
down to 50° below it.

Music taught in Common Schools.—I attended a lesson given
by Mr. Lowell Mason in vocal music to the girls attending the
Hancock common school in Boston. About 200 of them were

instructed for half an hour. They are taught only two half hours in the week, but their attainments are very considerable. They read music, analyse the notes, and detect false notes both in rhythm and melody, when played on the pianoforte or sung. They give the notes of the common chord in the various positions. They sang extremely well, observing both time and tune with great accuracy. The influence of this instruction in refining their taste, and opening up a source of innocent enjoyment to them, must be valuable. Mr. Mason is employed by the public authorities, and is remunerated from the common school fund.* He appears to be a first-rate teacher; and it is gratifying to see high talent devoted to the improvement of the common people in a branch of the fine arts which, a few years ago, was little prized even by the wealthy citizens of the United States. Although the food of the common people in Boston is abundant and nutritive, and these girls were well dressed, I regretted to observe that their bodily condition did not indicate robust health. Some appeared to have distorted spines, or depressed and narrow chests, and most of them presented that waxy, sodden appearance of the skin, which indicates breathing vitiated air, and absence of sufficient exercise. The school-room was well ventilated, so that they must have suffered at home. This is the more lamentable, as in this country these imperfections are the result not of poverty and physical degradation, as they often are in Britain, but of ignorance or want of resolution to act in conformity with the laws of health.

Dec. 20. Ther. 6°. *The Organ of Number.*—A gentleman who kindly undertook the management of the tickets for my lectures at Lowell, wrapped up the sum received from each bookseller in a separate paper, and made the person who paid it, mark on the parcel the amount it contained. When he paid the bills for advertising, &c., he took the money wanted out of one of the parcels, and put the receipts for the payments into it, and brought the whole sums collected to me in this form. Not understanding why he had done this, I placed the contents of the whole parcels together, and asked him how much he had received, and how much he had paid. He could not tell! I then observed that his organ of Number was deficient, and he told me that he had adopted this method to "avoid confusion." My own organ of Number being equally small, we tried, both by the pen and by counting the money, to discover the amount; but

---

* Not only do concerts *à la Musard*, at one shilling for the admission of each person, prosper in Edinburgh, but the laboring classes also have concerts this winter (1840–41) in Dun-Edin Hall, to which the admittance is only twopence, and these are crowded every evening. They are patronised by the Temperance Societies, and are valuable auxiliaries to civilisation.

neither of us could succeed! We finally parted, much to our own amusement, without either of us having been able to find out the aggregate sum either received or paid, and certainly it was not the magnitude of the amount that caused our difficulties. A deficiency of this kind, when it occurs in the organ of Number, occasions only amusement; but I never experience its effects without sincerely sympathising with those individuals who are as defective in the organs of Conscientiousness or Causality as I am in that of Number. They stand as much in need of external guides to virtue and wisdom as a man in my condition does of a ready reckoner; and they are equally unfit to fill situations in which active honesty and reflection are necessary to success, as such a man would be to discharge the duties of a teller in a bank.

Politics of American Authors.—The Whig party in America claims the wealth of the Union on their side, and the Democrats claim the genius. One of the Democratic papers cited the names of Irving, Cooper, Bryant, Leggett, Bancroft, Alexander Everett, Brownson, Nat. Willis, Fay, Prescott, Langtree, O'Sullivan, Nathaniel Greene, among other men of literary talents, as belonging to their party. The "Boston Atlas" answered this boast as follows. "We have only one observation to make, and that is, that somehow or other it has always happened, that, as a general rule, your poets, your story-tellers, your historians, your wits, nay, even your philosophers, have been great worshipers of *power*, in whatever hands for the time being it might happen to be deposited: and that, after all, the approbation or the praises of this sort of gentry must ever be regarded as a very uncertain test or proof of merit." I should like to see a list of men of genius classed under the heads of Whig and Tory. The general idea is that genius is liberal.

Dec. 21. Ther. 8°. *Mrs. Gove's Lectures.*—This day C—— attended one of Mrs. Gove's lectures to ladies. The subject was the effects of tight lacing and bad ventilation. The lecture was good, and the attendance was about 300, all females.

Dec. 22. Ther. 18°. *Fires.*—At 11 o'clock this night we felt a strong smell of burning in our parlor, and in a few minutes it was full of smoke. The hotel (the Pavilion) has shops below it on the level of the street, and one of them, directly beneath our apartments, was on fire. The porter of the hotel discovered the fire by the lurid light and smoke issuing from the shop window. The engines arrived with great promptitude, and it was extinguished. An iron stove full of coals had been left burning in the shop, and the radiation of the heat had ignited a wooden partition at the distance of three feet. The prospect of being driven to the street at midnight, with the temperature at 18°, was not very agreeable; but our only wonder is that we have escaped so long. There has been another very extensive fire in Cedar street, New York. The loss is stated at $500,000, and its origin is ascribed to incendiaries, who profit by stealing goods during the conflagration. The absence of a police force enables them to perpetrate this wickedness on a grand scale. A New York newspaper describes the scene as follows:—

"To those who were not witnesses of the conflagration on Saturday night, it is impossible to convey an idea of the scene it presented. Such a collection of blackguards and rowdies imagination can scarcely conceive, and the merchandize carrying about in all directions, without any one to look after it, or see that it was deposited in safe hands, would seem to say, that property had lost all value. As to the city watch, they scarcely troubled themselves to inquire—we know they rarely can tell—where the fire actually is when one does occur.

"The reports published by us of the fire commissioners show that, in their opinion, the great majority of fires which take place are intentional, and yet we hear of no prosecutions for arson, the most atrocious of crimes. As matters are now going on, it is impossible for insurance offices to stand the losses—it is impossible for the commerce or inhabitants of the city to pay them remunerating premiums. If the public authorities will not stir, will not take effective measures to arrest the evil, individuals, from every consideration of private interest and public duty, ought to combine on some plan to save themselves and the city of their residence from the destruction which hourly awaits them."

After this the merchants did institute a private watch, and in some degree mitigated the evil.

CHAPTER VIII.

1839

Dec. 25.   Ther. 26°.   This is Christmas day, and in Boston all the world is abroad enjoying the fine bright weather.   Public worship is performed in the Catholic and Episcopalian churches. but not in the others.   The stores belonging to members of these sects are closed. but the rest of the community who observe the day at all, dedicate it to feasting.

Frauds.—A fraud to the extent of a million of dollars has lately been exposed, perpetrated by the cashier of the Schuylkill bank in Philadelphia.   He sold shares to that amount in the bank of Kentucky, and appropriated the proceeds to his own purposes, or to those of the bank over which he presided, which also has failed.   On the 23d December, Judge Bouvier, sitting in the court of criminal sessions at Philadelphia, delivered the following charge to the grand jury:—

"Gentlemen of the Grand Jury:—Within a few days occurrences have transpired calculated to throw a gloom and dismay, not only in the commercial world, but also among the honest people in the middle and poorer ranks of society, which require from the court and the grand jury a full and impartial investigation.   Men who have heretofore stood erect in society, and whose integrity never was doubted, have been publicly accused of committing the vilest frauds.   Men who stood in high places have for a series of ten or fifteen years astonished the community by the boldness of their crimes.   Scarcely one shock of the moral feeling has subsided before another has succeeded, and the people, even those who have been robbed by these men of good standing, have viewed, after the first moment of indignation was over, the whole matter with apathy.

"Trace back the history of our public men for the last fifteen years, and you find some of those who have filled high official and other stations have been charged with forgeries, perjuries, and conspiracies. They have not been guilty of these offences, gentlemen, to get bread for their starving families, but to make a fortune by a dash, regardless of the means—to come out, if successful, in society, and by their wealth to claim distinction, and to be placed above the virtuous but poor man. The spirit of speculation has swept over the land, and carried away the frail virtue of those who became its worshipers. Enterprise, gentlemen, with industry, punctuality, and a high sense of mercantile honor, ought to be cherished; but the recklessnesss of the gambling and dishonest speculator ought to be discountenanced and discouraged, or the bands of society must be loosened, confidence between man and man destroyed, and fair trade must cease. •

"Let but the poor starving wretch break into a house to procure what he conceives he needs, and what perhaps he actually does want, and the public voice is raised to a clamor against the daring villain. He is arrested, and brought to trial and speedy and certain punishment. What idea, gentlemen, think you, he will entertain of human justice when he perceives 'respectable offenders' unpunished—when he sees the man who has robbed the helpless widow, age tottering on the grave, and childhood, unable to provide for itself, of their little aid—when he beholds one who has robbed of millions go unpunished, under the pretext that the law does not reach the case, or out of a sickly compassion to the offender or his family. This is the pity which spares the tiger that he may feed upon your children. Hold in your hands the scales of even-handed justice, and be not deterred in the performance of your duty from presenting offenders who have filled high places. Let not the poor man be able to say there is one kind of justice for him, and another for the rich. Do your duty 'without fear, favor, or affection.'

"You are aware, gentlemen, that I allude to the disgraceful disclosures which have been made within a few days, of alleged frauds by certain persons connected with the Schuylkill bank of this city. You have a right, and it is your duty, to investigate this business, and to send for persons and such papers as may be lawfully called for by a court of justice, and ascertain whether there has been any violation of law, and if so, by whom.

"You will be careful not to be carried away by your abhorrence of the crime so far as to present any one without reasonable proof of his guilt."

This charge embodies the sentiments which I heard generally expressed by the respectable members of the community on this occurrence. The cashier escaped to Europe; but a statement appeared assuring the public that the proceeds of the Kentucky Bank stock fraudulently sold, had been applied, not to his private use, but to support the Schuylkill Bank.

Debts of Cities.—The individual property of the citizens of Boston, New York, Rochester, and I believe of other towns, is liable, by the law of the states, to attachment for debts contracted by their civic rulers, and the liability has been enforced. When, in any of these cities, opposition is made to a tax for paying the interest of the public debt, a few of the largest creditors immediately commence processes against the parties who oppose, and speedily they petition for an assessment for their own relief. The law reserves to every citizen who has paid a debt under these processes, a claim for a rateable reimbursement from all the other inhabitants, but this form of redress is so tedious and expensive, that few resort to it. They prefer aiding the corporation to raise the necessary funds by general assessments. The bonds of these cities (which yield, those of Boston 6, and those of New York and Rochester 7 per cent.) are regarded as among the most secure investments in the United States. This state of the law under democratic institutions contrasts favorably with the provisions of the law under the aristocratic legislature of Great Britain. The civic corporation of Edinburgh borrowed large sums of money on bonds; built a high school, churches, and other expensive erections, for the use or ornament of the city; and then declared itself bankrupt. The law protected these edifices as public property, sacred to social purposes, and also the property of the individual citizens from attachment. The civic corporation which contracted the debts, essentially enjoyed the privilege of self-election, and the citizens had no efficient control over its actions. The law, therefore, regarded the lenders as having trusted for repayment solely to that portion of the corporation's property which could legally be alienated or attached for debt. In the American cities, the inhabitants at large elect their rulers, and are, therefore, justly held responsible for the debts which they contract. Since the Burgh Reform Act came into operation in Scotland, the citizens have enjoyed the right to elect the civic councils, but the law still exempts them from individual responsibility for the public debts.

Dec. 31. Ther. 0°. *Dr. Spurzheim's Birth-Day*—This is the anniversary of the birth-day of Dr. Spurzheim, and of the institution of the Phrenological Society of Boston. In the morning I waited on Mr. William Sturgis, who erected the monument in Mount Auburn, and thanked him cordially for the tribute of respect which he had paid to his memory. He said that he admired Dr. Spurzheim's sound sense and warm philanthropy, but knew nothing about Phrenology. He repeated, that it was his shrewdness of observation, simplicity of manners, and goodness of heart, that won his esteem. In the evening I delivered an address before the Phrenological Society in the Melodeon, lately the Lyon Theatre, which the public were invited to attend. The order of proceeding was the following:—Mr. Pierpont delivered an appropriate prayer; various airs were performed on an excellent organ; the address was read; and Mr. Green pronounced a benediction. The attendance exceeded 600 persons, and would have been larger, but for the circumstance, that at the same time Governor Everett delivered the introductory address to the Lowell lectures in the Odeon, and had an audience of at least 1500.

Phrenology and Education —So much interest was excited by my three lectures on education, that, in compliance with the request of numerous friends, I devoted the month of December to repeating them in the following places, and to all the courses the assistant-teachers of the common schools were admitted free.

In Boston, to the teachers in the Odeon, and again to the subscribers to the Lyceum. I was told that 1500 persons attended this last course.

In Salem, Lowell, and Worcester, each of which towns is accessible by a railway. The audiences who attended these lectures were numerous, averaging from two to three hundred each. I received more invitations to repeat these lectures than it was possible for me to comply with.

Having been invited to lecture in Albany in January, 1840, I left Boston on the 1st of that month, and remained at Springfield, where also I delivered the three lectures on education, and where again we passed a most agreeable week. I am under the necessity, from the length to which this work has already extended, of omitting many observations relative to these places, and the excellent persons with whom we became acquainted in each of them; and can only remark, that, in the New England villages, there is an amount of moral worth and intellectual attainment that redeems the country from the blots which its reputation sustains by the gambling speculators and ambitious politicians of the great cities, whose public actions attract the chief notice of a stranger, and give in his eyes their own character to that of the whole country. There is a sound kernel of honesty and worth in "old Massachusetts" that will preserve her amidst all her trials.

Lunatic Asylum at Worcester.—In vol. 1, p. 41-5, I have described this institution. On the 28th of December I visited it again, and met Mr. Salisbury, one of the trustees named by the state, commencing his official visitation. I was invited to accompany him, and entered every cell and apartment, and saw every patient in the institution, and nothing could exceed the

excellent condition in which it appeared. Only four or five
furious and filthy patients were found among the whole, and
they are lodged in a separate building, so distant that their noise
cannot annoy the general inmates of the hospital. Each of
these persons was in a distinct cell, the walls of which are of
brick, and the floors of mica-slate pavement, heated by fire applied below. The light is admitted from the passage. In one
of the cells was a musician, who tears every thing to pieces,
and is excessively dirty. He was seated on the warm stone-
floor, clothed in a very strong and thick cotton vestment, which
descended to his ankles. His organs of Time and Tune remained sound amidst the wreck of nearly all his other faculties.
I heard him, while thus seated, play several tunes on the flute,
with correctness and expression. His head is well formed,
with the exception of a predominating Destructiveness. His
temperament is nervous-sanguine, and the organs of Imitation
and Ideality, as well as those of Time and Tune, are largely
developed. Dr. Woodward gave the patients of the hospital a
ball on Christmas eve. They themselves decorated very taste-
fully one of the corridors, with boughs of evergreens, and converted it into a handsome ball-room, which I saw. They looked
forward to the entertainment with great interest for many days
before Christmas, and it is still affording them a pleasing theme
of conversation. It proved very successful, and even this musician performed a part in it.

Dr. Woodward is an enlightened phrenologist, and he assured
me that his conviction increases, the more he observes, that the
cases are extremely rare in which the whole of the mental organs
are involved in disease; and that this conviction led him to try
the experiment whether this individual could not be enabled to
command himself at the ball. He explained to him the preparations that had been made; asked him if he would like to attend.
This wakened up a thousand impressions received in his best
days of health and usefulness, and he professed his desire to
assist and to play in his professional capacity. Dr. Woodward
adverted to his dress, and said that he must appear in the costume
of a gentleman, and must conduct himself with decorum, as the
only conditions on which he could be admitted. He engaged to
comply with both stipulations. When all things were prepared
on the evening of the ball, the keepers entered his cell, dressed
him in a decent suit of clothes, and led him to his seat among
the musicians, and instantly the band struck up, and the dancing
commenced. He played in perfect tune and time. One of the
keepers was stationed behind him all the evening to prevent accidents, in case of his losing command of himself; but there was
no need for his interfering. For three hours he continued to

play and conduct himself with perfect propriety.   At the end of
two hours he complained of fatigue, and said that he believed
that formerly he used, about this time, to receive a glass of wine.
A glass of wine was given to him, he drank it, and played on,
till the close of the entertainment.   He was then reconducted to
his cell, and had hardly entered it when he recommenced tearing
his clothes.   In Dr. Conolly's instructive Report on the Hanwell
Lunatic Asylum, 1840, he remarks, that " the principle of changing all the circumstances surrounding a lunatic is evidently one
capable of application in certain cases, and in certain periods of
the malady, with singularly felicitous effects."   (P. 26.)   This
instance in the text shows how powerfully a change of circumstances may affect a lunatic even in the most hopeless condition.
In this case, the effect was temporary, but it was great while it
lasted.

Dr. Woodward mentioned that he allows about one-fourth of
the inmates of the Asylum to go into the village on specific
errands unattended, and only one man has escaped; and he did
so after being enticed by some acquaintance to drink.   Social
parties, with music and dancing, are given from time to time,
which, with religious worship on Sundays, have an excellent
effect on the minds of the patients.   The music is supplied
entirely by the patients themselves.

I saw in the hospital a woman, who, in a fit of religious and
destructive mania, had attempted to cut off the heads of two of
her children.   Philoprogenitiveness was deficient, and Destructiveness enormously large.   A man who is insane in regard to
wealth, imagining himself to possess incalculable riches, has the
organs of Acquisitiveness standing forth in such ample size and
well-defined forms, that they attract the eye in looking at him
even in passing.   Ideality is also large, and in his imagination
he applies his wealth to gorgeous purposes.   There were other
striking examples of the concomitance between the peculiar
features of monomania and the size of particular organs in the
brain; and Dr. Woodward expressed his surprise how any man,
living in charge of a hospital for the insane, and capable of mental analysis and physical observation, reasonably acquainted
with Phrenology, could avoid conviction of its truth. (a)

He mentions that he receives many shoemakers as patients.
This class is numerous in New England; but he believes that
insanity is produced beyond an average extent among them by
their breathing vitiated air in their hot, small workshops, without ventilation, and by their unfavorable position when working.

(a) Dr. Conolly, who has charge of the Lunatic Asylum at Hanwell near
London, holds similar opinions.

The frequent mention of bad ventilation in this work may appear to some of my readers almost like a monomania on the subject in its author, but the evidence of its injurious consequences meets one everywhere. "Dr. Lombard, whose researches (into the causes of pulmonary consumption) are founded on a total of 4300 deaths from phthisis, and 54,572 individuals exercising 220 different occupations, found by a comparison of all the professions carried on in the open air and in workshops, that the proportion of deaths from phthisis was *double* among the latter, and this proportion increased as the apartments were close, narrow, and imperfectly ventilated."* Dr. Woodward mentioned that he receives also many sailors as patients, whose insanity is produced by intemperance and exposure to severe hardships at sea. The cure in cases of less duration than one year amounts to 85 per cent. on an average of six years.

Dr. Woodward has published a valuable pamphlet, strongly urging the advantage of instituting "asylums for inebriates." His reasoning may be briefly stated thus: " 1. Intemperance is a physical disease. 2. It is curable in the great majority of cases, if not always. 3. The greatest existing difficulty in effecting this end commonly arises from the extent of the *temptation* to which the patient is uniformly exposed. 4. The best remedy for this state of things is to *confine* the individual, with a view to the avoidance of this temptation, and to the adoption of whatever other measures are necessary for this cure— till he *is* cured—under charge of an institution expressly adapted to the purpose." The subject has attracted considerable attention in the United States; and as Dr. Woodward's views are unquestionably sound, both physiologically and morally, I hope to see Massachusetts adding to her other claims to public admiration, that of being the first to carry his suggestions into effect.

History of Religious Freedom in Massachusetts.—No circumstance presents a more interesting subject of reflection than the change which has taken place in religious opinion in some parts of Switzerland, Protestant Germany, and Massachusetts, since the Reformation. Geneva was then the stronghold of Calvinism, and now it is, to a great extent, Unitarian; and, for a long period, Massachusetts was one of the most orthodox states in the Union, while now it is celebrated for its liberal religious opinions. Originally, also, a tax for the support of religion was levied in this state; now this is abrogated, and the voluntary system is adopted in its stead. I have endeavored to learn some particulars of the latter change.

* Article " Phthisis" in Penny Cyclopedia.

For many years after the colonisation of Massachusetts, nearly the whole population were rigid Calvinists, and none but members of the Church were freemen, or entitled to vote in the election of civil officers. As, however, nearly the whole settlers were of one faith, this scarcely operated as any restriction on civil liberty. At first, the parishes were territorial, the ministers were chosen by the members of the church, they were ordained by an ecclesiastical council, and, without any special legislative enactment on the subject, they were understood to be settled during life and good behavior, *ad vitam aut culpam*. In 1654 authority was given to the county court to assess upon all the inhabitants living within the parish a proper sum for the support of their minister. This law was re-enacted in 1669. For nearly two centuries no exemptions were admitted, except in the case of the Quakers. After Massachusetts ceased to be an English colony, she framed a constitution for herself; but still the old system prevailed. Some years later, however, a relaxation took place, and it was enacted, that if any individual conscientiously dissented from the Protestant Calvinistic faith of the parish minister, and actually attended on the services of another pastor, he should still pay the tax in support of religion, but that his own minister should be entitled to draw the amount from the public treasury. Afterwards, the dissenter was allowed to pay his tax directly to his own minister, the law having provided a process by which he could "sign off" from the minister of the parish, and attach himself to any other; but, until about the year 1830, every man was compelled by law to pay tax to some religious society. Since that date, certain amendments in the constitution of the state have been adopted by the people, in virtue of which every man is left free to support religious worship anywhere, or nowhere, at his option. This has entirely altered the relation between the people and the clergy. The latter are now dependent entirely on their flocks for support, as much so as a lawyer on his clients, or a physician on his patients. The number of churches has since increased, the attendance on them is greater, and I was assured that the sums now paid voluntarily in support of religion very considerably exceed the highest amount of the compulsory assessments.

These changes did not take place without severe contests. In 1641 the power of *electing* church-officers, comprehending the minister, was vested *in the church*. By this colonial statute the right of *ordaining* the minister was also given to the church, which enjoyed likewise the power of admitting, recommending, dismissing, and expelling, or otherwise disposing of its own members, upon due cause, " according to the rules of the Word." In 1668 it was thought necessary to enact again, that the church should elect her own officers; and in this statute the term *church* is defined to mean those who are in full communion only. The "teaching officer" of the church is also declared to be synonymous with the "minister of the whole people." This statute further provided that no inhabitant of any town should challenge a right unto, or act in, the calling or election of such officer or minister until he be in full communion, upon the penalty of being accounted a disturber of peace and order; and he is ordered to be punished by the court of the shire, either by admonition, security for good behavior, fine, or imprisonment, according to the quality or degree of the offence.

In the 4th of William and Mary, an act was passed by the legislature, vesting the appointment of ministers in the inhabitants of the town, and providing that if they neglected to exercise this right for six months, the court should provide a minister, and cause him to be settled within the town. This statute confirmed the other privileges of the church. In the same year another statute was passed, vesting the power of choosing the minister in the major part of the inhabitants of the town, but restricting them in the choice to a person of "good conversation, able, learned, and orthodox." In another statute it is declared that, upon farther consideration, the method here proposed for the choice of a minister, has, in divers towns, been found impracticable, and it is abrogated. By section 9th of this last statute, the power of election is restored to the *church*, on the condition that "the major part of such inhabitants as do there usually attend on the public worship of God, and are by law duly qualified for voting in town affairs," *concur*. It is also enacted that all the inhabitants should be liable for the minister's support.

In two years the system was again changed; for it was enacted, that, when the church should make choice of a minister, if the town did not concur, the church might call in a council of the "elders and messengers" of three or five neighboring churches; to which council the power was given of examining and deciding upon the question between the town and the church, and if they approved of the choice of the church, the minister might be settled notwithstanding the non-concurrence of the town.

No other law was passed upon the subject during the continuance of the provincial government. The "constitution" of 1780, and a statute passed in 1800, vested the right of election of the minister in the *majority of the parish*.

From these several colonial and provincial regulations, the efforts of the churches to obtain, preserve, and, when lost, to recover their power in the choice of ministers, is abundantly obvious. The circumstances which led to the final overthrow of this power were the following:—A church was defined by law to consist of those individuals only who were in full communion; and the clergy early discovered that, by adopting stringent rules relative to communion, they might concentrate the electors into a small body, and exercise considerable influence over them. They accordingly did so. Every candidate for admission to the table of the Lord, before being admitted, was called on to satisfy the church not only in regard to the soundness of his doctrinal belief, but of the fact that he had experienced a change of heart. In proportion as liberal opinions increased, the communion-table was more and more strictly fenced, until, in the progress of time, "the church," that is to say, the persons in full communion, became a mere fraction of the inhabitants of the parish. But the constitution of 1780, and the statute of 1800, vested the election of the minister in the "majority of the parish." In the parish of Dedham the church became vacant: a majority of the inhabitants elected Mr. Lamson, a Unitarian, as their minister; the majority of the communicants, who were rigidly orthodox, refused to acknowledge him. After a minister is chosen, it is the custom to call in an ecclesiastical council, composed of the neighboring ministers, to "ordain" him in his office. The majority of the inhabitants called in a council of clergymen of their own opinions, who proceeded in due form to "ordain" Mr. Lamson. The majority of the communicants, however, refused to concur in the invitation to this council, and maintained that without their consent it was void, and the "ordination" null; and their deacons insisted on retaining the property of the church.

Mr. Lamson and the majority of the inhabitants proceeded to elect church officers, who, although like their minister, rejected by the majority of the "communicants," brought an action of *replevin* in the supreme court against the orthodox deacons, "for the recovery of sundry bonds and other securities for the payment of money, together with the records and documents of the church aforesaid."

"The orthodox party, among other points, pleaded that "ordination" was indispensable to a settlement of a minister of the Gospel, agreeably to the usages and practice of the Congregational Churches in the state, and that Mr. Lamson was not "ordained" by a council chosen by the church. If this plea had been sustained, it would have given the church at least a *veto* on the minister chosen by the inhabitants, but the Supreme Court decided against it. The report of the decision mentions, that "the first minister of *Salem* was set apart by the lay brethren, accident having prevented the clergy who were expected from attending; and though, after they arrived, they

participated in the ceremony by giving the right hand of fellow-
ship. this act was not an essential part of ordination. We consider, then, the non-concurrence of the church in the choice of
the minister, and in the invitation to the ordaining council, as
in no degree impairing the constitutional right of the parish.
That council might have refused to proceed, but the parish
could not by that have been deprived of their minister. It was
right and proper, as they could not proceed according to ancient
usage, because of the dissent of the church, to approach as near
to it as possible, by calling a respectable council, and having
their sanction in the ordination. And it was certainly wise in
that council, finding that the points of disagreement were such
as would be likely to cause a permanent separation, to yield to
the wishes of the parish, and give their sanction to proceedings
which were justified by the constitution and the laws of the
land. They ordained him over the parish only; but, by virtue
of that act, founded upon the choice of the people, he became
not only the minister of the parish, but of the church still remaining there, notwithstanding the secession of a majority of the
members. Mr. Lamson thus became the lawful minister of the
first parish in Dedham, and of the church subsisting therein;
and he had a right to call church meetings, and do all other acts
pertaining to a settled and ordained minister of the Gospel. The
church had a right to choose deacons, finding that the former
deacons had abdicated their office; and thus no legal objection
is found to exist against their right to maintain this action."
The court found the new deacons entitled to the property of the
church.—*Eliphalet Baker and another* versus *Samuel Fales,
Norfolk October Term*, 1820, *Tyng's Reports*, vol. xvi, p. 488.

While the practice prevailed of supporting the clergy by a tax
raised on all the inhabitants, and of electing them by the votes
of the communicants only, the result was, that, under pretence
of purifying the communion-roll, they surrounded the table of
the Lord by their own adherents, and by amiable but weak-
minded persons; the first attached to them by deep devotional
feelings, and the latter prepared submissively to adopt whatever
they suggested:—while they alienated the strong-minded, enlightened, and independent members of the parish, by their wide
departures from charity, peacefulness, and common sense. The
Calvinistic churches all over the state became a kind of close
corporation; united by one common interest, and standing in
opposition to those who refused to bow the neck to their yoke.
The "communicants" were so thoroughly disciplined, that the
election of ministers, although ostensibly belonging to them,
was, *de facto*, effected by the clergy; because, when a minister
died, the orthodox brethren whom he had called in to assist him

in his ministrations, recommended a successor to him, when dead, and, as a general rule, the communicants piously gave effect to their suggestion. Under this system, Unitarianism and other forms of dissent from the ancient Calvinistic faith, multiplied and flourished abundantly, until, as in the case of Dedham, the "church" and its communicants became a mere fraction of the people, and often also the slenderest in point of influence and intelligence in the parish.

After the law was altered, and the ministers were rendered wholly dependent, not on the communicants, but on the people, the conduct of the Calvinistic clergy underwent a remarkable change. They found themselves dethroned from their ecclesiastical dominion, and, instead of directing all their measures to the sustenance of their own power, under the guise of guarding the purity of the communion-table, they threw themselves unreservedly on the affections and intelligence of their whole flocks, and became more diligent, more practical, more rational, and far less arrogant and exclusive. The consequence was, that the progress of dissent and Unitarianism received a check. At this moment, from the best information which I can obtain, Unitarianism is either not at all, or only very slowly, progressive in Massachusetts; many persons assure me that there has been even a reaction in favor of Calvinism;—Calvinism, however, is no longer presented in its ultra forms, and is itself undergoing modifications. All pretensions on the part of the clergy to a spiritual dominion, independent at once of the civil power and of the people, are completely laid aside.

These facts are instructive to the people of other countries. In Scotland, the clergy of the Established Church are laboring to bring matters into the condition from which the people of Massachusetts, after long and painful struggles, have only recently escaped. In Scotland, the law endows a minister for every parish out of the tithes or teinds payable from the lands lying within its boundaries. The right of nominating ministers is a privilege belonging in some instances to the Crown, in others to one or more private individuals, who are styled the patrons of the parish. The restrictions on the patron's right of nomination are twofold. He must choose a person previously licensed as a preacher, by a church court of the establishment; and, after the presentation, the nominee must apply to a church court to "ordain" him in his office. Before this court every objection to his character, doctrines, or competency, may be stated either by the people of the parish, or by the members of the court themselves; and, on cause shown, he may be rejected. A few years ago, however, the General Assembly of the Church of Scotland passed a law authorizing the male heads of families on

the "communion-roll" of the parish, to exercise a veto on the
patron's nomination, *without showing any cause;* and they instructed the territorial church courts, or presbyteries, to refuse
"ordination" to every nominee who did not obtain the concurrence of a majority of these "communicants." Certain nominees
who were "vetoed" under this law brought actions into the
Supreme Civil Court to have it found and declared that they had
right to the emoluments of the parish, notwithstanding the
veto and of the refusal of the presbytery to induct them into the
pastoral charge; and the civil court, and also the House of Peers
on appeal, sustained their claim. The General Assembly next
proceeded to deprive of their clerical character, and to depose,
certain ministers who had acted in obedience to the civil court,
and who were prepared to receive one of these nominees in
defiance of the veto. The civil court has threatened to enforce
obedience to the civil law; and in this state the dispute at present
stands.

The clergy, meanwhile, are preparing to change their ground.
They are now agitating for the entire abolition of patronage, and
for the passing of a law to enable the church, in other words,
"the communicants," to choose all the church officers. The
parallel between Massachusetts and Scotland, in regard to this
matter, is wonderfully complete: In Scotland, since the project
of placing either a veto, or the power of election, in the hands
of the communicants was started, the clergy have manifested
great zeal in "purifying the communion-roll;" in other words,
in doing what their brethren in Massachusetts did, placing on
the roll their own staunch adherents, and such other persons as
will be most easily led by their advice. They also are evidently
becoming more Calvinistic in their preaching, more lofty in their
pretensions to independent power, and they openly advocate the
principle of setting the civil law at defiance, where it threatens
to abridge their ecclesiastical authority.

The public mind in Scotland is scarcely awake to the most
important principle involved in this struggle. It is the same as
that which was implicated in the contest between the Calvinistic
clergy and the people in Massachusetts—religious freedom.
The question to be determined in Scotland is, Whether the nation
gave the endowments for the support of the religion of *the people,*
or for the maintenance *of the tenets of a sect.* If the former
was the object in view, then it is absurd to give either a right of
veto or of election to the "communicants." The "communicants" necessarily represent only the sect to which they belong,
and, according to the experience of other countries, they may be
converted into puppets, by pulling the strings of which, the
clergy of that sect will elect themselves to office, and claim to be

the spiritual lords of the whole community. The efforts of the clergy will then be directed to managing the "communicants;" the more seriously inclined, and less vigorously minded of every parish will be sought out, to sit at the communion-table, and in doctrine and practice the clergy will address themselves to the task of commanding and leading this portion of their flocks; while, by their pretensions to universal and independent ecclesiastical power, and their aberrations from common sense, they will oppose the advance of knowledge and of liberal education; and finally, after having alienated the minds of the enlightened and independent members of the community, they will accomplish their own downfall, and religious freedom will be established.

If the endowments were provided to support the religion of *the people*, then the election of the ministers in Scotland, as in Massachusetts, should be given to the *inhabitants of the parish.* This would at least ensure *progress* in religious opinions; for if the people of any parish came to entertain views different from those of the present predominant sect, they would enjoy the power of electing a pastor capable of edifying their own minds.

In short, in my humble opinion, religion will never flourish in its full vigor in Scotland until the example of Massachusetts be entirely followed out, and all endowments be abrogated: But if the majority of the people desire an endowed church, they will do well to profit by the example now set before them, and to avoid giving the clergy of the sect which they choose to endow, the power of self-election through the machinery of the communicants; for such a measure will destroy the usefulness of the clergy, forge chains of intolerance and bigotry for the public neck, and erect a barrier of the most formidable description to the moral and intellectual progress of the nation.

While I was engaged in this inquiry into the history of religious liberty in Massachusetts, I placed several Edinburgh newspapers, containing "non-intrusion" speeches and debates, into the hands of several intelligent friends who had furnished me with information. In returning them, after perusal, they made some remarks which are worth recording. One phrase that frequently occurred in the addresses of the established clergy, attracted particular attention; it was the assertion that "Jesus Christ is the sole head of our church." "We are contending for the crown rights of the Redeemer." One serious gentleman, on reading these expressions, said, "This sounds strangely to me. In Massachusetts every one of our sects, except the Roman Catholic, professes to have no head except Jesus Christ; that is to say, they disown all temporal heads; but we have no crown in this country to assign to the Redeemer, and we do not understand what a Christian means by the 'Redeemer's crown rights.' In this country, every one of our sects believes itself to be the true interpreter of the Divine mind, as it is revealed in the Scriptures, and, in this sense, each of them regards Jesus as their head, and themselves as his followers. but it would be viewed as unwarrantable presumption if each of them were to adduce Him as a guaranty for all its opinions and observances, and to ascribe these to him as his honors and privileges. The Unitarians might represent him, as their head, denying his own divinity: while the Trinitarians, also under his headship, might represent him as maintaining it: yet we do not see that he is, or can be, the head of the Church of Scotland, in any other sense than he is the head of our independent churches. The phrase seems to me to be used merely to operate on the feelings of the multitude: for we all know that Jesus never interferes with the proceedings of the clergy; and that under his headship they pursue whatever measures suit their own interests for the time. He was the head of our Calvinistic church through all the struggles of which you have read, yet he never appears to have directed its clergy to forego any item of power, as long as it was possible for them to retain it. Here we are republicans, and while we all acknowledge allegiance to Jesus Christ as our federal head, we do not identify him with the several acts of our separate church governments. We endeavor to discover and practise his will, but we do not call our own ecclesiastical powers and privileges either his 'state rights' or 'his crown rights.' We claim his protection; but we offer him nothing in return except the homage of our hearts." Another individual remarked, "Surely your Scottish clergy conceive their own church to be synonymous with Christendom. I have always understood Christianity to be cosmopolitan in its principles and application. Their language may suit themselves and their own flocks; but as it is offensive to the common sense of Christians who live under different forms of ecclesiastical government, I cannot acknowledge it to breathe the genuine spirit of universal Christianity."

I was frequently asked how this great change in the spirit of the Scottish clergy, since the days of Robertson and Blair, had arisen. The only account of which I could give was one which I had received, a few years ago, from an aged friend who was long an "elder" of one of the churches in Edinburgh, and who himself had witnessed the alteration. Before the breaking out of the French Revolution, said he, the Scottish clergy were distinguished for the liberality of their religious sentiments, and ublic rumor mentioned the intention of their leaders even to propose a revisal of the standards of the church. The men of property, the lawyers, and distinguished physicians. in general partook of the same spirit, and the people would have followed in their train without much hesitation. In this state of the public mind, the French Revolution broke out; the throne and the altar were overturned in France, and trampled under foot. The government and owners of property in Great Britain, became alarmed at the progress of French principles among their own people, and combined to resist them. Their great object was to rear bulwarks around the throne, for the protection, through it, of their private interests; and, viewing the altar as the principal pillar of the state, they became zealous supporters of religious institutions and observances. They patronised the church and courted the clergy; " I then saw," said the elder, "individuals of great political influence in Edinburgh, who for many years before had never entered a church door, ostentatiously walking up the High Street of Edinburgh, with bibles in their hands, to attend public worship; and they did not stop there, but hired evangelical tutors for their sons, and evangelical governesses for their daughters, and used all their influence to induce every loyal subject of King George the Third to follow their example. Their efforts were successful; the same spirit prevaded all classes of the community; a vast zeal was instantaneously evoked and put into action; and serious impressions were communicated to the young. This ardor originated in worldly motives, and its chief object was the security of property; but the children knew nothing of the designs of their parents, they received the impressions in all sincerity, and they now constitute the mass of modern society. I have lived to see some of these political supporters of the altar desert its shrines, and return to their habits of religious indifference: but their children not only did not fall away from the principles which had been instilled into them, but nearly broke the hearts of their parents by advancing into wild fanaticism, which the latter never contem·plated without disgust. We are now in the midst of the reaction, after the irreligious period of the French Revolution, and society must abide the maturity of another generation, or probably two, before reason will again exert any salutary influence over religious opinion in Scotland."

As the French Revolution had taken place long before I was capable of observing public occurrences, I am not able to judge of the merits of this explanation; but it bears strong indications of truth. One striking circumstance in the present contest between the church and the civil power in Scotland, is, that several men of talent, whose duty it was to view the question as statesmen, are found enlisted in the cause of the church, as mere religious partizans. The question, as I have already remarked, involves the religious freedom of the country. If the

church shall be allowed to hold her endowments and make her
own ecclesiastical laws, independently of the civil courts and
popular control, and to elect her own ministers and office-bearers
by means of the communicants, Scotland will speedily be involved in a spiritual despotism which will bring back the dark
ages, or lead to a new reformation. I have introduced these
remarks, because no topic is more generally interesting in the
United States than information concerning the condition and progress of religious institutions, practices, and opinions, in other
countries.

Jan. 9. 1840. *Journey from Springfield to Albany.*—The
cold has been as low as 8° below zero, and the ground is deeply
covered with snow. The distance to Albany is eighty miles, and
the road lies over mountains. It has been impassable for some
days, but is now open; and as the thermometer is 5° above zero,
the sky bright, and no wind, we resolved to proceed on our
journey. We hired an exclusive extra mounted on two sleigh-
runners and drawn by four horses. It was nearly twelve feet
long, and four broad, and was seated for twelve persons. We
occupied one end. and our luggage was piled up in the other.
The body of the "extra," as high as our elbows, was composed
of deal-boards, without stuffing or lining; from these boards to
the roof it was inclosed simply by green baize curtains very ill
fastened, the air entering freely in all directions. The bottom
was littered with straw; at our feet we had a heated soap-stone of
the size of a common brick, and a dressed buffalo skin, with the
hair next us, and on our persons we wore abundance of shawls,
fur-caps. cloaks, and great-coats. We set merrily off at nine
o'clock in the morning, and sleighed very smoothly for about
twenty miles to Blandford, where we stopped and had an excellent dinner of fresh fried cod, brought up frozen from Boston,
roast-beef, cranberry sauce, &c. Notice of our approach had
been given by the mail-sleigh in the morning, and all was
prepared for us. After dinner we proceeded on our journey;
the snow became deeper, and only one track was open.
When we met a vehicle of any kind, the two drivers dis-
mounted, plied their spades vigorously, which they carried for
the purpose, dug a hole in the snow on one side of the track
sufficient to contain one of the carriages, drove it into the
recess, made the other advance past it, and then extricated it,
put it also on the track, after which each proceeded on his way.
This occurred every half hour, and our advance was very slow.
Sometimes our leaders, sometimes those of the opposing team,
were unfastened and applied to drag the other carriage, or they
were stowed away up to the belly among the snow to make
room for other evolutions. The drivers were uniformly civil
and good natured to us and to each other; but occasionally they

would cry, "The woman must come out, and the man must come and hold on upon this here side to prevent her (the sleigh) from pitching over;" which orders we implicitly obeyed. The "woman" stood in the snow, the two drivers and the "man" hung by the rail on the roof of the coach, on one side, to prevent it toppling over and rolling down the side of the hill; while the horses, at the word of command, dragged it forward through immense wreaths of snow. We constantly overheard such scraps of conversation as these—"We'll take care any how, this d——d old thing (our vehicle) will tumble over as easy as not." "Well, has she been over to-day yet?"—"Well, not yet," and so forth. On one occasion we met a heavy wagon drawn by three horses, and, to make way for us, its master moved it so much to one side that it was completely and deeply imbedded in snow. He assisted our coachman for half an hour with his spade, before a way for us could be excavated, and at last, when we got fairly past, all hands and horses were applied to extricate his wagon, but in vain. We were ready to start, leaving him alone with his three horses on a steep acclivity, and the sun already set, when he said, in perfect good humor—"Well, I guess I'll not get out of this fix this night, but I am glad that you are through any how." I asked him what he would do. "Take out my horses and go back," said he. At half-past 9 P M. we reached Stockbridge, and found an excellent room provided for us in Mr. Gilpin's inn, by the kind attention of Mrs. Charles Sedgewick. This excellent family we found in affliction. Miss Catharine Sedgewick is in Italy with her brother, who is laboring under very infirm health, and Mr. Theodore Sedgewick senior lately died suddenly of apoplexy at Pittsfield. They are distinguished in the United States for their superior talents and virtues.

I select the following description of this day's journey from C.'s Journal:—"I never saw so much snow in my life, except at the Grindelwald Glacier, as on this journey, and never any so brilliantly, beautifully, bluely white. Wherever the wind had drifted it into little irregularities, or chinks had opened, we looked into crannies and miniature arches of the most intense sky color, often appearing like the porticos to fairy palaces, and so mysteriously lovely that I longed to be a sylph and explore them, if so be that sylphs be insensible to cold. In other places the lovely unsullied wreaths were hanging about the snake fences and the small evergreen trees, in the most graceful draperies, and on some of the inequalities in the ground beside us, as we moved along, lay as in little waves, or were spread out in chiselled smoothness. The sun's rays reflected so many diamonds from the surface of the snow, that I was forced to close my eyes.

The clearer atmosphere of this country must tend to these appearances, which I never noticed at home."

Next morning we proceeded towards Albany, and again I
borrow C.'s description.—" The worst of the road was to
come. We found it full of ' pitch-holes,' and unfortunately our
next sleigh was one of a very inferior description. Pitch-holes
mean holes in the snow into which the runners of the sleigh
descend with horrid jerks, and in rising out of which the traveller is pitched up high off his seat, on which he again descends
with a solid thump. The jolts and jars were so incessant and
so severe that my spine literally felt as if shortened a couple of
inches by the crushing of the cartilages between the several
bones. We dined at Chatham, and were again transferred to
another sleigh; it was an old, dirty, wooden box, with the cobwebs of last summer hanging from the top and interstices between
the deals of the roof, through which sun, wind, rain, and snow,
had full liberty of ingress when they chose. A little before dark
we crossed the Hudson on solid ice, and immediately drove to
the Mansion House hotel."

Albany from 10th January to 11th February.—We remained
in Albany during this interval. I delivered a course of twelve
lectures on Phrenology in the Hall of the Female Academy, and
was honored by the attendance of an audience exceeding 200
persons, who received the lectures in the best spirit, and, at the
close, passed the resolutions printed in the Appendix, No. X.
On the 17th of January the thermometer fell during the night to
30° below zero, and it was frequently 10°, 15°, and 20° below
that point. I suffered no inconvenience from it; and on three
nights of the week emerged from a temperature of 70° or 75° in
the lecture-room, to these low degrees in the external air, without the slightest unpleasant sensation, except that I felt cold in
the balls of my eyes. a feeling which I never experienced before.
Occasionally the wind was high, and the cold was then intole-
rably severe; when the weather was calm, it was comparatively
little felt. It was amusing, on these intensely cold days, to
observe the efforts of the pigs, dogs, and poultry, to screen themselves from the wind and obtain a few consolatory rays of heat
from the brilliant sun. Fortunately the wind came from some
points north of west, and they most ingeniously found out the
lea and sunny side of projecting stairs, logs of wood, banks of
earth, and other masses of matter, and stood in groups drinking
in the heat. The horses that had been driven into perspiration,
came into the town like moving automatons of frost work, every
long hair being the centre of an icicle. I was surprised to discover the extraordinary degree of cold which these animals
sustain with impunity. I saw them standing round the churches,

tied to stakes or trees, with only a rug or buffalo skin thrown over them, for hours in succession, during divine service. The stables are made of only half-inch boards, and the joints are not covered; so that they form a slender protection from the cold; yet the horses are said to be healthy. One gentleman, who had passed some winters in Canada, told me that he saw a curious compact carried into effect in his own stable between his horse and his poultry. The moment that his horse was unharnessed and tied up in its stall, in winter, a whole flock of ducks, geese, turkeys, and hens, descended on his person and covered every inch of his horizontal surface from his eyes to his tail, and squatted down upon him. They gave and received warmth, much to the comfort and gratification of both parties. I saw the work of excavation proceeding in forming a new street. The earth, when newly exposed, steamed with excessive heat; it was 70° or 80° warmer than the air. Innumerable steamboats, barges, sloops, and boats, were frozen up in the river and docks, and the ice, 15 or 18 inches thick, seems like adamant around them. One wonders how they will ever get out. There is much sleighing on the river, and the mail-coaches, coming from New York, travel many miles on it. The interiors of the houses are preserved comfortably warm by means of large fires of anthracite coal.

Dissection of the Brain.—During my stay in Albany Dr. Hoyt came from Syracuse, a distance of nearly 150 miles, in intensely cold weather, bringing with him a brain prepared in alcohol, for the sake of seeing it dissected in the method taught by Drs. Gall and Spurzheim. The dissection took place in one of the rooms of the Albany Medical College, and I was honored by the attendance of some of the professors and other medical men. Dr. M'Naughten had seen Dr. Spurzheim dissect the brain in Dr. Barclay's class-room, in presence of Dr. Gordon, in 1816; but to the other gentlemen the method was new. It was gratifying to see so much zeal for knowledge as Dr. Hoyt displayed in making so long a journey, at such a season, for a purely scientific purpose.

Albany Female Academy.—This may be described as a college for young ladies, administered by trustees, and supported to some extent by the state. In this institution Captain Marryat has forfeited some reputation. He mentions, that at the public examination he secretly assisted the young ladies with their French exercises, and received their acknowledgments confidentially for the favor; the young ladies maintain that all the rules of gallantry prescribed to the Captain an inviolable and eternal secrecy on the subject, instead of observing which he has published an account of the whole transaction in his work on

America; betraying their confidence, and, as they say, at the same time, indulging his own vanity. The teacher in whose department the alleged assistance was given, denies the possibility of such an incident having occurred without her having detected the Captain's interference; but this point must be settled between themselves. There is only one opinion, however, among all the ladies, young and old, plain and pretty, of the United States, who have read the Captain's narrative—that, if his own story be literally correct, it was very unlike a British naval officer to reciprocate confidential favors with young ladies, and then to boast of his own achievement. I attended part of the semi-annual public examination of the academy, which commenced on Tuesday the 4th February 1840, and was continued on the Wednesday, Thursday, and Friday immediately follow-, ing. The programme of the examination will convey an idea of the nature of the institution, and of the subjects taught. The departments under examination (two proceeding at the same time in different rooms) were on

"Tuesday, A. M.—The 5th and 6th departments, and the classes in Mathematics belonging to the 1st and 2d departments.

"Tuesday, P. M.—The French classes under the care of Prof. Molinard.

"Wednesday, A. M.—The 4th department, and classes in Watts on the Mind, Mental Philosophy and Evidences of Christianity.

"Wednesday, P. M.—The 2d division of the 3d department, and classes in Physiology and Chemistry.

"Thursday, A. M.—The 1st division of the 3d department, and classes in Ecclesiastical History, Arnott's Physics, and Kaimes' Elements of Criticism.

"Thursday, P. M.—The class in Astronomy, under the care of the President.

"On Friday, at 2 o'clock P. M., the usual exercises will take place in the Chapel of the institution, when the compositions, both English and French, will be read.

"The examination commenced each day at 9 o'clock A. M. and 2 o'clock P. M."

The senior classes were composed of young ladies apparently from fifteen to seventeen years of age, and their attainments were highly creditable to themselves and to their teachers. They had committed to memory a vast extent of details in history, astronomy, chemistry, physiology, and the other branches before enumerated. It was mentioned by some persons, however that they are stimulated to excess by emulation, and that they occasionally ruin their health by their exertions to gain prizes. This error is a serious one, for when knowledge is acquired by laborious efforts, not for its own sake, but to gratify the feelings of Self-Esteem and Love of Approbation, its *practical* value is not appreciated and it escapes from the memory when the gratification for which it was acquired has been attained. Information, on the contrary, recommended to the intellect by its inherent interest, and embraced by the moral affections from its practical utility, will become the stock and furniture of the mind through life, and, however limited in amount, it will be all real and permanently available.   Much solid instruction, however, is obviously communicated in this academy.   In the examinations, in chemistry, for example, the young ladies, without assistance or directions, performed numerous experiments, and gave the theory of the chemical actions involved in them.   In the examinations on astronomy, they referred to an admirable orrery, as to a text book, with clear intelligence; and so in the other branches.   It was in history that the memory seemed to be chiefly overtasked, and, viewing their studies in the aggregate, the quantity of matter included in them appeared to be too burdensome to ordinary minds.

Dr. Sprague's Collection of Autographs.—Dr. Sprague's collection of autographs surprised me more than any other object in Albany.   It is exceedingly extensive, rich, and valuable, and has been formed entirely by himself.   He has whole volumes of autographs of literary men, embracing both the kingdoms of Europe and the United States, and more than one devoted to those of crowned heads, and extending over several centuries. He has correspondents in the European cities who procure for him new treasures as they appear.   There are probably few more valuable collections in Europe.

The extreme cold, added to the severe suffering inflicted on C—— during the drive from Stockbridge to Albany, unfortunately involved her in much indisposition.   She was confined to bed, and continued an invalid during our whole stay in Albany. We experienced fresh instances of American benevolence.   The Rev. Dr. Sprague kindly offered to receive us both into his house, and his daughter offered to become C——'s nurse; other female friends offered unreserved attendance on her in her illness. Dr. M'Naughten, a Scotch physician, was most assiduous and successful in his treatment of her, and altogether, although I was prevented by this occurrence from going into society, or extending the circle of my acquaintances, we received renewed proofs of the generous kindness of the inhabitants.   Just as the lectures terminated, C—— was able to travel, and Dr. M'Naughten recommended to her to set out as speedily as possible for a more genial locality.

Having received an invitation to deliver a course of twelve lectures on Phrenology in New Haven Connecticut, the seat of Yale College, we left Albany on the 12th, sleighed to Hartford, and proceeded thence by the railroad to New Haven, where we arrived on the 15th of February. On the 16th February the thermometer stood at 15°, which seemed a mild and almost a bland temperature. after having been accustomed to —15°, —20°, and —28°, at Albany.

New Haven.—We remained in New Haven from the 15th of February to the 20th of March. The audience attending my class included most of the professors, and a portion of the students of Yale College, and a large number of the citizens. It was the largest class, in proportion to the population, which I have had in the United States. Our accommodations in the Tontine Hotel were excellent; the town even in winter is beautiful and peaceful; we enjoyed the most agreeable and enlightened society; and C——'s convalescence was rapid and satisfactory. We had the pleasure of cultivating the acquaintance of Professor Silliman, whose scientific reputation stands high not only in the United States, but in Europe. "The American Journal of Science and Arts," which has now reached its thirty-eighth volume, has long been, and still is conducted by him with the most indefatigable zeal, and serves as the grand channel by which the discoveries of the old and new continents are reciprocally interchanged. He is a man of the most amiable and interesting character, full of kindness, and his manner is so pleasing that it is a common observation in Boston and New York. where he occasionally delivers lectures, that he can speak more plain truths to his class, without giving offence, than almost any other lecturer they hear. In the United States no man's status is lowered by employing his talents usefully, and the most distinguished professors in colleges lecture occasionally to popular audiences in the different towns without any derogation from their dignity In New Haven we met also Professor Olmsted, Dr. Taylor, whom I have already mentioned. Mr. Noah Webster, the Johnson of New Haven. Mr. Trumbull. the distinguished historical painter of the United States, the friend of Washington and Franklin, and who still uses his brush, Professor Hooker, Mr. Skinner. and other highly accomplished men. The comparative repose which this residence permitted I employed in throwing together some general ideas founded on the observations which have already been detailed. These I shall now present to the reader.

CHAPTER IX.

American Civilisation.

1840.

March 20. *American Civilisation.*—Mons. Guizot, in his "History of Civilisation in Europe," has well observed that the degree of civilisation which any age or country has attained is indicated by the "development of social activity, and that of individual activity; the progress of society, and the progress of humanity. Wherever the *external* condition of man is quickened and ameliorated—wherever the *internal* nature of man is exhibited with lustre and grandeur—upon these two signs the human race applauds and proclaims civilisation, often in spite of fundamental imperfections in the social state." Let us apply these principles to the United States.

In no country, probably, in the world is the external condition of man so high as in the American Union. The enterprise, intelligence, activity, and economical habits of the people have multiplied to an astonishing extent all the physical elements of human enjoyment. It was observed to me by a gentleman who is minutely and extensively acquainted with the United States, that in this country no man who is able and willing to work need to go supperless to bed. In this he far understated the fact. Laborers here are rich compared with the individuals in the same class in Europe. Their food is wholesome and abundant; their dwelling-houses comfortable and well furnished; they possess *property*, and enjoy many of the luxuries which property, in a state of civilisation, is capable of purchasing. The American cities contain great wealth; and reckoning the whole property, and the whole population of the Union, and dividing the value of the one by the sum of the other, my impression is that the product would show a larger amount of wealth for each individual in the United States, than exists in any other country in the world, Great Britain alone probably excepted. In the United States this property is so equally diffused, that it is really national.

The formation of railroads and canals, the multiplication of steamboats, ships, machinery, manufactories, and houses, the extension of the productive soil; in short, the advance of all that ministers to the well-being of " the external condition of man" proceeds in the United States on a gigantic scale, and with extraordinary rapidity. We must grant, therefore, that whatever other " imperfection" may exist " in the social state," this fundamental element of civilisation abounds in a high degree.

The condition of the "*internal nature*" of man is the next index to civilisation. The human mind is endowed with animal propensities, moral and religious sentiments, and intellectual faculties fitted for observation and reflection. The propensities and sentiments are blind impulsive powers, which inspire man with desires, and impel him to seek for their gratification; but they do not discern either the mode of obtaining their own objects, or the extent to which they may be advantageously indulged. It is the province of intellect to study and to acquire knowledge, and when enlightened by knowledge to direct, guide, and restrain all the impulsive powers. The mind of an individual is perfect in proportion as it is capable of extensive action, of regulating itself in accordance with the rules of duty, and of finding its way to good in every sphere of its existence. If its scope of action be narrow; if it need external guidance; or if it fail to accomplish its own permanent welfare, it is imperfect in the degree in which it comes short in any of these particulars. I apply these data to measure the condition of the *internal* man in the United States.

The Anglo-Saxon race, which chiefly has peopled the United States, has been richly endowed by nature with mental qualities. It possesses, in a high degree, all the faculties classed under the three grand divisions before mentioned, but, to attain their complete development, they need cultivation. In the United States the development of the mind of the mass of the people is accomplished by the following influences —1*st*, By domestic education. 2*dly*, By district schools. 3*dly*, By religious instruction. 4*thly*, By professional instruction, and, *lastly*, By political action.

1*st*, *By Domestic Education.*—The object of education in the family circle is to develope and regulate the affections, as well as to instruct the understanding. So far as a stranger can discover by observation, or learn by inquiries, the family education in the United States is exceedingly various, and depends for its character much more on the natural dispositions of the parents, than on any system of instruction. In general the parents are in easy circumstances, are happily matched, are good-natured, active, and frugal, and these qualities insensibly cultivate similar dispositions in the young; but there are of course numerous exceptions; and education has not advanced so far among the masses as to render domestic training systematic.

Every family has its own manners, maxims, and modes of treatment. Speaking generally, the faculties of the child are allowed
free scope in the family circle, without sufficient enforcement of
self-denial, or of the subordination of the lower to the higher
powers. The first useful lesson to a child is that of self-restraint, or of foregoing a present enjoyment at the call of duty,
or for the sake of a higher, although more distant, good. Many
American children appear to be indulged in their appetites and
desires, and to be too little restrained in the manifestation of
their propensities. Egotism, or the idea that the world is made
for them, and that other persons must stand aside to allow them
scope, is a feature not infrequently recognised. The consideration of the manner in which their sentiments and modes of
action, will affect other individuals of well regulated and well
cultivated minds, is not adequately brought home to them. In
short, the active manifestation of the moral sentiments in refined
habits, in pure and elevated desires, and in disinterested goodness, is not aimed at systematically as an object in domestic
training. I speak of the masses composing the nation, and not
of the children of well educated and refined individuals.

In intellectual cultivation, domestic education is still more
defective, because in the masses the parents themselves are very
imperfectly instructed.

On the whole, therefore, the domestic training and instruction
appear to me to be imperfect, viewed in relation to the objects
of enlarging the mind's sphere of action, of conferring on it the
power of self-restraint, and also the ability to discover and successfully to pursue its own permanent welfare.

2dly, Of Common School Education.—From the various
remarks which have already been presented in these volumes,
the reader will be prepared to draw the inference that, viewed
in relation to the three objects before mentioned, the common
school education in the United States is also imperfect; I should
say very imperfect. The things taught (chiefly reading, writing, and arithmetic) are not in themselves education. If sedulously and wisely applied, they may enable the individual to
obtain knowledge; but the common schools stop short of supplying it. They even communicate very imperfectly the art of
acquiring it; for some of the teachers are themselves ill qualified; their modes of teaching are defective, and the attendance of
the children at school is brief and irregular. The addition of a
library to each school-district was dictated by a perception of
the magnitude and importance of the deficiency in this department. It appears to me that besides great improvements in
existing schools, still higher seminaries are wanted, in which
the elements of natural, moral, and political science, with their

applicatfons to the purposes of individual and social enjoyment, may be taught to the whole people.

One, and probably the most important, element in an education calculated to fit an individual for becoming an accomplished member of the American democracy, is *training* the faculties to their proper modes of action. This can be accomplished only by calling them all into activity, and by communicating to the higher powers the knowledge and habit of governing the lower. Mere intellectual instruction is not sufficient for this purpose; the propensities and sentiments must be trained in the field of life. The anecdote mentioned in vol. i, p. 305, is illustrative of this proposition. This end will be best accomplished by communicating to children the knowledge of their own faculties, and of their spheres of use and abuse, by placing them in circumstances in which these may be called into action, and superintending that action in such a manner as to cultivate the powers of rapid judgment and steady self-control. The play-ground is an important field for conducting this branch of education. The principles and practice of it are explained in the works of Wilderspin and Stow already referred to. This department of education is in a very humble condition in the United States; and yet to them it is all-important. Every one of their citizens wields political and judicial power; he is at once the subject of the law and its pillar; he elects his own judges, magistrates, and rulers, and it is his duty to obey them. If ever knowledge of what is right, self-control to pursue it, and high moral resolve to sacrifice every motive of self-interest and individual ambition, to the dictates of benevolence and justice, were needed in any people, they are wanted in the citizens of the United States. A well *instructed* citizen will consider the influence of any law on the general welfare before he consents to its enactment, and a well *trained* citizen will not only obey that law when enacted, but lend his whole moral and physical energies, if necessary, to enforce its observance by all, until repealed by constitutional authority. An *ill-instructed* citizen will clamor for the enactment of any law which promises to relieve *him* from an individual inconvenience, or to confer on him an individual advantage, without much consideration concerning its general effects, and an *ill-trained* citizen will seek to subject the magistrates judges, and the law to his own control, that he may bend them in subserviency to his interest, his ambition, or his inclinations, from day to day, as these arise and take different directions. The *ill-trained* citizen takes counsel of his self-will; and self-will, uninstructed and untrained to the guidance of moral principle, leads to destruction.

Phrenology is calculated to benefit the people of the United

States, by enabling both teachers and pupils to act with intelligence and co-operation in instructing and training. It presents views of each mental power, and of its spheres of use and abuse, so simple and intelligible that children can understand them, and teachers can act upon them.

Lecturing to the people in lyceums is extensively practised in the United States, and as a mode of public instruction it is well calculated to advance their intelligence; but hitherto, owing to the defects of their education in the primary schools, it has not yielded half its advantages. As formerly mentioned, the lectures delivered in lyceums are generally of a miscellaneous character, developing no subject systematically, and sacrificing profound interest to variety and temporary excitement; yet no other lectures would attract persons of mature age, whose minds had not been opened up, in their elementary education, to the value of scientific knowledge. If the simpler elements of the natural sciences were taught in childhood, the mind, when it expanded into vigor, would long for fuller developments of their principles, and the lectures in the lyceums might then assume a high character of usefulness.

Viewing the object of education, then, to be to communicate knowledge by which the sphere of the mind's action may be enlarged—to train each individual to self-control and the love of good—and to enable him, by these means combined, to pursue successfully his own welfare, the educational institutions of the United States appear generally to be defective.

3dly, *Of Religious Instruction.*—The objects of religious instruction are twofold; first, To obtain Salvation in a future life; and, secondly, To conduce to practical virtue in this world. I regard the first as belonging to the sphere of theology, and as beyond the jurisdiction, equally of the philosopher and the civil magistrate. By the principles consecrated at the Reformation each individual has the exclusive right of judging on this subject for himself, and for those whose souls Providence has intrusted to his care. I merely remark, that I perceive great differences existing in the opinions of American sects regarding, first, the extent of the danger to which the human soul is exposed in a future life; and secondly, the means by which this danger may be avoided; but that each sect exhibits a means of salvation which it considers commensurate with its own ideas of the danger. All profess to found their belief on a sound interpretation of Scripture; and as only the Great Judge of all can decide which has reached the largest portion of truth, we may hope that they may all prove essentially successful in accomplishing this important end. Instruction in the nature and extent of the danger, and in the nature and use of the means to avert it, constitute a large

portion of the religious education communicated to the young.
The clergy of the various sects appeared to me to be most
assiduous in the discharge of this duty; and from the extensive
attendance on religious worship exhibited in every part of the
Union which I have visited, their teaching appears to have excited that deep interest in the subject, which is the only legitimate proof, in this world, of their success. The grand motive
of the clergy of all sects is, no doubt, the love of souls; but there
is a secondary circumstance which is, probably, not without
some effect in securing their exertions, namely, the knowledge
that the acceptance of their peculiar doctrines regarding salvation
is the bond which binds the people to their ministrations, and
that the more successfully they impress a firm conviction of their
views on their flocks, the more secure do they feel in obtaining
the means of their own subsistence, and the greater also are their
power and influence over their people. This branch of religious
instruction, therefore, appears to be in a salutary and satisfactory
condition in the United States.

But religious instructors teach also the morality and religion
which ought to regulate human conduct in this world. In the
great outlines of secular duty, all the Christian sects are agreed;
and the clergy of all sects teach them to their flocks. In the
course of my attendance in the churches of the United States, I
could not, however, avoid making two remarks on this subject;
first, that, in proportion as the tenets of any sect represented the
dangers of eternal perdition to be great and imminent, and the
means of salvation to be difficult, the clergy of that sect taught
their own doctrinal views on these points more zealously and
more extensively, and the practical duties of Christianity rela-
tively less frequently; and *vice versa.* Secondly, That the
teaching of practical duties was in the vast majority of churches
exceedingly general, rarely descending to specific instructions
regarding the proper line of conduct to be pursued in the most
momentous and difficult departments of life. This defect attaches to nearly all Christian churches, and appears to me to
account for the rapid oblivion which overtakes sermons, as
described in p. 167. If I were to draw a comparison in this particular, I should say that the practical affairs of life are more
extensively introduced into the pulpits of the United States than
into those of Scotland, and the notices of sermons which have
been given will partly enable the reader to judge on this point
for himself. Still, in this respect, religious teaching is generally
defective, and I lament that it is so, because when the Creator
introduced into the world a system of causation, in virtue of
which, when circumstances are the same, one event follows
another in invariable succession; and when He bestowed on man

faculties of observation and reflection, rendering him capable of observing circumstances, and tracing the connection between causes and effects, he imposed on him the duty of observing, reflecting, and acting on system; and the moral world forms no exception to this rule. If the constitution of the world, mental and physical, be systematic, and if causation run through every department of it, then, while man acts without sufficient knowledge of, or reference to, the system of causes in the midst of which he exists, while he acts impulsively and blindly from the mere dictates of his inclinations, and upon superficial, limited, and inaccurate views of the qualities and adaptations of things which surround him, and which really determine his happiness or misery, he does not rise to his proper rank of a rational being. When God framed him and the external world on these principles, He clearly conferred on him the rational character, and it is man's duty to conform to it. If this view be sound, every element of external nature, and every organ and function of the human mind and body which are capable, when properly used, of promoting human happiness, and when abused, of leading to misery, is a divine institution presented to man for his study, and as a guide to his practical conduct. The pulpit, in my opinion, will never discharge its duty to mankind, until it shall become the expositor also of " these doings of the Lord," and shall inculcate the observance of them *under the sanction of religion.* The pulpit thus employed would contribute more effectually than it now does towards enlarging the sphere of the mind's action—presenting motives to self-control—and directing each individual to pursue successfully his real welfare both for this world and the next. Sermons of this nature would also add greatly to the utility of the lyceums; because the people, finding the elements of natural knowledge invested with a religious interest, would apply themselves with more earnestness and patience to extend their studies under the guidance of scientific teachers.

4thly, Professional Callings.—The great majority of the people of the United States are engaged in arts, manufactures, commerce, navigation, agriculture, divinity, law, and medicine; and their pursuits are therefore useful, and productive of enjoyment. As the paths of industry are rarely obstructed by bad laws or artificial obstacles, American civilisation, in this department, will bear a favorable comparison with that of the most advanced nations. These avocations, however do not fully develope the highest faculties of the mind. They cultivate Acquisitiveness, Self-Love, and the love of distinction, more than Benevolence, Veneration, Conscientiousness, and Ideality. They call the intellect into activity, but many of them do not neces-

sarily direct it to moral objects.   They are deserving of all
praise as important elements of civilisation, indeed as necessary
to the very foundations of it but in order to exhibit the "*internal*
nature of man with *lustre* and *grandeur*," higher pursuits must
be added to and mingled with them.   The schools, colleges, and
the pulpit, must supply the lustre and grandeur in which the
avocations of common life are necessarily defective.   Great
improvements in professional attainments remain to be made in
the United States.   American divines are not in general so
learned as those of England, but they appear to be more practical; while the professions of law and medicine in the rural districts, comprising nineteen-twentieths of the whole United
States, stand in need of large accessions of knowledge to bring
them to a par with the same professions in the enlightened
countries of Europe.(*a*)   The improved education which I
have suggested would render the practice of the professions in
some degree scientific or philosophical pursuits, in which each
individual would endeavor, in his vocation, to appropriate the
laws which the Creator has established as essential to success,
and the calm calculations of reason would, to some extent, regulate the impulsive and empirical movements (p. 55) which
have hitherto been fraught with so much suffering to the people.

   5*thly, Political Institutions.*—The American Declaration of
Independence announces that "all men are created equal," a
proposition which, however liable to be disputed in some respects, has (leaving out of view the African race) been practically
adopted as the fundamental principle of all the institutions and
legislation of the United States.   It is the most powerful maxim
for developing the *individual*, in all his faculties and functions,
that has ever been promulgated, and it has certainly produced
great results.   It is probably the first abstract proposition that
is cloathed with an intelligible meaning in the mind of the American child, and it influences his conduct through life.   It sends
forth the young citizen full of confidence in himself, untram-
melled by authority, unawed by recognised superiority in others,
and assured of a fair field for every exertion.   When he attains
to the age of twenty-one years, the institutions of his country

   (*a*) If professional knowledge be measured by its ready adaptation to the
exigencies of the case, the disparity between the professions in Europe and
in the United States is far from being so great or so evident as is implied
in the text   The European physicians, for example, may be better lexico-
graphers or linguists, but they are not, proportionately to this kind of learning, better read in medicine nor better practitioners than the Americans.
On the score of composition and style, the communications in the American Medical Journals, are in the average, superior to those in the British
periodicals of a similar character.   This statement is not made hastily
nor without due consideration.

provide him with the following arenas of political influence and exertion.

Each town is to a certain extent and for certain purposes a body corporate. " The citizens of the several towns qualified to vote for elective officers annually assemble and hold town meetings; and, when so assembled, they have power, not only to elect town officers, but also to determine what number of assessors, constables, and pound-masters shall be chosen for the ensuing year; to direct the commencement or defence of suits and controversies in which the town is involved or interested, and a sum to be raised for conducting the same."* The extent of their powers may be judged of from the officers whom they elect, and who are all responsible to them. I select the state of New York as an example; the constitutions of towns and counties are similar in most of the other States.

The qualifications of a voter are, that he must be a citizen of 21 years of age; he must have resided in the state one year, and in the county where he offers to vote for six months before an election. He must vote in the town or ward where he resides. Persons of color must have been citizens of the state for three years; and must have possessed for one year previous to the election a clear freehold estate of the value of $250. The town-officers annually chosen are,

1. *A Supervisor,* " who receives and pays over the principal moneys raised by the town for defraying town charges."

2. " *A Town-Clerk,* who has the custody of all the books, records, and papers of the town."

3. " *Assessors,* whose chief powers and duties consist in the assessement and valuation of the real and personal property of the inhabitants of the town, for the purpose of taxation."

4. " *The Collector.* He receives a tax-list with a warrant annexed, from the board of superiors of the county, and he then proceeds to collect the taxes mentioned in the list."

5. " *Overseers of the Poor.*"

6. " *Commissioners of High-Ways.*"

7. " *Commissioners of Common Schools.*" Of these there are three for each town. They have power to divide the town into a convenient number of school districts, and to regulate and alter them. They receive from the treasurer of the county, the moneys apportioned for the use of the common schools of their town, and they also receive from the town-collector, all moneys raised by the town, and by him collected, for the use of schools. These moneys are apportioned by the commissioners among the

* Civil Offices and Political Ethics by E. P. Hurlbut; New York, 1840. p. 95.

several districts, in proportion to the number of children in each district, who are above 5 and under 16 years of age, as the same appears from the last annual reports of the trustees of the several districts. They have power to sue for and collect certain penalties. which are added to the school funds.

8. *" The Inspectors of Common Schools."* They examine all persons offering themselves as candidates for the office of common school teachers of their town; also visit once a-year, or oftener if necessary, all the common schools of their town; examine into the state of them, the progress of the scholars in learning, and the good order of the schools; and give advice and directions to the trustees and teachers of the schools as to their government, and the course of studies to be pursued in them.

9. *" Trustees of School-Districts."* Their duties are to call special meetings of the districts when necessary, and make out a tax-list for the sums voted to be raised at a district meeting, annex to it a warrant of collection, and deliver it to the district collector. They build, hire, purchase, keep in repair, and furnish the school-houses, and employ and pay the teacher.

10. *" The Constables."*

11. *" The Town Sealer."* Who compares all weights and measures with the standard, and seals them.

12. *" Overseers of Highways."*

13. *" Pound-Masters."*

14. *" Fence Viewers."*

15. *" Commissioners of Excise,"* who grant licenses to keepers of inns and taverns.

16. *" Auditors of the Town Accounts."*

17. *" Commissioners of Deeds,* who take proof and acknowledgment of conveyances of real estate, the discharge of mortgages,"* &c.*

Some of these officers are not elected directly by the people, but appointed by persons chosen by them. Thus the Commissioners of Deeds are named by the Judges of the county courts and the boards of supervisors in each county; but directly or indirectly the people appoint them all.

" The next grand political division is the *County:* and the officers, most of whom are annually elected by the people, are the following:—Sheriff, Coroners, District-Attorney, Judges of the county courts (they are nominated by the Governor, with consent of the Senate, and hold office for five years), County Clerks, Surrogate, Superintendents of the Poor, County Treasurer, Board

* Lib. cit. p 95 to p. 120.

of Supervisors, Grand Jurors, County Sealer, Auctioneers, and Inspectors of Commodities.

" *The Legislature* consists of 32 Senators, and 128 Members of Assembly, with subordinate officers. The Senators are chosen by the people and by districts, and their term of office is four years. The Members of Assembly are chosen annually by the people.

" *The State.* The *Executive officers* are a *Governor*, chosen by the people at a general election, and who holds his office for two years. *Lieutenant-Governor*, appointed as before. *A Secretary of State*, appointed by the Legislature for three years. *A Comptroller*, appointed and holds office as the Secretary. *A Treasurer*, appointed annually by the Legislature. *An Attorney-General*, appointed for three years by the Legislature. *A Surveyor-General*, the same. *A State Printer*, appointed by and holds his office during the pleasure of the Legislature.

" *The Judicial* and *Administrative* officers of the state are appointed either by the Governor, with consent of the Senate, or by the courts. The higher judges hold office during good behavior, or till sixty years of age, when they are no longer capable of holding office. The Judges of County Courts and other inferior judges hold office for five years, Masters and Examiners in Chancery for three years.

" Finally, *The United States.* The President of the United States is chosen by the electors of each state, appointed in such a manner as the legislature of each state directs by law, and these electors are equal in number to the whole number of senators and representatives to which the state is entitled in Congress. He holds office for four years, but may be re-elected for a second term of four years.

" *The Vice-President*, is elected in the same manner, and for the same term.

The Legislative Body, or Congress, consists of *a Senate* and *a House of Representatives*.

" *The Senate* is composed of two Senators from each state, who are chosen by the Legislatures of their respective state, and hold office for six years.

" *The House of Representatives* is composed of members chosen every second year by the people of the several states. At present they cannot exceed one for every 47,700 of inhabitants, but the ratio is changed with every census taken by the United States.

" The President, or President and Senate, nominate Executive and Judical Officers, and also Naval and Military for the United States."

In contemplating this fabric of government, it appears as a

mighty school for developing the social nature of man; and it is
a school of that kind which nature dictates. The social body
controls its own destiny, suffers for its own errors, and enjoys
the benefits of its own wisdom and virtue. It gives power to
every elector to raise or depress his own fortunes and those of
his neighbors; but he must affect both; he cannot isolate himself
from his fellows, and pursue, in his electoral capacity, private
ends and individual advantages. He must "Love his neighbor
as himself," for his neighbor is his equal, and will not submit
to injustice. This form of government calls on individual citizens to discharge many public duties, and offers to their ambition numerous situations of public honor. It quickly brings
home to society the experience of the consequences of its own
actions —if it commit errors, suffering speedily indicates the
necessity for rectifying them; if it adopt wise laws and pursue
salutary measures, it is rewarded with certain prosperity; but its
influence in developing the *internal* faculties of the mind is the
chief object of my present remarks.

On perusing the list of officers elected by the American citizen, and of whose proceedings he is the ultimate judge, we discover that there is scarcely an interest relating to human nature
in this world, which is not directly or indirectly brought before
him for consideration, and placed to some extent under his control. The institutions appear to me to develope the whole faculties of the individual, with little modification. He is educated
by them in the belief that he can control every thing but public
opinion, and that little self-denial is required from him, except
in preserving a civil bearing in society. If, therefore, Nature
have bestowed on an American citizen a large endowment of
the animal organs with defective organs of reflection, and of the
moral sentiments, he is speedily developed into an audacious
and accomplished rogue. If to the propensities she have added
intellect, but still left the moral faculties deficient, he appears as
a speculative merchant, an ambitious and unprincipled politician,
or a dexterous and unconscientious lawyer—in each character
unscrupulously turning the institutions of his country, and the
good nature of his fellow-citizens, to his private advantage. If
Nature have given the citizen a high developement of the moral
and intellectual organs, with subordinate propensities, the institutions of his country unfold the best of human characters; such
an individual is a philanthropist, a man of practical sense, of
sterling honesty, and sturdy independence; in short, an ornament
to human nature. I have known many such. The American
citizen whose mental endowments are naturally high, and whose
education has been liberal, is reared in a noble field. There is
no glare of aristocracy to obscure his moral perceptions and

misdirect his ambition.   There is no established church to trammel his religious sentiments and obstruct his path in following the dictates of truth; there is no servile class to corrupt his selfish faculties by obsequiousness and flattery.   He is an excellent specimen of humanity, enlightened, benevolent, and just, and animated by an all-pervading activity.   There is another class of minds, by far the most common, on whom the three orders of faculties, animal, moral, and intellectual, are bestowed by nature in nearly equal proportions.   The American institutions evolve their faculties almost in the proportion in which nature gave them.   Men of this class are observed to be habitually selfish, yet occasionally generous, frequently cunning, yet often open and direct; at times carried away by passion and prejudice, but on other occasions manifesting sound judgement and honesty.

In short, the grand feature of American society is the fulness with which it developes *all* the faculties of its individual members, without impressing peculiar biases on any of them; and hence its heterogeneous aspect in the eyes of foreigners.   There is no evil and no good which may not be predicated of it with truth.   Numerous examples could be adduced in support of every picture representing good, better, best; bad, worse, worst, in American society.   Perhaps the reader may suppose that the same may be said of society in every country; but certainly not to the same striking extent as in the United States.   In Europe the different classes are cast in distinct moulds, and some of the faculties of the individuals constituting each class are suppressed, while others are highly developed, to fit them for their conditions.   In the United States the individual man stands forth much more as Nature made him, and as freedom and equality have reared him.

It is this extraordinary activity of all the faculties which forms the most striking feature in the people of the United States, and it affords the best guaranty that they are essentially in the right road to a high civilisation.

The imperfections discovered by strangers lie not so much in the American institutions as in the people.   The fierce political contests, the sudden elevations and depressions of public affairs, the frequent changes of laws and projects, and the want of smoothness and harmony in the action of the social machinery which have been observed in that country, are the natural indications that the impulsive power which is moving, and also the intelligence which is directing this vast social body, are both operating to a great extent at random; now attaining, and now missing their objects, but ever driving onward towards new experiments and evolutions.

In the exercise of nearly all their high elective, legislative, and administrative functions, the people and their rulers generally proceed on the mere dictates of common sense; and as Archbishop Whatley has well observed, common sense is never recognised as a sufficient guide in the management of important affairs, except when the individual is ignorant of scientific principles of action. A sailor will probably admit that common sense is sufficient to enable a man to preach or to practise medicine, but he will deny that it is adequate to the steering of a ship: He knows little of the difficulties of preaching and practising the healing art, and therefore believes that slender attainments will suffice for them; while he is intimately acquainted with the perils of navigation, and justly decides that scientific knowledge and experience are both indispensably necessary to render a man an accomplished navigator. Instinct does not guide man as it does the lower animals; and reason cannot act without extensive knowledge and laborious training. The education of the American people being still essentially defective in relation to their powers and duties, their institutions, when seen in action, do not render justice to the wisdom which framed them. A higher education, discipline in obeying the natural laws under the sanction of religion, and practical moral training, appear to me to be the remedies for these evils.

One test of civilisation, both in individuals and nations, is the power of self-command amidst temptations; and a second is the capacity of discovering and following out through difficulties, the path that leads to ultimate good.—In regard to the first test, it is a common remark in Scotland, that the sons of excessively rigid clergymen occasionally run into wild immoralities when they are emancipated from paternal restraint. The explanation is, that their own moral and intellectual faculties have never been disciplined to resist and to control the solicitations of the propensities amidst temptations. The restraining and directing power has been *external;* and good conduct depended on its presence. No youth is ever safe or well-trained unless these powers be *internal;* for then only are they ever present and ever at their posts. The same rule holds good in the case of nations. Before the revolution, the French people were restrained from action by priests, police officers, and a numerous soldiery. French society then presented fewer mobs, fewer defiances of the law, and fewer gigantic frauds, in proportion to the population, than American society does at this moment. But were the French of those days in a higher state of civilisation than the modern Americans? No. Their propensities were restrained by *external* powers, and little scope for self-action was permitted to any of their faculties. The consequence was, that when the pressure of the priests, the police, and the army, was removed, and a strong impulse was communicated to their minds, the propensities blazed forth with frightful energy—there was a lack of self-control—all was distraction and anarchy; and Napoleon restored order only by *reapplying the external restraints.* The American people live under no *external* restraints, except those established by God and by themselves. Their regulating influences are situated in their own minds; and they live, not in a state of apathy, but in one of high excitement. They contend for gain, for honor, for power, and in all their contests, only the law of God, the power of conscience, the fear of public opinion, and the laws which they themselves have made and may abrogate at pleasure, repress their ebullitions, and give direction to their efforts. Do they exhibit the wreck of social order, and the degradation of virtue? No! The progress of civilisation has been steady and rapid. In proportion as the new territories have been filled up by a numerous population, religion, law, and order, have been evolved in them. I was told by gentlemen in advanced life, that in their younger days Kentucky was the theatre of fierce duels, gouging, murders, and other gross outrages, as the new states of the West at present are; but in our day Kentucky is comparatively industrious, moral, and civilised. The latter fact I saw during my visit to the West in April 1840. In the older and Eastern States the supremacy of the law, the security of property, and the respect for religion, are unquestionably great. In the previous pages, I have described exceptions, but they are only exceptions; and there is a constant disposition and never-ceasing effort to prevent the recurrence, and remove the causes of them.

When this state of social affairs is regarded as the result of the *free internal* action of the mind *of the whole people,* I recognise the presence of a *higher general civilisation* in the United States than is to be found in any European country, except probably Switzerland, which has similar institutions. What European monarchy could throw such an extent of power into the hands of the whole people as is done in the United States, and afterwards boast of equal order, law, and justice? The oppressed, the injured, the ignorant, and untrained masses would, in all probability, during the first exercise of their power, rush headlong into anarchy. The prominence which outrages and frauds assume in American society is the consequence of the impulse given to all the faculties by their institutions, and of the comparative feebleness of *external* artificial restraints. As already mentioned, the rogue is developed in all his might and malignity, and his greatness attracts attention; but the good are developed in an equal proportion; and if they do not appear equally conspicuous on the public stage, it is because religion and virtue are in their own nature meek, retiring, and unostentatious qualities. The first step towards self-government is the most difficult; the Americans have made, and partly succeeded in it. Their future progress will be less difficult.

Captain Marryat bears testimony to a fact which is at once the consequence and evidence of this power of self-control in the American people in one department of social life. It is so important that, in my opinion, although he had not recorded one other circumstance in elucidation of American civilisation, he would have done good service to ethical and political science by contributing it alone. "I do not think," says he, "that *Demo-cracy* is marked upon the features of the lower classes in the United States; there is no arrogant bearing in them, as might be supposed from the despotism of the majority; on the contrary, I should say that their lower ranks are much more civil than our own. In his usual demeanor the citizen-born is quiet and obliging. The insolence you meet with is chiefly from the emigrant classes. I have before observed that the Americans are a good-tempered people, and to this good temper I ascribe their civil bearing. But why are they good tempered? *It appears to me to be one of the few virtues springing from Democracy.* When the grades of society are distinct, as they are in the older institutions, when difference of rank is acknowledged and submitted to without murmur, it is evident that if people are obliged to control their tempers in presence of their superiors or equals, they can also yield to them with their inferiors; and it is this yielding to our tempers which enables them to master us. But under institutions where all are equal, where no one admits the superiority of another, even if he really be so; where the man with the spade in his hand will beard the millionaire, and where you are compelled to submit to the caprice and insolence of a domestic, or lose his services, it is evident that every man must, from boyhood, have learned to control his temper, as no ebullition will be submitted to, or unfollowed by its consequences. I consider that it is this habitual control, forced upon the Americans by the nature of their institutions, which occasions them to be so good-tempered, when not in a state of excitement."

The facts and the philosophy here are equally sound, except that *American-born* "domestics" are trained under the same influences with the rest of the community, and, if paid at the common rate of labor and justly treated, they, as a class, are not insolent and capricious. Bad temper arises from unjust manifestations of Self-Esteem and Destructiveness, directed against individuals who have offended our egotism; while good temper is the result of Self-Esteem and Destructiveness kept in abeyance, and Benevolence, Veneration, Conscientiousness, and Love of Approbation, or some of them, actively manifested. If artificial differences of rank afford temptations to indulge in bad temper, they, to that extent, foster unchristian states of mind; while democratic institutions, if they cultivate self-restraint, good-nature, and civility, are unquestionably, in so far, the allies of virtue, and cherish Christian dispositions.

With regard to the second test, I cannot bear the same testimony in favor of the power of the American people to discover and follow forth, through difficulties, the path that leads to general prosperity. They greatly need a higher intellectual illumination to enable them to do so.

But it is said that the institutions of the United States have produced a frightful result in establishing the *tyranny of the majority*. This subject deserves serious consideration.

In all political, legislative, and corporate assemblies, the minority must, from the nature of things, yield to the majority. The mere fact of the majority in such bodies, carrying their own measures into effect, cannot justly be called *tyranny*. From the way in which the tyranny of the majority is generally spoken of, a stranger to the United States might be led to suppose that the majority enact laws in favor of themselves to the prejudice of the minority; but this is not the case. Except when legislating for the colored race, the majority uniformly include themselves in the laws which they pass; and if they be guilty of injuring the minority, it is only in consequence of an error in judgment, which equally affects themselves. A few cases probably might be discovered, in which the majority in the legislature of a particular state, had a common interest which they pursued at the expense of the minority. In 1840, for example, the majority of the legislature of New York may reasonably be suspected of having been composed of debtors. On the 14th of May in that year, they passed an act, ostensibly to curtail attorneys' fees; but, by section 24, they enacted that writs of *fieri facias* may be issued, and tested at any time in term or vacation, *after thirty days from the entry of judgment*, and such writs shall be returnable sixty days from the receipt thereof," &c. The plain meaning of this provision is, that, after the creditor has pursued his claim to judgment, he must wait thirty days before he can issue execution: in other words, that the debtor shall have thirty days to dispose of his personal property, and thus enjoy the privilege of defeating the claims of the creditor entirely. But, as the legislators are changed very frequently, all statutes which are found to favor one class at the expense of another, are likely to be speedily repealed.

Again, such cases as are referred to on page 213 of this volume occasionally occur, where the majority sacrifice the rights of the few, under the plea of promoting the general good; but unquestionably the *tendency* of the democratic legislatures of the United States is to embody justice in their laws. For example, the want of a registry of voters is an undoubted defect in the election law of the state of New York; but if such a regulation were proposed by the one political party, the other would represent it as "an abridgement of popular rights," and make "political capital" out of it. In the *city* of New York, however, the Democratic party had the ascendency in 1840, while the *Whig* party prevailed in the *legislature* of the state. The Whigs availed themselves of the opportunity afforded by the gross frauds practised at the New York *City* election in April, 1839, and of their ascendency in the legislature, to pass a *registry-law* for that city. They could not have done so for the state, because the cry of "popular rights" would have been successfully raised against them. They could lose nothing, however, by such a clamor in the city, because it already belonged to their opponents. They, therefore, by establishing a registry for the city, did the good that was in their power; and other occasions may occur in which it will be possible to extend this law to other places. In Great Britain the two houses of Parliament represent only the *minority of the nation;* yet they appear to me to exhibit many more examples of *tyranny* in law-making over the unrepresented majority, than I have been able to discover perpetrated by the majority over the minority, in the legislatures of the United States. A list of unjust laws enacted by the majority in the United States in order to benefit themselves at the expense of the minority, (omitting those regarding the African race,) would be remarkably brief. A similar list of unjust enactments by the minority in Britain against the majority, would, on the contrary, be extensive.

But it may be supposed that the tyranny of the majority consists in elevating their own will into supremacy over the law; in trampling on it, for instance, in their character of mobs; in setting it at naught as jurymen; or in forcing the judges to pervert it, under fear of dismissal from office. That examples of such evils do occur, it is impossible to deny; but they are the results of excitement, which is generally both temporary and local, and there is constantly a reaction in favor of law and order. These are merely ebullitions of unguided feeling, and do not assume the character of concerted or intentional tyranny of the majority over the minority. Indeed, my impression is, that they are generally perpetrated by the *minority*, without the approval of the majority, because, so far as my means of observation extended, I was led to the conviction that a vast majority of the citizens of the United States condemn these outrages, although they lack legal force and moral courage to prevent them. The newly settled, and therefore semi-barbarous, states of the west, and the slave states of the south, should be distinguished from the eastern and more civilised states, in discussing this question. The former may be compared to Ireland in 1824, when an army of 36,000 men was needed to preserve the peace, and the latter to Scotland now, where 1500 soldiers suffice. It would lead only to error to regard the British Isles as one nation, and to detail Irish outrages as examples of the lawlessness of the Scotch; and it is equally fallacious to cite the crimes and horrors of the south and west as examples of the influence of democracy in the United States. In judging of political institutions, we are bound to view them in those circumstances where they have been longest tried, and have had freest scope.

Assuming, then, for the present, the eastern states as the objects of our contemplation, I remark that their mobs proceed, in my opinion, from two causes—the constant excitement in which the people live, *which pervades all their faculties*, and the want of *training* and *dicipline in youth*. Their outrages are the result of impulse, vivid and general, but momentary; and not of deliberate action on any principle. One feature, moreover, distinguishes an American from an European mob. The moral and intellectual faculties are in a higher state of cultivation in the former than in the latter, and for this reason, the people are more suscepitble of moral or legal influence, even in their highest state of excitement. A European mob is like a wild beast, cruel but cowardly; the animal propensities rage with violence, and completely carry captive the moral powers. An American mob, on the other hand, if fairly opposed by men of courage in support of the law, has so much more of the higher elements of mind in its composition, that it may be arrested. In Philadelphia, a few years ago, Mr. B. W. Richards, when mayor, mounted his horse—dashed into the midst of a mob, and seized some of the ringleaders, when the other guardians of the peace, finding that they were led by a man of spirit, acted boldly, and speedily restored order. This act was loudly and universally commended. Again, in 1840, Daniel Neall, an old man, with his wife, and some other members of the Society of Friends in Philadelphia, had gone to visit the members of their society in Delaware, and they were assailed by a mob under the pretence that they were abolitionists. At night, while seated round the fireside of a friend two miles from Smyrna, in that state, Mr. Neall " was seized by force, dragged from the arms of his affrighted and agonised wife, and compelled to walk to that town

' to answer for his disorganising doctrines.' * * The mob hurried him off to the place of their destination, where they consummated their deed of shame by tarring and feathering him, and riding him on a rail. After having thus satisfied their fiendish malignity, they set him loose, and allowed him to join his friends. Friend Neall bore the indignity with his accustomed meekness, offering no resistance, evincing no fear, and manifesting a spirit which drew even from these fellows evidence that they were half ashamed of their conduct. When he was set at liberty, he turned to the mob, and, in his gentle manner, told them that if any of them should ever come to Philadelphia, and call at his house in Arch Street, he would treat them in a manner very different from what they had treated him."

This is the account which appeared in the newspapers, and the press poured out the warmest indignation against the perpetrators of this crime, but the most characteristic part of the occurrence was not published. Mr. Neall was altogether innocent of the offence alleged against him, but he both professed and acted on the doctrine of non-resistance. As he walked along, he spoke calmly, and with great moral force and dignity, to his persecutors, and urged on them the unchristian nature of their conduct. They were shaken, and had they not been afraid of the ridicule of their associates, they would have liberated him. They merely besmeared about six inches square of the back of his coat with tar, stuck some feathers on it, lifted him off his feet on a rail, carried him a little way, and did him no farther injury! This statement I received from a friend of Mr. Neall, and its truth is unquestionable. While no one can abhor these disgraceful outrages more than I do, I am deeply impressed, from what I saw of the American people, with the conviction, that even a moderate exercise of moral and physical courage by the well-disposed members of society, would check their mobs in the bud; and that individuals who should thus discharge their duty to their country would not encounter one-half of the danger to their own persons from an American, that they would do in encountering a European mob. There seemed to me to be, in the eastern states, an increasing and deepening sense of the disgrace which these and similar occurrences bring upon the country, and a strong tendency in public opinion to arrest them.

The tyranny of the majority may be supposed to mean merely that in matters of opinion nobody dares to think, or at least to avow what he thinks, in opposition to the majority; and this is really the only tyranny that exists. It is not correctly named, as I shall subsequently show; but, in point of fact, a very great extent of moral cowardice, or of fear to maintain the right, in opposition to public sentiment, even when it is unquestionably wrong, does prevail in the United States. Before attempting to give an explanation of this phenomenon, it may be instructive to state a few examples of its mode of operation. When the cry for war with England, mentioned in vol. i, p. 283, broke forth, the popular excitement was so deep and universal, that, with extremely few exceptions, the most enlightened patriots who condemned, did not dare to oppose it, but suffered it first to expend its force in the manner already described, and then only, ventured, cautiously, to offer to the public mind the suggestions of prudence and reason. Again,—in conversing with the friends of education on the imperfection of their schools in the department of *training*, and suggesting the advantages of inviting Mr. Wilderspin to come to the eastern cities and show them infant training in practice,—they acknowledged the defect, expressed themselves convinced of the benefit of a visit from Wilderspin—and said that there would be no difficulty in raising by subscription, the sum of money requisite to try the experiment; but one and all added that public opinion would not sanction such a step, and that if they ventured on it, they would do more harm than good to the cause of education. Again, when a scheme was hatching in Massachusetts to overthrow the Board of Education, there were not a few influential persons in different parts of the state, who, in private, acknowledged themselves to be the friends of the board, and who justly estimated its value, yet who had not sufficient moral courage publicly to declare their convictions, and to support it. I was informed of this fact by a gentleman deeply interested in education, resident in another state, who travelled through a large portion of Massachusetts at the time in question, and who made it an object to ascertain the state of opinion on the subject. Once more, when agitation for the abolition of slavery commenced in the New England states. public opinion gave up the individuals who favored it almost to martyrdom.

This tyranny of opinion proceeds still farther; it takes cognisance of private actions. When walking in the streets of a city with a clerical friend, he observed the cloak which I wore (a short light *demisaison* garment, which I had brought from Edinburgh,) and admired it, as suited to the American spring and early summer. " Why don't you get one?" said I. " Because," said he, " public opinion would not sanction it: I should be pointed at as the ' Dandy Parson!' " Some Americans of large fortune who have been much in England, and who have adopted the late hours and the style of English dinners, are condemned by public opinion as guilty of foreign predilections and aiming at aristocracy.

Public opinion in these, and in many similar instances, possesses so much force, that few individuals have courage to oppose it.

In contrast to these instances, I may remark that no man is afraid to avow himself to be a Whig or a Democrat, even in localities where his opinions may be those of the minority; nor to acknowledge himself to be a Calvinist, a Baptist, or a Roman Catholic; because these are powerful sects: In short, wherever the individual is *backed by an influential number of persons holding the same opinions with himself,* he is safe. It is only where one or a few individuals venture to oppose a decided public sentiment that they are in danger. Hence, in cities where there are few Unitarians, an individual, if not afraid, is slow, to acknowledge himself to belong to that sect. It is an error, therefore, to speak of the tyranny of the *majority* over the minority of the nation in matters of opinion; the tyranny is rather that of the public over the individual. To a private citizen the public is merely those who move in his own circle, and who may influence his prosperity or his social estimation.

The question next presents itself—What is the nature of the danger which threatens individuals who venture to avow opinions generally disapproved of? In the case of the politician it is exclusion from office. to become unpopular ruins all a man's prospects of rising to distinction in the state; and to every American citizen the career of office, from that of constable to that of president of the United States, is open. The constable is as deeply interested about his popularity, as the senator who sees the presidentship within his grasp. I have read advertisements addressed by constables to the electors, soliciting their votes and explaining their own principles and conduct, as anxiously as if they had been competing for the office of governor. If the reader will cast his eye over the list of public officers whom the people elect (pages 249-50-51), and bear in mind the frequency of the elections, he will perceive a reason why a large portion of the most active and aspiring men of every town and county in the Union, should live habitually under the influence of the desire for popularity. They court popular favor as the ladder by which they expect to mount to honor and consideration.

To gain popularity, the public mind must be addressed on its most accessible side. I have already described the great majority of American voters as young, ardent, impulsive, active, and practical, but deficient in profound and comprehensive views, and also in the capacity of pursuing a distant good through temporary obstacles and difficulties. I have stated, also, that their education, in relation to their powers and duties, is very defective. To gain the favor of a people in this condition of mind, actual fitness for office, with honesty and independence in the discharge of public duty, do not of themselves suffice. The candidate must render himself acceptable to the electors individually; he must address their predominant feelings, enter into their leading aversions and predilections, and attach himself warmly to the party or cause which he knows them to regard with the highest favor. He may vouch for his own fitness for office, and his own certificate will often be received, provided, in other respects, his conduct and principles are approved of. If he egregiously fail in the discharge of his public duties, he will be turned out of office at the end of the term for which he was appointed; but the most conscientious and skilful execution of his duties will not, in general, secure the endurance of his tenure, if he publicly advocate unpopular opinions, although altogether unconnected with his station, or if he belong to a party which has lost public favor and been displaced from power.

The best remedy that can be proposed for the evils now described, appears to me to consist in a higher education and a better training of the electors: if they were thoroughly instructed in youth, concerning the laws which regulate the prosperity of nations; in the qualities of the human mind, and in the indispensable necessity of judgment and integrity in public officers to the right management of their affairs—higher qualities would be required in their public men in order to gain their favor, and useful and faithful public servants would be retained in possession of their offices, out of respect to their fitness alone. The idea that it is possible to educate and train a people to act in this manner is regarded by many persons as altogether visionary and Utopian; but to deny this is to maintain that man is not a rational being. A certain advance in the knowledge of his own faculties and of the external world, and of their adaptations to each other, was necessary before the development of his rational nature could fairly commence, and this knowledge has not yet been generally communicated to the young, nor have they been trained in accordance with it, in the United States. That, in their actual condition, their actions and judgments should partake of the character of impulse and direct perception, is inevitable; but their capacity to advance to a higher state of civilisation is not by this circumstance necessarily excluded.

The danger which besets an individual *in his private capacity* in consequence of openly advocating unpopular opinions, may be best elucidated by referring to the instances already adduced. If any citizen propose improvements in education for which the public mind is not prepared, those individuals whose interests or whose pride would suffer, or whose habits of thinking and acting would be invaded by the change, naturally oppose them.

The common schools are placed under the management of directors and inspectors chosen by the people, and the reformers must obtain these offices before they can give effect to their benevolent designs. But the people, being ignorant of the nature and utility of the proposed changes, are easily operated upon by the insinuations, misrepresentations, and declamations of the hostile parties, who are scattered every where among them, and who by these means experience little difficulty in rendering the reformers unpopular, and thus preventing their election. The gentlemen who told me that the proposal to invite Wilderspin to the United States, would retard, instead of forwarding, the desired improvements in training, were sound in their judgment; because the prejudices of the people against foreigners, and their dislikes to innovation in their school systems, would, while they were ignorant of the nature of the proposed improvement, have ensured the exclusion of its projectors from office, and placed its opponents in power over the schools. The remedy for this evil is gradually to open up the subject to the public mind in lectures and through the press: or to carry the scheme into execution in some private seminary, and then show it to the people in action. After they comprehend its advantages, they will adopt it. And accordingly, the project of improvement by training is not abandoned by those who perceive its value; but they are proceeding prudently to prepare the people to receive and sanction it. So far from this condition of things being an unmitigated evil, it is attended with many benefits. It leads moral reformers to consider their measures thoroughly, and by anticipating opposition, to detect the weak points of their schemes. It also imposes on them the necessity of addressing the reason and moral sentiments of the people, and of *thus aiding in cultivating their rational nature*; and, in my opinion, the ultimate test of the merits of all institutions, is the degree in which they promote the accomplishment of this end.

The dangers which individuals incur from braving public opinion in their personal habits or pursuits bear a relation to two circumstances—the extent of their own dependence on that opinion—and if they be independent of it, on the degree of their own sensitiveness to disapprobation. In the case of clergymen, physicians, and lawyers, the dependence of the individual on public opinion is direct and striking, and in most mercantile pursuits, also, opinion may, to a considerable extent, influence individual prosperity. Besides, the example of bowing to it, set by the aspirants after public offices, who are generally the boldest, most active, and influential members of the community, generates and cultivates the habit of doing so in those who move in a private sphere, and the habit being once established, sensitiveness increases in proportion to its universal prevalence and duration, until at last, in many instances, it degenerates into a dread of public disapprobation, so powerful that it paralyses virtue, and deserves no milder epithet than that of moral cowardice.

This extreme sensitiveness is a peculiar characteristic of the Americans. But, as I have already described the minds of the people to be developed by their institutions in all their faculties, each man according to his own nature, and as each may be discerned pursuing his individual objects with a predominating egotism, there appears to be a contradiction between these two portraitures of society. The representations wear the air of paradox, and, in point of fact, nothing struck me so forcibly in the United States as the inconsistency between one aspect of the character of the people and another. Phrenologically, I explain these anomalous appearances by the impulsive activity of *all* the faculties, undirected by any great land-marks either of established custom, sentiment, or reason. The faculties themselves are heterogeneous in their objects and feelings, and if they be manifested freely, one in one set of circumstances, and another in another, without a presiding guide, inconsistency will be evolved by Nature herself. Within the limits permitted by public opinion, an American will pursue his pleasure and his interest, as if no other being existed in the world; his egotism may then appear complete, but when he meets an opposing public opinion, he shrinks and is arrested. The state of manners allows a pretty wide latitude of self-indulgence, and foreigners reporting on this phasis of character describe the people as personifications of egotism, but when the limit of public opinion is reached, this egotist may be seen quailing before, although virtue, honor, and religion, should call on him to brave it. Again, he will not pursue his self-indulgence so far as to give personal offence to his neighbor, because this would be resented. In short, he has that vivid regard to opinion, that he restrains himself whenever he incurs the risk of its condemnation; and if he act improperly, it is because opinion tolerates the wrong.

British authors, however, have in general erroneously estimated the comparative influence of public opinion in their own country and in the United States. It appears to me to be pretty nearly as active and influential in Britain as it is in America, certain differences in its modes of operation being taken into consideration. In Britain (see page 153) society is divided into a number of distinct classes, each of which has standards of opinion of its own. There is a public opinion peculiar to each class, and that opinion has acquired definite forms by the influence of ancient institutions. The opinions and modes of feeling of the individuals in each class, grow with their growth and strengthen with their strength, and in the maturity of life these conventional impressions appear to be absolutely natural. The differences between the grades of society produce corresponding differences in opinion and modes of action; and when an observer surveys individuals of each class acting according to their own perceptions of propriety, he may imagine that, because they differ, each is manifesting a fine moral independence, in following the dictates of his own judgment. But this is an error. In America all men are regarded as equal; there is no distinct separation into classes, with a set of established opinions and feelings peculiar to each. As society is young, and the institutions are recent, there are no great influences in operation to mould opinion into definite forms, even within this one circle, which nominally includes all American citizens. The proper contrast, therefore, is between the power of public opinion in an English grade and in the American single circle; and, if so viewed, the difference will not be found to be so greatly against the Americans as is generally supposed.

The English candidates for public offices do not bow to popular opinions, because the people have no offices to bestow; but if we select the fashionable circle in London, and consider how many of the individuals who move in it could be induced by the dictates of reason, or even by motives of moral or religious duty, to brave its opinions, and to pursue a line of conduct, however virtuous, that was stigmatised by the whole circle as vulgar or unfashionable, we should find the number very small. The same lack of moral courage which is considered so peculiar to the Americans, would be found almost universally prevalent in it. If we proceed to another grade, the same fear of incurring disapprobation will be found to pervade its members; and so down to the lowest, where public opinion ceases to act. In regard to private conduct the same result presents itself. In Edinburgh, a certain style of entertainment is in use in a certain rank; and, although many condemn the pomp, circumstance, and heavy vanity of the style, not one individual out of fifty will venture to depart from the established usage. In Scotland, instead of the tyranny of the majority, we live under " the fear of the folk;" and the most inattentive observer must have remarked that it is a most potential fear. It sends thousands to church who privately confess that they derive little edification from the exercises; it withholds thousands from countenancing their inferiors in society lest they should be regarded as ungenteel; and it impels countless multitudes to give an ostensible adherence to opinions and observances of which they, in their consciences, disapprove. Recently a religious party in Scotland, animated with an extraordinary zeal for the observance of the Sabbath, has denounced as sinful, and suppressed, interments of the dead on that day. This prohibition does not affect the rich, among whom it is not the custom to bury on Sundays; but it is a cruel tyranny over the poor, who, by interring on that day, more speedily remove a corpse from their small houses, who find their friends and relatives prepared to accompany the funeral without the loss of a day's wages, and who themselves are saved the loss of a day's labor at the time when disease and death are pressing most severely on their means. Besides, a service more solemn and more congenial with a religious frame of mind than a funeral, can scarcely be imagined. Nevertheless, few defenders of the poor man's rights have appeared among the upper ranks of society; and it is my firm conviction that the fear of being charged with countenancing Sabbath-breaking and infidelity, has been the chief cause of the silence of thousands who in their consciences do not approve of the prohibition.

The view here presented of the mode in which opinion operates in Britain may be illustrated by an example, in which the opinion, not of a circle only, but of the whole of society, was invaded. When the discovery by Dr. Gall of the functions of the brain, and of a system of mental philosophy emanating from it, was first presented to the British public, it contradicted the opinions of physicians, lawyers, divines, men of letters, and philosophers generally, as well as those of the people, respecting the subjects to which it related. How was it received? Did the reviewers, the men of science, the physicians, and the doctors in divinity, investigate it, and brave public opinion by proclaiming its merits? No! It was intuitively felt that the discovery, if true, would convict numerous persons of ignorance in matters of importance, in which they had hitherto been believed by the public to be learned, and that this mortification, above all things, was to be avoided. By a nearly unanimous consent, therefore, the press and public delivered over Dr. Gall, Dr. Spurzheim, and their few followers, to the most unmeasured ridicule and abuse; while hundreds who saw that the public was wrong, shrunk with terror from even whispering such an impression; and at the present day, when a quarter of a century of investigation and debate has considerably diminished the discredit of avowing a leaning to Phrenology, I could present a pretty considerable list of physicians of reputation, of divines of talent and consideration, and of accomplished private gentlemen, who entertain an unhesitating conviction of its truth and importance, and who nevertheless are afraid publicly to acknowledge this conviction, or to act on it. I have often been counselled to lay aside Phrenology, and employ myself in investigations approved of by public sentiment, and been told that the career of honor would then be opened to me; while I have been warned of the unpopularity and other evil consequences that would attend an opposite course of action. It did not fall to my lot to witness in America any greater prostitutions of conscience and judgment at the shrine of public opinion than I daily witness in my own country; and if in America the necessity for such sacrifices be greater than it is in Britain, the only cause of the difference is, that in Britain we are able to address a larger class of educated and reflecting men, who will bestow a second consideration on matters of social importance, and whose opinions will ultimately sway those of the people. In the American states, individuals of the educated class do not feel conscious of their own power, not so much on account of their being few in number, as because they are little united among themselves, and address a mass of their fellow citizens who wield power without possessing commensurate intelligence, and on whom, therefore, it is difficult to make an impression by means of reason.

The inconsistency of the phenomena presented by American society, strikes a stranger still more forcibly when he observes, not only the impunity, but the success, with which public opinion is occasionally braved by certain individuals. There are men to whom nature has given a predominant development of Self-Esteem and Firmness, with deficient Love of Approbation, who, so far from courting the approval of society, erect themselves into standards to which they expect the world to conform, and who never hesitate to set public opinion at defiance when it suits their interest or ambition to do so. No individuals prosper more than these in the United States. Quackery and bold pretension in every form meet with extraordinary encouragement and success. There is in that, as in other countries, not only a large share of credulity, the offspring of ignorance, ready to swallow every bait presented by ingenious impudence, but there is a sort of admiration of the courage of that man who can boldly walk in his own path, regardless of the scorn, and taunts, and opposition of society, his very impudence confers on him a species of importance; and if he only avoid gross personal immoralities, he may make his way to fortune or distinction with surprising success. There is another class of men, to whom nature has given predominant organs of Conscientiousness and Firmness, who also occasionally brave public opinion in obedience to the dictates of duty. Of these Dr. Channing is an illustrious example. They do not, however, proclaim disagreeable truths to their countrymen without suffering pain in their feelings, and a temporary abatement of their personal consideration; but the quality of moral courage in this form is so rare, and its value so highly appreciated, that they draw towards themselves a profound sympathy and warm admiration from the virtuous and enlightened, and they actually produce a powerful effect. In short, the Americans are themselves ashamed of their own lack of moral intrepidity, and they highly honor the quality when it is displayed by one of their number in virtue's cause. How are these apparent contradictions to be reconciled?

Before answering this question, we may first consider the origin of the influence of public opinion on the minds of individuals. Man is a being obviously destined by nature to live in the social state. The same fundamental faculties are common to all, but they are conferred on different individuals in different degrees of strength. While, therefore, there is an identity of nature, there are striking individual differences in mind, which give rise to diversities of feeling, talents, and dispositions. These differences may be regarded as, to some extent, the repulsive elements of society; but nature has bestowed on us also a very powerful faculty of Love of Approbation, (its organs are among the largest in the brain,) which inspires us with the desire of the approval of our fellow men. This faculty presents us with motives to smooth down our peculiarities, to forego our individual indulgences, and to conform as far as possible to the opinions, manners, and habits of our neighbors, in order to obtain their approbation; in short, it Macadamises the highway of social intercourse, and renders it agreeable and smooth. But this faculty needs the illumination of knowledge and the guidance of moral and religious principle to prevent it from degenerating into an universal complaisance, equally ready to acquiesce in the pretensions of vice as to approve of the excellence of virtue. When the quality is deficient in a people, the intercourse of society is harsh and disagreeable; but, when it is too powerful and ill-regulated, it may expend itself in an universal approval of the opinions of the day, and induce them to shrink from condemning any generally received object or opinion, lest they should give offence, or incur disapprobation. It then undermines truth, by sapping the foundations of moral courage.

When this faculty acts along with the love of wealth or of power its selfish influence is augmented, because the approbation of society conduces directly to the gratification of these desires. In the United States, these objects are eagerly pursued by a large majority of the people, and thus the vast influence of public opinion among them is accounted for. But Love of Approbation, when combined in action with the sentiments of Benevolence, Conscientiousness, Veneration, and enlightened intellect. takes a loftier aim; it then desires distinction on account of intellectual attainments, holiness, charity, and truth, and it desires only the approval of men of virtuous lives and cultivated understandings.

Far, therefore, from regarding the great power of public opinion in the United States as in itself an evil, I view it as a gigantic controlling influence which may become the most efficient ally of virtue. It is delightful to see the human mind, when emancipated from artificial fetters, evolving from its own deep fountains a mighty restraining power, far superior in force and efficacy for the accomplishment of good, to all the devices invented by the self-constituted guides of mankind. At present, this power is operating in the United States essentially as a blind impulse; many of the artificial standards erected in Europe by monarchy, aristocracy, feudalism, established churches, and other ancient institutions for its direction, have been broken down, and no other standards have yet been erected in their place. No manners or maxims have yet received the stamp of general acceptation, to enable opinion to settle on them with security.

That this is the true theory of the phenomena of public opinion, is rendered probable by the fact that its mighty influence is of recent growth. For many years after the Revolution, it was not felt to the same extent as at present—opinion continued to be modified by the monarchical feelings in which the people had been educated, long after they became their own rulers. It is only within these five and twenty years that the people have discovered and chosen to wield their own sovereign authority; and as if for the very purpose of controlling them, public opinion has within the same period developed its stupendous powers. The ground is gradually becoming cleared of the antiquated posts and rails that directed public sentiment into particular paths; and the question occurs, what is destined to supply their place? Christianity will readily occur, as the most desirable guide; but at present, and for some generations, its influence will be limited by the conflicts existing between the different sects. Besides, the pulpit still devotes too little of its attention to secular affairs, and there are yet too few instances of combination among Christians of all denominations to accomplish general practical good, irrespective of their several doctrinal views. May not some aid be obtained from the maxims of moral and political science, founded on a sound interpretation of the nature of man and of the external world, and of their reciprocal relationship? If the mere forms of monarchy, aristocracy, feudalism, and religious establishments, often at variance with reason and the best interests of mankind, have become fetters with which opinion has been bound as in adamantine chains, why may not the dictates of God's wisdom, when developed to the understanding and impressed upon the moral sentiments from infancy, produce as powerful and a much more salutary effect? The United States must look to instruction in moral and political science, aided and sanctioned by religion, for the re erection of standards and guides of opinion; and to the accomplishment of this object the new philosophy will constitute a valuable assistant.

One distinct cause of the fear of individuals to oppose public opinion, when wrong, is the want of reliance on the moral tendency of the public mind, and on its inclination to correct its own errors, and to do justice to those who have braved its disapprobation in defence of truth. The vivid excitement under which opinion is formed, is one element in producing this terror; but another unquestionably is the uncertainty which is felt regarding both the principles and motives by which, at any moment, it may be swayed. The public intellect is practical and direct, and it neither investigates principles nor embraces distant or comprehensive views; while the public feeling is composed of a confused jumble of selfish and moral impulses, the course of which, on any particular emergency, often defies calculation. Nevertheless the race is ever onward, there is little looking back, little calm reflection, little retracing of steps once taken, unless some unsurmountable obstacle presents itself, which, from its magnitude and immovability, deflects the public mind, or makes it recoil upon itself. It appears to me also that the organs of Benevolence and Veneration are larger and more powerful than those of Conscientiousness in the Anglo-Saxon race in general; and that in consequence, both the Americans and British are more distinguished for benevolent and religious feelings than for an acute sense of justice. This defect renders it more arduous for individuals, either in Britain or America, to take their stand on high moral principle in opposition to public opinion, because the faculty which prompts to the rectification of error, and the redressing of injustice, is comparatively feeble in the commoe mind. But this imperfection may be removed by a more assiduous cultivation of the faculty of Conscientiousness in the young. If the common schools embued the youthful mind with a clear knowledge of its own faculties, of the laws appointed by the Creator for their guidance, and also of the natural laws which regulate the progress of society, this information might come in place of monarchical and feudal institutions for the guidance of opinion, and might afford fixed starting points, from which the moralist and statesman, the divine and the philanthropist, could advance with safety, in their endeavors to check the people when bent on erroneous courses of action.

In short, if the gigantic regulating and controlling power of public opinion evolved by the free institutions of America, were enlightened and guided by the principles of Christianity and Science, instead of being left to act impulsively and as it were blindly, it would prove itself not a tyrant, but a protector to virtue, law, order, and justice, far more efficient than any that has hitherto been discovered. It would leave thought and action absolutely free, within the legitimate limits of all the faculties, (which none of the guides of opinion erected by human invention has ever done), while it would apply an irresistible check at the very point where alone a check would be wanted—that which separates the boundaries of good and evil.

I have made these remarks unhesitatingly, because I believe them to embody some truth; but I admit that it may be long before the American people will appreciate them, and longer still before they will attempt to carry them into effect; but with a nation, as with the God of nations, a thousand years is as one day, and if the views be sound, they will not lose their character or importance by delay.

Whatever estimate may be formed of the adaptation of the new philosophy to the wants of the American people as a guide to opinion, there can be little doubt that some general moral influence which should command respect and pervade the Union, would be highly useful. The division of the country into states, and these into counties and townships, each of which becomes an absorbing focus of interest to its own inhabitants, retards the diffusion of much valuable knowledge, and to some extent paralyses moral effort. I met with highly intelligent persons in Connecticut, interested in education, who knew nearly nothing of the organisation and action of the board of education in Massachusetts, although this state is divided from Connecticut only by a line. Not only so, but before I left the United States, the Common School Journal of Connecticut had ceased to be published, owing to the want of subscribers. It was a very ably conducted, useful, and cheap periodical, but it did not discuss politics, nor theological controversy, nor news; it was full only of high moral and practical information relative to the improvement of education, and this object interested so few persons that it could not find subscribers sufficient to support its existence! In Pennsylvania still less is known by the public of what is doing in Massachusetts or the other states in mere moral pursuits; and so with other portions of the Union. Large numbers of religious papers are published in the states, but the circulation of nearly the whole of them is local.

In New York several weekly papers devoted to general literature have recently been instituted, gigantic in point of size, and intended, by their contents and moderate price, to command a circulation throughout the Union; but their success also has been limited. The circulation of Chambers's Edinburgh Journal in Great Britain and Ireland, with a population of 24,000,000, is stated be about 70,000 weekly, while the highest circulation of any one of these New York papers, I was assured, does not exceed, on an average, 15,000 weekly, among a population of 18,000,000. There is a great difference also in the matter contained in these publications. Chambers's Journal is reprinted in New York, but has only a small circulation. It is too didactic and too little exciting to possess general interest in America. The New York publications are composed of the plunder of European novels and magazines; of reports of sermons by popular preachers; of stories, horrors, and mysteries; of police reports, in which crime and misery are concocted into melo-dramas now exciting sympathy, now laughter: with a large sprinkling of news and politics. As they obtain the largest and most general circulation of all the publications in the Union, they may be regarded as representing to some extent the *general* mind; and certainly they are not calculated to convey a high opinion of it. It would be a great advantage to the Union if a paper, composed partly on the principles of Addison's Spectator—taking cognisance of manners and minor morals. and partly on those of Chambers's Journal—combining didactic instruction with a reasonable amount of entertaining reading, could be established and widely circulated, a paper which should serve as the gazette of the philanthropist, of the moral and intellectual of all parts of the Union, which should inform each of what the other is doing in the great cause of human improvement, and diffuse useful intelligence into every town and county of every state.

Such a publication might, in time, serve to create a moral public opinion, and do vast service to the civilisation of the Union. But it should be conducted by a person of much wisdom and discretion, and be cosmopolitan in its principles. The difficulty is great in finding such a person. The success of Chambers's Edinburgh Journal is owing partly to the sagacity, perseverance, and industry of both its editors; but it has also been materially promoted by the genius and peculiar bent of mind of one of its conductors, Mr. Robert Chambers—in whom a combination of mental qualities, rarely met with, occurs. Hence, the work has been marked from its commencement by an unity of design, a variety of matter, popular interest, and scientific solidity, never before exhibited in any similar work— added to which is a presiding morality and sound sense. that recommend it equally to the peer and to the peasant. I deem it necessary to make these remarks respecting the special qualities employed in conducting Chambers's Journal, because I do not consider that any association of men of talent, although backed by ample funds, could render such a periodical successful either in Britain or the United States, without at least one conductor peculiarly fitted for the task by his mental endowments, tastes, studies, and attainments, and any attempt to institute such a work which should end in failure and disappointment would retard instead of advancing the accomplishment of its objects. The local newspapers, in general, do not circulate moral intelligence. I frequently read in the Common School Journal of Massachusetts articles of great interest connected with the advancement of public instruction; but, except in a few instances, they were not copied by the press with a view to diffuse them through the state. It was not because the School Journal's circulation superseded the necessity of this, but because the editors of the newspapers were not sufficiently interested in education to perceive the value of the information to their readers.

CHAPTER X.

1839.

New Haven, March 20. *Phrenology.*—The subject of the following case was introduced to me by a medical friend. On 15th September 1833, Lemuel Camp, now aged 36, temperament bilious-sanguine, keeper of an oyster tavern in this city, was shooting, when the gun burst, and the iron which closes the end of the barrel was driven into his skull, and buried in his brain, in the region of Eventuality. He fell, but soon recovered sensation, and walked home, a mile and a half, assisted by two young men. He was conscious all the time; felt little pain, and sustained little loss of blood. Dr. Knight travelled three miles to reach him, and then extracted the iron. He felt a terrible wrench when it was withdrawn, but no other severe consequences. The broken portions of the skull were extracted, part of the brain came away, the skin closed on the wound, and in five weeks he was able to walk abroad. He gave me this information himself, in presence of a medical friend of his own, and added that his mind has never been affected; but his friend informed me that Camp's wife declares that, since the accident, he has been oblivious of things and occurrences. He will come into the house, lay down his whip, and in a minute forget where he has put it. After being exposed to severe cold, and after drinking, he is liable to be seized with involuntary muscular action, amounting to convulsions. In other respects, his health is good. He took a box out of his pocket and showed the iron and the broken pieces of bone which he carried in it, and he quite seriously assured me, that for the first year after the accident, if any person rattled these in the box, or meddled with them, his wound would ache, although he were a mile distant from the box and bones, and had no previous suspicion of any such interference! After the first year, this acute sensibility ceased! I felt the edges of the wound in the skull, and found them irregular, and the injury seemed to be chiefly on the left side. There is, however, in the box a portion of the frontal bone to which the falx had been attached, and both Dr. Knight and Dr. Hooker afterwards mentioned, that they considered that both sides of the brain had been injured at the point in question. Dr. Knight had no doubt that the longitudinal sinus was ruptured, and accounted for the small hæmorrhage by the wound being low in the forehead. Dr. Hooker said, that the patient's intellectual faculties are not impaired. This was all the light I could obtain on the case. The injury was confined almost entirely to the organs of Eventuality, and I could form no accurate estimate of the state of efficiency of this faculty, from the short interview which I had with the patient, who, besides, was not a reflecting man. I must therefore leave the reader to form his own opinion, whether the mind of the patient was *entire* or not.

The audience attending my lectures passed resolutions at the close of the course, which are printed in the Appendix No. XII.

Professor Hooker mentioned to me, that my lectures had made few converts to Phrenology in New Haven; in answer to which remark, I repeated the statement made in my introductory lecture, that the truth of Phrenology could be ascertained *only by observation*, and that the object of my lectures was, *not to prove its truth*, but simply to teach *what* was to be observed, and *how* to observe; and, therefore, that the more scientific any audience was, the fewer would be the believers through sheer credulity, an order of converts which I did not desire. Professor Silliman, on the other hand, in seconding the resolutions adopted by the class, mentioned that he had attended four courses of lectures on phrenology, and that he was satisfied that the great principles of the science were well founded; thus showing that, in his case, conviction bore a relation to the extent of observation on the subject. His speech was subsequently published in the American Journal of Science and Arts for July 1840, and an extract from it is given in the Appendix No. XI.

Reversed Organs.—Many objections to Phrenology are founded on the supposed want of symmetry between the two sides of the brain. The differences between the arrangement of the convolutions on the one side and the other are not greater than between the distribution of the veins in the right arm and the left. Nature occasionally makes considerable deviations from the common position of particular organs in the body; and, indeed, in some instances, entirely reverses their usual locality.

This is well known to medical men, but for the sake of the non-medical reader, I present Dr. Hooker's description of a preparation of a human subject which I examined in his anatomical museum.

"In the winter of 1638-9, a subject brought into the anatomical rooms of the Medical Institution of Yale College, was found to have a perfect lateral transposition of the viscera of the body. The heart was on the right side; the right lung had two, the left three lobes, the descending aorta lay on the right side of the spine, the vena cava on the left; the liver with the gall-bladder on the left, the spleen on the right side. The blood-vessels, nerves, and other parts, were examined with the utmost minuteness, and not the least exception was found to a perfect transposition of all the parts, every thing appearing perfectly normal except in position. The subject was a man apparently fifty-five years old, and had undoubtedly been a hard-laboring man, as was indicated by the thickened cuticle of the hands, the large muscles, and other circumstances. He appeared to have died from acute disease of the lungs."

Professor Hooker showed me a skull bearing an inscription—Richard J. Wethby, died Dec. 10, 1829, aged thirty-one, on which I remarked that the organs of Constructiveness must have been very large, because they had depressed the edges of the super-orbitar plate on which they had rested, towards the eth-moidal fossæ, and also raised a considerable elevation externally at the usual place on each side, while the organs of Language must have been very small, because the super-orbitar plate was convex, instead of being concave, which is usually the case, where they had rested on it. Dr. Hooker mentioned that the man whose skull this was had been a stone-cutter; he had died of consumption, and, during his illness, had given himself to be made into a skeleton after death. He was a very expert artificer in stone, and so deficient in language that in conversation he was not only slow, but used extraordinary words, through deficiency in commanding the usual vocabulary.

Attack on the Board of Education in Massachusetts.—The assault against this institution, which I have repeatedly alluded to, has at length been made in the legislature of the state. On the 3d of March, 1840, the committee on Education was directed by the House of Representatives to consider the expediency of abolishing the Board of Education and the normal schools; and on the 7th of March, the majority of the committee presented a report, which merits serious attention. The reader will find the constitution and powers of this Board described in vol. i, p. 52; and he is reminded that Mr. Dwight, a citizen of Boston, had made a gift of $10,000 to the state, on the condition that the legislature should provide a similar sum, and apply both to

the institution of normal schools, which was accordingly done.
The report possesses more than a local and temporary interest.
It is indicative of the state of intelligence of a considerable portion
of the citizens of Massachusetts, whose opinions it expresses;
and besides, it embodies views which, in all probability, would
be urged by one party or another against education under the sanction of government in other countries. I shall therefore briefly
advert to it.

Two reports were presented, one by the majority, and another
by the minority of the committee. The majority object to the
Board for the following among other reasons —

"The Board has a tendency, and a strong tendency, to engross to itself the entire regulation of our common schools, and
particularly to convert the legislature into a mere instrument for
carrying its plans into execution."

Remark.—The Board has *no power* except that of communicating information and recommending measures to the school
committees, teachers, and other persons interested in education.
Therefore, it can engross to itself the regulation of the schools,
only by convincing the understanding of those who manage
them of the wisdom of its proposals, and this is not a power
of which any rational being can be justly jealous.

"If the Board has any actual power, it is a dangerous power,
trenching directly upon the rights and duties of the legislature;
if it has no power, why continue its existence at an annual expense to the commonwealth?"

Answer.—By the wisdom of its suggestions and the character
of its members, it may exercise a *moral power* which may prove
highly beneficial, while it does not, and cannot, trench on the
rights and duties of the legislature. Its members serve without
salaries or fees, and the annual expense which it occasions does
not exceed one-tenth part of a cent. per annum to each of the
inhabitants of the commonwealth.

"As a mere organ for the collection and diffusion of information on the subject of education, the Board seems to your committee to be, in several respects, very much inferior to those voluntary associations of teachers which preceded the existence of
the Board, and which, perhaps, suggested the idea of it." * *
* "The school committees of the several towns and districts
are qualified to superintend the schools, and might best be trusted
with that superintendence."

The slightest knowledge of the actual condition of the schools,
school-houses, teachers, modes of teaching, and things taught, in
the commonwealth, will suffice to convince any reasonable person that this is a most lame and untenable assertion. Before it
was made, the Secretary to the Board of Education had publicly

stated that, "In this commonwealth, there are about 3000 public schools, in all of which the rudiments of knowledge are taught. These schools, at the present time, are so many distinct independent communities; each being governed by its own habits, traditions, and local customs. There is no common superintending power over them; there is no bond of brotherhood or family between them. They are strangers and aliens to each other. The teachers are, as it were imbedded each in his own school district; and they are yet to be excavated, and brought together, and to be established, each as a polished pillar of a holy temple. As the system is now administered, if any improvement in principles or modes of teaching is discovered by talent or accident in one school, instead of being published to the world, it dies with the discoverer. No means exist for multiplying new truths, or even for preserving old ones. A gentleman, filling one of the highest civil offices in this commonwealth—a resident in one of the oldest counties, and in one of the largest towns in the state—a sincere friend of the cause of education—recently put into my hands a printed report drawn up by a clergyman of much repute, which described, as was supposed, an important improvement in relation to our common schools, and earnestly enjoined its general adoption, when it happened to be within my own knowledge that the supposed new discovery had been in successful operation for sixteen years, in a town but little more than sixteen miles distant!" This representation is indisputably correct, and in the face of it to deny the utility of the Board of Education, must have required no small obliquity either of understanding or of conscience.

There are countries which have outstripped Massachusetts in some branches of education, and in the art of teaching, and her teachers stand in need of nothing more than the active agency of an enlightened central board to collect and diffuse information on these subjects—to urge them to adopt improvements—to give advice to local committees, and to submit to their consideration rules which would benefit the pupils. Such are the duties of the Board of Education; and its constitution is framed with express reference to the people themselves continuing to govern their schools. It can operate only by convincing the teachers and school committees that they may do something better than they have previously accomplished. It is not to be expected that voluntary associations of teachers, the members of which are scattered through the state, and engrossed with local objects, interests, and duties, should acquire, digest, and diffuse information with the same success as a public board; and besides, they would want that moral weight to induce the acceptance of improvements, which gives the Board its chief value.

" 'The establishment of the Board of Education seems to be the commencement of a system of centralisation, and of monopoly of power in a few hands, contrary, in every respect, to the true spirit of our democratical institutions, and which, unless speedily checked, may lead to unlooked for and dangerous results."

The Board of Education can wield only the power of moral suasion; they cannot coerce, they cannot bribe, they cannot exercise even a veto on any measure or appointment. Their influence, then, must bear a proportion to the extent of the reason which they present to the understandings of those whom they address, of the practical advantages which they show as likely to result from their recommendations, and from no other source. The real proposition embodied in the foregoing objection is, that democracy, for its own security, must resist the dictates of reason, and reject the most obvious measures of utility, when propounded by its own servants, lest by accepting them these servants should acquire a moral influence over the minds of the people' But this is tantamount to a denial of the rational nature of man. A virtuous and enlightened mind cannot avoid admiring superior wisdom, and yielding to the suggestions of superior intelligence; and if the Board of Education display those qualities, why should its influence be dreaded? If it do not, it can exercise no control over the public mind, unless we assume that both its members and the people are irrational, and will voluntarily adopt injurious errors.

So far from such a board being dangerous, it is what above all things is wanted in every state in the Union. There is a want of a *moral power* which shall address itself to the higher faculties of the people, and assist in forming and giving consistency and permanence to opinion, and which, without conflicting with the political, religious, or money powers at present exclusively prevailing, may serve, through the influence of reason, to elevate, temper, and guide them all. Such a board, named by the legislature in every state, and invested with a pretty extensive range of moral functions, seems of all imaginable institutions that which is most directly fitted to prove useful to a democracy which must rest on the intelligence and morality of the people, or perish. In its addresses to the people, it would confine itself to objects of moral import alone; but it would appeal to *principles*, expound consequences, recall the admonitions of experience, and, in short, supply to some extent the grand deficiencies which palpably exist in the public mind—the want of knowledge, of reflection, and of regard to distant but inevitable results.

" The right to mould the political, moral, and religious opinions of his children is a right exclusively and jealously reserved by our laws to every parent; and for the government to attempt, directly or indirectly, as to these matters, to stand in the parent's place, is an undertaking of very questionable policy."

The Board of Education operates on the children only through the medium of the parents; for the parents themselves either constitute or elect the school committees and school inspectors, who, again, appoint, superintend and dismiss the teachers. The Board, therefore, can neither order nor forbid any thing, except by convincing the electors, and those who obey them, of its utility.

The report next attacks " The School Library." " It is professed, indeed, that the matter selected for this library will be free both from sectarian and political objections. Unquestionably the Board will endeavor to render it so. Since, however, religion and politics in this free country are so intimately connected with every other subject, the accomplishment of that object is utterly impossible, nor would it be desirable, if possible."

This argument is founded on the assumption that there is no portion of religion which is not matter of contention between the sects, and no scientific principles in politics and political economy which are not subjects of party disputation. With all deference to the authors of this report (see p. 175), there is a vast field of Christian, ethical, and political truth which is highly interesting and instructive to the young, and which, nevertheless, is happily without the pale of contest, and may appropriately form the groundwork of the treatises prepared for the common school libraries.

" Another project, imitated from France and Prussia, and set on foot under the superintendence of the Board of Education, is the establishment of normal schools. Your committee approach this subject with some delicacy, inasmuch as one-half the expense of the two normal schools already established has been sustained by private munificence." * * * " Academies and high schools cost the commonwealth nothing, and they are fully adequate, in the opinion of your committee, to furnish a competent supply of teachers." * * * "*Considering that our district schools are kept, on an average, for only three or four months in the year, it is obviously impossible, and perhaps it is not desirable, that the business of keeping these schools should become a distinct and separate profession* which the establishment of normal schools seems to anticipate."

This is a striking acknowledgement of the low state of education in the commonwealth, and if the committee had been composed of enlightened men it would have perceived that this fact furnished the most forcible reason for establishing normal seminaries, and for increasing the length of the attendance at the common schools; but they, on the contrary, recommended the abolition of the Board of Education, the school library, and the normal schools, and proposed to refund the money " generously contributed" to the support of the latter by Mr. Dwight! They appended to their report the draft of an act to carry these recommendations into effect!

In my humble opinion, all that has been written by European travellers against the people of the United States, their manners and institutions, will not depreciate the character of their civilisation in the judgment of reflecting men to one-half the extent that will be done by this document alone. It appears, indeed, to contradict much that I have already said in favor of the American people; and at the hazard of standing still farther condemned, I am under the necessity of reporting that it found 182 individuals in the house of Representatives of Massachusetts, the most enlightened of the States, to vote for its adoption. In point of fact, however, I have endeavored to convey the idea that there is a vast extent of ignorance in the Union, and even in Massachusetts; and this report signally sustains the assertion. But there is also another side to the picture, which I am happy now to exhibit.

The minority of the committee, consisting of " Mr. John A. Shaw and Mr. Thomas A. Greene," gave in an admirable report in support of the Board of Education and the normal schools; some of the Boston newspapers warmly espoused their cause. Dr. Channing published in one of these an eloquent and cogent defence of them, and in the House of Representatives a highly interesting debate ensued on the merits of the whole question, the result of which was, that 248 members voted *for the rejection of the first mentioned report*, making a majority in favor of the Board of sixty-six members. One of the most luminous and effective speeches in support of education was delivered by a member who is well known as an able phrenologist.*

* Since the text was written I have received the " Abstract of the Massachusetts School Returns for 1839-40," and regard it as affording a triumphant vindication of the law, which established the Board of Education—of the Board itself, and of its Secretary. These returns have been made by 301 out of 307 towns in the commonwealth, and they are accompanied by selections from the Reports of the School Committees. The " Returns," and " Reports" taken together, present a most instructive and interesting view of the condition of the schools at the present time. They appear to me to show that the condition of the school-houses is, in many instances, deplorably deficient; so much so as to be injurious to the health and sym-

On 20th March we left New Haven at 8 A. M., and arrived at New York by Long Island Sound at 2 P. M.

The Manhattan Bank.—This has long been regarded as one of the most substantial and well managed banks in New York; but lately the stock has undergone a rapid and serious depression

metrical growth of the children; that the schools generally have been sadly neglected by the more wealthy and intelligent citizens, and that many of the teachers, although men of excellent moral character, are, in consequence of their own deficiencies in education and in the art of teaching, ill qualified for their situations. This is an alarming picture of a commonwealth, whose prosperity rests on the morality and intelligence of its people. It indicates, that the first step towards a despotism, that of rearing an ignorant population, had been taken. But the "Abstract" shows a cheering counter part. The exposure of these defects is already stimulating public opinion to enforce their removal. The Reports of the School Committees while they indicate that a highly enlightened zeal in educational improvement exists in many of the towns, throw a flood of light not only on what is deficient, but on the means of supplying what is wanting. The accurate knowledge, sound sense and classical eloquence, of some of these reports do honor to the state, and by placing their bright corruscations of moral sentiment and intellect, side by side with reports of a different character, the most vigorous emulation will be excited in all, to improve. The fact of all the towns having reported except six, shows that the machinery is efficient. The "queries" circulated by the board, and which the committees in most instances, have answered, are of the most searching description, and well calculated "to hold the mirror up to nature," and to show to every town its own imperfections or accomplishments

The public mind must be vividly awakened to the importance of education by such a document as this, and it is indispensable that it should be so. Under a despotism like that of Prussia, the whole intelligence and power of the state can be wielded by the Sovereign and applied to the improvements of schools, but in the United States, unless the people, *the whole people*, see the necessity of a high education, understand what constitutes it, and become animated with an active zeal to attain it, the common schools cannot prosper. As water cannot rise higher than its fountain, so, in the United States, education, morality and religion, cannot rise higher than the level of the intelligence of the people. The law in Massachusetts is wisely framed, with a view to this fact. The Secretary to the Board by travelling round the state, by correspondence and interviews, obtains all the knowledge he can reach, respecting existing defects and practical improvements; he communicates this information to the Board; from them it goes to the legislature, by whom it is printed and sent into every school district of the state. The law requires that the committee of each town shall make a report to *the town*, a copy of which must be sent to the board, and from these reports, the annual abstract is composed. (See Fourth Annual Report of the Board of Education, together with the Fourth Annual Report of the Secretary of the Board Boston, 1841.) Although in all this there is nothing of compulsion, and although the Board acts by moral influence alone, yet the system, by appealing to the benevolence and intellect, the Self-Esteem and Love of Approbation, the Philoprogenitiveness and Conscientiousness of the whole community, is calculated to produce great results.(a) It will beget

(a) The following paragraph, to be met with in p. 59 of the Report of the

in consequence of the fact having been divulged, that the cashier and majority of the directors had lent out a great part of the capital on permanent loans to themselves and a few of their friends. Mr. Robert White, the cashier, was removed from office, and in revenge he assaulted in Wall street with a stick Mr. Allan Thompson, the director (seventy years of age), who had divulged his transactions, and injured him severely. Mr. White is bound over in $5000 to stand trial for the outrage.

March 23. Ther. 37°. Presentation of a Silver Vase.— This evening a beautiful and richly ornamented silver vase was presented to me in Howard's Hotel by the ladies and gentlemen who had attended my two courses of lectures in New York. It was delivered by Mr. E. P. Hurlbut, the author of the work on "Civil Office and Political Ethics," formerly alluded to, in their names, in presence of an assemblage of the subscribers, and prefaced by a speech, of the merits, of which it is not suitable for me to speak, but which, with a description of the vase, is printed in the Appendix No. XII.

March 25. Ther. 27°. Visit to Ohio and Kentucky.— This day we left New York, accompanied by a much valued American friend, on a visit to Cincinnati and Kentucky, not with the view of lecturing, but to see something of the interior of the country before returning to Europe. We went to Philadelphia, and thence to Baltimore, by the Philadelphia, Wilmington, and Baltimore Railway.*

that deep and general interest in education, in the whole people, without which, as already remarked, schools cannot flourish in an American commonwealth. I shall regard it as a bright day for Great Britain when she shall have such a machinery at work, directed by such able hands, to raise the moral and intellectual condition of her people.

Secretary of the Board of Education, Mr. Mann, is worthy of insertion in this place.

' It will ever remain an honor to the commonwealth of Massachusetts, that, among all the reports of its school committees, for the last year, so many of which were voluminous and detailed, and a majority of which, probably, were prepared by clergymen, belonging to all the various denominations in the state, there was not one, which advocated the introduction of sectarian instruction, or of sectarian books, into our public schools, while, with accordant views—as a single voice coming from a single heart—they urge, they insist, they demand, that the great axioms of Christian morality shall be sedulously taught, and that the teachers shall themselves be patterns of the virtues they are required to inculcate."

* The second annual report of the directors of this Railway Company, dated 1st January 1840, states the expenditure in making the road (94 miles), and all other expenses, at $4,379,225 17

Deduct bills receivable,	$4000	
Cash in hands of assistant treasurer,	19,205 28	
		23,205 28
		$4,356,019 89

April 2. Ther. 32°. We proceeded to Frederick, (Maryland,) a distance of sixty miles, by a railway which runs for a great part of the way along the bank of a small river, the Patapsco, flowing in a beautifully wooded narrow valley. At Frederick we hired an exclusive extra to carry us by the National Road to Wheeling on the Ohio river, and travelled the distance, 221 miles, in four days, having stopped each night to sleep. We descended the Ohio in a steamboat, and arrived at Cincinnati at 6 A. M. on the 8th of April. The thermometer then stood at 40°. The town disappointed me, not in consequence of its own defects, but of the exaggerated descriptions of it which I had read. It is a handsome city of 50,000 inhabitants, and a marvellous example of the rapid increase of the country in wealth and population. In 1795, Cincinnati contained 500; in 1800, 750, in 1810, 2500; in 1820, 10,000; in 1830, 25,000; and now, in 1840, it is estimated to contain 50,000 souls. Mrs. Trollope's bazaar is converted into a lecture room, and is an object of curiosity to strangers.

April 13. Ther. 32°. *Visit to General Harrison.*—General Harrison, the Whig candidate for the Presidency of the United States at the election in November, 1840, lives at North Bend, on the Ohio, 16 miles below Cincinnati, and one of his friends having offered to introduce us to him, we sailed down the river, and waited on him. As he has since been elected President, a few particulars of his history may be interesting to the reader. General Harrison was born in Virginia, on the 9th February, 1773.* He was educated at Hampden Sydney College, and then repaired to Philadelphia to pursue the study of medicine under Dr. Benjamin Rush. In 1791 he abandoned the profession of medicine, and obtained from General Washington a commission as ensign in the first regiment of the United States Artillery. He served in the war with the Indians, in the Northwest Territory; and an old soldier, speaking of his appearance at this time,

The receipts for the year 1839 were	$490,635 55
The disbursements were	296,131 58

Balance applicable to dividends,		$194,503 97
Dividend paid 1st August 1839, 4 per cent ,	$84,480	
Do. 1st Feb. 1840, 3½ per cent ,	77,418 25	
		161,898 25

Surplus fund,	$32,605 72

The description of this railroad, and the expense of its different works and materials, may be interesting to some readers, and I present them in the Appendix No XIII , extracted from the report.

* Sketches of the Civil and Military Services of William Henry Harrison, by C. S. Todd and Benjamin Drake. Cincinnati, 1840.

remarked, " I would as soon have thought of putting my wife in the service as this boy; but I have been out with him, and I find those smooth cheeks are on a wise head, and that slight frame is almost as tough as my own weather-beaten carcass." Peace was concluded with the Indians in 1795, and Captain Harrison was appointed to the command of Fort Washington, (now Cincinnati,) where he married the daughter of John Cleves Symmes, the founder of the Miami settlements. He subsequently retired to his farm near Cincinnati, and soon acquired that taste for agriculture which, through a long life, has prompted him, when not engaged in public service, to return to the plough, and where we found him at our visit.

On 13th July 1787 an "ordinance" was passed in Congress " for the Government of the Territory of the United States Northwest of the River Ohio," Article VI of which, proposed by Mr. Dana of Massachusetts, as an amendment, and adopted, bears that " there shall be neither slavery nor involuntary servitude in the said territory, otherwise than in punishment of crime, whereof the party shall have been duly convicted." This clause has done more to promote the prosperity of that region than language can express. Early in 1798, Mr. Harrison was appointed secretary, and *ex officio* Lieutenant-Governor of the Territory. In 1800 he was sent as a delegate to represent the Territory in Congress. " His first effort was to effect a change in the mode of selling the public lands, which had hitherto been offered in large tracts—a system well suited to the rich speculator, but adverse to the interest of the poor man, however industrious and enterprising." He partly succeeded in this object, and obtained an act which facilitated the purchase of land by poor but industrious settlers, and thereby contributed essentially to the prosperity of the Territory.

In 1800, he was appointed Governor of Indiana: In 1803, upon the admission of Ohio into the Union, the region of country which now forms the state of Michigan was added to the Indiana Territory; and during the subsequent year, Mr. Harrison was made *ex officio* Governor of Upper Louisiana. On the 7th November 1811, he fought the battle of Tippecanoe against the Indians, led by their celebrated chief Tecumthe, and gained a decided victory. The forces engaged amounted to about 900 on each side, and the loss was equal; about fifty men being killed belonging to each army, and double the number wounded. This is the exploit celebrated in innumerable electioneering songs, and which gave name to hundreds of political clubs.

In 1812, when the British and Indians threatened the Northwest Territory, he was appointed commander-in-chief, and maintained a gallant defence of " Camp, now Fort Meigs," against these assailants. On the 5th October 1813 he met the British General Proctor, commanding 800 or 900 men, and Tecumthe, with 1800 or 2000 Indians, on the bank of the River Thames, near the Moravian Towns, and completely defeated them. " General Harrison personally gave the directions for the charge to be made when the right battalion of the mounted men received the fire of the British: the horses in the front of the column recoiled from the fire; another was given by the enemy, and our column at length getting into motion, broke through the enemy with irresistible force. In one minute the contest in front was over. The British officers, seeing no prospect of reducing their disordered ranks to order, and seeing the advance of infantry, and our mounted men wheeling upon them, and pouring in a destructive fire, immediately surrendered." The result of this charge decided the fate of the day. The Indians also were defeated. The Americans lost about twenty killed, and from thirty to forty wounded; the British had eighteen killed and twenty-six wounded, and the Indians left on the ground, and in the pursuit, between fifty and sixty killed. This battle also has been the fertile subject of many electioneering songs.

In 1816, General Harrison was elected to Congress by the district in Ohio in which he resided, and some charges having been preferred against him by an army contractor, his conduct was investigated by a committee of Congress, which unanimously reported his conduct to stand above suspicion. Congress subsequently awarded to him a gold medal and the thanks of that body. " He exhibited in Congress an intimate familiarity with the civil and military affairs of the country, and the possession of a vigorous and cultivated mind. As a debater, he was ready, fluent, and forcible, always courteous and dignified, eminently happy in illustrating his arguments by the history of other nations, both ancient and modern, with the philosophy of which his mind is deeply and accurately imbued."

In 1824, he was elected to the Senate of the United States by the legislature of Ohio, and in 1828 appointed, by President Adams, Minister Plenipotentiary to the Republic of Columbia. " While in Columbia, the proposition was entertained by one of the political parties, of putting aside the constitution, and raising Bolivar to the Dictatorship. During the agitation of this question, General Harrison, as the personal friend of Bolivar, and not in his official capacity, addressed to him a letter on the subject of this change of government. This document, which has been extensively circulated and greatly admired in the United States, is written with great force and eloquence of diction, and breathes the pure spirit of republican liberty. After General Harrison's return from Columbia, he retired to his farm at North Bend, and resumed the peaceful pursuits of agriculture. In 1837, he was put in nomination for the Presidency, but was then unsuccessful.

" While Governor of Indiana, and Superintendent of Indian affairs, during a period of twelve years, he disbursed, at his discretion, and with but few, if any checks, very large sums of money; and, in the course of the late war, he drew on the Treasury for more than $600,000 for military purposes. Yet General Harrison retired from public service poorer than he entered it, and has never been a defaulter to his government."

These representations of General Harrison's services, character, and attainments, although drawn from a work edited by his friends, contain, so far as I could learn, essentially the truth. Indeed his writings, which are pretty copiously quoted, prove that his intellectual attainments are highly creditable, while few American public men, since Washington, can boast of greater uprightness, disinterestedness, and devotion to the best interests of his country. When Governor of the Northwest Territory he wielded nearly the powers of a Dictator, and his administration was marked by singular equity. moderation, and judgment.

General Harrison's residence at North Bend consists of a centre house of two stories, now covered with clap-boards, but which the General told us is really built of logs, and two clap-boarded wings of one story each. It stands about a quarter of a mile from the Ohio, in a grass park, having a few cherry trees in the distance, and several laburnums close to the door The park may contain forty to fifty acres, enclosed with a rail-fence. A foot-path, worn in the grass, but not formed by art, leads from the gate to the door of the house. The floor of the house is about fifteen or eighteen inches above the grass, and three stones of increasing thickness, undressed, not built on each other, but each lying on the ground, at successive distances, serve as steps to surmount this height. The centre house has much the appearance of a log-cabin. The principal room in it is coarsely finished, and the wooden fire blazes on the hearth. One of the wings, however, is finished like a modern house, and comfortably furnished as a drawing-room. Between the park and the river a canal is forming, to connect Cincinnati with the interior of the state.

General Harrison was suffering from a violent headache when we arrived, but Mrs. Harrison gave us a kind welcome, and the General at length appeared. He is now sixty-seven, rather above the middle stature, slender, and he stoops considerably. His temperament is nervous and bilious, his head is long, of full average height, but not remarkably broad. The anterior lobe is above an average both in length from front to back and height; and both the observing and reflecting organs are well developed. The head is obviously flat in the region of Acquisitiveness. The moral region seemed to present an average development. His eye is vivacious, and his countenance is highly expressive of thought; indeed his whole appearance is much more that of a literary or scientific man, than that of a military commander. His habitation presented unequivocal indications of humble fortune: indeed I may say (and I say it without the least feeling of disrespect) of poverty; yet his manner and appearance were those of a man of the world, who was familiar with the best society, and who, in the retirement of his farm at North Bend, retained the polish and appearance of a gentleman.

In making these remarks I may appear to be trespassing beyond the limits of legitimate publication, and trenching on the privacies of domestic life; but at the time of my visit, and for many subsequent months, all the circumstances of General Harrison's conduct and condition, private as well as public, were described and discussed in almost every periodical of the Union; and I state little here which is not as public in the United States as the noon-day sun.

Immediately after dinner we retired and walked with him over part of his farm. It is his own property, and we were told extends to about 1500 acres, part of his wife's dowry. From the rising ground behind his house the view is highly beautiful, embracing two bends of the Ohio and its picturesque banks. At first it was intended to plant on this spot the great city of the west; but it is said that the commanding-officer of the district entertained an affection for the wife of a sergeant who was then stationed at Cincinnati, and that this induced him to remove his troops there, from which circumstance that town sprung into being.* Behind the General's house is a large garden, in which we saw a white-headed eagle, with only one leg. It was presented to him by a convention of his political friends; and the gentleman who delivered it, in name of the rest, observed, in his speech, that as an eagle was seen hovering over Fort Meigs when the General fought the battle in its defence, this may possibly be the identical bird! The General remarked to us that

* The original name of Cincinnati was Losantiville, compounded in the following manner by Captain Robert Filson, a teacher apparently of great classical attainments. A small stream flowing from Kentucky, enters the Ohio opposite to Cincinnati, and is named the Licking —L, therefore, stands for Licking; *os*, Latin, mouth, *anti*, Greek, opposite; and *ville*, French, town, make Losantiville, or the " town opposite to the mouth of the Licking." It was hard on such an ingenious scholar to drop his erudite appellation, and to substitute for it Cincinnati, derived from the name of a self-constituted military order which met there.

eagles were then so numerous in that country that they might be
seen hovering over many places. The captors of the eagle had
dislocated its leg, and Dr. Thornton, the General's son-in-law,
believing it to be broken, had amputated it. The friend who
introduced us to the General said, " General Harrison has
promised to keep the eagle till the 4th of March next, when we
hope he will go to the White House," (the familiar name of
the President's official residence in the city of Washington.)
" Ah!" said the General promptly, and in the most natural tone,
" there is one other condition about that. If Mr. Van Buren
abandons his mischievous policy, he may stay in the White
House, and I shall remain in mine." He mentioned that in
agreeing to be put in nomination for the Presidency, he had distinctly announced his resolution to retire at the end of the first
term of four years.

He spoke of Bolivar and General Paez of Columbia. The
former he praised, but regarded him as corrupted and ruined by
his ambition. The latter he described as a true and excellent
man. He was, he said, destitute of education, but studied when
he became a man, and he is now a respectable scholar. He
first distinguished himself by a singular exploit during the War
of Independence. Two Spanish gunboats lay in the river near
which Bolivar's army was encamped, and annoyed them seriously. Bolivar had no boats of any kind by which he could
approach them. Paez offered to capture them with his division
of cavalry. Bolivar thought him in jest, as the idea of attack-
ing two ships of war in a navigable river by means of cavalry
seemed far removed from reason. But Paez, assuring him that
he was quite serious, obtained leave; and the next morning presented the gun-boats to Bolivar as trophies of victory, and their
crews as captives. His mode of accomplishing the feat was the
following.—Paez and his division were " reared" in a district
which is overflowed by a large river every spring. The houses
are built on eminences, and stand, during the inundation, like so
many islands in an ocean. Communication is maintained between the families by boats, and also by swimming on horseback. Paez proposed to his men, accustomed to this kind of
travelling, to enter the river on horseback, about half a mile
above the gun-boats, at night, and to swim down to them with
the stream. They readily volunteered; Paez led, and simultaneously both sides of the two gun-boats were entered sword in
hand, and captured without a struggle. The horses swam to
the shore and joined their regiment.

In the evening we left North Bend, and had a delightful drive
along the right bank of the Ohio to Cincinnati. I was impressed
by this visit with strong feelings of respect for General Harrison.

After a long life spent in the service of his country, he lives, poor indeed, but he seemed cheerful and happy. He does not conceal his poverty, nor does he make the least parade of it. He alludes to it simply as a fact, and he betrayed not one emotion of envy or jealousy of any human being, and still less did he indicate any feeling of disappointed ambition.

Since this visit General Harrison has been elected President of the United States, and enters to his office on the 4th March 1841. The circumstances that have led to his elevation are curious. The year 1838 was one of great "prosperity" in the United States; that is to say, many of the states borrowed largely on bonds, and prosecuted vast internal improvements. These bonds were purchased on favorable terms by the bankers and merchants, who sent them to London, where they sold readily at high prices, and formed extensive funds of credit. On the faith of these credits not only were large orders for European goods transmitted to England and France by the merchants, but the American banks issued their paper in floods. This abundance of currency quickened internal commerce and manufactures; prices rose, and speculation flourished. At this time Mr. Van Buren appeared immovably seated, for two terms, in the "White House." But in 1838 the crop of grain in England failed, large quantities of corn were imported from the Continent of Europe, and a drain commenced on the Bank of England for gold. This led to a contraction of the currency in Britain, followed by commercial distress. The American stocks speedily felt the effect of the shock, and in 1839 became nearly unsaleable. The banks and merchants who had drawn on England on the faith of them, suddenly found their means of meeting their engagements and paying for their large importations cut off; and suspension of cash-payments by most of the banks in the south and west followed. This produced derangement in the exchanges (see vol. ii, p. 157), a stagnation of commerce, and a great fall in the prices of commodities. Cotton, wheat, and tobacco, the great articles of export to Europe, also fell, and their value as remittances to extinguish the American debt in Europe, proportionately diminished. In short, universal distress prevailed. So general was the suffering in the latter end of 1839, and the first half of 1840, that every class in the United States was involved in it. Many of the capitalists were ruined; the merchants and manufacturers sustained enormous losses; the farmers could scarcely obtain money for their produce at any price, and the laborers were thrown out of employment. The Whig party, then in opposition, traced all these disasters to the measures of their Democratic rulers, beginning with the veto exercised by General Jackson on the renewal, by Congress, of the charter of the United States' Bank as a national institution, down to the Sub-Treasury Bill; and they promised another national bank, restoration of credit, and renewed prosperity, if the people would only place them in power. In any country such an appeal to the interests of a suffering people would have had great influence in determining their choice; in the United States it was irresistible. Its effects were seconded by the character and circumstances of General Harrison himself. He had gained victories, and the American people have an excessive admiration of warriors. They, therefore, formed "Tippecanoe" clubs, and celebrated all his victories in songs. He lived in a log-house; and log-cabins were constructed and carried in proud triumph in the political processions, and this charmed the humblest class, who felt as if, in electing General Harrison, they were raising one of their own number to the Presidency. For twenty years he had drunk only cider, because he was not rich enough to pay for wine, and his political opponents said in derision that it was "hard" cider. Cider casks also became emblems which enlisted the sympathies of hundreds of thousands who used this beverage. These means secured the people, and as the Whigs had long had the majority of the wealthy on their side, General Harrison triumphed by a large majority.

That he was worthy of the honor, and that with many there was generosity of sentiment in honoring his poverty, I most willingly admit; nevertheless, judging philosophically of all the influences by which his election was accomplished, I cannot say that they were such as an enlightened patriot could boast of as proofs of the intelligence and moral elevation of the people.

The excitement of the public mind during a contest for the Presidentship is great and universal; the tongue ceases to utter, and the ear to hear, any words except those relating to the election, the press groans under the weight of the subject, and all the functions of life seem to be exclusively devoted to it. It is the parent of much drinking and debauchery, of fraud, lying, bribing, cajoling, and intimidating. But it also evolves good. The measures of government are severely scrutinised by reason as well as decided on by passion; the whole Union is moved by one interest, and the impression that they all belong to one nation is vividly excited. Local interests are for the moment forgotten, and one pulse appears to beat from Maine to Mississippi. My fear is, that without the recurrence of these elections, the people of the different states would rapidly come to regard each other as strangers and rivals, and insensibly slacken the bonds which bind them together as one great nation. The elections of members of Congress have not this effect, for although that assembly is national, each of its members represents only a section of the country. The President alone derives his power from the people of the whole Union.

April 15. Ther. 55°. *Kentucky.*—We sailed down the Ohio to Louisville in Kentucky, distance 135 miles, and found it a large thriving town, and apparently destined to become a formidable rival to Cincinnati. My chief object was to pay a visit to Dr. Charles Caldwell, with whom I had corresponded for upwards of twenty years, but whom I had never met. He is one of the most powerful and eloquent medical writers in the United States, and has scarcely a rival west of the Alleghany Mountains. He has been the early, persevering, intrepid, and successful advocate of Phrenology; and in his character of medical professor, first at Lexington and latterly in Louisville, has exerted a great influence in its favor. To our regret, he was still suffering from the effects of a recent severe indisposition, and was able to see us only for a few minutes, a circumstance which on every account, we deeply lamented. He recovered; and before we sailed for Europe I had the pleasure of receiving a passing visit from him in Staten Island. He is now advanced in life, but so full of fire and vigor, that I look forward to his still laboring in the cause of science for many years.

We travelled by an excellent road to Frankfort, the capital of Kentucky, thence by a railroad to Lexington, near which Mr. Clay resides, but who was then engaged in the Senate at Washington, and afterwards to Maysville, where we again met the Ohio. Nothing can exceed the fertility and beauty of Kentucky, yet slavery prevents it from fully flourishing. In passing through a portion of Virginia, and also in Kentucky, I narrowly observed the extent of labor performed by slaves, whether as waiters, house-servants, laborers, or tradesmen, and in all these capacities it was greatly inferior both in quantity and quality to that performed, not only by white men, but by free negroes. In the inns, the slaves run about with a wonderful display of muscular activity, but there is a sad lack of mind in it; they are active in body to avoid vituperation, but their minds are dormant, because they have no interest in their work. The condition of many of the inns, the servants of which are slaves, is very bad. They are sadly dirty and sorely dilapidated; and even in Louisville and Lexington, where they are managed in the best manner possible with such assistants, they are far inferior to the hotels of the same class in the free states, in many of which, too, free Africans are the chief servants. By comparing the amount of exertion, and the progress in work made by the white laborers and tradesmen in Ohio, with those of the slave-laborers and tradesmen in Kentucky, I became convinced that a vigorous German or British emigrant, working by the piece, performs more work than two slaves, and does it better; and that two white laborers, taking them on an average, accomplish more than three slaves. Kentucky, with this inferior quality of labor, competes with Ohio and Indiana and their free labor, separated only by the river, and certainly it is not advancing in prosperity nearly so fast as they do, and this in fact is a relative decline. There is a prevailing expectation, therefore, that her own interests will prompt Kentucky to abolish slavery within a few years, independently of any general movement on the subject by the other slave states.

Great religious revivals were in progress at Frankfort when we visited it. The governor of the state had been converted, and prayed publicly every morning at sunrise in one of the churches. The Supreme Court also was in session, and at table we met the judges and many lawyers. The following dialogue took place at the public breakfast table, and was obviously not of a confidential nature, but on the contrary intended, at least by one of the parties, for general edification. The Rev. Mr. ———— said, that the governor had, that morning, given them a most impressive prayer in the church, and, turning to the chief justice, he continued, "When shall we see the chief justice in the church giving us a prayer?" Chief Justice—"Why you see I have so many duties to discharge, that I have no time for it." Minister—"But, Chief Justice, these are all little matters of this world's concernment, and this is the one thing needful!" Chief Justice—"True, and I have been intending, the first leisure three months I can command, to give the whole subject a thorough consideration." Minister—"But, Chief Justice, you *believe*, and no time is necessary for consideration. If you begin at once and pray, the kingdom of Heaven will be opened unto you." Chief Justice—"Well, that is very true, but I don't like to set about a thing without a complete investigation. I want to consider the whole question, and to satisfy myself properly. You see that my time is entirely occupied with these causes; it is my first duty to attend to them, and I have not an hour to bestow on any other subject. I must go to court immediately." This dialogue is characteristic of the professions of the speakers, and it shows, also, that, although there is no Established Church in Kentucky, there is no lack of zeal and earnestness in religion.

In Kentucky, slavery exists in its mildest form, and agriculture is the chief employment of the slaves. A farmer buys his ploughman as he does his horses and cattle, and his price is from $700 to $800. Nevertheless, Thomas Jefferson's picture of the effects of slavery is realised even here. In his "Notes

on the state of Virginia,"* he says, " There must doubtless be
an unhappy influence on the manners of our people produced
by the existence of slavery among us. The whole commerce
between master and slave is a perpetual exercise of the most
boisterous passions, the most unremitting despotism on the one
part, and degrading submission on the other. Our children see
this, and learn to imitate it; for man is an imitative animal.
This quality is the germ of all education in him. From his cra-
dle to his grave he is learning to do what he sees others do. If
a parent could find no motive either in his philanthropy or his
self-love, for restraining his intemperance of passion towards
his slaves, it should always be a sufficient one, that his child is
present. But, generally, it is not sufficient. The parent storms;
the child looks on, catches the lineaments of wrath, puts on the
same airs in the circle of smaller slaves, gives a loose to the
worst of passions, and thus nursed, educated, and daily exercised in tyranny, cannot but be stamped by it with odious peculiarities. The man must be a prodigy who can retain his manners and morals undepraved by such circumstances." * * *
"And can the liberties of a nation be thought secure when we
have removed their only firm basis, a conviction in the minds of
the people, that these liberties are the gift of God? That they
are not to be violated but with his wrath? Indeed, I tremble
for my country when I reflect that God is just; that his justice
cannot sleep for ever, that considering numbers, nature, and natural means only, a revolution of the wheel of fortune, an exchange of situation, is among possible events; that it may become
probable by supernatural interference! The Almighty has no
attribute that can take side with us in such a contest."
    It is impossible to add to the force of eloquence of this expo-
sition of the inherent evils of slavery. I had the pleasure of
meeting a gentleman, a native of Virginia, who mentioned, that
he had emancipated his slaves and removed to a free state, because, among other effects, he saw that slavery was corrupting
the minds of his children. He added, however, that his slaves
had not profited by their freedom; the incapacity for self-action
and self-control which slavery engenders, renders emancipated
Africans, in general, unfit to struggle successfully with the difficulties which surround them. These difficulties arise from the
existence of slavery and slave-laws, and of habits of feeling connected with them, in the society into which they are thrown.
By them the negroes are degraded and oppressed after they are
free, and often become immoral and miserable. Universal emancipation, which should raise all the Africans at once to the con-

* Eighth American Edition, 1801, p. 240.

dition of free men, and impose on the whites the twofold duty
of treating them with kindness and directing their industrial
efforts, will probably prove the only safe and beneficial means
of terminating slavery.

Return to New York.—We descended the Ohio from Maysville to Cincinnati, and there engaged a comfortable state-room
in a steamboat going up the river to Pittsburg, where we arrived
on the 26th of April. There were only two modes of reaching
Philadelphia, one by the Pennsylvania Canal and Portage Railroad across the Alleghany Mountains, the other by the public
road. We were assured by every one, that the road was in the
worst possible condition, and the inns indifferent, and that the
canal was preferable. We accordingly embarked on board of
the "James Madison" at 9 P. M., and the scene may be thus
described. The boat is fitted up exclusively for carrying passengers. The gentlemen's cabin was about 42 feet long, 15
broad, and 7 high; and the ladies' cabin 12 feet long, 13 broad,
and 7 high. Behind the ladies' cabin was a dressing-room for
them, 6 feet by 7 or so. Before the gentlemen's cabin was the
bar-room and the kitchen. There were windows all along on
both sides of the boat. There was one small sky-light in the
roof of the gentlemen's cabin. Into this space were stowed 35
men, 19 women, and 10 children, 7 of whom were at the breast.
The rate of travelling by the boats was four miles an hour. The
distance from Pittsburg to Harrisburg is 286 miles, of which we
travelled by the canal 249, and by the Portage Railroad 37 miles,
occupying four nights and three days. The beds were ranged
continuously along each side of the boat, in three tiers, all within
the space of 7 feet in height, and they ran directly across the
windows; every one of which was anxiously closed, to prevent
the ingress of cold and damp air. The passengers, whose beds
reached to the door, insisted on closing it also to keep out the
cold; so that there was only the small sky-light in the gentlemen's cabin for ventilating thirty-five pair of lungs, and it, too,
was packed round on every side by luggage, and covered on the
top on account of rain. During the day the beds, consisting of
mattresses, sheets, pillows, and cotton quilts, were piled one
above another, as close as they could be packed, in a corner of
the boat, and inclosed withing folding-doors and a curtain, so as
to be out of sight, and to occupy as little space as possible.
They were stowed away the moment the passengers left them
in the morning, and continued so until bed-time. The smell of
animal effluvia, when they were unpacked, was truly horrid.
The mattresses and quilts, from their construction, could not be
washed, and they were saturated with the perspiration of every
individual who had used them since the commencement of the

season, or probably from the time when they were first taken on
board. There was no provision for holding the clothes of the
passengers during the night, except laying them on stools which
were speedily upset, or on the floor, which all day had been spit
upon by innumerable chewers of tobacco. The sense of suffocation in bed was distressing, and on rising the feeling of discomfort and fatigue proved that nature had not been refreshed.
During the day we breathed fresh air on deck, and opened the
windows. The cooking was astonishingly well accomplished,
considering the small accommodation; and the meals were unex-
ceptionable; but I should willingly have lived on bread and water
for a clean bed and fresh air at night. The second night revealed
a new horror. The beds had been packed up promiscuously,
and they were tossed out in the same manner; so that each night
every man got a different sheet, mattress, and quilt, as they
chanced to come to hand, which had been used by his neighbors
the night before, who in their turn received his!

At Hollydaysburgh eight or ten clergymen, of various denominations, with the wives and children of some of them, joined the
boat, and we had now upwards of seventy passengers on board.
The Captain said that we should soon be "damning" him on
account of our discomfort; but he was guiltless, and nobody,
within my hearing, said an uncivil word to him. He was at-
tentive, and did all that he could to contribute to the welfare of
the passengers; but little was in his power. At night one of
these clergymen put the question to the vote of the passengers,
whether they would have religious exercises. The majority
voted in favor of his proposal, and we had prayers and psalms.
The majority knelt on the floor, which had been defiled all day
by tobacco saliva; and after shutting up all the avenues to fresh
air, and preparing to sleep in unwholesome bedding; in short,
after setting aside all the laws of health, and assembling around
them the natural causes of croup and fever for the children, and
of pulmonary affections for themselves—they prayed fervently
to God for spiritual blessings, and also for refreshing slumbers
and sound health, and to be raised up next morning invigorated
and cheered for the labors and duties of the day! They were
not rough, wild, excited fanatics; on the contrary, with one exception, they were gentle, kind, cultivated, Christian men.
Their exercises were not only clothed in the words, but breathed
the very spirit of benevolence and veneration, and their language, always appropriate, was in some instances even elegant
and touching. But they were sadly deficient in the knowledge
of God's physical creation. Their prayers for health, in these
circumstances, appeared to me little short of a mockery of
Heaven; they did not mean them as such, and of course were not

guilty of irreverence; but God must have suspended his natural laws before he could have given effect to their petitions; and when the question is put, whether rational beings should expect that God should work miracles in order to save them from the consequences of their own ignorance and neglect of his laws— or whether they should ventilate their boat, and preserve decent cleanliness in their night apparel, as a preliminary condition to receiving the blessing of health—there can scarcely be two opinions on the subject. It was their duty to observe the laws of health, before praying for the blessing appointed by the Creator to flow from that obedience. In point of fact their prayers, on this subject, appeared to me not to have been answered; for in the morning I heard one of them complaining that he felt as if he had no life in him—that his head was as if filled with some heavy inanimate matter; another complained of pain in his head, a third of nausea; and two who were affected with bronchitis, mentioned how much worse they felt in the morning; while the wife of one of them wondered how, on rising, she was seized with faintness, and continued for hours to feel as if she should sink down insensible on the floor. I did not hear one of them connect these sufferings with the bad air and uncleanly condition in which they had passed the night. We had prayers and psalms in the morning, and again on the second evening; but as it rained incessantly, and the cabin was kept, if possible, still more close, the suffering increased; and, for my own part, I did not recover my usual feelings of internal comfort and mental alacrity for several days after we had escaped from this torturing prison.

These clergymen, certainly, were only passengers, and could not alter the circumstances in which they and we were placed. But if they had known and respected God's natural laws, they might have used the great influence which they obviously possessed over the minds of the passengers, in inducing them to admit at least some portion of fresh air, and also in giving effect to a general complaint to the owners of the boats against arrangements so manifestly injurious to health, and which a little skill and expense could unquestionably have remedied.

Some of these ministers were Methodists, and they mentioned that their society allows each preacher $100 for himself, besides his travelling expenses; $100 for his wife, if he be married; $16 for each child below seven, and $24 for each child above seven, and below fourteen years of age, all per annum. Each preacher has a district which he must traverse every six weeks, and at the end of every two years his circuit is changed. These are all the allowances, except gifts from their flocks. By this machinery the thinly-scattered population of the west is preserved within reach of Christian ordinances and cultivation. The love of souls alone can induce men of ordinary attainments to embrace so laborious and ill-requited a profession.

Part of the scenery through which we passed is said to be exquisitely beautiful, but a heavy rain descending through a thick mist prevented us from seeing any object at a distance exceeding a hundred yards from the boat.

One of the passengers in conversing with me asked—" Have you been to the west?"—"A short way only."—" Have you been long in the country?"—" Only about twenty months."—" Did you go to · ·tle?"—" No."—" Were you at St. Louis?"—" No, not so far."—" On the Ohio, then?"—" Yes, as far as Louisville."—" Were you thinking of buying land in Kentucky?"—" No."—" Do you go to Baltimore?"—" No, to Philadelphia."—" Are you settled there?"—" No."—" Farther east perhaps?"—" Yes, a good way farther east."—" What is the name of the town?"—" Why, if you have any particular interest in knowing, I will tell you."—" Oh no, not any particular interest, only one likes to know the gentlemen one travels with. If we hear them inquired about, we can say that we saw them."—" I do not think that there is much chance of your being asked about me." Here the dialogue terminated; but all this was said quite civilly, and without the least intention of rudeness.

The day after this conversation C—— missed a silver fruit-knife, which she valued highly; and I used every means to discover whether she had dropt it in the boat, but in vain. It was given up as lost; when some hours afterwards, I saw it in the hands of the individual who had interrogated me so minutely. "That's my wife's fruit-knife," said I, "which she lost yesterday; where did you find it?"—" Oh, I found it last evening on the deck between two trunks; I have since been inquiring to whom it belonged, and could not find an owner."—" But my wife's initials are on it—C. C."—" True. I saw these letters, but as you would not tell me any thing about yourself yesterday, I had no idea that these were your wife's initials." The inquisitive gentleman kindly returned the knife; and I felt that he had got completely the better of me on this occasion.

April 30. Ther. 55°. We stayed a day at Harrisburg, and admired exceedingly the beauty of the Susquehanna River, on the left bank of which it stands. The village itself, although the political capital of Pennsylvania, is small, plain, and unpretending.

May 1. Ther. 56°. We started this morning at 7 o'clock by a railroad for Philadelphia. The country through which it passed is all cleared, highly fertile, well cultivated, and possesses much natural beauty. The farm-houses and offices looked

substantial, clean, and neat; we were told that a great part of
the population is of German descent, and that they preserve the
language and manners of their original country. At 1 P.M. the
engine was allowed to run off the track; and we lost two hours
before it could be restored to its place, by means of tackle and
a multitude of men. No injury was done to it or any of the
passengers; but we had not proceeded far when the engine stood
still. All the coals had been consumed, and the engineer had
supplied their place with green oak, which would not burn. At
last a baggage train came up and pushed our train before it to
the next station, where we got a supply of combustible fuel.
The engine then performed its duty well, and at 7 P.M. we arrived at Philadelphia, three hours behind the usual time. The
distance was 105 miles. During all these delays, the result of
sheer carelessness, not an angry or discontented word was heard
from the passengers, who were very numerous. The railway
train from Philadelphia to New York started at 5 P.M., and we
should have arrived an hour before that time, instead of two
hours after it. Many individuals who had urgent business and
appointments in New York found their plans deranged, and suffered serious inconvenience; yet they bore the disappointment
with most exemplary patience and good humor.

May 9. Thermometer 45°. *Philadelphia and Boston.*—
I have now seen something of both Boston and Philadelphia,
and they present distinct mental characteristics. In Boston literature is more cultivated than science, and speculation is preferred to physical investigation. A person gains reputation
there, by having at command all the striking passages of Shak-
speare, and knowing every reading of his text, and the opinions
of his commentators; by studying Italian, and being able to quote
Dante; by learning German and becoming eloquent in Göethe.
It is not necessary that he should know chemistry, natural philosophy, natural history, physiology, or even geology. The
Bostonians are learned in literature, write well. and speak well;
but an ingenious theory has more charms for them than a laborious inquiry into scientific truth. The educated men of Philadelphia study science more generally and extensively. They
are precise and accurate in their knowledge of facts and natural
phenomena, and solid in their inductions and conclusions; but
they know less of books, commentators, theories, and opinions.
The temperament of the educated class in Boston presents more
of the sanguine and nervous elements than that of the same class
in Philadelphia; and in them also, the anterior lobe is, perhaps,
a little larger, while the moral organs are generally large in both.
In their present condition, the Philadelphians are the more
scientific thinkers, and more in harmony with the first class o

minds in Europe. Boston, however, takes a deeper interest than Philadelphia in moral, intellectual, and religious pursuits. Boston resembles Edinburgh in the days of Dugald Stewart, when great reputations were founded on acquirements in metaphysics and belles-lettres, and when distinguished literary men were unacquainted even with the rudiments of physical science.

Debts of the American States.—I have frequently been asked whether, in my opinion, the American states will preserve faith with their public creditors and pay their debts. A vast extent of information beyond what I can pretend to possess, would be necessary to enable any one to deliver a satisfactory answer to this question; but some ideas may be presented which may serve to enable others to elucidate it in a more satisfactory manner. The subject divides itself naturally into two heads; 1st, The ability of the states to redeem their obligations; and 2dly, Their willingness to do so. Ample and correct information in regard to the first head, may be obtained from Mr. Trotter's " Observations on the Financial Position and Credit of such of the states of the North American Union as have contracted Public Debts." This work was commended by the American press, and in the United States its details are regarded as worthy of being relied on. I frequently conversed with bankers and capitalists on the subject of the state debts; and in travelling into different parts of the Union, I endeavored to form some estimate, necessarily a vague one, of the resources of the states. Premising, then, that the debts of the different states have been incurred, not to prosecute wars and measures of destruction, but chiefly to form canals, roads, and railroads, and to institute banks, I remark, that the general opinion which I heard expressed was, that from one-half to one-fourth of the sums constituting the debts of most of the states, have been wasted through unskilful application and lavished expenditure—the inevitable accompaniments of works undertaken by a popular government; but that the remainder has been beneficially invested. The waste differs much in different states; but allowing for its utmost magnitude, and viewing the extent of surface, the salubrity of the climate, the fertility of the soil, the mineral riches, and all the other natural advantages of the country, together with the industry and ingenuity of the people, the debts appear to me to be a mere trifle in comparison with the resources of the states. Wealth and population are augmenting so rapidly, that twenty years hence, the present amount of state debts, with few exceptions, would scarcely be felt as a burden according to European notions, although both principal and interest were raised by direct taxation. I never heard a man of the least judgment doubt the *ability* of all the states to meet their obligations; and so far as my own means of judging extend, I concur in this view.

After travelling through a considerable portion of Pennsylvania, and contemplating the amazing richness of her soil and mines, and the very great advantages which she derives from her canals and railroads'(with all their faults), and after witnessing the industry, economy, and wealth of her people, the amount of her debt appeared to me to be no formidable incumbrance on her resources.

It is stated in the American Almanack for 1840, as follows:—

For canals, bearing 5 per cent. interest,		$16,576,527 00
Railroads, do do.		4,964,484 00
Turnpikes and bridges, do.		2,595,992 00
Miscellaneous, do.		3,166,787 00
	Total,	$27,306,790 00

In the American Almanack for 1841, the total stock and domestic debt of Pennsylvania are stated to amount to $33,016,149, or a little more than six millions and a half sterling

In 1830, her population amounted to 1,348,232, and it must now reach nearly to 1,800,000, while her soil is capable of supporting probably ten millions in abundant comfort. Her financial embarrassments, therefore, arise not from the magnitude of her debt in relation to her means of payment, but from difficulties in bringing the latter forward to meet her engagements; and the same may be predicated of every other state which has paused in the discharge of the interest of its debts.

If the revenues of the canals, railroads, and banks, to which the borrowed money has been applied, should prove sufficient for repayment of the debts, no doubt can reasonably be entertained on the subject. Any proposal to devote these revenues to other public purposes, and to defraud the public creditors, would, in my opinion, be rejected by the legislatures of all the states without a moment's hesitation. But in some instances these revenues have already proved insufficient to discharge the interest of the debts; and in Pennsylvania in particular, the alternative has presented itself, of submitting to taxation in order to raise funds to pay the interest, or of declaring the state insolvent. This occurred in the beginning of 1840, when the interest of the public debt remained unpaid for one day. The difficulty was then surmounted, by a loan from the suspended banks, and the interest was discharged: but this was a mere temporary expedient; and during the session of that year the proposition was fairly brought before the legislature, to impose taxes to make up the deficiency between the revenues yielded by the canals and railroads, and the interest of the public debt.   The majority of both houses of the Legislature, and also Governor Porter, were Democrats, and they had obtained the ascendency in the state, in a great measure, by reason of their hostility to the banks and the paper-currency system, and especially to the Bank of the United States.   By a singular coincidence, also, it happened, that at the time when recourse to taxation became necessary to avoid insolvency, the United States' Bank, by suspending specie payments, had forfeited its charter, and fallen prostrate under the power of these legislators.   The electors and legislators of Pennsylvania, besides, are by no means so enlightened as those of some of the Eastern States; so that, altogether, a combination of circumstances presented itself, well adapted to bring the second question to trial, whether an American state legislature will venture to impose taxes on the people in order to discharge public debts.

To the honor of Governor Porter, he never hesitated for a moment, but from the first occurrence of the difficulties, declared himself in his messages to the legislature ready to support the public credit by dealing discreetly with the suspended banks, and by resorting to taxation to supply the deficiency of the revenue; and called on the two houses to do their duty to the state in the same spirit.   The measures which he suggested met with great opposition.   Several bills were brought in to deprive the United States' Bank of its charter, and some of them passed one of the houses; but the attempts to pass a bill for raising taxes to pay the interest of the debt were again and again defeated.   Individuals were not wanting, in the legislatures both of Pennsylvania and other states, who openly advocated bankruptcy, and seemed to rejoice in the prospect of cheating the public creditors, especially the bond-holders in Britain.   I was told that the conferences, arguments, explanations, and entreaties used by the more enlightened members of the legislature of Pennsylvania, chiefly belonging to the cities, to induce the farmers and country members to pass a tax-bill, were innumerable.   The session dragged on, and no bill was passed.   Speeches were delivered, and articles written in the newspapers, discussing the question with the utmost zeal, and still the opposition raged.   At last, however, at the very close of the session, a tax-bill was passed, and the bank-charter was spared.   The farmer-proprietors, however, in the legislature, imitating the British Parliament, preserved all real estate free from assessment, and imposed the taxes on personal property alone.   The following extract from the New York Weekly Herald of June 20, 1840, contains the particulars of the bill.

The legislature of Pennsylvania have again adjourned, after passing the tax-bill, the bill to pay the interest on the State loans, and the improvement bill.   The tax-bill provides as follows:—

SYNOPSIS OF THE PENNSYLVANIA TAX-BILL.

On all dividends by banks or corporations of one per cent. or
    over—on $1, a tax of   .   .   .   .   1½ mills.
On $1 of all taxable property, occupations, &c. .   1 mill.
On $1 of all bonds, stocks (except state), moneys at interest,
    &c., on which 1 per cent. dividend may accrue,   .   ½
On all household furniture, and plate exceeding $300—per $1 of
    value, ...   5
On pleasure carriages, ...   1 per cent.
On gold watches, ...   1 dollar.
On gold and silver watches,   .   .   .   75 cents
On other watches, ...   50 cents
On all salary offices, ...   1 per cent.

This, it is estimated, will yield $1,000,000.   This, it is supposed, will be sufficient to obviate the necessity of resorting to new loans to pay interest on state stocks.   The revenues and expenditures of the state last year were as follows:—

Revenue.

Canal and railway tolls,	.	.	.	$821,780
Auction duties,	.	.	.	101,728
Dividends of banks, &c.,	.	.	.	207,097
Tax on bank dividends,	.	.	.	133,440
Bank charters,	.	.	.	100,000
Other sources,	.	.	.	257,074
				$1,621,119

Expenditures.

Government expenses,	.	.	.	$412,751
Canal repairs, &c.,	.	.	.	376,336
Common schools,	.	.	.	385,253
Interest on loans,	.	.	.	1,296,010
Other expenses,	.	.	.	238,513
				2,708,863
Deficiency,	.	.	.	$1,087,744

The State treasurer's estimate for 1840 was as follows —

On hand, January 1, 1840,	.	.	.	$1,337,170
Estimated receipts,	.	.	.	2,914,275
Total means,	.	.	.	$4,251,445
Estimated payments,	.	.	.	5,267,333
Deficiency,	.	.	.	$1,015,888

From this it appears that the new tax will be sufficient to cover the deficiency.   The bill to pay the interest on the state loans, provides that in future all interest upon loans shall be paid in specie; and also provides for the payment to holders of state stock the difference between bank notes and specie on the sums paid for interest during the suspension. The senate amended the improvement bill by striking out the clause requiring the United States Bank to loan the money at 4 per cent., and substituting a resolution authorising the governor to borrow in the market at an interest not exceeding 5 per cent.

Thus far the example is salutary, and calculated to inspire confidence in the honor of the American states; and my conviction is that it will be generally followed. Mr. Trotter, in enumerating the motives which may be relied on to induce the American democratic legislatures to pass tax-bills to fulfil their public engagements, trusts chiefly to the influence of religion and education; but, in addition to these, the operation of the powerful motives of self-interest, and fear of public opinion, may be mentioned. In compliance with a resolution of the House of Representatives, the Auditor-General communicated the following information relative to the banks, savings institutions, and loan companies of Pennsylvania, returns having been made from fifty-two institutions:—

Statement of the stock of the Bank of the United States of Pennsylvania, January 1, 1840.

Number of persons holding stock to the amount of 5 shares and under, 864

Do.	Do.	10	"	661
Do.	Do.	20	"	732
Do.	Do.	50	"	994
Do.	Do.	100	"	588
Do	Do.	500	"	814
Do	Do.	over 500	"	80

Par value of the Stock, $100 per share.

The number of shares held by

Females,	29,876
Executors and Guardians,	4,256
Trustees,	16,248
Benevolent Institutions,	1,758

Number of Stockholders in the United States.

Maine,	16	Brought forward,	2,665
New Hampshire,	23	North Carolina,	27
Vermont,	4	South Carolina,	340
Massachusetts,	106	Georgia,	36
Rhode Island,	40	Ohio,	22
Connecticut,	60	Kentucky,	13
New York,	230	Tennessee,	4
New Jersey,	117	Indiana,	2
Pennsylvania,	1,481	Illinois,	4
Delaware,	51	Alabama,	1
Maryland,	289	Missouri,	2
District of Columbia,	37	Mississippi,	1
Virginia,	211	Louisiana,	11
Carry forward,	2,665		3 133

Number of Stockholders in Europe and elsewhere, excepting United States.

Great Britain and Ireland,	1,185		Brought forward,			1,324
France,		36	Denmark,	-	-	2
Spain,		59	Switzerland,	-	-	4
Portugal,		6	West Indies,	-	-	52
Germany,		10	East Indies,	-	-	1
Holland,		26	South America,		-	2
Belgium,		1	Mexico,	-	-	3
Prussia,		1	Nova Scotia,	-	-	2
Carry forward,	1,324					1,390

Statement of the amount of five, ten, and twenty dollar notes of the Bank of the United States in circulation on the 1st of January, 1840.

Five dollar notes issued under the eighth section of the improvement act, passed July 19, 1839, - - -	$20,000 00
Ten dollar notes, - - - -	1,831,110 00
Twenty dollar notes, - - - -	1,138,380 00

When the Democratic party was in opposition, they breathed unmitigated hostility against the United States Bank, and why did they not destroy it when it fell fairly under their power in 1840? One answer will be found in the foregoing statement of the number of shares held by females, executors, guardians, and trustees, and in the number of stockholders in the United States. To have withdrawn its charter, would have carried loss and suffering into thousands of families, which would have reached either directly or indirectly almost every individual in the legislature. Public opinion also would have raised its powerful voice in denunciation of such a measure, and most of the members who should have voted against it, would have been rejected at the next election. Hence the very men, who in opposition clamored most loudly for the destruction of this institution, were spell-bound by public interest and public sentiment when they acquired the power to execute their own aspirations!

I was told by a member of the legislature, that one great objection to the bill for raising a tax was thus stated by the farmers. "Why should we be oppressed by taxes to support the nobility of England?" they believing that the state debt was held chiefly by the British nobility. I paid little attention to this report, supposing that it referred probably to the case of one, or at least very few individuals; but it derives some countenance from another head of the Auditor-General's return relative to the Bank of the United States, which is in these words. "The nobility holding stock are: Earls, 2; Marquises, 2; Counts and Countesses, 8; Lords, 2; Knights, Barons, and Baronets, 28." If the stock of the United States Bank had belonged altogether

to foreigners, the two powerful motives before stated, to spare
its charter, would have operated with less weight, and the result
might have been more doubtful.

The same remarks apply to the state debts. They are not
due exclusively to European creditors, but in almost every state
of the Union, large investments have been made in them by the
banks, and also by private persons who have realised capital.
A state bankruptcy, therefore, would be a highly unpopular
measure, and would carry misery far and wide into private
circles: from which it would directly operate against the individuals whose votes in the Legislature had permitted it to happen.
The aversion to taxation is great every where, and particularly
in the United States: and no surer road to popularity can be
found than in resisting a tax; but on the other hand, a state bankruptcy would, if possible, be a still more unpopular measure,
from the ruin of families, of banks, insurance offices, and charitable institutions, and also the universal insolvency which it would
draw after it; and, supposing American morality be neither
greater nor less than that of other nations, it appears to me that
the faith which the financiers and best informed merchants of
the Eastern cities entertain in the ultimate security of almost all
of the state stocks, is well founded.   These views will be better
appreciated after perusing the following additional extract from
the Auditor-General's Report.

" The returns from fifty-one other banks, loan companies,
and savings institutions in Pennsylvania, show the following
result:

Amount of $5 notes in circulation, 1st January, 1840,	$1,175,535
Amount of $10 in circulation, 1st January, 1840,	1,660,161
Amount of $20 in circulation, 1st January, 1840,	776,740

Number of Stockholders,				12,548
Number holding 5 shares and under,				3,422
Do. 10 do				2,905
Do. 20 do.				2,831
Do. 50 do.				2,647
Do. 100 do.				1,408
Do. 500 do.				933
Over 500 shares,				52
Number of shares held by Females,				39,860
Do. do. Executors,				10,956
Do. do. Guardians,				5,541
Do. do. Trustees,				10,185
Officers of Benevolent Institutions,				1,685
Title of Nobility,				none.

As a single specimen of the extent to which state stocks are
held by the banks in the United States, I present the following
extract from the Utica Observer, (state of New York,) of 3d

March, 1840, written, as I was informed, by a gentleman possessing accurate information and sound views on the subject of
banking.

" *The Scarcity of Money.*—The comptroller's late report to
the legislature, shows that up to December the 1st, the free
banks of this state, New York, had invested but a trifle short of
five millions of dollars in state stocks; the whole of this, with the
exception of less than half a million, was in the stocks of Illi-
nois, Arkansas, Alabama, Indiana, Kentucky, Missouri, and
other western states. The investment is in effect a loan to those
states—and it accounts very plainly for the unexampled scarcity
of money at home.

Oneida county has thus loaned to states, - -	$190,000
Erie, - - - - - - -	1,030,000
Monroe, - - - - - -	221,000
Niagara, - - - - - -	175,000
Onondaga, - - - - -	160,000
St. Lawrence, - - - - -	130,000
Genesee, - - - - - -	136,000
Wayne, - - - - - -	110,000
Herkimer and Montgomery, - - -	130,000
Seneca, - - - - - -	97,000
Orleans, - - - - - -	81,500
Tompkins, - - - - - -	65,000
Jefferson, - - - - - -	76,000
Broome, - - - - - -	75,000
Livingston, - - - - -	75,000
Steuben, - - - - - -	75,000
Tompkins, - - - - -	65,000

" Any person can see that the more we have of such banks the
poorer we must become. They commence by collecting all the
money that exists in their neighborhood, and loaning it to distant states, whence it is practically never to return. From the
county of Erie, more than a million of dollars have been thus
sent, and no county in the state is so prostrated as Erie, in all
its business operations. If all the investments had been made in
the stocks of our own state, the effect would be equally impover-
ishing to the neighborhood, for the stock, after it is procured, is
only locked up in the Comptroller's office. The neighborhood
receives no benefit in return, except that the new bank has the
privilege of issuing bank notes to the amount of money that it
has sent abroad for state stock. And even this benefit is fallacious, because experience proves that the bank notes thus issued,
effect no more than to drive out of circulation an equal amount
of safety fund bank notes; so that the operation ends by making
the community poorer than they were before in funds, to the
whole amount that has been invested in state stocks. Nor is

this quite all the mischief. The safety fund banks are so weakened by the loss of circulation, and the more rapid return than formerly, of what they issue, that they are compelled to reduce their loans to a much greater amount than the loans of the new banks can compensate for."

It requires little reflection to perceive that if the states, whose bonds have thus become the subjects of such large investments by the New York country banks, were to declare themselves bankrupt, the loss and misery would be unspeakably great, and I therefore consider that the different states are bound together, in some degree, by their debts; that a strong guaranty for good faith to the foreign creditor is implied in the interest which the American people themselves feel in preserving their public credit; and that this interest reaches the vast majority even of the Democratic voters. I therefore look forward to the states preserving their faith with their creditors, whether foreign or domestic.

Laws relative to Banking in the State of New York.—I have procured, by the kindness of a legal friend, a brief summary of the laws relative to banking in the State of New York, which I present in the Appendix No. XIV. Athough these banks were bound by law to redeem their circulating notes either in specie or by a draft on New York, yet, during the suspension of specie payments in Pennsylvania and the south and west in 1840, their paper fell to a discount of from 2 to 5 per cent.; and in May 1840 the comptroller of the state was almost daily bringing large amounts of stocks and other property deposited with him by " the Free Banks" to sale by public auction, to redeem their circulation; and in some instances the proceeds of the sales were not sufficient for this purpose.

The Manhattan Bank.—In December 1840, Mr. Robert White was tried in New York for the assault on Mr. Jonathan Thompson, already mentioned, and he was sentenced to pay a fine of $250, and to be imprisoned for fifteen days.

Negroes of the Amistad Schooner.—The trial which was to decide the fate of these negroes (see vol. ii. 138), took place in January 1840, and an appeal was entered to the Supreme Court of the United States. I have delayed noticing the decision, in the expectation of the appeal case being disposed of; but as I now learn that it will not be heard until long after my departure from the United States, I present the following summary of the District Judges.

" *Amistad Trial--Termination.*—Having just returned from New Haven, where, on behalf of the committee acting for the captured Africans, I have been attending the district court, I hand you an Extra of the New Haven Palladium containing the opinion of the Judge, of which the following is an abstract. The opinion is not very accurately printed, owing to its being done in haste, and in the night. On Wednesday, the Judge read an elaborate opinion, in which he decided:—

" 1. That the district court of Connecticut has jurisdiction, the schooner having been taken possession of in a legal sense on the ' high seas.'

" 2. That the libel of Thomas R. Gedney and others is properly filed in the district court of Connecticut.

" 3. That the seizers are entitled to salvage, and an appraisement will be ordered, and one-third of that amount and cost will be decreed just and reasonable.

" 4. That Green and Fordham of Sag-Harbor, who claim to have taken original possession of vessel and cargo, can not sustain their claim, and therefore their libels be dismissed.

" 5. That Ruez and Montez, through the Spanish Minister, have established no title to the Africans, as they are undoubtedly Bozal negroes, or negroes recently imported from Africa, in violation of the laws of Spain.

" 6. That the demand for restitution, to have the question tried in Cuba, made by the Spanish Minister, cannot be complied with, as, by their own laws, it is certain they cannot enslave these Africans, and therefore cannot properly demand them for trial.

" 7. That Antoine, being a Creole, and legally a slave, and expressing a strong wish to be returned to Havana, a resolution will be decreed under the treaty of 1795.

" 8. That these Africans be delivered to the President of the United States, under the 2d sect. of the act of March 3, 1839, and the 1st sect. of the law of 1818, still in force, to be transported to Africa, there to be delivered to the agents appointed to receive and conduct them home.

" 'The Court stands adjourned to meet at Hartford on the 23 d instant, and meantime the decree will not be entered, to give an opportunity to the parties to appeal, if they see fit.

" Respectfully yours,   '· Lewis Tappan.

[The opinion of Judge Judson in the Evening Palladium, fills nearly eight closely printed columns, the substance of which seems to be embodied in the abstract given above.] (a)

On the Spirit of British Legislation.—In the preceding pages of this work, I have spoken freely of the defects of American legislation, but it is instructive to compare it with that of our country. Before the passing of the Reform Act in 1832, the majority of the House of Commons was elected by the influence of the landed aristocracy; and as they also constituted the House

(a) The Supreme Court of the United States has declared that the negroes of the amistad shall be liberated.

of Peers, the legislature of the kingdom represented substantially only one class of the community. The middle ranks were able to return a few members to the House of Commons, who gave utterance to their sentiments and wishes, but who were powerless in protecting the rights of that portion of the nation against the power of the higher, while the lower orders were not represented at all. The few members elected by the freemen of some of the burghs cannot be named as representatives of the laboring population. In those days the Government of Great Britain was that of an aristocracy; and the following, among many others, are specimens of the spirit of their legislation.

In the reign of William III, the land-tax was fixed at 4s. in the pound upon the valuation of all real estate, and then yielded 1,997,000*l* annually. It amounted to about two-fifths of the whole public burdens, and it was equal to nominally one-fifth, but allowing for a low valuation, probably to one-sixth of the real land rents of the kingdom.

This tax has never been raised since the reign of William III; while the taxes which bear on the lower and middle classes have been enormously increased.

At the Union, the land-tax of Scotland was fixed at 48,000*l*., which amounted probably to one-third of the whole revenue of the country, and was probably equal to *one-fifth* of the real rents of the land-holders. It has never been augmented—it does not now exceed one-hundredth part of the real rents of the land; and it forms only about one-hundredth part of the taxes paid by the country. Sir John Sinclair* estimates it at twopence per pound, which is less than one per cent. on the rents.

The British Parliament imposed heavy inventory duties on the personal property of persons deceasing, when passing to their executors, but exempted real estate from this burden.

They imposed heavy legacy duties on personal property, but exempted real estate from them also.

They imposed a duty of 3s. per cent. on the *value* of all property *insured* by the subjects of Great Britain, but exempted *agricultural stock, produce, and implements*, from the tax.

They imposed taxes on dogs and horses, from which agriculturists, with few exceptions, have been exempted.

They imposed a heavy window tax, from which agricultural tenants who pay under 200*l*. a-year of rent are exempted.

They exempted real estate from attachment for personal debts, and this law has been only lately repealed.

They authorised entails, by means of which real estate is preserved to a series of heirs, unattachable by the claims of creditors.

* General Report, i, p. 109.

They authorised the impressment of seamen, and compelled them to serve in the navy for less wages than they could have obtained in the merchant's service; the effect of which was to deprive this class of persons of their liberty, and of the legitimate value of their labor, in order to protect the property, and save the pockets, of the rich.

They nominally compelled all ranks, when ballotted for, to serve in the militia, but made the fine for non-enrolment 20*l*. for each person. This was tantamount to the enactment of personal service by the poor, and exemption for the rich, because the fine was equal to half a year's income of a laboring man, while it did not exceed a week's income to the middle ranks, and not a day's income to the higher.

They prohibited the laboring classes from combining to raise the price of their labor, but left the higher classes at liberty to combine to depress it; and this law has only lately been repealed.

They prohibited the exportation of machinery, thus shutting out the product of the laborer's industry and skill from foreign markets: and only lately has this law been repealed.

They have imposed heavy duties on the importation of corn and other necessaries of life, the effect of which is to raise the rents of land at the expense of the consumers, who are the great body of the people. The tax on corn varies with the price of grain in the home market.

Under the present existing Corn Laws of Great Britain (Act 9th Geo. IV, cap. 60) the duty on Foreign wheat is as follows, viz:

When the average price of wheat is at and above

73*s*. 0*d*. per qr., duty is	1*s*. 0*d*. per qr.	On Flour	0	7	7.32 per bl.
72 0	2 8		1	7	1.4
71 0	6 8		4	0	1.8
70 0	10 8		6	5	
69 0	13 8		8	2	21.32
68 0	16 8		10	0	5.16
67 0	18 8		11	2	3.4
66 0	20 8		12	5	3.16
65 0	21 8		13	0	13.32
64 0	22 8		13	7	5.8
63 0	23 8		14	2	27.32
62 0	24 8		14	10	1.6
61 0	25 8		15	5	9.32
60 0	26 8		16	0	1.2
59 0	27 8		16	7	23.32
58 0	28 8		17	2	15.16
57 0	29 8		17	10	5.32
56 0	30 8		18	5	3.8
55 0	31 8		19	0	19.32
54 0	32 8		19	7	26.32
53 0	33 8		20	3	1.32
52 0	34 8		20	10	1.4

51	0	-	-	35	8	-	-	-	21	5	15 32
50	0	-	-	36	8	-	-	-	22	0	22 32
49	0	-	-	37	8	-	-	-	22	7	29.32
48	0	-	-	38	8	-	-	-	23	3	1.8
47	0	-	-	39	8	-	-	-	23	10	11.32
46	0	-	-	40	8	-	-	-	24	5	9.16
45	0	-	-	41	8	-	-	-	25	0	25.32
44	0	-	-	42	8	-	-	-	25	8	
43	0	-	-	43	8	-	-	-	26	7	7.32

On bar'ey and Indian corn, if the average price is 33s. and under 31s. the duty is 12s. 4d. per imperial quarter, and for every 1s. per quarter of advances in price the duty is increased 1s. 6d., until it reaches 41s. per quarter, at which price and upwards, no more than 1s. per quarter is levied, and the duty increases in like manner 1s. 6d. per quarter as the price declines 1s. or part of 1s. under 33s. per quarter. On oats, if the average price is 25s. and under 26s., the duty is 9s. 3d. per quarter, decreasing 1s. 6d. per quarter as the average price advances 1s. until it reaches 31s., when at that price or more the duty is only 1s. per quarter, and in like manner it is increased 1s. 6d. per quarter for every 1s. or part of 1s. per quarter the average recedes below 25s. to 24s. per imperial quarter.

The import duties on the following articles, are, I believe, stationary. They show a tendency of the landowners to avail themselves of political power to promote their own interests, by excluding foreign competition:—

	£.	s.	d.
Bacon, per cwt. -	1	8	0
Beer, per 32 gallons,	2	13	0
Butter, per cwt. -	1	0	0
Cider, per ton,	21	10	4
Cheese, per cwt. -	0	10	6
Cucumbers, *ad valorem*,	20	0	0
Hops, per cwt. -	8	11	0
Hay, per load,	1	4	0
Hemp, dressed, per cwt. -	4	15	0
Oil, Rape, and Linseed, per ton,	39	18	0
Perry, per ton, -	22	13	8
Potatoes, per cwt.	0	2	0
Seeds, Clover, &c.	1	0	0
Spirits, foreign, per gallon, (I. M.)	1	2	6
Timber, per load,	2	15	0

Beef, lambs, mutton, pork, sheep, and swine, are prohibited to be imported.

A high duty is laid on rice, arrow-root, and sago, in order to encourage the use of British corn and potatoes.

A duty of £1. 2s. 6d. per gallon is levied on brandy, and 9s. 6d. per gallon on rum, in order to encourage, or rather force, the use

of British spirits, which must be made from British grain, and
pay high duties of excise.

While they have thus protected land from a due share of taxation, and have enhanced its value by prohibitory duties, at the
expense of the people, they have not scrupled to throw a vast
amount of taxation on the non-represented masses.

Under the Reform Act the non-electors (including all the males
of 21 years of age and upwards) are to the electors in England
as 5 to 1, in Scotland as 7 to 1; and in Ireland probably as 14 to
1. The average of the whole United Kingdom is that the non-
electors are to the electors as $8\frac{2}{3}$ to 1. The average of Great
Britain, exclusive of Ireland, is 6 to 1.*

In 1831 the population of Great Britain, exclusive of Ireland,
was 16,500,000. Of this number, about eleven millions were
workmen, agricultural or manufacturing, including their families;
and all the other classes, including their families, amounted to the
remainder, or five and a half millions. In this estimate the
word "workmen" is used as including those only who hire their
labor to masters for wages, and their families, and not those who
labor directly on their own account, or their families.

The first requisite of life is food, the second clothing, the third
comforts, and then come luxuries. Taxation is founded in
justice, in proportion as it absorbs equal portions of the incomes
of all classes. If all the taxes, direct and indirect, paid by a
family which spends 1000*l.* a year, amount to 200*l.*, and all
those paid by a family which expends 50*l.* a year amount to
10*l.*, the ratio of taxation is just. But the British taxation is
imposed to so great an extent on the *necessaries* of life, that a
very large portion of the laborer's income is absorbed by it, in
comparison with that of the rich man. Nine-tenths of a laborer's
income must be expended on food and clothing, while probably
not the tenth part of a rich man's income is devoted to these
objects. The unrepresented eleven millions of laborers, therefore, not only pay a very large portion of the following duties
because they are most numerous and the great consumers, but
the duties bear a larger proportion to *their* incomes than the
taxes which affect the rich bear to theirs.

1. *Sugar*, a necessary of life, pays 24*s.* a cwt., equal to the
prime cost of the article if it be the produce of British colonies,
while 63*s.* is charged on all foreign sugars whatever. On 25th
May 1829, Mr. Huskisson, in his place in the House of Commons, said, "that, owing to the present enormous duty on sugar,
he did not go too far when he stated that *two-thirds of the poor-*

---

* I am indebted to my esteemed friend, Dr. Thomas Murray, Lecturer on
Political Economy, for the above and other calculations in this section.

er consumers of coffee drank that beverage without sugar."
The rich scarcely feel the pressure of the duty.

2. *Tea.* The duty on tea, also a necessary of life, is 2s. 1d.
per lb., equal to 200 per cent. on Bohea, and it affects the poor
much more heavily than the rich.

3. *Coffee.* The duty is 6d. per lb. when imported from our
own colonies; but 1s. 3d. when from any foreign country. The
same remark applies to it.

4. *Soap.* This is an indispensable necessary of life to all
classes, and the want of it is the direct cause of disease: yet the
manufacture of it is impeded by excise restrictions; the materials
of which it is made, tallow, barilla, and turpentine, are loaded
with duties, and a direct tax is charged upon it, making in all a
charge upon it equal to sixty or seventy per cent. *ad valorem.*
The importation of it is *prevented* by a custom-house duty of 4l.
10s. per cwt. on hard soap, and 3l. 11s. 3d. on soft.

The following articles may be regarded as the *luxuries* of the
poor, which they chiefly consume, and on which they pay the
legal duties in a proportion far exceeding the ratio of their numbers to those of the rich, because the rich use them to a very
limited extent.

5. *Tobacco and Snuff.* The duty on these amounts, in ordinary years, to 3,400,000l.

6. *Home-made Spirits.* The duty on these, including Ireland, is upwards of 5,000,000l. per annum.

7. *Malt Liquors.* These may almost be regarded as necessaries of life in the humbler ranks. The duty on them has
amounted in some years to upwards of 5,000,000l. per annum.(a)

The general result is, that the taxes levied on spirits, malts,
hops, corn, soap, sugars, and molasses,—tea, coffee, tobacco,
and snuff, amount annually to about 26,000,000l. odds, and are
paid chiefly by the laboring and middle classes. The land-tax,
window-duties, and taxes on servants, horses, dogs, carriages,
and other minor duties, which are borne exclusively by the upper
and middle classes, do not exceed 4,000,000l. yearly.

Here, then, while the humbler classes in Britain are excluded
from all influence over the legislature, we perceive that the
classes above them, who have monopolised the privilege of conducting the government and law-making, have so managed the

(a) Luxuries, the direct enjoyment of which serves more or less to impair
the health and strength of the people, cannot be taxed too heavily. Of this
nature are the articles enumerated in the three preceding paragraphs in the
text. If tobacco, spirits, and malt liquors could be taxed out of use, and,
in their stead, abundant fruits and the allowably sensual enjoyments of public
gardens and squares, and of music were made common or easily accessible to
all, a nation would gain in the improved health, morals and happiness of its
people.

public affairs that they have created the necessity for levying taxes to the amount of fifty millions of pounds annually to pre-serve the national faith and honor—that they have exempted themselves to an extraordinary extent from these burdens—that they have imposed them unsparingly on the unrepresented classes; and, finally, that they have prohibited the unrepresented from purchasing agricultural produce in foreign markets, where it can be obtained at low prices, in order to increase the revenues of their own estates.

Farther, the criminal law of Great Britain and Ireland, which has been enacted by the rich, and applied chiefly against the poor, was long atrociously unjust and severe, and still retains too much of the same character. If the reader will peruse the Prison Reports which are now made to the Secretary of State for the Home Department, he will see that neglected children of twelve, fourteen, and fifteen years of age are condemned to trans-portation or imprisonment for periods of seven and ten years for petty thefts. In the " Reports relating to Parkhurst Prison (Isle of Wight) for 1840," one of the most judiciously conducted prisons in the kingdom, I find: Prisoner, No. 7. "Age—15." " Offence—*stealing a sovereign.*" "Sentence—*seven years.*" "In custody—*once.*" "Convicted or imprisoned—*once.*" "Father—*living.*" "Mother—*dead.*" " Character which ac-companied the prisoner—*good; connections respectable,*" "Re-marks—*temptation through master's carelessness, and tempta-tion of fellow-servant.*" p. 11. This is only one of many cases of a similar nature. The treatment of prisoners has been of the most debasing description (see vol. ii, p, 187), and the people have been too often ruled as with a rod of iron. Since the Reform Bill was passed there has been an amendment in the condition of prisons and the treatment of prisoners and also in the criminal law; but much remains to be accomplished before this branch of our civil administration shall become worthy of a civilised and Christian people.

The Legislature has refused adequate grants for the education of the people. Considering that the national debt was incurred exclusively under the administration of the aristocracy, and that its existence is the cause of much of our heavy taxation, it would be an equitable arrangement to apply the 8,400,000*l.* raised annually from tobacco, snuff, and home-made spirits (the luxuries, and, in my opinion, the injurious luxuries of the labor-ing classes), to the education of the people, and to raise a corres-ponding sum by imposing inventory duties, legacy duties, and direct taxes on real estate.

As the law now stands, the unrepresented masses are able to influence the classes who make the laws only in two ways, either by outrages against social order and property, which are speedily repressed and punished, or by becoming burdens on them as paupers. I am far from believing that legislation can remove all the evils with which the lower classes in Great Britain and Ireland are afflicted, and much farther from recommending universal suffrage as the remedy even for those which legislation may reach. I have elsewhere* said that " no rational person will maintain that one ignorant man is a proper ruler for a great nation, but additions to numbers do not alter the species. Twenty, or a hundred, or a thousand ignorant men, are not wiser than one of them; while they are much more dangerous. They inflame each other's passions, keep each other's follies in countenance, and add to each other's strength."———

I acknowledge also that the great cause of the prosperity of the people in the United States appears to me to be their contiguity to extensive regions of fertile and unsettled land, which drain off the restless and enterprising spirits from all the older states, absorb the population as fast as it increases, pour in plenty to every market, and still preserve the wages of labor high. I met with few British subjects, who, however much they might have advocated universal suffrage at home, continued to admire it after experiencing its effects in the United States. But while I make these admissions, I regard it as undeniable, that just and wise legislation is capable of accomplishing much to benefit— and partial and unwise legislation much to injure, a people; and it appears to me that British legislation is probably both unjust and injurious to the unrepresented masses. The Established churches in the three kingdoms have not yet succeeded in inducing the higher classes, whose laws created and support them, to practise the first and fundamental precept of Christianity towards the people, " Love your neighbor as yourself;" and if centuries of teaching of the Gospel, by the most pious and learned of mankind, have been so unsuccessful in this respect, it is not unreasonable at length to try the effect of additional means.

The despotisms of Austria and Prussia are in many respect† less injurious to the people than the government of Britain.‡ The rulers of these countries do not oppress the people with taxes, and leave the rich free; nor do they deliver over the poor to become the uncontrolled subjects of the legislation of the rich. Physically, therefore. they do not injure the masses so deeply.

* Moral Philosophy, Chap. 7.
† The influence of these governments on the minds of their subjects is treated of in the next chapter. With respect to taxes, I may notice, that in France, Germany, Austria, and other continental states, the chief burden of them is borne by land. The *Contribution Foncière* in France is a permanent property-tax of about 10 per cent. on land and houses.

Again, these rulers prevent political and social action in *all*
classes of their subjects; and the minds of the people become
so far dormant as to be in some degree in harmony with their
external condition.   In Britain, the most ample scope for political and social action is permitted to the higher and middle
classes, but to the people none.   Their minds, however, are
agitated and roused by the vivacity of mental action which exists
around them, and they feel their own exclusion from the exercise
of political power far more keenly than the Austrian people,
who, in this respect, see themselves on a level with the noble
and the rich.   It is a delusion to suppose, that, because the
higher ranks are open to receive individuals from the lower,
there is no abridgement of their field of political action.   Only
men of superior talents can emerge from the lower, and take a
place in the upper ranks, and, as the masses do not boast of
more than average abilities, this liberty of rising can benefit only
a few individuals.   Besides, while the present state of social
arrangement continues, the men of superior minds of their own
class are tempted, when they acquire wealth, to leave them, and
to assume the prejudices and dislikes of the higher orders, the
more effectually to recommend themselves to their new associates.

I have endeavored, in this work, to expound the principle,
that mental action is the first requisite to moral and intellectual
improvement.   If we expect to confer, on the British people,
intelligence—we must educate them; if self-restraint—we must
intrust them with political power, and train them to use it.   It
appears to me, therefore, that retaining the two Houses of Parliament as at present constituted, a limited representation might,
with safety and advantage, be granted to the people.   The objections to remodelling the House of Commons, and introducing
universal suffrage for all the members, are formidable.   The
majority of the people in Great Britain and Ireland are uneducated, possessed of little property, and untrained to political
action.   A legislative assembly which should represent and give
effect to their feelings and ideas, would probably lead directly
to anarchy.   Both in physical circumstances and mental enlightenment, they are inferior to the majority in America; yet even
in America the people are not prepared to do justice to their
institutions.   Universal suffrage in that country is attended with
many evils; and I therefore should deprecate its adoption in
Britain, at present, as dangerous to the best interests of society.
To household suffrage, or any other limited representation,
there would be this objection, that it would still leave a large
non-represented class, which would become more discontented
and impatient, the nearer it was brought to the line which sepa-

rated it from the represented. To leave the people unrepresented, and to attempt to perpetuate the selfish reign of the upper classes, is neither desirable nor praticable. The working classes are God's creatures, and are as well entitled to justice as the higher ranks. By the peculiar institutions of this country, the middle classes have been trained to admire and act with the higher; but when their eyes are thoronghly opened to the injustice which has been inflicted on the lower, this idol-worship will cease. Besides, the increasing intelligence of the laboring classes will render their calls for justice irresistible.

If we assume, then, the population of Great Britain and Ireland to amount to twenty four millions, and that the non-electors are to the electors as eight to one; this will give twenty-one millions of unrepresented persons in the whole of the United Kingdom; or, to obtain round numbers, we may assume them to amount to twenty millions. Suppose the kingdom were divided into 100 districts, each containing a population of 200,000 unrepresented persons. If universal suffrage, limited only by requiring in an elector six months' residence within his ward or county previous to an election—freedom from conviction for felony —and twenty-one years of age, were established, and the power of electing one member of the House of Commons were given to each district, the following results might be expected probably to ensue:—The mental faculties of the laboring classes would be provided with a legitimate field of political action, which I consider useful in prompting them to improve their moral and intellectual condition. There would be no non-represented class to foment secret discontent and resistance to the laws: There would be no danger of anarchy, because the members who represent the property of the country would still constitute a large majority in Parliament. The laboring classes would have legitimate organs in the legislature capable not only of making their grievances known, but of obtaining, to some extent, the redress of them: In all measures regarding which the representatives of property were nearly equally divided, these hundred members could cast the scale on the side which was most favorable to the people. The higher classes, seeing the people possessed of political power, would be prompted by their own interest, as in the United States, to respect them more, to do them justice, and to assist in elevating their moral and physical condition, and thus by slow degrees our vicious system might be purified, and the British Constitution be adapted to the wants of increasing civilisation. The House of Commons is already too numerous; and probably 100 members might well be spared from its present number, whose places might well be supplied by the representatives of the people. *Property* would still have five and a half votes to one, even supposing these representatives to be disposed to assail it, which is far from being a probable occurrence.

Whatever may be thought of these suggestions, my humble opinion is, that the present condition of affairs in Britain is so palpably unjust and injurious to the masses, that its permanence is impossible, consistently with man's rational nature, and the obligations of Christianity. Those persons, therefore, who regard the Reform Act as a final measure seem blind to the nature of man, and unaware of the age of the world in which they live. It was obviously only the *beginning* of improvement: If it be not, then, in the words of Jefferson, "I tremble for my country when I reflect that God is just;—his justice cannot sleep for ever."

Return to England.—On the 1st June 1840, we sailed from New York in the British Queen. In leaving the American shores we were agitated by profound emotion, awakened not only by parting from many dear and highly valued friends, but by an overwhelming impression of the grandeur of the moral experiment which is now in progress in the United States. Glorious and cheering hopes for its success mingled with fears lest it may have been begun too soon. As we receded from the scene, however, we reflected that Providence has granted to this people for their moral training and intellectual improvement, the period between the present day, and that on which their vacant lands shall be fully settled, and that existing circumstances indicate that they will employ this interval with a deep sense of its importance, and in the end prove true to themselves and to the cause of universal freedom. As we bounded over the sea to the home of our fathers, Hope joined with the understanding in lending bright colors to the future destiny of the land which we had left. We had a prosperous and agreeable voyage; and so admirable were the accommodations of the British Queen, and so full of urbanity and attention her commander Captain Roberts and her other officers, that we left the deck of a ship for the first time in our lives with regret. We arrived at Portsmouth on the 16th, and in London on the 17th of June. It is only justice to England to say that, in passing my multifarious effects through the Custom House of London, I experienced the same facilities and attentions which I have mentioned as afforded to us in Boston. The subject of the next chapter is an address to the people of the United States, which I have been led to believe may be useful, and with which I close this work.

CHAPTER XI.

The Application of Phrenology to the Present and Prospective Con lition of the United States.*

1840

To the Citizens of the United States:

I have visited various European countries, Prussia, Austria, Bavaria, Holland, France, and Switzerland, besides the British Isles, for the purpose of observing the condition of the people living under different forms of civil and ecclesiastical government, and one of the motives which led me to repair to your shores was to obtain the means of judging of the influence of democracy on the physical prosperity and mental condition of your nation. I am deeply sensible of the sources of error to which a stranger is exposed in observing and speculating on the institutions of a foreign country; but you will be able to detect and correct the errors regarding your own country into which I may inadvertently fall, and I may be permitted to hope that amidst these will be found some admixture of truth.

The people of the United States are justly proud of their political independence, won at the expense of many sacrifices; and also of the institutions which the distinguished founders of their government framed and bequeathed to them for their guidance; but if I were to ask different Americans in what the superiority of these institutions consists, I should receive a multifarious variety of answers. Does Phrenology enable us to attain to any precise views on the subject?

In my previous lectures, I have endeavored to explain to you that happiness consists in the activity of our faculties, and that the greater the number of them called into action, the higher rises our enjoyment. Any object that should delight the eye would be agreeable; but an assemblage of objects that should

---

* This Chapter contains a great part of my last Lecture on Phrenology, delivered before thirteen different audiences, and which I was frequently solicited to publish. There are a few omissions and some additions; but the substance and arrangement are essentially preserved. My American readers will find a full, able, and accurate report of the entire course of lectures, prepared and published, by my respected friend Dr. Andrew Boardman of New York.

simultaneously gratify the eye, the ear, the palate, and the senses
of touch and smell, would be universally regarded as yielding a
still larger measure of gratification, and so with the internal
faculties of the mind. There are three conditions, however,
under which this activity must exist to render it productive of
the greatest amount of happiness. *First*, It must never exceed
the limits of health; *Secondly*, The subordination of the inferior
to the superior faculties established by nature must be preserved;
and, *Thirdly*, The action of the different faculties must be har-
monious. The highest enjoyment, therefore, is produced by
the *virtuous activity of all the faculties*. The question then,
presents itself—What effects do different forms of government
exercise on the activity of the mental faculties?*

We may consider, *First*, the influence of a despotic form of
government; and I select Austria as an example of a civilised
despotism. In Austria, the emperor is at once the fountain of
the laws and the executive power which carries them into effect.
His will rules the empire, and is subject to no constitutional
control on the part of the people. The religion of the state is
Roman Catholic; and the pope and priests rule as despotically in
ecclesiastical as the emperor does in temporal affairs. Nevertheless, the Austrian is a civilised despotism, and rests essentially on opinion. The emperor is not a tyrant ruling by means
of dungeons and bayonets. He is more like the father of his
people: he may be seen walking among them without military
guards, or other means of protection, safe in their reverence and
affections. I have seen the present emperor going to church in
the town of Ischl, attended by a servant carrying his prayer
book, and two or three gentlemen of his household, so unosten-
tatiously that when he passed as near to me as I am now to
you, I could not have discovered his rank, if I had not been told
that he was the sovereign of Austria. Austria, moreover, is
governed by laws, and the emperor acknowledges that, in regard
to rights of property, these bind him as well as his subjects. In
the village of Baden, about twenty miles from Vienna, where
there are celebrated baths, the emperor is proprietor of a house
in an ordinary street, in which he resides when he visits the
springs. The house is in no respect distinguishable in its ex-
terior from those on each side of it. I was told that the late
Emperor Francis found it too small, and wished to purchase the
contiguous tenement; but that the owner asked an enormous
price. The emperor would not submit to what he considered

* The reader who is not familiar with the phrenological faculties is respectfully requested to read the list of them presented at the end of the Introduction, in vol. i, with their uses and abuses, which will render this
Chapter more clear and interesting.

an imposition, and the proprietor, to force him to his terms, let it for a sort of club-house or tavern. The emperor made no complaint, but insisted that the laws of decorum and propriety should be observed by the inmates; and when I saw it in 1837, I was assured that it still continued the property of the individual. In the same year I saw the present emperor and his household, living in a common street in Ischl. He had purchased or hired four ordinary dwelling-houses standing together, and, by internal communications, converted them into one; but in no respect did they differ, in their external aspect, from those of the other inhabitants of the same quarter of the town. I mention these unimportant details to convey to you an idea of the spirit of the Austrian Government as it exists in the emperor's hereditary states, because many individuals in America, from reading descriptions of its rule in its conquered Italian provinces, imagine it to be everywhere a despotism of fire and sword.

In what respect, then, does this government favor or permit the activity of the mental faculties of its subjects? Viewing the group which constitutes the domestic affections, I answer that it allows them ample scope: Life and property are secure, the soil is reasonably fertile, and industry abounds: The Austrian subjects, therefore, may enjoy the happiness of conjugal life and domestic affection as perfectly as you do under your democratic institutions. Again, looking at the propensities of Acquisitiveness, Self-Esteem, and Love of Approbation, those mainsprings of exertion in the United States, the Austrian is allowed scope for them all. The farmer, the manufacturer, and the merchant, may accumulate and preserve wealth in Austria as in America; distinctions of rank are recognised, and the field of ambition is open for men to rise from humbler to higher grades: By public service and the favor of the emperor, nobility even may be obtained.

What, then, is wanting? In what respect does the Austrian Government, as a means of diffusing enjoyments and advancing the civilisation of its subjects, fall short of yours? In this—that extremely little scope is allowed for the action of the moral and intellectual faculties beyond the sphere of private life. Man is a social being, and the field of public interests is the one in which his higher powers expand and find their appropriate objects. In Austria this field is shut up to the people, and is appropriated exclusively by the government. The Austrian people do not manage their own schools and colleges, the affairs of their own towns, and counties, or appoint their own civil and military officers; nor do they choose their own religious instructors, as you do. The government performs all these duties for them. But Phrenology shows us that the very fundamental element of happiness is *activity*, and that the higher the faculties which are vividly employed, the more intense and lasting is the pleasure. Now, when man pursues private and domestic objects only, he gratifies chiefly his propensities, which are selfish and inferior in their nature to his moral faculties: It is when he comes forth into the circle of social life, and becomes an agent in producing public good or evil, that his higher powers begin freely to play. A single incident will serve as an example:—The Emperor lately issued an edict intimating that as his subjects had been injured by accidents occurring on railroads, he will levy a fine of 10,000 florins on the directors of the railroad company for every person who shall in future be injured; and if this shall prove insufficient to arrest the evil, he will suppress the railroad altogether. This edict may in itself be wise and paternal; but the power which issued it has no legal limits. And even this, in my opinion, is not its worst feature. In your democracy, in such a case, you would put into action a grand jury, an attorney-general, a judge, a common jury, and many lawyers, and finally the legislature, before you could accomplish the ends reached by the simple edict of the Emperor; and the advantage of all this social machinery does not end merely in protecting your people from oppression: It exercises, and, by exercise, strengthens and carries forward the moral and intellectual faculties of your citizens. The impulse given to the intellect and moral faculties by one of your trials, does not terminate in the court-house, any more than a lesson ends in the school. In both instances the ideas and the activity communicated, remain in the mind, and the individual is wiser and better in consequence. He follows his private vocation with more effect, rules his family better, and altogether stands forth a more amply developed rational creature, when trained to use his powers in the important arena of social life. This is the grand effect produced by your institutions, which allow you to manage every interest of the community yourselves.

If an Austrian subject, under the influence of powerful benevolence and enlightened intellect, desire to improve the schools, the roads, the police of his town, the laws, or the mode of administering public offices, the government arrests him in every effort, unless he be employed by itself. If, under the influence of Conscientiousness, Veneration, and enlightened intellect, he wish to purify the religion of his country, he is silenced by priests whom the civil power supports in the exercise of a complete despotism over religious opinion. For instance, in 1839 the Church of Scotland sent the Rev. Mr. McCheyne, the Rev. Mr. Bonar, the Rev. Dr. Keith, and the Rev. Dr. Black, to Jerusalem to inquire into the condition of the Jews. They returned through Constantinople, Moldavia, Wallachia, and Austria, making investigations into the state of the Jews wherever they went. On the 20th November, 1839, the Rev. Mr. McCheyne, in reporting the proceedings of the deputation to the commission of the General Assembly of the Church, informed them that " in Austria, the government will suffer no missionaries. There we were treated with the utmost severity. All our Bibles, our English, our Hebrew, our German Bibles were taken away, our papers were searched to see if they could discover whether we were missionaries, and what were our intentions. In that country it is out of the question to carry the gospel to the poor misguided population. A missionary might stand up for once, but it would be for the first and the last time. There they would not allow you to preach the gospel even to the Jews, who were most ready to receive us; and though they knew they could bring us into difficulty, and get us sent out of the country immediately, we found their synagogue a sanctuary. A Jew, to whom a Bible had been given, said in his own tongue, ' none shall see it; none shall see it,' and, so far as the Jews are concerned, they are open for the preaching of the gospel."*

Education is the first means by which the faculties may be roused into activity. It not only furnishes them with the materials of thought, but wakens and calls forth their latent energies. The Austrian Government assumes the control of education, and permits just so much of it to reach the minds of its subjects as will fit them for their condition. The people are instructed in the Roman Catholic as the only true religion, and are taught to look upon themselves as bound to yield implicit obedience to the priests and the emperor. They are allowed to learn mathematics, Greek, and Latin; but moral and political subjects are interdicted, because, where imperfection is detected, these lead to efforts for improvement. If an individual see any

* These complaints come with rather a bad grace from the clergy of the Church of Scotland, because the General Assembly has long had a committee of its own members specially charged with the duty of watching, and, as far as lies in their power, preventing, the spread of Roman Catholicism in Scotland. From the spirit of their reports, I am led to fear that, if they wielded the same temporal power which the Roman Catholic Church does in Austria, they would serve a deputation of bishops sent from Rome by the Pope to convert the Scottish people and Jews to their faith, much in the same manner as the Austrians did them; and, like the Austrians, they would not doubt that, in dealing with them in this manner, they were contributing to the glory of God and the salvation of souls. I can make no distinction between sects, when they organise themselves with the special object of watching and obstructing the progress of each other. Perfect freedom of discussion, and the absence of all pains, penalties, disabilities, and dislikes, are, in my humble opinion, indispensable to the eliciting and diffusing of religious truth

thing wrong in the social machinery, he is not encouraged to complain of it even to the government. Any servant, except the highest and most confidential of the Austrian emperor, who should say that things are better elsewhere, and suggest improvements at home, would be told that he might leave Austria and go into his own Utopia. The government will not permit its subjects even to reside in other countries, to obtain a higher education than their own schools afford. If an individual were to ask a passport to carry his son to France, Switzerland, or England, to complete his education, it would be refused, and he would be asked, " Why should you send your son abroad to spend your money and imbibe false notions? Our schools and colleges are sufficient to teach all that a good subject needs to know."

The general effect of this form of government, then, is, that it is fitted to render happy all the humbler class of minds, those individuals who have neither desire nor talents to extend their efforts beyond the private sphere; but that it chains up, and thereby obstructs the enjoyment of the men of powerful intellect and high moral endowments, whose sphere of action is public life. The nobler the mind, the more heavily does the leaden load of despotism weigh upon its powers. Farther, it imposes fetters on the general mind of the nation, and retards progression. The government must move before the people are allowed to stir; and where all rational motives for progression are withdrawn from it, its advance must be slow, or if its pace be accidentally quickened by the genius of an individual sovereign, the effects of his liberality and energy are lost, because the people are not prepared to follow in the path which he opens to them.

The government of Prussia was in much the same state as that of Austria, until it was overthrown by Napoleon in the war of 1807. After its restoration, however, it saw its error. Under the old regime, its subjects had been kept in such profound ignorance, and so thoroughly oppressed, that they possessed neither mental energy nor national feeling, and so fell an easy prey to the invading French. It became the interest of the government to rouse its people from this lethargy, and to excite sentiments of patriotism. This was accomplished by making the serfs free, and instituting a system of universal and comparatively high education. The effects of the change were marvellous· In one generation Prussia stood forth a regenerated nation—full of energy, activity, intelligence, and profound national feeling. But the form of the government was little changed. It continues to be a despotism, but a more liberal and a much more enlightened despotism than that of Austria. The education which it provides for its people is superior to that of any other country in Europe, and I believe superior to any which even you can boast of. The government is well administered. It regulates every thing, but it does it well. Its police and custom-house officers are civil gentlemanly men; its post-office department is regular and safe, but it opens letters without scruple when it wants political information; it keeps the stage-coaches, post-horses, and roads of the state in excellent condition, but it monopolises them all. If, however, a single passenger more than the stage will carry presents himself at the hour appointed for its starting, another vehicle is instantly provided for him. The laws are just, and impartially administered. Life and property are as safe as in any country in the world; industry is fostered, and learning and philosophy are patronised. In what, then, is the Prussian government inferior to yours?

I have said that happiness is the result of the activity of all the faculties. The Prussian government, while it does every thing *for* the people, and does it well, allows the people to do exceedingly little for themselves. It educates them, and elicits talent, but it allows that talent little scope in the social circle, except in its own service. It permits the towns to choose some of their municipal officers, but their number and powers are small. A few simple illustrations will enable you to judge of the restrictions which this government imposes on the activity of the higher faculties of the mind. When I visited Prussia in 1837, one serious evil in their educational system had begun to develope itself. The education of females under the national system has been so much inferior to that of the males, that a body of young women has grown up who are strikingly behind the men of the same generation in general intelligence and accomplishments. The consequence of this inequality in mental attainments is a diminution in that respect for women, which has long been a beautiful feature in the Prussian character. The cause of this evil was understood and regretted by many persons; but it was whispered in society, that the government was more inclined to diminish the education of the men than to increase that of the women. "But," said I to a Prussian gentleman, "why do not your enlightened men themselves institute higher schools for females?" "You speak," said he, "like a Briton. Here nothing can be done without the government. Should any private individuals attempt to establish improved academies for female education without the sanction of government, they would speedily be stopped." The people are not allowed to meet for the discussion of public affairs. Missionary and other religious and benevolent societies exist, but their rules are first sanctioned by the government, and then police spies are sent to their meetings to see that they do not transgress them. Again, the government is so enlightened that its censors of the press will permit the higher minds to publish works of a liberal cast, even on government itself, provided they employ reason, and resort neither to ridicule nor inflammatory declamation, in order to rouse the people to action; and provided also that the books appear in the form of octavo volumes of not less than 300 pages. They do not fear the philosophers of Berlin, and of a few other cities, who alone will read such works; but if any man were to move faster than the government, and to propose plans of practical reform for which it was not prepared, it would immediately arrest his progress. In short, under this monarchy, as under the empire of Austria, self-action in regulating social interests is denied to the people, and the object of the government is to draw into its own service all the energy, talent, and attainments of the nation, and to leave the mass the passive recipients of its impressions. It desires intelligence in the masses, because it needs mind and energy for its own defence against hostile nations; but it refuses to allow free scope to the mind and energy which it has evoked, lest they should subvert its own authority, and introduce self-government. Here, therefore, as in Austria, commonplace persons are happy; but the higher minds are cribbed and limited in their natural and best spheres of action, except when enlisted by the government in its own service. As civilisation must be measured chiefly by the intelligence, power of self-action and self-control of the masses, the Prussian government, by denying the right of political action to the people, limits their advance in mental improvement. It, however, allows religious freedom; for men of all forms of faith are equally eligible to fill public offices.

Let us now advert to the government of Great Britain and Ireland. That country has enjoyed political liberty for centuries, and claims to be the parent of your freedom. In Britain we enjoy the right to say and print what we please, in what form we see proper, and also to go where, and to do what, our own inclinations dictate, on the simple condition that, in pursuing our own gratifications, we shall not unjustly interfere with the rights of our neighbors. We may worship God, also, in any manner that appears to our own consciences to be most acceptable to the Divine Majesty. Life and property are secure, and the paths to wealth and honor are open to all. In Britain, then, it may be supposed that every faculty has as ample a scope for action as in the United States; but there are two bulwarks which arrest, or misdirect, the activity of the intellectual powers and higher sentiments of the people. The first of these is the hereditary peerage, invested with political power and special privileges. It maintains in possession of great legislative, moral, and political influence, a body of men who owe their superiority, not to personal attainments, but to birth alone. If man be a rational being, the objects of his reverence, and the standards by which he forms his manners and opinions, should possess the highest natural gifts, most assiduously and successfully cultivated. A hereditary peerage presents to the public mind of Great Britain and Ireland, standards which do not possess these attributes of natural and acquired superiority. It, therefore, obscures the moral perceptions of the middle and lower ranks, by training them to pay that profound homage to high birth which is due alone to intelligence and virtue. By its influence it also misdirects the ambition of the aspiring minds in all the lower grades, and renders them more desirous to be admitted into its ranks, by any means, them to merit distinction for superior wisdom and morality. It is not open, as a matter of right, to all, but is to be attained by favor, with or without merit. It maintains a class so far removed from contact with, interest in, or dependence upon, the mass of the people, that it is little moved by their sufferings, and little disposed to elevate their moral and intellectual condition, or to do them justice in the exercise of its legislative powers. (See page 310—320.)

The hereditary peerage operates injuriously also on the lower and middle classes of society, by leading their active and ambitious members to turn away from their fellows whom they should protect and advance, and to adopt the interests and prejudices of the aristocracy, into whose ranks they aspire to gain admission.

The second obstacle to the free action of the mind in Britain is the existence of established churches. These have consecrated opinions formed, in the dawn of modern civilisation, by theologians who partook much more of the character of monks and school-men than of that of philosophers or practical men of the world, and these opinions stand immovably enacted and ordained by Parliament as the legal guides to salvation, against which advancing reason and science employ their demonstrations in vain. A vast priesthood, amply endowed to maintain these opinions, resist improvement as innovation, and denounce free inquiry as profanity and infidelity. The consequence is the reign of hypocrisy, and the prostration of the religious sentiments by many individuals at the shrines of interest and ambition.

To avoid the charge of misrepresenting the state of Christianity in the British Isles, I present you with the following description of it given by the Reverend Baden Powell, Savilian

Professor of Geometry in the University of Oxford, in his work on " The Connection of Natural and Divine Truth," published in 1838.

" Too many nominal Christians entertain only the most miserable idea of the nature of the Gospel they profess to believe; their only notion too often consists in a confused general impression of a certain sacredness in Scripture, which produces little effect beyond that of making them afraid to enter its precincts, and search its recesses for themselves, and yet more fearful lest its sanctity should be invaded by others. And their dread of openly encountering any contradictions, and their anxious desire to shelter themselves under even the most frivolous explanations, if it does not betray a lurking distrust of the proper evidences of their faith, at least evinces the lowest and most unworthy conceptions of the spirit and meaning of the Bible, and an almost total absence of due distinction between the design and application of the several portions of which it is made up.

" With others again, the sincere, but (as we must consider it) misguided spirit of religious fanaticism, produces similar effects. Blinded to all but the internal light of his spiritual impressions, the enthusiast will always entertain a deeply-rooted and devoted hostility against any such distinctions as those here advocated. Maintaining the literal application of every sentence, every syllable of the divine Word, he rejects, as impious, the slightest departure from it. Human reason, along with all science, which is its offspring, is at best carnal and unsanctified, and should any of its conclusions be advanced in contradiction to the letter of a scriptural text, this completely seals its condemnation as absolutely sinful, and equivalent to a rejection of revelation altogether.

" In such cases we may most readily make every allowance due to sincerity, however mistaken. But there are other instances, in which, unfortunately, little claim to such indulgence can be found. There are some who join most frequently in the cry against science in general, and geology in particular, as dangerous to religion, *upon no sincere grounds of religious conviction.*

" 'Their adoption of a certain form of faith is dictated by motives of *expediency,* and the mere value of its practical effects on society. Not themselves recognising its claims as founded in *truth*, they uphold the established creed, as well as all received errors popularly engrafted upon it, as a convenient and effectual instrument for securing the influence of practical restraints on the multitude. Hence they condemn all inquiries which may come into collision with any portion of the popular belief, and

against the agitation of any question which may shake established prejudices, or suggest any distinctions in the application of
Scripture, there is an immediate and indiscriminate cry raised,
that they unsettle men's minds, and are heretical doctrines of a
most dangerous tendency, and such as will weaken and efface
all sense of religious and moral obligation.

"But even among the best men and most sincere believers,
there exists too often a sort of dread of meeting such questions
in a strictly *honest* frame of mind. Those who have the most
conscientious regard for truth in every thing else, seem to think
it dispensed with in supporting the cause of religion; and while
they earnestly condemn those who, in former ages, could justify
the ' pious frauds' introduced in support of the received faith, are
yet themselves influenced by the very same spirit, only in a different form, in dreading the dissemination of knowledge, if even
imagined to be at variance with established religious belief. The
one party seeking to support religion by the propagation of falsehood, the other by the suppression of truth, both agree in treating truth as if it were falsehood, and thus give its enemies the
fairest ground to think it so." (pp. 242-4.)

Fortified by this authority, I may venture to assert that legislative articles of faith and endowed churches trammel the wholesome activity of the superior faculties of the human mind; and
thus far serve as impediments to the advancement of civilisation.

I am far, however, from affirming that the hereditary peerage
and Established Churches are felt by every British subject as
obstacles to his enjoyment; or that hundreds of thousands of intelligent, good, and sincerely Christian men of all ranks are not
reared under their sway. The Austrian government, civil and
ecclesiastical, has moulded the opinions of the people into harmony with itself, and common minds in that country are happy
under it, and desire no change In Britain, also, the institutions
of the state have communicated their own forms to opinion; and
millions of British subjects admire and honor the hereditary
peerage, while their souls rejoice under the wings of rectors,
bishops, and archbishops. But it may nevertheless be true that
the British institutions, like the Austrian, misdirect the minds
even of those who are comparatively happy, and certainly contented, under them. The British clergy will recognise the truth
of this proposition when applied to the Austrian people, and
concede that their blind, though willing, subjection to Popery,
is an obstacle to their advance in civilisation; but they will probably deny that a blind, although voluntary, subjection to Calvinism, produces any injurious effects on the public mind. It
appears to me, however, that in Britain, as in Austria, these
institutions operate as weights repressing free mental action; and

that the more upright, searching, and independent the moral sentiments and intellectual powers of any individual are, the more severely do they check his pursuit of happiness. I disavow, however, every desire to see them abrogated by force, or prematurely abolished by a temporary and unenlightened excitement of public feeling:—reason and moral suasion are the only weapons by which they can be overthrown, without producing evils much greater than themselves.

Another form in which the Established Churches of Britain oppose civilisation, is that of hostility to popular and liberal education. They profess to desire the education of the people, but demand the entire control of the means which the government may devote to this object. This demand is not only unjust to the dissenters, whose contributions form important elements of the national wealth, but injurious to the whole community, because its avowed object is to obtain the right of fashioning the religious opinions of all future generations in the moulds of antiquity, which are already worn out; or, in other words, of exercising a spiritual tyranny over unborn multitudes of men. The authoritative declaration by Parliament of certain points of faith, as the only true expositions of the will of God, the offering of large endowments to those individuals who choose to embrace these interpretations, and visiting with obloquy, exclusion, and disqualification, those who doubt them, and especially the investing of these dogmas with the attribute of infallible truth, to so great an extent that every member of the church who publishes serious doubts of their soundness is liable to be expelled for heresy, and excluded from Christian privileges—is at once to anchor theology—to prevent it from advancing with increasing knowledge—and to bind up the moral and intellectual faculties of the best minds from all free, honest, and independent inquiry in this great department of human interests.

What, then, is the influence of the Democratic form of government under which you live, on the activity of the mental faculties? The answer is obvious—you leave all the faculties free to find their own way to happiness as they best are able. You have no hereditary or artificial aristocracy to mould your opinions according to erroneous standards, nor to misdirect your ambition: you have no Established Church to chain up your moral and religious sentiments in the trammels of antiquated articles of belief; you have no self-constituted executive to take out of your hands the administration of your own affairs, and no legislatures formed of privileged classes to restrain your industry by obnoxious laws, or to repress your mental energy by prescribing boundaries to your exertions. Your government leaves all your faculties free, presents to them the highest and best field for their exercise, and leaves every individual to reap the natural reward or punishment of his own conduct. If the first and most important condition of happiness be the activity of all the faculties, your government complies with it in the most ample manner.

The institutions of the United States not only allow but encourage the activity of *all* the faculties. In your vast unoccupied territory, a fruitful soil presents its attractions to those individuals in whom Acquisitiveness and Ambition predominate. The cultivators raise millions of bushels of grain from their lands, and rear on them innumerable herds of cattle, and offer these rich productions in exchange for articles of utility or luxury manufactured by your Atlantic cities, or imported by them from Europe. All over the wide expanse of your national domain, industry and enterprise are busy, and Acquisitiveness is stimulated by rich rewards. In your political institutions, Self-Esteem and Love of Approbation find unlimited scope. If the humblest citizen thirsts for power and distinction, there is no constitutional obstacle to his becoming President of the United States. The career of activity is equally open to your moral sentiments and intellectual faculties. Every citizen may not only profess whatever religious or philosophical creed seems best suited to his own mind, but he is at liberty to preach and teach that doctrine; to found churches, schools, lyceums, colleges, and libraries in support of it, and to form associations for its propagation and defence. In short, there is no sphere of action of the human faculties, consistent with the common dictates of morality, that is not here encouraged. Nay, so extensive is your liberty, that it occasionally degenerates into licentiousness—your citizens, in paroxysms of excitement, occasionally indulge their animal propensities in violence, outrage, and injustice, and the law is too feeble to protect the objects of their displeasure, or to punish those who have set it at defiance.

You perceive, then, the mighty difference between your institutions and those of despotic countries. But I call your attention to another principle.

Happiness consists in the free play of all our faculties within their legitimate spheres of action, and this kind of action can exist only when the animal propensities are subjected to the control of the moral sentiments and intellect, and where these latter powers are sufficiently enlightend to be capable of distinguishing between good and evil—between the right course and the wrong—in every department of individual, domestic, and social action. I earnestly press on your attention the great truth, that our affective faculties, both animal and moral, are in themselves blind impulses, and that they stand in need of constant guidance.

There must be subordination, restraint, self-denial, the power of self-direction, in short, there must be *government*, and enlightened government, before happiness can be attained. We have seen that your institutions have done every thing to set your faculties free: but what have they done to guide them in the right path? So far as I can discover, the answer must be—too little.

In Europe a National Church professes to cultivate the sentiment of Veneration, and to teach morals and religion. Here you leave every man to embrace whatever religion is approved of by his conscience, or to cast off the restraints of religion at his pleasure. In Europe, artificial rank and hereditary titles profess to inculcate deference and subordination in the different departments of society. Here you have no distinction of ranks, and, while you encourage Self-Esteem and the Love of Approbation in their boldest flights, you have no artificial institutions, either for restraining or directing them. In Europe, independent courts of justice, and a strong executive, direct or repress the animal propensities. Here, your executive is feeble; and when a general excitement seizes your people, your laws are as cobwebs in restraining the propensities. Your institutions have relied on one sole power to regulate all the faculties in their manifestations— the power of public opinion. But what is public opinion? It is the outward expression of the particular group of faculties which may happen to predominate in activity in the majority of the people for the moment. It is the sum of the active impulses of many individual minds. In questions, however, of moral conduct, of religion, of political economy, of law, or even of common prudence, it is not the number of minds, but the degree of their intelligence and virtue, that gives value to their decisions; and I ask, what do your institutions do to communicate to the mind of each person who forms one of your majorities, that wisdom which alone fits him to act as a directing and controlling power over his own propensities and those of his fellow-men? I fear that we must again answer—too little.

The idea seems to be entertained by some of your politicians, that propensity in one man will restrain propensity in another;— that sentiment in one will direct sentiment in another; in short, that out of the conflict of interest against interest, justice will be evolved, and that out of the conflict of reason with extravagance and error—whether in religion, in morals, or in political action, wisdom and truth will be brought to light, and that the social body will at length grope its way to repose, prosperity, happiness, holiness, and virtue. If this result shall ultimately be reached by such a process of mental action, it can only be by the exhaustion of errors, and the endurance of countless miseries in the process.

Do not imagine, from these remarks, that I am the advocate of European despotisms, and the enemy of your institutions. Quite the reverse; but it is my object to point out to you, that, in providing an organised moral and physical machinery for regulating the propensities, and directing the sentiments of their subjects into what they consider to be their legitimate spheres of action, monarchs act on a sound and philosophical principle. The propensities are energetic impulses, which must be restrained and guided by some power, external or internal, superior to themselves, otherwise they will deviate into wild abuses. In the European monarchies *external* restraints are chiefly resorted to; and these, too, unfortunately, are, in many instances, applied by ignorant and selfish men in such a manner as in some degree to crush intellect and stifle virtue, as well as to suppress vice. Although, therefore, you have done well in liberating all your faculties from thraldom to legislative churches, aristocracies, and despots; yet you cannot set them free from the laws of God, written not only in the Scriptures, but on your mental constitution, and on the external world. Some persons appear to conceive liberty to consist in the privilege of unlimited exercise of the animal propensities. The head of Liberty stamped on the earlier medals, commemorative of the French Revolution, is the very personification of this idea. She is a female figure with a villanously small, low, and retreating forehead, deficient moral organs, and ample development of the base and posterior regions of the brain, devoted to the propensities. Her hair is flying back in loose disorder, and her countenance expresses vivacity and passion, but neither morality nor wisdom. The same figure appears on the earlier coins of the United States. Liberty, as I should draw her, would possess large moral and intellectual organs, with moderate propensities. I should arrange her hair in simple elegance, and imprint serene enjoyment, benignity, and wisdom on her brow. She should represent moral liberty, or the unlimited freedom to accomplish all that is good, and the absence of every desire to do evil. Such alone is the liberty after which you should aspire.

I desire, then, to see in this country a moral and intellectual machinery put into vigorous action, calculated to teach the young the legitimate spheres in which all their faculties should act, and to *train* them to impose that restraint upon themselves, to practise that self-denial, and that self-direction, which are indispensable to happiness and prosperity. I desire to see public opinion, which is here your great restraining power, composed, not of the sum of the ruling prejudices, passions, or interests of the day, but of the concentrated wisdom and virtue of millions of trained and enlightened minds. Such a public opinion I should regard as the best and safest of all governing powers. An ignorant public opinion is, to the wise and good, a revolting tyranny. In this country you have chosen public opinion for your chief regulating influence, and it is impossible for you to substitute for it any other. You have established universal suffrage, placed supreme authority in the hands of your majorities, and no human means, short of military conquest, can deprive that majority of its sway. You have, therefore, only one mode of action left to reach the goal of national happiness: enlighten your people, teach them whatever is necessary for them, in order to guide their faculties aright—*train* them to self-control—*train* them in youth to bend all the inferior feelings under the yoke of morality, religion, and reason. In short, educate them—and educate them well.

Most of you will probably acknowledge the advantages of education, point to your common schools, to the large sums appropriated by the states for public instruction, and ask what more can any reasonable man desire? With every feeling of deference towards your learned men and divines, I would answer that you stand in need of a philosophy of mind capable of guiding your steps in your efforts to bestow education on your people. Many will say—Is not common sense sufficient to enable us to manage with success both our political and educational institutions? I repeat the observation of Archbishop Whately, that men never acknowledge the sufficiency of mere common sense to the accomplishment of any important undertaking when they fully understand its nature and the difficulties that must be surmounted to ensure success. A blacksmith will probably assure you, that common sense is sufficient to enable you to farm, if he knows nothing about farming; but if you ask him whether common sense will enable you to shoe a horse, he will unhesitatingly answer, that if you try the experiment, you will probably get your brains kicked out for your rashness and presumption. Do you imagine, then, that the successful direction of the affairs of a great nation, and the training of the human mind, demand less of scientific skill and experience than shoeing horses?

But allow me to ask, what do you understand by common sense, which is supposed to be such an all-sufficient guide in the United States? What is called common sense means the notions which have entered the mind of any individual, from such occurrences and sources of information as he happens to have enjoyed. Men's capacities differ, their opportunities of observation differ, and hence their common sense differs. The individual who professes to have no theory, no hypothesis, no system, but to follow plain common sense, has a theory: it is that formed by his innate capacity, aided by his own individual experience.

In some of your academies, the talent for English composition is supposed to be the most valuable attainment that can be communicated to the young, in others arithmetic and mathematics are regarded as the best studies for developing all the faculties; while one female teacher assured me, in all seriousness, that the human mind is a blank, that all minds are alike in their native capacities, and that she can evoke whatever talents and dispositions she pleases. This is her theory, and she has practised on it for many years! You must have observed how the practices of teachers differ; you cannot suppose that each adopts his own method without some reasons for preferring it,—these reasons, however limited and lame, constitute his theory. In point of fact, they all have theories, and the vast differences in their notions prove that nature is not the author of them; because she is always consistent with herself, and gives one response to all. When we have studied nature we agree. Hence, the great principles of astronomy, chemistry, physiology, and of other branches of natural science, are no longer in dispute. But on the subjects of morals, religion, and education, the diversity and conflict of opinion are boundless. Does not this indicate that our notions on these subjects do not yet rest on a scientific basis? in short, that we enjoy no sound and practical philosophy of mind?

To you this state of mental science is an evil of the greatest magnitude. In this country you need not only education, but an education that shall communicate to youth the knowledge, maxims, and experience of age. Here you commit political power to the hands of nearly every man who has attained majority. Your population doubles every twenty-three or twenty-five years. The actual majority of your voters is probably under thirty-five or thirty-six years of age. There is no other country in the world which is ruled by men so young and so inexperienced. I was told before I came here, that the Americans are the most excitable nation on the globe; that you take fire in a moment, and instantly rush to action, whether it be in speculation, in legitimate enterprise, in war, or in political change; and since my stay among you, I have heard the deep-toned war-cry uttered with a force and unanimity which is full of fearful omen. And the cause of this may be discerned. The mind, till thirty-five, acts more under the impulse of the feelings than under the guidance of intellect. By the very laws of our nature, Combativeness, Destructiveness, Self-Esteem, Love of Approbation, and Acquisitiveness, are then more energetic than they are at fifty or sixty; and at that period also experience is most deficient. Life has not been long enough to enable us to accumulate wisdom, to detect the illusions of passion or of vain glory—to supply the deficiencies and correct the errors of an imperfect education.

In your country, then, above all others, your school education should teach your youth the specific knowledge of the constitution and powers of physical nature, and the means by which they may be applied to the promotion of human happiness—of the constitution of the body, and the laws of health—of the constitution of the mind, and the means by which we may be best trained to the discharge of our duties in the private, domestic, and social circles—of the laws by which wealth is created and distributed; and of the influence of morals and legislation on the welfare of the individual and society. As you do not wait until your voters, who wield the destinies of your country—who make peace and war—who make and unmake banks—who make and unmake tariffs affecting industry to the core—and who make and unmake even your schools, colleges, and churches—I say, as you do not wait until age has given them wisdom and experience, but place the helm, at once, in their hands, and allow them to act, while they are still full of young blood, and all the energy, confidence, and rashness that attend it—you are called on by every consideration to perfect your schools, so as to communicate to them the dictates of a wisdom which cannot be dispensed with, and which will not otherwise be attained.

In the election which took place in November 1839, the question of the currency was actually brought to the polls in the state of New York. The mottos were—banks and paper currency on the one side—hard specie and sub-treasury laws on the other. These are questions on which Dr. Adam Smith, Ricardo, M'Culloch, and the profoundest political economists, have differed in opinion. Does your education enable your people to understand them, and decide on them? No! Yet your people *act* whether they understand them or not. They vote the supporters of paper into power; and paper flourishes. If evil ensue, they vote the advocates of specie into power; and paper and credit go to the wall. They try the experiment. But what an awful experiment! How many thousands of individuals and families are ruined by the violence of every change!

In Austria and Prussia the safety-valve of the body politic is loaded with the weight of an established church and 100,000 bayonets. In cases of discontent, opinion cannot escape, until it has burst through these compressing powers, and then it will explode with terrific violence. Here the safety-valve bears no load except the sense of each individual mind. Any strong internal excitement, or the application of external provocation, causes the propensities and sentiments to glow, and to express themselves with instantaneous energy. Their voice is heard in Europe, and the timid hold their breath, waiting for a grand explosion. Perhaps it never comes. In your country, ten times ten thousand valves let off excited opinion so rapidly that the body-politic cools down to its natural heat, as quickly as its temperature was raised. But every one of these excitements shakes credit, deranges trade, ruins fortunes, is attended by suffering, and leaves many pangs behind. Load, then, your safety-valves with knowledge of nature and religion, and train your young minds to control passion by virtue, and you will find these means more effectual than millions of armed soldiers, to insure your prosperity and happiness. Mr. Wyse, in his work entitled "Education Reform," says, "A period of total quiet resulting from a long continued acquiescence in old institutions, leaves a very different imprint upon the national mind from that which is the necessary consequence of a general breaking up of old principles and forms, and an earnest search after new. In the first instance, an education of stimulants becomes necessary. It is essential to the healthy activity of the body-politic. In the second, steadiness, love of order, mutual toleration, the sacrifice of private resentments and factious interests to general good, should be the great lessons of national education." Vol. 1. p. 48. Such, assuredly, should be the education of your sons.

Yours is a noble destiny. Providence has assigned to you the duty of proving by experiment, whether man be. or be not, a rational and moral being, capable of working out his own way to virtue and enjoyment, under the guidance of Reason and Scripture, unfettered by despotic power, and unchained by law-enacted creeds. Your institutions and physical condition call all your faculties into vivid action. Among these, the animal propensities, as I have remarked, are not dormant; but those observers err, who allow their attention to be arrested only, or chiefly, by the abuses of the propensities which appear in your people. Virtue consists in meeting and overcoming temptation. As you, then, by possessing freedom are tempted above other nations, you will show a virtue above them all, if you nobly resist every seducing influence, and march boldly onward in the paths of rectitude and wisdom. The subjects of a despot, whose every thought and action are ruled by other minds, have little merit in exhibiting order and decorum in their public conduct. You will prove the true strength of your moral principles, when you restrain your passions by your own virtuous resolves, and obey just laws enacted by yourselves. It is to aid you in this admirable course of action, in so far as the feeble abilities of one individual will go, that I now address to you these observations. And I again ask, Do your schools teach all that your young voters should know? all that the best of your citizens would wish them to know, when they act as electors and arbitrators of the public welfare?—I believe not. If you ask how they can be improved you will be answered by as many projects and proposals for education, as if you had inquired for the philosopher's stone.

So far from education supplying this knowledge, it appears to me, that a vast proportion of your people have not yet obtained a glimpse of what, I hope, is destined to constitute the real greatness and glory of your country. I find here, the ambition of many individuals directed towards raising the United States to the rank of the richest and the most powerful nation in the world. They bend their whole minds to the increase of her commercial, agricultural, naval, and military grandeur. This is not wrong, but it is not *all*. Thousands of your young men pant for war, in order to wreath the laurels of victory round the brow of their native country; and they call this patriotism. I desire to see higher and better views entertained of the glories and destiny of the United States. History presents only the records of wars, devastations, and selfish aggrandisement pursued by all governments that have ever existed;—republics, oligarchies, monarchies—all have run one wild career of immorality and ambition. If your nation consider herself to have no higher vocation than these, she ceases to be an object of moral interest to the philanthropist and philosopher. If her annals be destined to record the contests only of faction against faction, of party against party, or of the nation against foreign nations—the friend of human improvement must turn from her in despair. The grand duty assigned to Americans is to raise up and exhibit to the world, a nation great in virtue, to show, for the first time, since history began, a people universally educated, a people prosperous, refined, happy, and gigantically great, by the realisation in their institutions, in their private lives, and in their public actions, of the principles of Christianity.

The founders of your constitution, when they established universal suffrage, assumed it as a fundamental principle, that man is a moral, religious, and intellectual being; and that, if thoroughly instructed and left to direct his course by the truths of Scripture and the dictates of reason, he will found and maintain institutions calculated to promote virtue, religion, and universal peace, with all the physical enjoyments and mental gratifications which attend them. Phrenology confirms this opinion, by unfolding to us the great facts that we possess moral and intellectual faculties invested with authority to rule over and direct the animal propensities; and the propensities themselves have all a legitimate sphere of action. When the founders of your institutions threw unlimited power into the hands of the people, they assumed it as a fundamental principle, that the people are capable of being trained and instructed; and that, when so trained, their desires will be towards that which is good, holy, useful, and just; and Phrenology is the only philosophy, with which I am acquainted, which warrants and sustains this assumption. The despotisms and the established churches of Europe are founded, and defended, on a principle directly the reverse of this, viz., that the mass of mankind are so selfish, so ignorant, and so prone to prefer an immediate individual gratification to the general advantage—that the people cannot be trusted with knowledge and power—that it is Utopian to imagine that the masses can be rendered capable of applying self-restraint, and of reaching virtue and happiness by the spontaneous action of their own minds; but that they must be ruled, like children, by the more enlightened members of society, and chastised when they infringe the laws enacted by their superiors for their guidance. These two sets of principles are subjects of constant debate between the liberal and despotic parties in Europe; and both, with the deepest interest, look to you to solve the problem on which they differ. All your aberrations from the dictates of morality; the "colonising" and false swearing at your elections (see vol. ii, p. 19); the practice of betting on elections; your mobs, your Lynch laws, your wild speculations, your bank suspensions, with the injustice to so many of yourselves which accompany them; your Negro slavery, your treatment of the Indians (vol. ii, p. 85); the incessant abuse which the one of your political parties heaps on the distinguished men of the other; the elopements of persons placed in situations of trust with the funds of the nation, or of their constituents; the excessive number of bankruptcies; the very imperfect police for the prevention of crime which characterises some of your great towns, such as New York; the enormous and calamitous conflagrations which scourge your cities, the results either of recklessness or incendiarism; the great self-complacency of the mass of your people, who, although very imperfectly educated, are persuaded by political orators that they know every thing, and can decide wisely on every question; the general absence of reverence for authority or superior wisdom, displayed first in childhood, and afterwards in the general progress of life, the regardlessness of the obligations of contracts and agreements that occur in trade, commerce, and personal service;—all these, and every other fault and imperfection, real or imaginary, which can be ascribed to you with any shadow of plausibility, are carefully collected, blasoned, and recorded in Europe—not to *your* disparagement alone, but to the degradation of human nature, and to the unspeakable injury of the cause of liberty all over the civilised world.

And I ask—What have you to oppose to these charges? Generally your press hurls back accusations of crimes and follies as bad or worse, as fairly chargeable against European governments and nations. But admitting this to be true, the philanthropist, using a common phrase, replies that two blacks do not make a white, and that this forms no legitimate defence for your imperfections. You have proclaimed the supremacy of man's moral and intellectual nature over his animal feelings, and adopted this principle as the basis of your social fabric, and of your hopes. In the old despotisms of Europe, the very opposite principle is avowed. It is assumed by the rulers of these nations, that if man be free, he will only do evil continually. You profess to impose the restraints of religion and morality on yourselves; they impose the restraints of armed force on their people, to lead them to order and obedience. If you, therefore, realise only a social condition no worse than those which are founded on the opposite principle, the friends of liberty feel that their cause is lost. You are bound to exhibit *higher* intelligence, a *purer* morality, a *deeper* reverence for all that is great, good, and holy—a more rational prudence, a juster estimate of the real value of physical wealth, a greater abhorrence of war and all forms of injustice, and a higher interest in every pursuit that tends to elevate man's moral, religious, and intellectual nature—than are to be found in countries in which the activity of the higher faculties is suppressed by force, or misled by ignorance or fraud—in short, you are bound to impose an enlightened self-restraint on all your faculties; and if you do not do so, you betray the great cause of freedom which Providence has entrusted to your care.

And I ask—Are your schools, your literature, your daily maxims and pursuits, and the spirit which animates the masses of your people, steadily, systematically, and successfully directed towards the attainment of these high and honorable objects? are they adequate to the formation of a public opinion under which a virtuous and enlightened mind may live in peace, and rejoice, and with which it can cordially co-operate? When I converse with your wisest citizens many of them concede that such should be the objects of your institutions, manners, and pursuits; and they labor to reach them; but they often lament the vast interval which lies between these great conceptions and their accomplishment. The enlightened philanthropists of this country desire to see commenced in earnest a system of training and instruction which shall be really capable of preparing the young republican for the discharge of the highest duties which a rational being can be called on to execute, in a manner and in a spirit becoming their grandeur, dignity, and utility; but they experience extraordinary difficulties, arising from the ignorance and the power of the people, in realising their aspirations. Many who now hear me, and who participate in these desires, will confirm what I say. I was invited to come to this country by some philanthropists, who believed that this philosophy would aid your people, in discovering, at once, their own need of better instruction and the means of obtaining it. Phrenology lays open, even to the most ordinary mind, an intelligible view of the human faculties; it carries home a striking conviction of the indispensable necessity of education to their improvement and direction, and presents tangible principles for administering this instruction.* I have long been an admirer of your institutions, and an advocate of man's capability of raising his moral, religious, and intellectual powers to supremacy over his animal propensities; and I obeyed the call which was sent to me. Far from disapproving of your institutions, I admire them, and have confidence in them; but it is my duty to express my conviction, that your people need a vastly improved education to render them equal to the faithful and successful discharge of the important duties committed to them by the institutions of the states and of the Federal government, and to form a public opinion adequate to the due performance of the high duties assigned to this power.

In the preceding lectures I have already explained my views of education, and left them to your judgment. I am far from pressing them on your attention as infallible; I only submit them in all humility to your consideration; "prove (or try) all things, and hold fast that which is good." If you know a sounder and more practical philosophy of mind than that which I have expounded, adopt it, and carry its principles into practice. All that I mean to maintain, without limit and qualification, is, that, in the United States, the moral and intellectual condition of the people must be raised far above its present standard, or your institutions will perish. If you agree with me in regard to the end, you are the proper judges of the means.

You are engaged in trying many momentous experiments in regard to the nature and capabilities of man; and you are now also in the act of evolving the true nature and power of Christianity. You leave reason and Scripture, science and theological doctrines, to adjust their several claims to acceptance, and to work out a harmony among themselves. Though your wide extended country be overrun by contending sects, still fear not for religion. If Austria boast of almost unanimity in her faith, it is not because she has found infallible truth, but because she has extinguished in her people the desire and the capacity of independent thinking on religious doctrines. Your numerous sects prove to my mind one great truth, that Christianity is not

* The reader is respectfully reminded that this address was delivered at the close of a full course of lectures on Phrenology, and that it was not necessary to describe to my audience what Phrenology is.

vet fully understood, that in past ages, the Scriptures have been
interpreted, too often without knowledge of the philosophy of
mind, and without regard to the dictates of reason and of science.
In Britain many persons suffer under feelings of insecurity about
religion.   They seem to regard it as a pyramid resting on its
apex; Bishops and Archbishops may be pictured on one side;
rectors and endowed clergy on another, the Lords and Commons
on a third; and many excellent laymen on the fourth; all straining
ing themselves to preserve it erect, each, apparently, believing
that if he were to withdraw his support, it would fall and break
into a thousand fragments.   Professor Powell, in the work already quoted, ably describes the mental condition of these appre-
hensive Christians. "Adopting their creed," says he, "blindly
from education, custom, or party, too many hold their religion
only by a most loose and uncertain tenure, and are lamentably
confused in their notions of its nature.   Hence they dread a
formidable shock to Christianity in every physical discovery;
and in the obscurity which surrounds them, imagine danger to
the truth in every exposure of error.   Insensible to the real
strength of their position, they live in groundless alarm for its
security; and, accustomed to cherish faith in ignorance, they ap-
prehend in every advance of knowledge, the approach of the
enemy of their salvation."   But when we discover by means of
Phrenology, that religious feelings spring from the innate faculties of Veneration, Hope, and Wonder, we perceive that religion
can never be shaken.   The churches, creeds, emblems, and
ceremonies, which many individuals mistake for religion, are
really its effects.   They are the outward symbols by which the
innate religious sentiments manifest their desires, and seek for
gratification.   They are no more the causes of religion, than
clarionets and violins are the causes of that love of melody which
exists in the human mind, and which prompts the intellect to
produce them for its gratification.   I request of you, then, clearly
to distinguish between the sentiment of religion—which is inherent in the human mind;—and its outward symbols—which may
assume various forms at different times and in different countries,
yet religion itself be not for one moment in danger.   The
founders of your institutions have acted on this view; and in
your country they have placed the pyramid of religion at once
on its basis.   Here, it is seen standing in all its native solidity,
simplicity, and beauty, without needing the aid of human power
to preserve it in its place.

In the same spirit, you have trusted the preservation of the
purity of the Bible to the moral and religious principles, and the
interest, of your printers and publishers.   You have conferred
no patent monopolies on individuals, and established no boards,

with well paid secretaries, to superintend the printing of the
Scriptures; yet in your country the text is as pure as it is in
Britain. You have learned by experience that an edition in
which errors are detected, becomes, by the unanimous verdict
of your community, mere waste paper in the hands of those who
have produced it, and that this operates as a most efficacious
check against corruption.

The attention of the Christian world has lately been called
to a singular fact, which is instructive, and I think encouraging
to you; It is this—that Protestantism has made little progress
in extending itself in Europe, since the " end of the thirty
years' war, and that the expansive power," which we believe
all truth to possess, has not been manifested by it since that
epoch. " It is truly remarkable," says a recent critic, " that
neither the moral revolution of the eighteenth century, nor the
moral counter-revolution of the nineteenth, should, in any per-
ceptible degree, have added to the domain of Protestantism.
During the former period, whatever was lost to Catholicism was
lost also to Christianity; during the latter, whatever was regained
by Christianity in Catholic countries was regained also by
Catholicism."* One cause of this phenomenon appears to me
to be, that the Protestant Kingdoms of Europe, in general, have
imitated the Roman Catholic so closely, that they have in many
respects instituted Popish Churches under a different name.
The Reformation proclaimed freedom of religious opinion; but
the Protestant monarchies enacted creeds and endowed churches
to maintain them. They stifled opinion, and bound up the
human mind in the fetters of authority;—and how could Protestantism, in other words, religious freedom, prosper or expand
itself in such circumstances? You, almost alone, have done
justice to Protestantism; you have given it a fair field; and if, in
your country, Popery shall not ultimately yield to it, Popery
must contain the greater extent of truth.

In attending the places of religious worship of several of your
sects, I have received a profound impression of the vivacity of
the religious sentiments among you. I, therefore, consider religion in this country as in the most prosperous condition.
Honest and earnest zeal for the glory of God and the welfare of
human souls, evinces itself in innumerable forms: It is true that
I perceive a great diversity of doctrines (a statement of which
will be found in the Appendix, No. XV); but this fact leads me
simply to the conclusion that much yet remains to be done
before the true interpretation of Scripture shall be completed;

* *The Ecclesiastical and Political History of the Popes of Rome during
the sixteenth and seventeenth centuries, by Leopold Ranke, Professor in the
University of Berlin. Edinburgh Review, vol. lxxii, p. 258.*

and that many improvements remain to be introduced into
Christian theology, before it shall stand side by side with reason
and science, and exhibit all the symmetry and beauty of a har-
monious compartment in the great temple of universal truth.
Far from regarding the diversity of your sects as an evil, I view
it as an unspeakable advantage. The existence of wide diversity of the opinions of Christian sects is to me irrefragable evidence that error is not yet fully expurgated from popular Christianity.

How, then, is the religion of Jesus to be purified? Not by
adopting one form of its corruption and declaring it, by statute,
to be true. This has been tried, and has failed. Not by the
recondite studies and commentaries of cloistered monks, or state-
endowed and state-chained divines. for what human research
and learning could accomplish has been achieved by them already;
The doctrines, generally known under the name of Puseyism,
afford a specimen of the improvements in Christianity which
learned priests, even in the nineteenth century, propose when
left to follow the dictates of their own judgment. Christian
theology is not destined to advance by such aids as these. The
conflicts of your sects will do more for its improvement than
has been accomplished by all the commentators who have labored
in the field since the Reformation.

One palpable advantage of a number of religious sects, all
equal in the eye of the law, is, that that their clergy discuss each
other's interpretations of Scripture and the doctrines founded
on them, with a degree of fearlessness, energy, and effect, which
rarely characterises the efforts of laymen in the same field.
Each sect brings the doctrines of its opponents to the touch-
stone of reason, although some of them shrink from applying
reason to their own. In a discussion on points of Scriptural
doctrine, between laymen and religious teachers, the latter are
prone to charge the former with infidelity, as the short answer
to all objections; and the religious world too often makes common cause with the teachers, in giving effect to the accusation.
But when the clergy of one sect contend with those of another,
their religious characters protect them against this brief method
of dealing with their arguments, and the subject must be treated
on its merits. By this means, truth is advanced, and theology
and reason are brought more and more into harmony. If a layman, for instance, had attacked the Calvinistic doctrine of Election, he would probably have been at once denounced as an
infidel. But when the Rev. John Wesley, himself a high
authority in religion, in commenting on the Rev. James Hervey's
advocacy of this doctrine in his "Theron and Aspasia," says,
"But what becomes of other people? (that is, besides the Elect).

they must inevitably perish for ever? The die was cast ere even they were in being. The doctrine to-pass them by, has

> 'Consigned their unborn souls to hell,
> And damned them from their mother's womb.'

I could sooner be a Turk, a Deist—yea, an Atheist, than I could believe this; it is less absurd to deny the very being of God, than to make him an Almighty tyrant;"—when a religious man writes thus, he must be answered in reason, and in Scripture reconcilable with reason.

Again, when the Church of Scotland, claiming Christ as its only head, asserted, that in contending for its own power and privileges with the supreme civil court of the country, it was only defending the "Redeemer's crown rights," any layman who should have stigmatised this as an act of unwarrantable and irreverend assumption, would probably have been accused of infidelity; and the religious portion of the community would have given effect to the charge; but when the Rev. And. Marshall of Kirkintulloch, a speaker at a great meeting of Evangelical Dissenters, held in Edinburgh on the 16th December 1840, used the following words, the religious public could not treat them thus, but must have pondered them well and answered them in reason. The system of non-intrusion, said he, is "an attempt to set up an institution (the Church of Scotland) in the name of Christ which Christ never sanctioned—an institution breathing a spirit and clothed with a character which the religion of Christ utterly disowns—an institution calling itself national, and claiming a large portion of the national property—an institution claiming a right to dispose of the national property, the national honors, and the national emoluments; yet at the same time refusing to be controled by the national authority, and setting at defiance all laws but its own. Is this a Christian institution? Is this an institution to be tolerated in any free State? Yet, such is the institution which the non-intrusionists are trying to set up, and of this institution they say that Christ is the head. I deny the assertion. I consider it an assertion bordering upon blasphemy; an assertion throwing a stain, a foul and injurious stain, upon the great name by which we are called The head of the Church of Scotland! Christ is the head of his own mystical body, the foundation and chief corner-stone of that spiritual living temple which is composed of all Christian men in all parts of the world; but I have yet to learn that the Church of Scotland, either as it has existed hitherto, or as it would exist, provided the non-intrusionists had their will—I say, I have yet to learn that the Church of Scotland and this living temple are one and the same thing. I grant, indeed, that there

is a sense in which Christ may be said to be the head of the
Church of Scotland; but that is just as he is the head of the
Church of England, just as he is the head of the Church of
Rome; and just as he is the head of any other existing society,
or any other portion of human beings—as the head, for instance
of the British empire, or the empire of the Chinese. I will
grant that there is a sense in which Christ orders the concerns of
the Church of Scotland, and in which he superintends all their
affairs, great and small; but that is exactly as he superintends
the affairs of the French, or the affairs of their friend Mehemet
Ali." Such arguments as these, proceeding from religious men
and directed against the doctrines of religious men, open up the
understandings of the people, and give them courage to think;
and by them theology is advanced.

Fear not evil, then, from the multitude and conflicts of your
sects.

Many of them reject the authority of reason when applied to
themselves, but they all use it to expose and refute the errors of
their opponents; and by this constant appeal to reason, I anticipate the ultimate purification of Christian doctrine, and the increasing approximation of all sects towards unanimity. There
is one God, and one truth, and no interpretations of Scripture
can be sound, or secure of universal acceptance and permanent
existence, which contradict reason or clash with natural science.
Scripture may legitimately go beyond what reason can reach, as
in teaching the resurrection of the dead, but no sound interpretations of it can evolve doctrines that distinctly contradict natural
truth.   The process of improvement appears to me to be evidently begun.   A large portion of your Presbyterian Church has
dropt some of the peculiar doctrines of Calvinism (vol. i. p. 312),
and even Yale College (vol. ii. p. 118) has modified the ancient
views of original sin.   These are steps, however small, by
which the professors of Calvinism are approaching towards the
opinions of those who adopt Universalism and Unitarianism.
Be not alarmed; it is not my intention to express an opinion in
favor of the superiority of any sect; this does not become a
stranger, and one whose element is philosophy; but as a philosophical observer, I beg leave to state my conviction that the progress which Christianity is destined to make in your country, is
one of approximation to unity in belief, that, in proportion as the
knowledge of mental philosophy and physical science is extended
among your people, your sects will drop one doctrine after
another, as it is discovered to clash with reason and natural truth,
and that they will elicit purer, and sounder, and more practically
useful doctrines in their place; until truth, commanding unanimity, shall stand forth before an admiring world.   This must be

the ultimate effect of free discussion, if man be really a rational and moral being; and, however distant the prospect, it is still discernible by the eye of reason and of faith.

If such be the probable result to which your religious discussions will lead, Phrenology will serve as a beacon-light to guide you on your way. The starting point of innumerable religious differences lies in different views entertained in regard to the nature of man: Phrenology will settle this point beyond the possibility of controversy. While every individual takes his own consciousness and observations as the standards by which he measures human dispositions and capacities, metaphysical divines may assign or deny to the human mind whatever moral and intellectual qualities best suit their several religious opinions; but when the faculties are studied in connection with organs, this becomes impossible. Organs are visible and tangible, and owe their existence directly to God. The mental qualities, therefore, attached to them, are all equally the direct gifts of the Creator; and be they what they may, they are His workmanship. Hitherto, Scripture has generally been interpreted without the knowledge of the organs and of their influence on the mental manifestations; and it appears to me that, when this knowledge becomes general, many popular interpretations will not bear investigation. Again, Phrenology shows us that, to improve the human mind, we must begin by improving the condition of the brain; and that, to attain success in this object, all moral, religious, and intellectual teaching must be conducted in harmony with the laws of physiology. While, however, it foretells of changes in the interpretations of Scripture, and in religious opinions, it affords us a guaranty for the safety, the permanence, and the ever-extending power of religion itself, sufficient to assure the most timid. It brings before our eyes, organs specially destined to the manifestations of religious sentiments. It thereby shows us that religion itself is inherent in our nature, and that it is as enduring as the race. It enables us to compare our mental nature, such as God has constituted it, with the precepts of Jesus, and shows us the most admirable harmony between them. It forcibly demonstrates that great differences exist in the relative strength of the faculties in different individuals, and leads us to infer that many of our religious differences are referable to this cause; each of us being impressed most forcibly by those texts of Scripture which speak most strongly to his own predominant faculties. While, therefore, it foretells the dissolution of many dogmatical opinions, which at present put enmity and strife between Christian sects, it presents the strongest confirmation of the great truths about which all are agreed, and gives, if possible, an enlarged prominence and importance to the influence which, when freed from heterogeneous errors, these are destined to exercise over human civilisation.*

One great obstacle to your moral, religious, and intellectual progress appears to me to be the influence which the history, institutions, manners, habits, and opinions of Europe are still exercising over the minds of your people. Study these in order to imbibe their wisdom and to adopt their refinement; but avoid the errors which they exhibit, and shun them as guides in your religious and political progress. Society is in a state of transition, and old things are passing away. I have endeavored to point out to you, that your institutions, and those of the governments and churches of Europe, rest on widely different views of human nature and its capabilities. A religious creed, founded on the opinion that man is " wholly defiled in all the faculties and parts of soul and body," may be adapted to a monarchy, which, acting in the spirit of this dogma, denies political power to its millions, and supports religion by statutes, enforcing these, if necessary, by bayonets; but it may be very unsuitable to you, whose whole social arrangements rest on the assumption that man is by nature a religious, moral, and intellectual being. When, however, your sects, in the exercise of freedom, renounce that opinion, and embrace views of man's nature more in accordance with your social institutions, the chained clergy of Europe may accuse them of heretical errors. But do not allow yourselves to be shaken by their disapproval. If you are right, they are in the wrong; and they are not willing to decide against themselves. Every religious community whose faith has been anchored by the edicts of popes, emperors, kings, or parliaments, will represent your departures from their standards as backslidings and pernicious errors, and the conflicts of your sects as the harbingers of the extinction of religion. But fear not. Before your religion can become capable of exercising a powerful, and a much-needed influence, over the public conduct of your people, it must be brought into harmony with the principles of your social institutions and as you have laid aside European forms of government it is to be expected that you may depart from European standards of faith. After a long night of troubled controversy, a brighter dawn will rise on your religious world; Truth is omnipotent, and free discussion is her glorious arena. She will come forth triumphant, and you will ultimately exhibit Christianity in her purity and might, acknowledging Science as her brother and Learning as her sister, mingling harmoniously and gracefully with this world's interests, and guiding your people securely in the paths of virtue and peace.

* I have discussed this topic more fully in my lectures on Moral Philosophy, to which I beg leave to refer.

The influence of the American citizen reaches to all the interests of his country; and I have already endeavored to point out to you how Phrenology may aid you in the discharge of your important duties. Assuming it to be the philosophy of mind founded on the physiology of the brain, it will furnish valuable lights to your understandings when you act,—

As jurymen, and decide on questions of insanity, involving the most important private rights and responsibility to the criminal law;—

As directors of common schools, and superintendants of education;—

As visitors and inspectors of houses of refuge and of prisons;—

As visitors and inspectors of lunatic asylums; and

As electors of legislators, governors, and a vast variety of public officers. Allow me to remark, that, as the whole fabric of your institutions rests on a moral basis, and is devoid of artificial supports, you, of all nations, stand most in need of high moral and intellectual qualities in your public men. It is too obvious that you do not yet possess adequate means of discriminating and selecting individuals possessed of these qualities; for in no country which I have visited, has such an array of delinquencies, committed by men in confidential public situations, been exhibited, as has met my eye since I came to the United States. Many of you will smile when I express my opinion that Phrenology is calculated greatly to aid you in avoiding this monstrous evil. I have stated to you that the native power of manifesting every mental faculty bears a reference, other conditions being equal, to the size of its organs; and that the magnitude of the organs may be estimated. If you wish, therefore, that your public administrators should be vigorous and active, choose men with high temperaments, large brains, and large lungs. If you desire that they should possess native integrity, choose men with predominant organs of Conscientiousness. If you desire that they should possess native benevolence and piety, select individuals in whom the organs of these sentiments are largely developed. If you desire that they should be distinguished for intellectual superiority, select persons with large anterior lobes of the brain. If you require activity, you must attend to the temperament, see vol. i, p. 84; if general power, to the size of the brain in general; if general morality, to the size of the region above B; if general intellect, to the size of the region before A A; and if animal vigor, to the size of the region below B and behind A. This figure represents the proportions of a head in which the moral region above B is generally large, the intellectual region, before A A, respectable; and the animal region, below B and behind A, moderate.

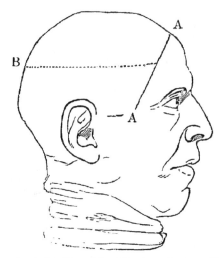

It is the head of the Rev. Mr. Martin, who was distinguished for this combination of qualities.

If you desire to avoid committing your destinies to men of great animal vigor, but deficient in moral and intellectual qualities, shun individuals whose heads resemble or nearly approach to the following form. It represents the head of William Hare, the atrocious associate of Burke in murdering sixteen human beings for the sake of selling their dead bodies for dissection.

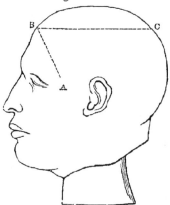

Contrast the proportions of the different regions in these figures; go to Nature and judge for yourselves.

I have explained to you that the size of the organs indicates only the presence of *native* mental power. If size and temperament be deficient, I know of no earthly means by which high capacity can be conferred: but these may be possessed without being cultivated. Phrenology affords no key to the extent of cultivation; but this may be ascertained from other sources. What I desire, therefore, to say is, that if you select men with favorable temperaments, large moral and intellectual organs, adequately educated—and moderate animal organs, disciplined to obedience—you may rely on their virtuous qualities when you employ them as public servants, in all emergencies, not involving disease, as securely as upon the physical elements of nature;—if you choose men deficient in the moral and intellectual organs, and greatly gifted in those of the animal propensities, be their education and religious professions what they may, you will, in the hour of trial and temptation, find that you have relied on broken reeds, and on vessels that retain no water.

I expect these remarks to draw from many of you a smile of incredulity, and from some even one of derision; but nature can wait her time. You and your sons will probably long contemn this method of distinguishing the native qualities of the candidates who solicit your votes; but you and they will suffer as you have done in times past, and now do, from the inferior qualities of many individuals whom you elect, until you open your eyes to your own interest and duty. It is God who has established the facts which I now explain to you, and what he has appointed can never fail. Your vast constituencies cannot, by personal experience and observation, enjoy the advantage of judging of the qualities of all the candidates who solicit their suffrages; and nothing is more fallacious than the testimonies of friends and political partisans; but the brain cannot be moulded to suit the interests of the day, and it will not deceive you. It affords an index to native qualities which, with honest intention and assiduous care, may be read; and I unhesitatingly anticipate that the day will come when your posterity will acknowledge that it sheds a light from heaven upon the entangled path of their public duties.

Finally—Phrenology, when generally taught, will not only render your citizens far more discriminating in their estimates of the qualities of public men, but it will give them confidence in moral and intellectual principle; it will induce them to seek for, draw forth, elevate, and honor, the good and the wise, who at present are too often borne down and excluded by noisy egotism and bustling profession, and left unemployed in the shade. It will also enable the good to recognise each other, and to combine their powers; it will give definite forms to their objects, and union to their efforts. In short, it appears to me to be a great instrument presented to you by Providence, to enable you to realise that grandeur and excellence in your individual and social conditions which the friends of humanity hold you bound to exhibit as the legitimate fruits of freedom.

In presenting these views to you, I exercise that freedom of thought and of speech which your institutions declare to be the birthright of every rational being: but I do not construe your attention in listening to them into approval of their substance; nor do I desire that your countrymen should hold you answerable for either their truth or their tendency. We must hear before we can know, and reflect before we can understand; and truth alone can bear investigation. Embrace, therefore, and apply whatever I may have uttered that is sound; and forgive and forget all that I may have stated in error. By your doing so, the cause of civilisation will be advanced; while we, although differing in opinion, may live in the exercise of mutual affection and esteem. With my warmest acknowledgments for your kind attention, I respectfully bid you farewell.

APPENDIX.

No. I.—Referred to (erroneously as No. III) on p. 9.*

RESOLUTIONS OF THE SECOND CLASS AT PHILADELPHIA.

The average attendance at each lecture in the second course in Philadelphia was 357.

The following resolutions were adopted, and presented by a committee:—

"At the close of Mr. George Combe's second course of Lectures on Phrenology, in the Hall of the Musical Fund, April 6, 1839,

' On motion, Professor Samuel B Wylie was called to the chair, and George M'Clellan, M.D., appointed Secretary.

"The Rev. Chairman addressed the meeting on the propriety of making some public expression of the satisfaction which the very numerous class in attendance had derived from the lectures.

"On motion, the following resolutions, offered by Mr. Thomas Fisher, were unanimously adopted.—

"Resolved,—That this class have listened with great interest to the able and highly instructive exposition of Phrenology which Mr. Combe has offered us.

"Resolved,—That whatever may have been our previous acquaintance with the subject, the lectures of Mr. Combe have impressed us with much respect for its practical importance, and with the kindliest feeling for the learned lecturer.

"Resolved,—That Phrenology is recognised and commended as a science founded in nature, by a large portion of the most distinguished anatomists on both sides of the Atlantic, and that we believe it to be the only adequate illustration of the existing wonderfully various manifestations of the human mind.

"Resolved,—That it will afford us pleasure, and that we believe it will be highly acceptable to this community, that Mr. Combe should make it consistent with his arrangements in other cities to give, during next winter, another course in Philadelphia.

"Resolved,—That a committee of seven gentlemen be appointed to communicate to Mr. Combe a copy of these resolutions.

---

* In some instances the same number serves to designate different articles in the Appendix. This error has arisen from some mistakes in the numeration in the English edition, and also from the circumstance of the sheets of the body of this volume having been printed before the Appendix to it was received.

" The following gentlemen were accordingly appointed —
"Samuel B. Wylie, D.D.   Joseph Hartshorne, M D.
"Samuel George Morton, M.D.   Thomas Gilpin, Esq.
"George M'Clellan, M.D.   Thomas Fisher."
"Charles S. Coxe, Esq.

No. II.—Referred to on p. 35.

CORRESPONDENCE BETWEEN MR. TAPPAN* AND MR. KEY.

(*From the African Repository for April*, 1839.)

Augusta, (Me.) July 31, 1838.

My Dear Sir:—Some years since I had the pleasure of travelling in company with you from Philadelphia to Baltimore, and was indebted to you for the privilege of being introduced to the acquaintance and hospitality of the much beloved and respected Dr. Nevins. I know not whether you will recollect the circumstance, but I must make it my apology for writing to you now with somewhat more of freedom than I would feel in addressing a stranger.

The subject of slavery has frequently come up, within two or three years past, in the meetings in New England of ecclesiastical bodies, and resolutions have been passed expressing their views respecting it. At a late meeting of the General Conference of Maine (consisting of clerical and lay delegates from the county conferences of Congregational churches throughout the state), a committee was raised, of seven clergymen, to correspond with ecclesiastical bodies at the south. After some consultation, the committee were of opinion that it would be advisable, in the first place, to correspond, individually, with individuals at the south. In conformity to that opinion, I am taking the liberty, dear sir, to address this communication to you. You, I am persuaded, will not accuse us of intermeddling, in this matter, with that which does not belong to us. You have welcomed the aid of your fellow-citizens at the north in the colonisation enterprise, in the hope (if I have not misunderstood your views) that the influence of that enterprise would be conducive to the termination of slavery. You will not, therefore, object to the inquiry, whether our influence may not be exerted at the north, as well as at the south, bearing more directly upon such a consummation.

Our first object, in the correspondence proposed, is to obtain information. Permit me, then, to request your attention to the following inquiries.

Does the opinion generally prevail among the ministers and members of southern churches that slaveholding, as practised in this country, is sanctioned by the Word of God? If this is not their opinion, how do they justify themselves in holding slaves?

Do professors of religion forfeit their Christian character by *buying* and *selling* slaves, as they may find it convenient? or do they subject themselves to censure and discipline by any immorality or ill treatment of which they may be guilty towards slaves?

Since the discussion of slavery in the legislature of Virginia a few

---

* Rev. Dr. Tappan of Augusta, Maine.

years since, has there been in that state any change of opinion more favorable to the continuance of the present system? If so, to what causes is that change to be attributed?

Is it the general belief of humane and Christian Colonisationists at the south, that slaves *ought* not to be emancipated, unless they are also sent out of the country? If this is their opinion, on what is it founded? Were they set free, would not their labor still be needed, and might it not be rewarded on terms more advantageous to both parties than under the present arrangements?

Is there any good reason to believe that any thing of importance will be done, generally speaking, to prepare the slaves for freedom before they are made free?

Is there not an under-current of opinion and feeling in the south, among the more enlightened and philanthropic, and is it not widening and strengthening, against the continuance of the present system, and an increasing conviction that it may safely and advantageously be abolished?

What will probably be the influence upon the southern mind of the experiment now in progress in the West Indies?

What, in your opinion, has been the effect, on the whole, at the south, of the efforts of abolitionists? Were the letters, which passed the last winter between Mr. Ellmore and Mr. Birney, read (to any considerable extent) by southern members of Congress? So far as they were read, what was the impression produced by the statements and reasonings of Mr. Birney?

Can there be any useful co-operation between the good people at the north and south (except by means of the colonisation society) in efforts for abolishing or meliorating the present system of slavery?

What are the present prospects of the American colonisation society?

Have many of the officers of this society liberated and colonised their own slaves?

Begging you to excuse the liberty which I have now taken, and requesting an answer at as early a period as you may find it convenient,—I remain my dear sir, very respectfully, yours,

                                            BENJAMIN TAPPAN.

To Francis S. Key, Esq.

P. S.—It is not proposed to make any public use of your name, in connection with any facts or opinions which you may have the kindness to communicate.

MR. KEY'S REPLY.

Washington, October 8, 1838.

REV. AND DEAR SIR:—A long absence from home prevented my receiving your letter till lately; and, though I could wish for more time and leisure to answer it more fully and satisfactorily, I will endeavor to do it without further delay. I well remember our meeting on the occasion you mention; though that would not be necessary to induce me to treat with all respect and attention a letter from you on any subject, and particularly on one which has long and greatly interested me. Before I answer your questions, you will excuse my saying a few words for myself—as that may show how far I am competent to answer them, and what my answers may be worth.

I was born in Maryland, and have always lived in a slave state—am pretty well acquainted with the middle states, and have been as far as Alabama to the south. No northern man began the world with more enthusiasm against slavery than I did. For forty years and upwards, I have felt the greatest desire to see Maryland become a free state, and the strongest conviction that she could become so. That desire and that conviction have not abated in the least—I feel sure that it will be so. I have always been endeavoring to aid in promoting that object, and do so still. I consider it now in the course of accomplishment: and, could I give you all the facts in my possession, and the results of my observation and experience for many years, I believe you would come to this conclusion—that there is now a field open for the labors of all who wish to promote emancipation, to which they should direct and confine their efforts; and that such efforts, if pursued in the right way, would accomplish more in comparatively a few years, than has ever been yet effected: and with these great advantages—that the dissensions arising from this delicate and exciting subject would be everywhere quieted, and the condition of the slaves in the other states greatly meliorated. Had I time, I would like to go on to the north and maintain these propositions. As this cannot be the case, let me now say a word or two more about them.

You may ask why such efforts should be confined to Maryland? I answer: because, first, they would there be readily received; secondly, her people see the advantages of her becoming a free state; thirdly, she is the border state, and can obtain free labor; fourthly, that species of labor already prevailing in some part of the state, manifests its superiority by every sort of improvement. These, and many other causes now in full operation, show, what experience will prove, that no slave state adjacent to a free state can continue so. The people of Maryland are satisfied of this; and a vast majority of them are not only content, but pleased at the pros-pect. Her legislature has declared these views, and, with reference to such a result, has made liberal appropriations to the scheme of Colonisation.—The state has a colony of its own at Cape Palmas Its condition is flour-ishing, and, notwithstanding many difficulties, and the violent and most unreasonable opposition of the abolitionists, the colored people have con-sented to remove to it as fast as their establishment there could be pru-dently conducted, under present circumstances. It is true that her slave population is diminishing, at the same time, by other means. Her prox-imity to a free state enables many to escape. Indeed, near the Pennsyl-vania line, there are few slaves but such as are willing to continue so. Many are also sold, and many remove with their masters to the south, where their labor is more profitable. This, I agree, is not so favorable a disposition of them as colonisation; but it cannot be helped, and it is bet-ter for them than remaining slaves in Maryland, where the unprofitable-ness of their labor makes it difficult for their masters to maintain them comfortably.

You may also desire to know what I mean by qualifying these efforts to be made in Maryland, by saying they must be "*pursued in the right way*," —and you may ask if I do not mean, by this *right way*, colonisation. I answer, that it must be done in a way that the people of Maryland will agree to. Nothing can be more unreasonable than to attempt it in any other way. And if there is any way, to which they will consent, which is better for the slaves than their present condition, it ought to be acquiesced in even by those who may think that there is a better way. Now, there are some ways in which the people of Maryland will never agree to these efforts being made. 1st, Not by abolition publications—because they are dangerous and unnecessary. It is vain to argue about their being danger-ous. They know it from experience, and certainly are better judges of what is dangerous to persons in their situation than any men elsewhere can be. Further—whether better judges or not, they will be, and they ought to be the only judges for the danger is to themselves. And such efforts are proved to be unnecessary; for there are now, and always have been, more slaves ready to be emancipated than there are means to remove from the state, that condition of removal being, as the people of Maryland think (allowing some exceptions) indispensable. Of this I shall speak hereafter. 2dly, They will not allow an immediate and general emancipation, deeming it ruinous both to the slaves and themselves. And, 3dly, They require, as a condition, removal from the state, except in particular instances, where the slaves, on account of their good conduct and character may be allowed to remain, on certain conditions That such removal may be accomplished in a way advantageous to the liberated slaves, the door of colonisation has been opened. We believe (we think upon undoubted evidence) that, besides the obvious and immense advantages to Africa, this mode of disposition is the best for them; and we are sure that time will make this apparent to all But, if the people of the free states think otherwise, and are so sure that they may remain safely, happily, and usefully in Maryland, as to be willing to receive them into their own limits, there would be no objection to their doing so If there is this difference of opinion as to their remaining among the whites, between the people of the free states and the slave states, surely the only fair way of settling it is for those who are in favor of their remaining to take them. It is unnecessary, therefore, to discuss this question. If ever so necessary, I am sure it would be vain; for the people of Maryland have an experience upon the subject that no arguments could shake. And they will believe that they are more competent to decide it than the people of the free states can possibly be.

I will, however, state the results of my own experience. I have emancipated seven of my slaves They have done pretty well, and six of them, now alive, are supporting themselves comfortably and creditably Yet I cannot but see that this is all they are doing now; and when age and infirmity come upon them, they will probably suffer. It is to be observed, also, that these were selected individuals, who were, with two exceptions, brought up with a view to their being so disposed of, and were made to undergo a probation of a few years in favorable situations, and when emancipated, were far better fitted for the duties and trials of their new condition than the general mass of slaves. Yet I am still a slaveholder, and could not, without the greatest inhumanity, be otherwise. I own, for instance, an old slave, who has done no work for me for years I pay his board and other expenses, and cannot believe that I sin in doing so.

The laws of Maryland contain provisions of various kinds, under which slaves, in certain circumstances, are entitled to petition the courts for their freedom. As a lawyer, I always undertook these cases with peculiar zeal, and have been thus instrumental in liberating several large families and many individuals. I cannot remember more than two instances, out of this large number, in which it did not appear that the freedom I so earnestly sought for them was their ruin. It has been so with a very large proportion of all others I have known emancipated. A gentleman in Maryland, upwards of thirty years ago, emancipated by his will between two and three hundred negroes. They all took (as they were required to do) his name. For several years they crowded our cities, where their vices and idleness were notorious, and their sufferings extreme. I have not seen one for many years, and am informed that there are none in the county where they were liberated. There may be some in the free states. Their name was Barnes. I do not believe there could be now found in Maryland twenty of the name.

It is in vain, in the face of facts like these, which every man I have ever spoken with upon the subject avows his knowledge of, to talk of the British West India Islands and the apprentice system—at least, it must be vain to talk of these things till they are fully tried. I shall be surprised, though gratified, if the result of these experiments differ from that of similar attempts in Maryland. I observe that, at the last anti-slavery anniversary, it was admitted that the apprentice system was all wrong, and had failed; and now, the recent accounts from Jamaica represent the deplorable state of the island, in consequence of the refusal of the negroes to work, except for wages beyond the power of the planters to give

I will proceed now to answer your questions. This is the first.

"Does the opinion generally prevail among the ministers nd members of southern churches, that slaveholding, as practised in thi- country, is sanctioned by the Word of God? If this is not their opinion, how do they justify themselves in holding slaves?"

The ministers and members of southern churches will not attempt to justify themselves in any thing without the sanction of the Word of God: the latter part, therefore, of the question is unnecessary. You ask, then, if we believe that slaveholding, as practised in this country, is sanctioned by the Word of God. I answer, that they believe generally, I think, that Scripture contains neither an express sanction nor an express prohibition on the subject. It gives general rules to govern men's conduct towards each other, applicable to this and all other cases. If men cannot hold slaves without violating these rules, they must not hold them, and, if these rules permit or require us, under any circumstances, to hold slaves, then the Word of God sanctions *such* slave-holding. Take, then, the great rule of the Gospel—"Do unto others as you would they should do unto you." This must govern all possible cases of human conduct, and bears, of course, upon this question as to slave holding. Does it sanction slave-holding *under all circumstances?* or prohibit slave-holding *under all circumstances?* It does (and, I think, most wisely) neither—leaving it to be determined by circumstances whether this law of love authorizes or forbids it. If a Christian, then, considering whether he shall hold a slave or not, takes this rule, and applies it honestly, as in the sight of God, to his case, and comes fairly to the conclusion that he should, who shall condemn him? All that can be said is, that he is misled by prejudice or interest, and has come to a wrong conclusion: Hundreds and thousands of Christians, showing in their whole life undoubted evidences of the faith which they profess, have so applied this rule to their conscience, and so come to this conclusion. Their brethren at the north, knowing nothing of the peculiar circumstances under which they have acted, nor of the care and faithfulness with which they have inquired and decided, call upon them to justify themselves for violating the sanctions of God's word. This, I am willing to believe, is more owing to want of information than of charity: though, certainly, even without information, it would be only reasonable to indulge the hope and the belief that there was something of a justificatory nature in the circumstances surrounding their distant brethren, which should relieve them from such an accusation.

Consider what a proposition it is that must be maintained by those who thus denounce, in these sweeping terms, all slave-holders It is this: A man always violates the divine precept of doing as he would be done by when he holds a slave.

Strange as this proposition would sound to any one at all acquainted with the various circumstances under which persons in a slave state become the owners and holders of slaves, yet I doubt not many honest, but heated abolitionists are ready to maintain it. Indeed, it is often avowed in their publications. Yet I think it is easy to state a few instances in which it would seem impossible to deny that this precept not only permitted, but required, the holding of a slave; and they are instances continually occurring.

A man becomes (sometimes by no act of his own) the owner of an old or infirm slave, when emancipation would be the basest cruelty, and there is no way of maintaining him in comfort, but by holding him as a slave; is he to be emancipated? So of a slave who is idle, intemperate, &c. &c. who, without wholesome restraint, would be wretched himself, and a plague to all others; would this Christian precept require him to be emancipated? So of all cases where the holder of slaves conscientiously believes that their condition, from the peculiar circumstances of their situation, will be made worse by freedom—worse to themselves and others.

There are, again, other instances when a benevolent man will meet in a slave community with such appeals to his charity, that he will buy and hold slaves because he wishes to do as he would be done by. Many are so bought and held. A slave may have an unkind master—may be about to be sold away from his friends or family—a family of slaves may be liable to separation: in all these cases, a man who is known to be a good master, and who has the means of employing them so as to maintain them comfortably, will be importuned to purchase them. It will be a manifest improvement in their condition. Will not this Christian precept sanction his yielding to their entreaties? It may be said that he should buy them and liberate them. This, even if satisfied that it would be better for them, he might not be able to afford. And shall he refuse to do the lesser charity because he has not the means to do the greater?

I therefore answer your first question thus: "Slave-holding, as practised in this country, is sanctioned by the Word of God," when it is practised, as I know it often is, in such instances as I have stated, and in many others, consistently with the Christian precept of doing as we would be done by. And "slave-holding, as practised in this country" otherwise, as when slaves are bought and held for the mere purposes of gain by traffic, or by extorting their labor without any regard to their welfare (for it must be admitted that it is so practised by some,) is not sanctioned by the Word of God. So that slave-holding is right or wrong (as many other things are) according as it is practised. I have not thought it necessary to advert to some passages of Scripture which it seems hard to reconcile with the idea that slave-holding, under all circumstances, is within its prohibitions.

Your second question is as follows.—

"Do professors of religion forfeit their Christian character by buying and selling slaves, as they may find it convenient? or do they subject themselves to censure and discipline by any immorality or ill treatment of which they might be guilty towards their slaves?"

The persons among us who buy and sell slaves for profit are never, as I have ever heard or believe, professors of religion. Such conduct, or any immorality or ill treatment towards their slaves, would forfeit their Christian character and privileges, if their minister did his duty. And nothing more disgraces a man in general estimation than to be guilty of any immorality or ill treatment towards his slaves

Third question—"Since the discussion of slavery in the Legislature of Virginia, a few year since, has there been in that state any change of opinion more favorable to the continuance of the present system? If so, to what causes is that change to be attributed?"

A considerable change of opinion has taken place in all the middle states, particularly, perhaps, in Virginia and Maryland, such as your question suggests. Some who are favorable to the emancipation connected with removal now avow themselves against it altogether, and against the agitation of every thing connected with slavery, and show less kind feeling toward the blacks. I attribute this to the publications and efforts of the abolitionists.

Fourth question—"Is it the general belief of humane and Christian colonizationists in the south, that slaves ought not to be emancipated, unless they are also sent out of the country? If this is their opinion, on what is it founded? Were they set free, would not their labor still be needed, and might it not be secured on terms more advantageous to both parties than under present arrangements?"

It is, I believe, universally so thought by them. I never heard a contrary opinion, except that some conceived, some time ago, that a territory in our country, to the West, might be set apart for them. But few, comparatively, adopted this idea; and I never hear it advocated now. This opinion is founded on the conviction that their labor, however it might be needed, could not be secured but by a severer system of constraint than that of slavery—that they would constitute a distinct and inferior race of people which all experience proves to be the greatest evil that could afflict a community. I do not suppose, however, that they would object to their reception in the free states, if they chose to make preparations for their comfortable settlement among them.

Fifth question—"Is there any good reason to believe that any thing of importance, generally speaking, will be done to prepare the slaves for freedom before they are made free?"

As the colonisation scheme advances, I think much will be done. Many masters will prepare their young slaves for such a change. Many, who cannot afford to emancipate altogether, will make arrangements with their slaves to go to Africa, and remit a moderate price for themselves, as they may be able to do. And if a desire to return to their fathers' land should become general (as I trust it will,) both among the slaves and free blacks, nothing could be better calculated to improve and exalt the whole colored race. It would encourage them to good conduct, industry, temperance, and all those efforts that men make to better their condition.

Sixth—"Is there not an under-current of opinion and feeling in the South among the enlightened and philanthropic, and is it not widening and strengthening against the continuance of the present system, and an increasing conviction that it may safely and advantageously be abolished?"

I have not seen any appearance of such a current for several years past. I think it would be difficult to find any tolerably informed individual who holds such opinions or feelings. There was formerly some feeling of this kind in favor of a gradual abolition of slavery. I think there is none now, unless conected with the condition of removal. I assure you that I never hear, though I converse with men of all sorts, slaveholders and others, who hold no slaves, any opinion favorable to emancipation, except on that condition.

Seventh—"What will probably be the influence upon the southern mind of the experiment now in progress in the West Indies?"

If the southern mind becomes calm and unheated by opposition, and that experiment should succeed, it would, I think, have great effect—Removal from the country might not then be insisted on as a condition of emancipation.

Eighth—"What in your opinion, has been the effect, on the whole, at the South, of the efforts of abolitionists? Were the letters which passed last winter between Mr. Elmore and Mr. Birney read (to any considerable extent) by southern members of Congress? So far as they were read, what was the impression produced by the statements and reasonings of Mr. Birney?"

I think the efforts of the abolitionists have been most unfortunate. There is a great and unfavorable change of opinion and feeling in the whites towards the blacks, which, I think, cannot be otherwise accounted for; and the whole colored race have been injured by these efforts. The free and the slaves have been both subjected to more restraint. The publications mentioned have been very little read by southern men. They would rarely take up any thing understood to be written by a prominent abolitionist.

Ninth—"Can there be any useful co-operation between good people at the North and South (except by means of the Colonisation Society) in efforts for abolishing or ameliorating the present system of slavery?"

I think good men at the north if they will fairly inquire, will, both for the sake of Africa and our own land, prefer the colonisation plan to any other. They must do this soon, as they must know (what they may know now) what benefits Africa is receiving, and our colonists are enjoying, under its efforts. But, if any of our Northern brethren cannot see this, let them prepare an asylum for emancipated slaves among themselves, where they can be usefully employed and happily settled, and raise funds for their removal and settlement. I believe as many could be obtained readily as could be thus provided for. In this way they could essentially promote emancipation.

In "meliorating the present system of slavery," they could also do much. This might be done in several ways, but more particularly in assisting in their religious improvement—a subject which now greatly occupies the minds of southern men, particularly since the Southampton insurrection, which, you may know, originated with a religious fanatic, or a hypocrite playing the fanatic. From a variety of causes, the public mind particularly of religious professors, has been turned to this subject. The Assistant-Bishop of Virginia, a year or two ago, made a strong appeal to the churches of his diocese, and the ministers of all denominations are taking up the subject, and considerable efforts are making for their regular religious instruction. The Bishop of North Carolina told me, a year ago, of very interesting commencements of this kind introduced into that state. He stated that it was now common for two or three neighboring planters to join in employing a minister for their slaves, and he said he had then applications for ministers for six or seven such situations, and found it impossible to supply them. I was informed last winter of the arrangements made by Mr. Rhett, a member of congress from South Carolina, for the instruction of his negroes. He employs a minister, who lives on his estate, and devotes himself to the improvement of his slaves, for whom he has built a church, where they have regular service. I made several inquiries of Mr. Rhett, who gave me a very interesting account of his establishment, and says it has introduced order, good conduct, and happiness among his slaves to a remarkable degree, and that many of his neighbors are endeavoring to adopt similar arrangements. Now, we want ministers for all these places. The demand for them is now great and earnest; and I believe that, in every neighborhood where there are many slaves, in the middle states, such situations will be found. Let our northern brethren qualify their young ministers for these interesting charges—qualify them, by making them understand this delicate subject of slavery—or keeping them pure from all the fanaticism of abolition, send them with their minds open to conviction, where they may see and judge for themselves, and where they will learn that, while many Christians are holding slaves, from the necessity of their situation, they are holding them without forgetting

they are their brethren—and where they will see slaves far happier than
the laboring classes of many countries. At present, young men from the
North are excluded from these situations, because they are supposed to
be under the influence of abolition principles, and slaveholders are afraid to
trust them. Let this prejudice against receiving young men from the
North as teachers and ministers in such situations be removed, by a
more correct and charitable state of feeling and opinion at the North
towards slaveholders and a wide and most interesting field of labor
will be opened to pious young men from the northern states, in which
they will be able to do much for the melioration of the present system of slavery, and, in some situations, where it can be done with advantage to the slaves and without danger to the masters, to promote emancipation also.

I will here mention that the religious instruction of the slaves in the
middle states (I speak more particularly of Maryland) has been more attended to by the Methodists than by any other denomination I think
more than three-fourths of the whole colored population, where they have
access to Methodist churches, belong to that denomination. Nor is there
any prejudice against the Methodist teachers and preachers, on the part
of the masters, although that sect has been always considered friendly to
emancipation. A change has, however, taken place, not only in the opinions and feelings of that class of Christians, but in the discipline of their
church, which it may be proper to mention. It shows how Christians,
strongly prejudiced against slavery, and anxious to abolish it, have been
made to learn, by their own observation and experience, that, under certain
circumstances, it is perfectly consistent with Christian principles to purchase and hold slaves. Methodists formerly denounced slavery in general
terms, as it is now denounced at the north. They were never allowed, and
would not be now, to act as jurors in a suit for freedom. They were not
allowed by their discipline to continue in the church, if they purchased and
held slaves. If a member of their church purchased a slave, no matter
under what circumstances, the matter was brought before the monthly conference, and it was then determined, the age and value of the slave and
the price paid for him being all considered, what was a reasonable term of
service to be required of him as a compensation for what his master had
paid for him—that is, how many years' service at the usual rate of hire,
would reimburse the advance of the master—and he was then to be no
longer a slave, but a servant for that time.

The rule of discipline is now changed; and now, when a member of
their Church purchases a slave, it is brought, as before, to the consideration of the conference, and the circumstances are inquired into. If it is
considered that he has bought from a mercenary motive, for gain alone,
without any inducements of kindness or favor towards the slave, he is cen-
sured and suspended from his church privileges, and made to do what is
thought right or excommunicated, according to the circumstances of miti-
gation or aggravation that may be found in the particular case. If he has
bought from kindness to the slave, to prevent the separation of a family, or
in any way with the motive of bettering his condition, he is allowed to
hold him, and is considered as having acted consistently with Christian
principles. In this way Methodists now buy and work slaves as other
Christians do; and their church (as is the case with all other denominations)
only requires that they should treat them well. Cruelty to slaves, if
charged and sustained against any man belonging to a church of any
denomination, would exclude him from its privileges, and would also exclude him from all reputable society. I do not mean to say that the

slaves in Maryland are maintained as well as they ought to be; in some parts of the state, I know, I have already said, their masters are unable to do so.

It may seem strange to gentlemen unacquainted with our institutions how a man can buy a slave from mere charity; yet nothing is more common—as a very short residence in any slave neighborhood would convince them. Perhaps I may best show this by supposing a case—it is such a one as often occurs. To make it more apposite, I will suppose the person applied to to be a man from the north, with the strongest prejudices against slavery. He buys a farm in Maryland, which he cultivates with hired labor, both because of his opposition to slavery, and because it is, in his opinion (as in some parts of Maryland it is in fact), cheaper than slave labor. He has nothing but his farm and its stock, and it requires all its produce, with a good management and strict economy, to maintain his family. Such a man, who has lived in this way a year or two, and whom we will designate as Mr. B., is applied to on a Saturday evening by Tom, a stout, hearty, young negro, and the following dialogue takes place between them.—

Tom. Master, I am come to ask a very great favor.

Mr. B. Well, Tom, let me hear what it is. If what you want is reasonable and in my power, I shall be glad to do it.

Tom. Master, I think it is reasonable, and I hope it will lie in your power. My wife, you know, is a free woman, and has now been in your service some time. I was hired to you last harvest, and at other times, and you know what sort of a hand I am.

Mr. B. Yes, Tom, I have been well satisfied with both your wife and yourself, and you know that I offered, partly to accommodate you both, to hire you by the year, but your master thought he could not spare you.

Tom. Well, sir, he must spare me now. I am to be sold; and what I want, and what would make me and my wife happy for our whole lives, is for you to buy me.

Mr. B. Tom, that is out of the question. You know I hold no slaves—I am principled against it. I will go and see your master, and hire you. Surely he will not sell you.

Tom. Sir, he can't help it. They say he has had a power of money to pay for his cousin in town, who was broke up last spring; and another debt has now gone against him. last week, at the court. So he called me into the hall yesterday, and says he, "Tom, you have been a good fellow, and so was your father before you. You'll have to be sold by the sheriff, if you can't get a master in the neighborhood· go and see what you can do." So he gave me this note, and he gave notice to all but the old people. He said he had been to the gentleman who held the debt; and all he could do was to give him one week, to try and sell the people himself, that the sheriff might not have to sell them to the soul-drivers. I am sure I am sorry for him, as well as for myself; for he has been a good master to us all.

Mr. B. Tom, I am sorry for you, but I cannot buy a slave—I cannot give such a sanction to this horrible system. You must get somebody else to buy you: I will hire you, and give the highest wages. I know you are a good hand; but I cannot hold a slave—it is against my principles.

Tom could not well understand this, but he went to two or three other neighbors without success, and he and his wife were in great trouble.

On Sunday night they were (as usual) called in to family prayers, and it so happened that Mr. B., being in the habit of using, on such occasions, Doddridge's Family Expositor, came to that part of the book which contained the precept of our Savior of doing to others as we would they should do unto us. The exposition of Doddridge is, as we know, very plain and very strong. Tom understood it, and thought it a pity that Mr B.'s *principles* should prevent him from doing the favor he asked. Mr. B. was a Christian and he felt like a man who has two opposite principles to walk by. He saw it would be a kind thing to buy this poor fellow—that was plain—and that it was just what, in similar circumstances, he should wish done for himself. But slave-holding, he had long settled, was the height of wickedness—and how could he do it? If he could buy him and set him free, then his duty was plain: but this he could not afford to do with justice to his own family. It would leave him without adequate means to hire labor for his farm. Still he was not at ease, and he arose early in the morning, and called Tom, whom he found taking a sorrowful leave of his wife.

Mr B. Tom, I am sorry I have not the means of buying you and setting you free. If I could afford it, I would gladly do so.

Tom. Master, if you could buy me and let me work for you as long as I live, that would be all I could ask. You would have to run the risk of my dying or running away; but you would have my labor as long as I worked for you, and this would save you the hire of other hands—so that you might afford to do this, instead of buying me and setting me free for nothing.

Mr. B. That is true, and I am not afraid of your running away, Tom; but I cannot hold a slave—I must not be a slaveholder.

Tom. Master, then hold me, not as a slave, but something else—buy me, and you can call me what you please, you can tell me that I am not a slave and that I may run away when I please—you know I will not.

Mr B. Well, Tom, if I could get around this, I do not see how I can buy you. It would be owning your master's right to you as a slave, and his right to sell you.

Tom. Well, it is very hard. I don't see who has got any right to object to your buying or holding me as a slave, if I am agreed to it. If I ask such a favor, and you grant it, to save me from being sold away, who can complain of you for doing such a kindness—for doing as you would be done by?

Whether this argument succeeded with Mr. B., or he was overpowered by the distress of Tom's wife, and the sympathy of his own wife and children, who all came around him, it might be hard to determine; but he told Tom to stay where he was, and he rode over to his master.

Before I conclude what I have to say under this question, permit me again to solicit your attention, and that of your friends, to the present situation of Maryland. This state is a slave state, bordering on a free state. She is changing her condition, as Pennsylvania and other states have done. Her legislators and citizens very generally avow their determination that she shall be a free state. The free labor of Pennsylvania is flowing over into her, and she can change her laborers, and in many parts of the state bordering on Pennsylvania, there is now scarcely any slavery—certainly none that can be regarded as an evil—for there are no slaves there but such as choose to continue so. Such parts of the state also exhibit a remarkable degree of improvement, so as to convince all that Maryland, in the price, and improvements, and products of her land, in the increase and improvements of her population, and in many other respects, will derive incalculable benefits from the change.

I shall send you some documents and publications upon this subject, which will show you what the legislature of that state is doing, and what evident progress is making to accomplish the object of making Maryland a free state.

Thus will soon be worked out this political problem—"A slave state, lying by the side of a free state, will become a free state." I believe this as fully as any demonstration in Euclid.

What a prospect this opens to humane and benevolent men at the north, is obvious—particularly to such as desire to remove this blot from as many of our institutions as possible.

When Virginia becomes the border state she will be brought under the same process. Indeed, in some parts of that state, it is now in operation. Free labor will be brought to her, and she will find that she can change, and change most beneficially, her system. And so will it work on, till the dark line that separates the free from the slave states reaches the southern border of our land.

Thus, and thus only, is the slavery of the southern states to be approached. In many of them, now, it is absurd to propose any scheme of emancipation, or to address their people upon such a question.

But let the work be confined to the border states, and it will go on rapidly and safely.

The slaves of Maryland are diminishing every year, as will appear by the census. They are going off in various ways—many are sold to the south; many are emancipated; some run away.

Hundreds of masters in Maryland are ready to emancipate their slaves, if they can go away—a condition which they know, from the fullest experience, is beneficial both to themselves and those they liberate. They have already emancipated a great number—some of whom have remained, and others have gone to Africa—and they know how great and obvious have been the advantages of removal.

In some parts of Maryland slave labor is no longer profitable. They cannot be maintained there. Their masters must remove with them, or dispose of them in some way. Humanity to them requires this.

Must they, then, go farther south as slaves? or to Africa as free men?

This is the condition of the colored population of Maryland—this is the alternative presented for them to the consideration of the benevolent.

I agree that, if removal to Africa is that horrible act of cruelty that it is represented to be—if their condition in the colonies there established is as wretched as is asserted—humanity may stand still, and be indifferent whether they go south as slaves, or cross the ocean as freemen.

And this brings me to the last topic of your letter—the present condition and prospects of the colonisation scheme. Examine this thoroughly and impartially, and see whether any thing has been done, or can be done, to compare with it, in its beneficial results to the colored race here and in Africa.

All I need say of this (as I shall send you publications giving you full information on the subject) is, that I think I have seen more indications of the favor of Providence towards this object than any other I have ever considered—that its success is greater than that of any other similar enterprise ever undertaken, and that I have no doubt of its success—that the long-lost children of ill-fated Africa will be restored to their fathers' land, bearing with them the blessings of religion and civilisation, and thus

" Vindicate the ways of God to man."

I have no objection to your making use of this communication, and of my name, in any way that you think will do good.

I am, yours respectfully,

F. S. KEY.

P. S.—I did not observe that I had omitted to answer a part of your last question.

The publications of the society will show that many of its members have emancipated their slaves, and sent them to Africa, and others have made arrangements for doing so. Mr. Murray, of Maryland, sent out all his slaves (upwards of 30) nine or ten years ago, and he often hears from them, and they speak with great satisfaction of their situation Mr Fitzhugh, of Virginia, another member of the society, has made provision, by his will, for the removal of all his slaves (I believe about 200) to Africa. Most of those now in Africa have been emancipated with the view to their removal there. F. S. K.

No. III.*—Referred to on p. 48.

RESOLUTIONS OF THE CLASS WHO ATTENDED THE SECOND COURSE OF LECTURES OF PHRENOLOGY IN NEW YORK.

The average attendance on this course was the following —subscribers, 139, visiters, 35, complimentary hearers, 20; total average attendance each night, 194.

To GEORGE COMBE, Esq

NEW YORK, *May* 20, 1839.

SIR.—At a meeting of the class in attendance on your second course of lectures in this city, held on the 18th day of May 1839, the undersigned were appointed a committee to present the accompanying resolutions which were unanimously adopted by the class, as expressive of their opinions of the truth and importance of Phrenology, of your talents as a lecturer, and of your character as a man.

In fulfilling this pleasurable duty, the undersigned beg to assure you of their hearty concurrence with the opinions and sentiments therein expressed, and of their high personal respect.

THOMAS J. SAWYER,
LA ROY SUNDERLAND,
E. P. HURLBUT,
ANDREW BOARDMAN.

At a meeting of the class in attendance upon Mr. George Combe's second course of Lectures, on the 15th day of May 1839, the following gentlemen were appointed a Committee to prepare and report a paper and resolutions expressive of the sentiments of the class, upon the subject of said lectures, and their feelings toward Mr. Combe as a lecturer, to-wit: Rev. Mr. Sawyer, Mr. Boardman, Rev. Mr. Sunderland and Mr. Hurlbut.

On the 18th day of May instant, Mr. Hurlbut, from that Committee, reported the following paper and resolutions, which were adopted unanimously by the class·

The second course of lectures upon Phrenology, delivered in this city by Mr. George Combe, of Edinburgh, having closed, the members of his class are desirous of expressing their views of the science which he has taught, and the sentiments entertained by them toward the distinguished lecturer personally.

* See p. 357.

He has presented to us the wonderful discovery of Dr. Gall, and its practical influence upon the character and condition of man. That discovery was characterized by the most minute attention to the laws of our organization—by the most patient observation of facts— and by the deduction of inevitable conclusions from them.

Dr. Gall abandoned the school of metaphysical speculation, and taking to the observation of nature, he at length presented to the world his great discovery of the true functions of the brain, and of its various parts.

We now look to nature for the foundation of the science of mental philosophy, and the enlightened mind of the old world and the new is now engaged in illustrating and establishing it.

Our own country has been twice honored by visits from the earliest and most gifted advocates of this science. The noble and accomplished Spurzheim (a name sacred to every friend of man) fell a victim to disease upon our shores, whilst just opening the rich fountain of his well-stored intellect to an American audience.

The language of eulogy fails altogether when employed upon so noble a nature as his But for this we thank him—that he directed the mind of a Combe to the sublime truths he had himself embraced, and allowed his mantle to descend upon the gifted individual to whom we have all listened with intense interest and delight. How nobly has he executed in our country the work which his " great and lamented master" had begun!

He came not among us to earn applause, for of that he had already enough; nor treasure, for we are happy to know of that he had no occasion to go in search. He came not seeking controversy, being no less distinguished for his love of peace than for his devotion to science But he came as a minister from the enlightened mind of the old world, to treat with the intellect of the new upon matters of the deepest concern to the human race.

His message was of the highest importance to us all It interested us as students of Nature's laws, as observers of their manifestations, as speculators in mental philosophy, and friends of education. It opened new views of man's moral and intellectual character, and well nigh explained the mystery of *thought*—that most subtle emanation from the divinity of Nature. It taught the discipline of youth. how to inform their intellect, to elevate their sentiments, and to moderate their passions. It pointed the way of happiness to man, by exhibiting the sources of human virtue and its effects; the causes of vice, and its effects upon his condition in life. It presented the most rational and humane view of moral responsibility, and explained and enforced the whole duty of man, and, in this his last and crowning lecture, Mr. Combe has opened the treasures of his knowledge of the political institutions of the old world—faithfully portrayed their defects, their subversion of human liberty and happiness—and contrasted with them the free institutions of our own country and their happy influences upon the moral and intellectual condition of our citizens.

And now, having attended upon the gifted lecturer through his various illustrations, his well authenticated facts, and heard his sound deductions drawn from them, we hasten to express our profound sense of obligation to him for the instruction he has afforded us, and our high appreciation of the doctrines he has so ably maintained.

Be it therefore—

1. Resolved, That we regard Phrenology as having its foundation in the truths of Nature—and as entitled, in point of dignity and interest, to rank high among the natural sciences

2. Resolved, That we regard the practical application of Phrenological principles, to physical training, to moral and mental education—to the

treatment of the insane, and to criminal legislation—as of the highest importance and utility; and we indulge the hope of witnessing in our own day the beneficial results of such application in the increased happiness of our homes, in the improved condition of our seminaries of learning, in more enlightened legislation, and in the more benign influences of our civil and religious institutions

3 Resolved, That the extensive knowledge and sound philosophy which Mr. Combe has exhibited in the course of his lectures, have inspired us with a profound respect for his intellectual power and attainments; and, while the simplicity of manner and purity of style with which he has conveyed the most interesting truths, evince a highly cultivated taste, the generous enthusiasm with which he has embarked in the cause of humanity commands our admiration of his sentiments equal to the respect we entertain for his understanding.

4. Resolved, That, entertaining such opinions of the science with which Mr. Combe has identified his life and fame, and such sentiments toward him as a lecturer and a man, we beg to tender to him an expression of our heartfelt gratitude for the instruction and delight he has afforded us, and our kindest wishes for his prosperity and happiness through life

On motion, it was farther Resolved, That the gentlemen constituting the Committee who reported the foregoing, be instructed to present the same to Mr. Combe.

T I. SAWYER, *Chairman.*
ANDW. BOARDMAN, *Secretary.*

No. IV.—Referred to on p 68

(*From the Albany Daily Advertiser*)

THE LAW OF THE ROAD.

AN esteemed correspondent sends us the following communication, which is of especial interest to the great moving mass of travellers, who at this season of the year throng our steam-boats, stages, and railroad cars Most persons attach a vast deal of meaning to the brief notice, "All baggage at the risk of the owner," when in truth it imposes no additional care on the traveller, and certainly relieves of no responsibility the different transportation companies. *Their* duties as *common carriers* are clearly shown in the annexed communication, and no notice of the above or any other description can free them from the obligations which they assume when they undertake to transport passengers and property.

"ALL BAGGAGE AT THE RISK OF THE OWNER."—Syracuse and Utica Railroad.

"All goods, baggage, freight, specie, bank-bills, or any kind of property taken, shipped, or put on board of these boats must be at the risk of the owners, &c,"—New York, Albany, and Troy Steam-boat Line.

"Freight and baggage at the risk of the owners thereof."—Troy and Albany Steam-boats.

"All baggage positively at the risk of the owner *Way passengers will attend personally to the disposition of their baggage at Schenectady*"—Utica and Schenectady Railroad.

"All baggage at the risk of the owners thereof."—Saratoga and Schenectady Railroad, Troy, Ballston, and Saratoga Railroad.

"All baggage at the risk of the owner."—Auburn and Syracuse Railroad.

"All baggage, specie, and freight at the risk of the owners thereof."—New Steam-boat arrangement between Albany and New York.

To the Editor of the Albany Daily Advertiser:

The above notices are taken from advertisements in a single column of the Albany Argus.

As quiet or ignorant people may perhaps be induced to submit to the imposition of a loss of their freight or baggage rather than litigate with a great monopoly, especially when the above notices are thrust in their faces, and they are told *they were bound to take notice of them,* it will perhaps be doing the travelling public a service by referring them to two decisions of the Supreme Court of this State, to wit Holster *v* Nawlen, 19 Wendell's Reports 234, and Cole *v.* Goodwin, ibid. 251, both decided at the May term, 1838, in which it is expressly decided, that stage-coach, railroad, and steam-boat proprietors *are common carriers,* and are, like all other common carriers, answerable for the baggage of passengers, that they are regarded as *insurers,* and must answer for any loss not occasioned *by the act of God, or the public enemies.* That the fact that *the owner is present,* or sends his servants to look after the property, does not alter the case. That common carriers cannot restrict their common law liability, by a general notice like that which I have taken above as the text of this article—that a notice, "ALL BAGGAGE AT THE RISK OF THE OWNER," *even if brought home to the knowledge of a passenger* in a stage coach who lost his trunk, was no protection to the proprietors of the coach in an action against them for the loss of the trunk That *common carriers* are bound to deliver to *each passenger* at the end of *his* journey *his* trunk or baggage That *the whole duty* in this respect rests upon the carriers. That the exercise of ordinary care in marking the baggage, entering it upon a way-bill, and delivering a check-ticket to the owner, renders easy its discharge. That the *passenger* is not required to expose his person in a crowd, or endanger his safety in the attempt to *designate* or *claim* his property.

What is the reason that the common law will not excuse the carrier unless he show the act of God, or the enemies of the republic, or the misconduct of the owner? "This," says Lord Holt, in Coggs *v* Bernard, 2d Lord Raymond's Reports, 918, "is a politic establishment, contrived by the policy of the law, for the safety of all persons, the necessity of whose affairs requires them to trust these sort of persons (*common carriers*) that they may be safe in their ways of dealing, for else these carriers might have an opportunity of undoing all persons that had any dealings with them, by combining with thieves, &c., and yet doing it in such a clandestine manner as would not be possible to be discovered.

Cowen, Justice, in Cole *v* Goodwin, cited above, says at page 280, " I have said that relaxing the common law rigor opens the high road to fraud, perjury, theft, and robbery. It does more. Looking to the present ordinary, not to say universal means of travel and transportation by coaches, railroads, steamboats, packets, and merchant vessels, the mere superaddition of negligence, in respect to the safety of passengers and property, would constitute a most fearful item. There is no principle in the law better settled than that whatever has an obvious tendency to encourage guilty negligence, fraud, or crime, is contrary to public policy Such, in the very nature of things, is the consequence of allowing the common carrier to throw off or in any way restrict his legal liability. The traveller and bailor is under a sort of moral duress, a necessity of employing the common carrier under those legal arrangements, which allow any number of persons to assume that character, and thus discourage and supersede the provision for other modes of conveyance. My conclusion is, that he shall not be allowed, in any form, to higgle with his customer, and extort one exception and another, *not even by express promise, or special acceptance,* any more than by notice. He shall not be privileged to make himself a common carrier for his own benefit, and a mandatary, or less to his employer. He is a public servant with certain duties defined by law; and he is bound to perform those duties."

No. V.—Referred to on p. 70.

The following table will exhibit the relative strength of the different brines from which salt is manufactured in the United States —

At Natucket, 350 gallons sea-water give a bushel of Salt.

Boon's Lick (Missouri), .	450 gallons brine, give	do
Conemaugh (Penn.), . .	300	do	do
Shawneetown (Illinois), .	280	do.	do.
Jackson (Ohio), ...	213	do.	do.
Lockhart (Miss.), . . .	180	do.	do.
Shawneetown (2d saline,)	123	do.	do.
St. Catharines (U.C.), . .	120	do.	do.
Zanesville (Ohio), . . .	95	do.	do.
Kenawha (Va), ...	75	do.	do.
Grand River (Arkansas),	80	do.	do.
Illinois River, do.	80	do.	do
Muskingum (Ohio), . .	50	do.	do.
Onondaga,* (N. Y.), .	41 to 45	do.	do

* This table is chiefly extracted from Dr. J. Van Rensselaer's Essay on Salt. The produce of the Kenawha brine, and of the Muskingum saline is added from Hildreth's observations on the saliferous rock-formation in the valley of the Ohio.—Silliman's Journal, No. XXIV. p. 65.

TABLE

SHOWING THE COMPOSITION OF VARIOUS BRINES, FROM ONONDAGA AND CAYUGA COUNTIES, NEW YORK.

LOCALITY OF THE WELL OR SPRING.	Total amount of solid matter in 1000 grains of brine	Carbonic Acid.	Oxide of Iron and Silica, with a trace of Carbonate of Lime.	Carbonate of Lime.	Sulphate of Lime.	Chloride of Magnesium.	Chloride of Calcium.	Chloride of Sodium, or pure Common Salt	Water, with a trace of Organic Matter, &c.	Total.
ONONDAGA.										
From the Well at Geddes,	138.55	0.06	0.04	0.10	4.93	0.79	2.03	130.66	861.39	1000
From the Well at Syracuse,	139.53	0.07	0.02	0.14	5.69	0.46	0.83	132.30	860.40	1000
From the Well at Salina,	146.50	0.09	0.04	0.17	4.72	0.51	1.04	140.02	853.41	1000
From the Well at Liverpool,	149.54	0.07	0.03	0.13	4.04	0.77	1.72	142.85	850.33	1000
CAYUGA.										
From a Well at Montezuma,	101.20	0.08	0.02	0.18	5.25	1.00	1.40	93.35	898.72	1000

No V.—Referred to on p. 120.

CERTIFICATES IN FAVOR OF DR. SEWALL's " ERRORS OF PHRENO-
LOGY EXPOSED."

1 *From Mr. John Quincy Adams to Dr Sewall, dated Washington, 5th
April* 1839

"I have read with great satisfaction your two lectures upon the science
of Phrenology, *which I have never been able to prevail upon myself to
think of as a serious speculation.* I have classed it with alchymy, with
judicial astrology, with augury, and, as Cicero says that he wonders how
two Roman Augurs could ever look each other in the face without laughing, I have felt something of the same surprise that two learned Phrenologists can meet without the same temptation "* Thus qualified to judge,
Mr Adams congratulates Dr. Sewall on the success of his work,
and thanks him for " furnishing him with arguments to meet the
doctors who pack up the five senses in thirty-five parcels of the
brain'"

2. *From the Honorable Daniel Webster, dated 8th March* 1839.

"I read your Examination of Phrenology when first published Of the
accuracy of the physical and anatomical facts which you state, I am no
competent judge, but if your premises be well founded, the argument is
conclusive." Mr. Webster here candidly states his own inability to form
any judgment through want of knowledge of the subject.

3 *From the Honorable John Maclean, Judge of the Supreme court of the
United States, dated 25th of June* 1837.

"I do not profess fully to understand the science of Phrenology, if it
may be called a science You have taken the most effectual method to expose the absurdity of the system, and so completely have you succeeded, that
I do not think the disciples of Gall and Spurzheim will attempt seriously
to answer you."†

4. *From the Rev Reuel Keith, D D , dated 19th March* 1839

"As I am one of those who believe the pretensions of Phrenology not
only to be false, but very prejudicial to the interests of morality and religion, inasmuch as they degrade man from the rank of a free and accounta-
ble being to that of a mere physical and irresponsible machine, I have
heard with great pleasure of the intended republication of your admirable
work on the subject,"&c

I had the pleasure of meeting this reverend gentleman five or six months
after this letter was penned, and discovered from his conversation that

---

* These remarks are not very complimentary to the good faith or honesty of Phrenologists; but the only revenge which I shall take on Mr.
Adams for the aspersion is, to mention that Phrenologists *do laugh*
when they meet, in his presence, and perceive his own head, which is
bald, and strongly marked proclaiming, in forms so distinct that those
who run may read, the truth of the science which he employs that head in
denying.

† Dr. Caldwell published an answer *so serious* that he did not leave one
shred of Dr. Sewall's argument adhering to another.

he was profoundly ignorant of the subject which he had so sweepingly condemned

There are many letters of a similar description, and one of the writers, the Rev. Dr Fisk, actually commends Dr. Sewall "for his fair-
ness and candor," a compliment which to imitate Mr. Adams's phrase,
must have drawn a smile from Dr. Sewall's own countenance when he
read it.

Instead of preparing any serious exposition of the worthlessness of such
certificates as these, I wrote and sent the following letter to the New York
Evening Post, in which it was published on 6th September 1839. A few
of the provincial papers copied it, but I was informed that many of them
declined to do so, on account of the ridicule which it attached to several
distinguished men. The whole was a *jeu d' esprit*, and if there be any
point in the letter, it has been derived from the inherent absurdity of the
original certificates themselves.

Letter of the Emperor of China to Dr Thomas Sewall, on the merits of
Phrenology.

Since the second edition of Dr. Sewall's work, "Errors of Phrenology
Exposed," was published, the following letter has been received. It
came too late to be printed along with the letters from Mr. John Quincy
Adams, Dr Reuel Keith, and other distinguished men, prefixed to the
volume itself. The Evening post is, therefore, requested to give it
a place in its columns. It is proper to observe that in the Chinese language the word "Barbarian" which occurs frequently in the letter,
has a signification very much resembling the word "foreigner" in English.
All who are not subjects of the Celestial Empire are "Barbarians" in the
court language of China; and the term is not intended to be offensively applied.

We, WHANG-HO-CHING, Brother to the Sun and Moon, Cousin to the
Stars, Grandfather to the Comets and Meteors, Supreme Ruler of the
Celestial Empire, and only Fountain of Universal Truth—To the learned
Barbarian Thomas Sewall, M D., Professor of Anatomy and Physiology in
the city of Washington, District of Columbia, in the United States of Ame-
rica, greeting

Thou hast done well, O learned Barbarian, to lay at our feet thy produc-
tion entitled "An Examination of Phrenology; in two Lectures;" for we are
the fountain of all science. Thou askest our judgment on thy grand proposition—"the brain is a unit" We condescend to inform thee that we
have never inquired into the dark mysteries of the human skull; but, in
virtue of our high relationship to the Sun and Moon, it belongs to us to
know all things without study, and also, in matters recondite and strange,
to judge infallible judgment even without knowledge. Learn, then, that
in the Celestial Empire, men distinguished for their stupendous wisdom
have no brains at all. It is only in the desolate outskirts of the universe,
in regions far removed from the dazzling glories of the Celestial Kingdom,
that brains are known to exist, and there they darken the sublime and im-
material spirit. We, and our treasurers and sub-treasurers, our post-
masters and collectors; our mandarins and judges, district and supreme,
men of surpassing wisdom: our wives and concubines, and the ten thousand
millions of subjects who live on the breath of our Celestial nostrils, are all
brainless.—Hence the greatness and glory of the Celestial Empire. Know,
then, that the great sun of science, Confucius, before whom all barbarian
sages are ignorant as unborn babes, hath written, "A hen's head to a wise
man, a big head to a fool small heads shall be exalted, because they are

light, large heads shall be abased, because they are heavy and full of brains." In the Empire which encircles the Universe, and is endless as time, we cut off all heads that are large, because they are troublesome.— Hence our everlasting peace.

But, O most learned Barbarian, we chide the presumption of thy friends. Know that it belongs to us alone, in virtue of our high prerogative, to judge infallible judgment without knowledge. To Barbarians this is not vouchsafed; yet a certain Barbarian, who in thy pages, indicates his existence by the hieroglyphic marks, " J. Q Adams," speaketh as one possessing wisdom, concerning the uses of the brain; nevertheless this Barbarian saith " I have never been able to prevail on myself to think of it as a serious speculation " We, the Great Whang-Ho-Ching, rebuke the barbarian Adams. It belongs to us ALONE to judge infallible judgment without knowledge

We rebuke, also, the Barbarian whose marks are " John Mc Lean," who useth these words. " I am, in a great measure, unacquainted with the anatomy of the parts involved in the question: but I have always supposed that there was a tenancy in common in the brain." Make known to this Barbarian that he insults our Celestial Majesty by his presumption, and, surely, in his brain wisdom has no tenancy It belongeth to the brother of the sun and moon alone to judge righteous judgment without knowledge. Thou stylest this Barbarian, " Judge of the Supreme Court of the United States." Truly hath the heaven-eyed Confucius written " Darkness envelopeth the Barbarian." How otherwise could a Barbarian Judge pretend to judge without knowledge?

We rebuke also those who are known among Barbarians by the hieroglyphic marks " John Sargeant," " H. L. Pinckney," " S. Chapin," " Justin Edwards," " Moses Stewart," and " Reuel Keith." Touching the brain they have all usurped the Celestial prerogative, which belongs to us alone— they have pretended to judge infallible judgment without knowledge.— Verily Barbarian brains obscure wisdom and engender presumption.

We commend the Barbarian whose marks are " Daniel Webster." He judgeth *cautious* judgment, as behoveth all Barbarians. He saith, " Of the value of the physical and anatomical facts which you state, I am no competent judge, but *if* your premises be well founded, the argument is conclusive." Our great interpreter of the Barbarian tongue, Hungi-Fuski-Chang, read to us, lately, forth of a Barbarian book, these words—" *A second Daniel* come to judgment." We condescend to greet this " second Daniel." His wisdom is worthy of a mandarin of the Celestial Empire: " If the brain be good for nothing; then good for nothing is the brain!!" Has not this Barbarian read the pages of the sublime Confucius? Only from the deep fountains of his inspired volumes could such discreet wisdom penetrate the mind of a Barbarian, obscured by a brain

We instruct our interpreter Hungi-Fuski-Chang, to render this our epistle into thy Barbarian speech, lest our celestial wisdom, radiating with too intense a brightness, should extinguish thy feeble and Barbarian mind, clouded by that " unit" styled by thee a brain.

Given at our Palace of the Moon, in the year of the Celestial Empire, the Seven hundred and fifty-fourth thousand, and of our reign the 399th year.

                    (Signed)   WHANG-HO-CHING.

Seal of   the

> FIGURE.
> A large man with a small head, sitting on a white cloud, the sun beneath his right arm, the moon beneath his left, a tiara of comets around his head, and a firmament of stars beneath his feet. His countenance is radiant with self-complacency, good nature, and foolishness.

(Signed)   Fum, Chancellor.

Celestial Empire.
A correct translation.
                 (Signed)   HUNGI-FUSKI-CHANG,
                                 Interpreter of Barbarian tongues.

Probably some of my American readers may consider that by accepting Dr. Sewall's hospitality in Washington, I was precluded from offering any strictures on his work; but I beg leave to observe, that on that occasion I told him personally that he had mistaken and misrepresented Phrenology; and that it was subsequently to this information that he reproduced all his mistakes, misrepresentations, fictions, and misquotations, as if he had never heard that they were objectionable. It was also long after Dr. Caldwell had demonstrated in print his errors and disingenuousness, beyond the possibility of hesitation on the subject. In these circumstances, his republication is a deliberate adherence to error, which no private considerations can palliate, far less justify.

No. VI.—Referred to on p. 156.

DESCRIPTION OF THE NORMAL SEMINARY OF GLASGOW, BY ROBERT CUNNINGHAM, ESQ. RECTOR OF THAT INSTITUTION.

To George Combe, Esq.   Glasgow, 207 St. George's Road.
    My Dear Sir   23d November 1840.

I shall rejoice to be in any way instrumental in advancing the cause of Common School Education in America. During my two years' residence in the United States, I devoted all my energies to that cause. I had the pleasure of holding intercourse with many of its most zealous advocates, and, though now precluded from direct co-operation with them, I cease not to cherish the liveliest interest in their success.

The great obstacle to the progress of common school education in America is the want of properly qualified teachers. This arises from two causes —the inadequate remuneration of teachers compared with other classes of the community, and the absence of any provision for training candidates for the office. These causes co-exist, and means must be taken to remove them simultaneously. The bettering of the condition of the teacher will not avail, unless provision is made for securing a higher standard of qualification. On the other hand, the establishing of training seminaries, will never insure a supply of properly qualified teachers unless measures are adopted for rendering their situations respectable and comfortable. In a country like America, where there are so many openings for talent and industry, it is not to be expected that educated men will continue to labor in situations, the emoluments of which are much below the average gains of every other profession.

For raising the status of teachers various plans were advocated by me in the Educator, a paper established by Dr. Junkin, President of Lafayette College, and myself, and of which I continued joint-editor during my stay in the United States. One of these was to place teaching on the same footing as the other learned professions, by prohibiting all persons from practising it who had not a regular diploma. For granting these diplomas, I suggested that boards of teachers should be established in each county of the different States, analogous to the County Medical Board in the State of New York, and over these a State board exercising the same functions as the county board, and to which there should be liberty of appeal. The justice, expediency, and practicability of this plan are argued at considerable length in the Educator of 7th July 1839. On various public occasions I recommended other measures for improving the condition of teachers, such as attaching to every common school a house and garden for the teacher, declaring the office to be one held during life or good behaviour, instead of the present system of annual elections, and augmenting their income by allowing a small fee to be exacted from each pupil in addition to their salary.

For the training of teachers, you are aware that in Pennsylvania, at least, I recommended the attaching of model schools, and a professorship of education to the existing colleges, rather than the establishing of distinct normal seminaries. My reasons were, 1st, The saving of expense in the erection of buildings, and endowment of professorships, thereby enabling the State to expend its bounty in providing scholarships for supporting indigent young men of talent during the period of their training. 2dly, The giving greater unity to the system of education, by connecting the common schools with the higher seminaries. 3dly, The avoiding the difficulty in regard to religious instruction, the colleges being connected with various religious denominations, and liberty of choice being thus afforded to persons qualifying themselves as teachers. 4thly, The raising the status of teachers, by associating them during the course of their studies with persons preparing for the other learned professions. Had the Legislature adopted the plan proposed, and applied the $10,000 asked by the superintendent of public schools for the endowment of normal seminaries, to the erection of 400 scholarships of $100 each (fifty scholarships to each of the eight colleges of Pennsylvania), taking an obligation from the persons benefitted, that they would either refund the cost of their education, or serve the state as common school teachers for three years, I have no hesitation in saying that the 200 teachers who would have been annually sent forth, supposing the course limited to two years, would speedily have raised the standard of common school instruction, and given an impetus to the progress of education throughout the state. That the superintendent's plan would not have succeeded, was, I think, clearly proved by an experiment made at Easton. The trustees and president of Lafayette College, at my suggestion, built a model school, invited a teacher from Scotland, and advertised in the New York and Philadelphia papers, that I was willing to give gratuitous instruction in the art of teaching to persons desirous of becoming common school teachers, and to superintend their training in the model school attached to the college. The advertisements were continued at intervals for several months, and the result was, that we had three applications, Had the normal seminaries been built, the superintendent could have offered nothing more than we did, and had no reason to expect different success. Persons willing, under existing circumstances, to become common school teachers, have not ordinarily the means of supporting themselves during the course of instruction, and those able to support themselves are not willing to become common school teachers

I have said that the plan which I proposed for Pennsylvania had a special reference to the circumstances of that state. In the New England States that the number of persons qualified, and desirous to become common school teachers, is greater, and the success of distinct normal seminaries less problematical In Massachusetts one such seminary had been establishedb efore I left America; and from the last report of the Connecticut Educational Board, I observe that the enlightened superintendent of public schools strongly recommends the establishment of at least one distinct normal seminary in that state. In the hope that the experience of the Glasgow Educational Society in their normal seminary may be useful to the managers of these and similar institutions, I shall endeavor to furnish you with the details which you request regarding that seminary. Professor Bache, in his admirable report on the state of education in Europe, has indeed described the seminary as it was at the period of his visit. Besides the changes since introduced, my position, of course, affords me greater facilities for acquiring a knowledge of its internal machinery than even he possessed.

From the accompanying plan, you will observe that the buildings consist of a central compartment, and two wings running back in the form of parallelograms, and inclosing on three sides a space used as exercise ground for the normal students. The buildings front the City Road, and a street runs parallel to the boundary wall on the north side On either side, and behind the buildings, there are vacant spaces occupied as play-grounds, each school having one attached to it

Standing in front of the seminary, you have immediately before you the central building, containing on the ground-floor a house for the janitor, and rooms for the secretary and rector, on the second floor a hall and class-rooms for the normal students, and on the attic story a room lighted from the roof, to be used as a class-room for drawing. On the ground floor of the right wing is the Infant School. On the second story the School of Industry, in which girls of ten years of age and upwards, in addition to reading the Scriptures, writing, and arithmetic, are taught sewing and knitting. Behind the School of Industry are apartments for the master of the Infant School On the ground-floor of the left wing is the Juvenile School for children of both sexes, from six to fourteen, under two masters, having each an assistant. The second story of this wing is occupied as a Private Seminary, in which the fees are higher than in the other schools, and the branches taught more numerous, but the method of instruction the same as in the other Schools Behind are apartments for one of the masters of the Juvenile Schools The Private Seminary alone is self-supporting. The fees of the other schools are intentionally low, so as to exclude none, the charge per quarter in the Infant School being 2s.—in the Juvenile, 3s —for children under eight, and 4s for those above that age, and in the School of Industry, 4s The buildings and grounds cost £15,000, of which £5000 were contributed by Government—£7000 remain as a debt on the property The interest of the debt, and the excess of the expenditure over the sum raised by fees, are met by private subscription. The normal students pay £3 3s to the institution, and support themselves during the period of their attendance, which at present is fixed at not less than six months. The directors

382   APPENDIX.

contemplate making it twelve The inability of the students to support
themselves for a longer period, is the sole obstacle to this

The seminary is open to persons of all the different religious denominations, and contains at present Presbyterians of all the different bodies, Episcopalians, Wesleyan Methodists, Independents, and one Baptist Candidates for admission are required only to bring certificates of their moral
character from the clergyman of the denomination to which they belong
On presenting this, they are examined by a board, composed of the rector
and principal masters of the Model Schools Candidates are examined on
whatever they profess to know, and as they differ widely in acquirements,
the nature of the examination varies accordingly, embracing occasionally
classics, mathematics, and the elements of natural and moral science, confined at other times to grammar, geography, arithmetic, and the history,
doctrines, and precepts of the Bible. If found to possess a competent knowledge of the subjects last specified, the candidates are recommended for admission   If found deficient, they are either advised to prosecute their studies
with a view to be again examined at a subsequent period, or dissuaded from
thinking of teaching as an employment.

After being admitted, the students enter on a course of training. The
shortness of the period of attendance precludes the idea of attempting more
in the way of instruction, than revising their previous knowledge, and ar-
ranging it anew, so as to give them a firmer hold of the general principles.
They attend forty hours weekly, of which during the last four months, sixteen are spent in receiving instruction, eight in observing the model schools,
and sixteen in giving lessons under the superintendence of the masters and
rector   During the first two months, a greater proportion of time is spent
in observing the normal schools, as they are not expected to give lessons
Reports of what passes in the schools under their observation, are given in
to the rector weekly The written exercises of the students of two months'
standing and upwards, are of a different character.

The method of imparting instruction pursued in the Model Schools of the
Glasgow Society is so peculiar that I despair of making it intelligible without actually exhibiting it in operation. One lesson from the Scriptures, and
another from the Book of Nature, are given daily to the children arranged
in a gallery opposite to the master Each of these lessons is given orally,
the children taking part in the exercise, answering questions, and filling in
ellipses. The idea is to present to the mental eye of the children a clear
picture of the object described, or point to be illustrated—to tell them nothing
which, by analogy, they can be led to discover for themselves—to proceed
from the known to the unknown—slowly and gradually using the simplest
language, and availing yourself of every possible mode of illustration—to
notice all the answers of the children, never dogmatically passing judgment
on these answers, but by a judicious series of questions, leading the child, if
in error, to discover his mistake, and after eliciting the true answer, to make
sure that it is received, by calling on all the children to fill up ellipses in
which it is involved   The method differs essentially from the verbal analysis of the Sessional School, in which the fragments of knowledge that occur
in reading are taken to pieces, but no attempt is made to re-construct them
so as to exhibit a connected view of any one point, far less of any one department of science. It approaches more nearly to that of Pestalozzi than
any other with which I am acquainted and yet I have reason to believe the
individual under whom it was wrought out, was unconscious of that re-
semblance   The person to whom I refer is, of course, Mr. Stow, the indefatigable secretary of the Glasgow Society, in whose recent work on "The
Training System" you will find a full exposition of his views   In the

method of teaching reading, writing, arithmetic, and geography, there is less difference betwixt this and other schools, although in all, the general principle of addressing the understanding before consigning to the verbal memory, is kept distinctly in view.

The masters accompany the children to the play-ground, and mingle in their sports. He is a silent, but not unobservant witness of what passes, and on their return to the gallery, calls their attention to any impropriety which may have occurred, applying the Scripture rule to the case, and leading the child to pronounce on his own conduct, without directing especial notice to him, unless under aggravated circumstances. The school, I ought to have observed, opens and closes with prayer and praise, and the greatest pains are taken to blend devotional feelings with the exercises of the day,— the children being trained to regard religion as consisting in love to God and to man, and to practise throughout the day the precepts which have been explained in the Scripture morning lesson. The effect of this is to do away with the necessity of corporal punishment, and the ordinary stimuli of prizes and taking of places. The sense of duty, the desire of the approbation of their masters, and the pleasure arising from the gratification of their thirst for knowledge, and the exercise of the powers of their minds, are found sufficient to secure a greater amount of attention during the giving of the lesson than is common in schools. The interference of the parents, or, in an extreme case, the expulsion of the offender, is had recourse to; but this last has occurred once only for several years.

Great attention is paid to physical exercises. The movements to and from the play-ground are performed in regular order, to vocal music, and whenever the attention begins to flag in the gallery, physical movements, or the singing of some lively air, are employed to rouse the sluggish. The influence of physical movements in training to habits of obedience is very important. Require of a child some intellectual effort, you cannot tell whether his non-obedience proceeds from want of power or of will. Ask him to raise his hand—you can be at no loss to determine which. The habit of obedience in one part of his conduct is extended to all. Vocal music is taught as a regular branch of instruction, and its beneficial influence is visible both on the temper and the spirits of the children, harmonising and softening the character, and cheering and enlivening them after mental toil.

To prepare a person accustomed to a different method, for conducting a school on such principles as these, within the limited period at present in use, is next to impossible. All that we can do is to put him on the way. Whether he will go forward or return to his former method, depends partly on the individual himself, partly on the directors of the school in which he is called to labor. The candidate teacher is first placed in the infant department. The necessity of using simple language, and of being clear and orderly in his statements, is here forced on his conviction. After he has acquired an idea of the system, he is employed in giving lessons to detachments of the children from the Model Schools, in the hall, under the rector's superintendence. The subjects of these lessons are prescribed, and the students are expected to prepare themselves carefully for giving the lesson. After the children withdraw, the voice and manner of the different students who have been employed, and the matter and language of the lessons themselves, are minutely criticised by the rector, who occasionally interposes even during the lesson to correct an erroneous statement, or bring out more fully a point slurred over. Once a week four of the senior students give each a lesson to the children in the gallery of one of the departments, on subjects prescribed the week before. These lessons are given in presence of the secretary, the rector, the master of the department, and all the students. At the close of the lessons, all except the master of the department and the children, withdraw to the hall, and the lessons are there subjected to a searching criticism by such of the senior students as feel disposed and by the master and secretary, the rector summing up the criticisms, and enlarging occasionally on one or more points of special importance. In addition to these exercises, the senior students once a week give lessons to their fellow students on prescribed subjects in presence of the rector The students on these occasions are enjoined to give no answers which a child might not be expected to give, and the ingenuity of the trainer is put to the test in bringing out answers without departing from the principles of the system The rector occasionally interposes to check wandering, and bring back to the point, or correct erroneous statements, and he can do this the more freely from the absence of the children He exemplifies the system in lessons to the students twice a week, one on Natural History, and one on Physics

The number of students varies from thirty to forty, of whom one-third are females Had we the means of aiding deserving persons to support themselves during the course, our numbers might be doubled or tripled.— As it is, the demand for teachers trained in the seminary far exceeds the supply, and this it is which keeps up our numbers. Had they not the hope of bettering their circumstances by submitting to a course of training, the mere desire of professional improvement could not be expected to induce so many to submit to the privations which they often find necessary for attaining their end. Our transatlantic brethren must keep this in view in planning Normal Seminaries No one will submit to a laborious course of training to prepare for a situation which is not worth the accepting after that training is terminated One other point I would urge on their especial notice. Normal Seminaries, if they are to be useful, must be so conducted as to inspire the candidate teacher with deep devotional feeling The remuneration of the teacher, under the most favorable circumstances, is so inadequate, and the duties which he is called to perform so laborious, that, to insure their right discharge, he must be animated by higher motives than the hope of earthly reward. To train him to act on these motives ought to be the great aim of rightly conducted Normal Seminaries

For the encouragement of benevolent individuals desirous of promoting the interests of education by the establishing of Normal Schools, let me remind them, in conclusion, that the Glasgow Society commenced their labors with one small infant school—that they have trained since they began their operations upwards of 600 teachers, most of whom are still laboring in different parts of the world, and that they have now under a course of instruction in the commodious buildings which they have erected, upwards of 600 children, and from forty to fifty candidate teachers with every prospect of increasing usefulness —I remain, my dear sir, yours faithfully,

                                        Rob Cunningham

No. VI.—Referred to on p. 165.

TABLE OF ATTENDANCE ON TWELVE LECTURES ON PHRENOLOGY IN HARTFORD, CONNECTICUT.

Date.	Weather.	Sub-scribers.	Visiters.	Young Men's Institute.	Compli-mentary
1839.					
Sept 27.	Fair.	50	25	—	12
" 30	Rain.	49	14	—	13
Oct 2	Fair.	—	—	35	—
" 4	Do.	66	6	46	11
" 7.	Do.	60	4	56	8
" 9.	Do.	62	12	54	10
" 11.	Do.	59	14	53	9
" 14	Rain.	47	1	50	9
" 16.	Fair.	57	6	54	10
" 18	Do.	55	8	52	10
" 21.	Do.	53	14	52	38
" 23.	Do.	56	15	54	43
" 25.	Do.	59	23	54	43
		12) 673	11) 560	11) 560	12) 216
		Average 56	11	50	18

HARTFORD, *25th October,* 1839.

At a meeting of Mr. Combe's Phrenological Class held immediately after the close of the last lecture of the course, the class was organised by calling the Rev. Dr Totten, president of Washington College, to the chair, and appointing Wm. James Hammersley, secretary.

On motion of Erastus Smith, Esq., a committee of three was appointed by the chair to draft resolutions for the consideration of the class. The committee consisted of the Rev. Mr Gallaudet, Erastus Smith, Esq., and Dr. A. Brigham.

The committee having reported, the following resolutions were discussed, and unanimously adopted.

Resolved—That we have derived pleasure and instruction from the interesting course of lectures now completed by Mr. Combe.

Resolved—That from this able exposition of Phrenology, we have learned numerous facts of practical utility in relation to intellectual, moral, and physical education.

Resolved—That we regard his exposition of the subject as highly valuable in teaching us the functions of the brain, and the philosophy of the mind; and believe that great benefits will result from the application of many of its principles to the education of youth, to legislation, jurisprudence, and the treatment of the insane.

Resolved—That a committee of five be appointed to convey to Mr. Combe these resolutions of his class, and an expression of thanks for the gratification his lectures have afforded them.

The committee appointed, in accordance with the above resolution, were Rev Mr. Gallaudet, Erastus Smith, Esq., Dr. A. Brigham, Rev. Mr. Hovey and Professor Stewart.

On motion adjourned.

SILAS TOTTEN, *Chairman:*

WM. JAMES HAMERSLEY, *Secretary*

No. VII.—Referred to on p. 198.

TABLE OF ATTENDANCE ON SECOND COURSE OF LECTURES ON PHRENOLOGY AT BOSTON.

Date.	Weather.	Sub-scribers	Visiters	Teachers	Compli-mentary
1839.					
Nov. 1.	Fair.	141	7	19	26
" 4	Do.	172	8	27	32
" 6.	Do.	190	8	36	31
" 8.	Do.	199	12	40	32
" 11.	Do.	192	6	42	26
" 13	Do	195	5	40	36
" 15.	Do.	151	10	35	28
" 18	Do.	157	11	41	32
" 20	Do	180	22	47	29
" 22	Do	178	18	47	36
" 25.	Do.	161	24	34	22
" 27.	Do.	139	37	43	30
		12) 2055	12) 168	12) 451	12) 360
	Average	171	14	37	30

No. VIII.—Referred to on p. 201.

SPEECH OF HIS EXCELLENCY GOVERNOR EVERETT ON ST. ANDREW'S DAY, 30TH OF NOVEMBER 1839.

The chairman of the Scots Charitable Society gave as a toast " Massachusetts, and her distinguished Chief Magistrate.

On the announcement of this toast, Governor Everett said—

I rise, Mr. President, to tender you my sincere thanks for the flattering notice with which you and the company have been pleased to honor me. I can say with entire truth, though I am unconnected by any national association with this occasion, that I have cordially entered into its spirit. Though I am a republican by principle and feeling, I am not so much of a stoic as not to have had my sympathies touched while your national anthem was sung with such spirit and feeling. It is a beautiful spectacle to witness this voluntary tribute of respect paid at the distance of three thousand miles, to the youthful sovereign of Great Britain, by a company like this who, though the children or descendants of Scotland with few exceptions (as was observed by H. M. Consul on my right), owe her at present no political allegiance. It would be a pleasing incident if it stood alone. But it is not your solitary act. You do but add your voices to a strain, which is almost literally echoing round the globe. On this day, dedicated to your patron saint, the tribute of respect which you have just paid to the maiden majesty of your father-land, is repeated by the sons of Scotland, wheresoever their lot is cast at home or abroad, from the utmost Orkneys to the Cape of Good Hope, and from Canada to Hindostan, with no difference but that of time, as the evening star, rising successively on each region of the world-encircling empire of England, appoints the hour of the social gathering, and summons the sons of Caledonia to their patriotic vespers.

I thank you, Mr. President, for allowing me to partake your hospitality on this occasion. I was not aware till I received your kind invitation, that there existed among us an institution like this, coeval almost with the settlement of the country. It would be doing injustice to a society of this description, though it may bear a foreign name, to regard it as an institution of foreigners. Some of you, gentlemen, trace your descent, I presume, from ancestors who came to this country with the second, perhaps with the first, generation of its settlers. Among the names of the original founders of the institution, as preserved in one of the ancient record books, kindly put into my hands by my friend Mr. Gordon, I recognise some which still subsist among us, and which stand as high in the respect of the community as they did one hundred and eighty years ago.

It is a principle deeply wrought in the destinies of America, that, settled originally in times of trial and convulsion in Europe, it should at all subsequent periods afford a refuge to those who might be driven abroad by the storms of fortune, or who, from a desire of bettering their condition in life, should go forth from the crowded population of the elder world, and follow the guidance of an honest spirit of adventure to the new-found continent. Accordingly we find that, in the higher paths of state, swept as they are by the tempests of revolution, regicide judges in ancient times, and in our own times fugitive kings, have found a safe retreat on our shores. In the quiet and happier walks of private life there has at all times been an active resort from Europe to America; and I doubt not that, at this moment, in more than one foreign country, many a loving and aching heart, waiting to receive the summons to follow those who have gone before, is able to respond to the plaintive strain of your immortal Burns—

> I turn to the west, when I gae to my rest,
> That happy my dreams and my slumbers may be;
> For far in the west is he I loe best,
> The youth that is dear to my bairn and to me.

Now, Sir, among all those, who, coming from every country in Europe, have brought hither the qualities by which they are characterised at home —whether it be the firm and manly Englishman, the ardent and generous son of Erin, the mercurial and generous Frenchman, the sedate and industrious Hollander or German, there is none who has proved a better citizen in his new home, than the punctual, intelligent, and conscientious Scot. We of New England ought to give you this credit, for both those who in a serious strain are disposed to pronounce our eulogy, and those who in a lighter mood, make merry with our foibles, ascribe to us pretty much the same merits and defects of character. I may say, therefore, though to this extent a party interested, yet with so much the greater claim to be believed sincere, that there is no people in Europe or America among whom the Scottish emigrant has reason to blush for his native land. You are not numerous here, Sir. I am sorry for it; and I hardly know why it is so, for I suppose we should be unwilling, on either side to acknowledge the validity of the reason, which has sometimes been assigned to the fact, viz that we Yankees are too canny for you.

Your society, Sir, as the secretary, in his very handsome report, has informed us, was founded near two hundred years ago. Scotland was then an independent kingdom. Not merely independent, she had more than half a century before sent her sovereign to sit upon the throne of the sister realms. Although in the particular year in which the society was established, in 1657, the monarch of his proscribed lineage was perhaps, like some of your founders, wandering in foreign lands dependent on the stranger for protection, yet three years had scarcely elapsed before he was triumphantly restored. At the close of the century, however, the separate sovereignty of Scotland was merged in the Union of the kingdoms, in consequence of the superior wealth and numbers of the English, the local sceptre of the ancient monarchy departed for ever, and the crown of Bruce was locked up in a dusty chest in Holyroodhouse, never more to be drawn forth, but as an object of antiquarian curiosity, or as a melancholy show. But let not the patriotic son of Scotland lament the change. The sceptre of mind can never pass away; she has won for her brows a diadem, whose lustre can never be obscured. Not to speak of the worthies of ages long passed; of the Knoxes, the Buchanans, and the early minstrelsy of the border, the land of your fathers, Sir, since it ceased to be a separate kingdom, has, through the intellect of her gifted sons, acquired a supremacy over the minds of men, more extensive and more enduring than that of Alexander or Augustus. It would be impossible to enumerate them all—the Blairs of the last generation, the Chalmerses of this, the Robertsons and Humes; the Smiths, the Reids, the Stuarts, the Browns, the Homes, the Mackenzies, the Mackintoshes, the Broughams, the Jeffreys, with their distinguished compeers, both in physical and moral science. The Marys, and the Elizabeths, the Jameses and the Charleses will be forgotten before these names will perish from the memory of men. And when I add to them those other illustrious names—Burns, Campbell, Byron, and Scott, I may truly say, Sir, that the throne and the sceptre of England will crumble into dust like those of Scotland; and Windsor Castle and Westminster Abbey will lie in ruins, as poor and desolate as those of Scone and Iona, before the lords of Scottish song shall cease to reign in the hearts of men.

For myself, Sir, I confess that I love Scotland. I have reason to do so. I have trod the soil of the

> Land of brown heath and shaggy wood,
> Land of the mountain and the flood

I have looked up to the cloud-capt summit of Ben Lomond; have glided among the fairy islets of Loch Katrine and, from the battlements of Sterling Castle, have beheld the links of Forth sparkling in the morning sun. I have done more, Sir, I have tasted that generous hospitality of Scotland, which her Majesty's Consul has so justly commemorated; I have held converse with her most eminent sons; I have made my pilgrimage to Melrose Abbey, in company with that modern magician, who, mightier than the magician of old that sleeps beneath the marble floor of its chancel, has hung the garlands of immortal poesy upon its shattered arches, and made its moss-clad ruins a shrine, to be visited by the votary of the muse from the remotest corners of the earth to the end of time. Yes, Sir, musing as I did, in my youth, over the sepulchre of the wizard, once pointed out by the bloody stain of the cross and the image of the arch-angel—standing within that consecrated enclosure, under the friendly guidance of him whose genius has made it holy ground, while every nerve within me thrilled with excitement, my fancy kindled with the inspiration of the spot I seemed to behold, not the vision so magnificently described by the minstrel—the light, which, as the tomb was opened,

> broke forth so gloriously,
> streamed upward to the chancel roof,
> And through the galleries far aloof

But I could fancy that I beheld, with sensible perception, the brighter light which had broken forth from the master mind, which had streamed from his illumined page all-gloriously upward, above the pinnacles of worldly grandeur, till it mingled its equal beams with that of the brightest constellations in the intellectual firmament of England.

No. IX.—Referred to on p 208

MODE OF INSTRUCTING LAURA BRIDGMAN, DEAF, DUMB, BLIND, AND WITHOUT SMELL.

An extract from the diary kept by her instructor will give an idea of her manner of questioning.

December 3.

"Spent one hour in giving Laura an idea of the meaning of the words left and right. She readily conceived that left hand meant *her* left hand, but with difficulty generalised the term At last, however, she caught the idea, and eagerly spelt the name of her arms, hands, fingers, feet, ears, &c, as they were touched, and named them, right or left, as might be; suddenly pausing, however, and looking puzzled, she put her finger on her *nose*, and asked if that were left or right, thus she continually puzzles one but such is her eagerness to find out one's meaning, such a zealous co operation is there on her part, that it is a delightful task to teach her.

" Uses to-day freely the prepositions *in* and *on:* she says, teacher sitting *in* sofa —do not dare to correct her in such cases of anomalous usage of the preposition, but prefer to let her be in error, rather than shake her faith in a rule given the corrections must be made by and by the sofa having sides, she naturally says *in*."

In her eagerness to advance her knowledge of words and to communicate her ideas she coins words, and is always guided by analogy. Sometimes her process of *word making* is very interesting; for instance, after some time spent in giving her an idea of the abstract meaning of *alone*, she seemed to obtain it, and understanding that being *by one's self* was to be alone, or *al-one*. She was told to go to her chamber, or school, or elsewhere, and return *alone;* she did so, but soon after, wishing to go with one of the little girls, she strove to express her meaning thus, Laura go *al-two*

The same eagerness is manifested in her attempts to define, for the purpose of classification for instance, some one giving her the word bachelor, she came to her teacher for a definition, she was taught that men who had wives were *husbands,* those who had none, *bachelors,* when asked if she understood, she said, " *man no have wife bachelor—Tenny bachelor:*" referring to an old friend of hers. Being told to define bachelor, she said " *bachelor no have wife, and smoke pipe.*" Thus she considered the individual peculiarity of smoking in one person as a specific mark of the *species bachelor.*

Then, in order to test her knowledge of the word, it was said by her teacher, Tenny has got no wife, what is Tenny?

She paused, and then said, *Tenny is wrong!*

The word widow being explained to her, a woman whose husband is dead, and she being called upon to define, she said, "*widow is woman, man dead, and cold,*" and eked out her meaning, by sinking down, and dropping her hand, to signify *in the ground.*

The two last words she added herself, they not having been in the definition, but she instantly associates the idea of *coldness* and *burial* with death

Her having acquired any idea of death was not by the wish of her teacher, it having been his intention to reserve the subject until such a development of her reason should be attained as would enable him to give a correct idea of it.

He hopes still, by aid of the analogy of the germination and growth of plants, to give her a consoling hope of resurrection, to counterbalance the almost instinctive dread of death.

She had touched a dead body before she came to the institution.

She easily acquired a knowledge and use of active verbs, especially those expressive of *tangible action;* as to walk, to run, to sew, to shake.

At first, of course, no distinction could be made of mood and tense; she used the words in a general sense, and according to the order of her *sense of ideas;* thus, in asking some one to give her bread, she would first use the word expressive of the leading idea, and say, "*Laura, bread give*" If she wanted water she would say, *water, drink, Laura.*

Soon, however, she learned the use of the auxiliary verbs, of the difference of past, present, and future tense; for instance, here is an early sentence, *Keller is sick—when will Keller well;* the use of *be* she had not acquired

Having acquired the use of substantives, adjectives, and verbs, prepositions and conjunctions, it was deemed time to make the experiment of trying to teach her to *write,* and to show her that she might communicate her ideas to persons not in contact with her.

It was amusing to witness the mute amazement with which she submitted to the process, the docility with which she imitated every motion, and the perseverance with which she moved her pencil over and over again in the same track, until she could form the letter. But when at last the idea dawned upon her, that, by this mysterious process, she could make other people understand what she thought, her joy was boundless.

Never did a child apply more eagerly and joyfully to any task than she did to this, and in a few months she could make every letter distinctly, and separate words from each other.

The following anecdote will give an idea of her fondness for teazing or innocent fun or mischief. Her teacher looking one day unobserved into the girls' play-room, saw three blind girls playing with the rocking horse. Laura was on the crupper, another in the saddle, and a third clinging on the neck, and they were all in high glee, swinging backward and forward as far as the rockers would roll. There was a peculiarly arch look in Laura's countenance—the natural language of sly fun. She seemed prepared to give a spring, and suddenly when her end was lowest, and the others were perched high in the air, she sidled quickly off on the floor, and down went the other end so swiftly as to throw the girls off the horse.

This Laura evidently expected, for she stood a moment convulsed with laughter, then ran eagerly forward with outstretched hands to find the girls, and almost screamed with joy. As soon, however, as she got hold of one of them, she perceived that she was hurt, and instantly her countenance changed, she seemed shocked and grieved, and after caressing and comforting her playmate, she found the other, and seemed to apologise by spelling the word *wrong*, and caressing her.

When she can puzzle her teacher she is pleased, and often purposely spells a word wrong with a playful look and if she catch her teacher in a mistake, she bursts into an ecstacy of laughter.

When her teacher had been at work giving her an idea of the words carpenter, chair-maker, painter, &c., in a generic sense, and told her that blacksmith made *nails*, she instantly held up her fingers and asked if blacksmith made them, though she knew well he did not.

With little girls of her own age she is full of frolic and fun, and no one enjoys a game at *romps* more than Laura.

She has the same fondness for a dress, for ribbons, and for finery as other girls of her age, and as a proof that it arises from the same amiable desire of pleasing others, it may be remarked that whenever she has a new bonnet or any new article of dress, she is particularly desirous to go to meeting, or to go out with it. If people do not notice it, she directs their attention by placing their hand upon it.

Generally she indicates her preference for such visiters as are the best dressed.

She is so much in company with blind persons that she thinks blindness common, and when first meeting a person, she asks if they are blind, or she feels of their eyes.

She evidently knows that the blind differ from seeing persons, for when she shows blind persons any thing she always puts their fingers on it.

She seems to have a perception of character, and to have no esteem for those who have little intellect. The following anecdote is significant of her perception of character, and shows that from her friends she requires something more than good-natured indulgence.

A new scholar entered school—a little girl about Laura's age. She was very helpless, and Laura took great pride and great pains in showing her the way about the house, assisting her to dress and undress, and doing for her many things which she could not do herself.

In a few weeks it began to be apparent even to Laura that the child was not only helpless, but naturally very stupid, being almost an idiot. Then Laura gave her up in despair and avoided her, and has ever since had an aversion to being with her, passing her by as if in contempt. By a natural association of ideas she attributes to this child all those countless deeds which Mr. *Nobody* does in every house—if a chair is broken, or any thing is misplaced, and no one knows who did it, Laura attributes it at once to this child.

It has been observed before that she is familiar with the processes of addition and subtraction in small numbers. Subtracting one number from another puzzled her for a time, but by help of objects she accomplished it. She can count and conceive objects to about one hundred in number—to express an indefinitely great number, or more than she can count, she says *hundred*. If she thought a friend was to be absent many years, she would say—will come hundred *Sundays*, meaning weeks. She is pretty accurate in measuring time, and seems to have an intuitive tendency to do it. Unaided by the changes of night and day, by the light, or the sound of any timepiece, she nevertheless divides time accurately.

With the days of the week, and the week itself as a whole, she is perfectly familiar; for instance, if asked what day will it be in fifteen days more, she readily names the day of the week. The day she divides by the commencement and end of school, by the recesses and by the arrival of meal-times.

She goes to bed punctually at seven o'clock, and of her own accord. For some time after she came under our charge she had some one to put her to bed every night, but soon it was thought best to send her alone, and that she might not wait for any one, she was left alone one evening; and she sat until quite late, a person watching her; and at last she seemed to form her resolution suddenly—she jumped up and groped her way up to bed. From that time to this she has never required to be told to go to bed, but at the arrival of the hour for retiring she goes by herself.

Those persons who hold that the capacity of perceiving and measuring the lapse of time is an innate and distinct faculty of the mind, may deem it an important fact that Laura evidently can measure time so accurately as to distinguish between a half and a whole note of music.

Seated at the piano forte she will strike the notes in a measure like the following quite correctly:—

Now, it will be perceived that she must have a clear perception of the lapse of time in order to strike the two eighths at the right instant, for in the first measure they occur at the second beat, in the second measure at the third beat.

There is no doubt that practice will enable her to subdivide time still more minutely. Possibly some attach an undue degree of importance to this power of measuring time, considered in a metaphysical point of view, for any one may make the same experiment upon himself, and by stopping his ears and closing his eyes, will find he can measure time, or the *duration of his sensation*, and know which of two periods is the longest; nevertheless we shall continue carefully to note the phenomena in the case of Laura for the benefit of whom they may concern.

It is interesting, in a physiological point of view, to know the effect of the deprivation of three senses upon the remaining two.

The sense of smell being destroyed, it seems a curious question whether the effect upon the organ of taste is general or particular. That is, whether the taste is blunted generally, and for all things alike, or whether one kind of sapidity is more affected than another? To ascertain this some experiments have been tried, but as yet not enough to enable one to state confidently the results in minute distinction. The general conclusions are these:

Acids seem to make vivid and distinct impression upon the taste, and she apparently distinguishes the different degrees of acidity better than of sweetness or bitterness. She can distinguish between wine, cider and vinegar better than substances like manna, liquorice and sugar. Of bitters she seems to have less perception, or indeed hardly any, for on putting powdered rhubarb into her mouth she called it *tea*, and on one saying *no*, and telling her to taste *close*, she evidently did try to taste it, but still called it tea, and spit it out—but without any contortion or any indication of its being particularly disagreeable.

Of course she has a repugnance to these kinds of experiments, and it seems almost imposing upon her good nature to push them very far; we shall, however, be soon able to ascertain certainly how far she can distinguish different sapid bodies. Those who are curious in the physiology of the taste know that the highest degree of *gusto* or the acme of pleasure is not obtained until just as the morsel has slipped over the glottis, and is on its way beyond the power of recall down the œsophagus. This seems to be a wise precaution of nature to prevent the stomach being cheated of its due, for if the highest degree in pleasure of eating could be obtained without absolutely swallowing the morsel—the epicure could have an exhaustless source of pleasure, and need never degenerate into the *gourmand*.

Some physiologists who have speculated upon this subject, consider that this final climax of the pleasure of taste is produced by a fine aroma which, rising from the morsel and mounting up the fauces, pleasantly titillates the ramifications of the olfactory nerve. The fact that, when we have a cold in the head and the fauces are obstructed, the taste is blunted, seems to bear out this supposition; but, from some observations on Laura, one would be inclined to think that some other cause must contribute to the effect.

She appears to care less for the process of mastication than deglutition; and probably it is only the necessity of mechanical trituration of food, which induces her to go through with it, before hastening to the pleasant part of swallowing. Now, as the imperfection of smell impairs the taste in the tongue and palate during mastication, it should have the same effect in deglutition, supposing this theory to be correct. but it seems not to be so—else Laura would have little inducement to swallow, save to fill a vacuity of stomach. Now, it seems doubtful whether the feeling of vacuity of stomach, strictly speaking, would show a child the road for the food, or whether it would not be as likely to stuff bread into its ear, as into its mouth, if it had no pleasurable sensation in tasting, and further, if the pleasurable sensation did not increase and tempt to deglutition, it is doubtful whether hunger or vacuity of stomach *alone* would teach a child to swallow the chewed morsel.

On the whole, she seems to care less for eating than most children of her age.

With regard to the sense of touch it is very acute, even for a blind person. It is shown remarkably in the readiness with which she distinguishes persons: there are forty inmates in the female wing, with all of whom of course Laura is acquainted, whenever she is walking through the passageways, she perceives, by the jar of the floor, or the agitation of the air, that some one is near her, and it is exceedingly difficult to pass her without being recognised. Her little arms are stretched out, and the instant she grasps a hand, a sleeve, or even part of the dress, she knows the person, and lets them pass on with some sign of recognition.

The innate desire for knowledge, and the instinctive efforts which the human faculties make to exercise their functions, is shown most remarkably in Laura. Her tiny fingers are to her as eyes, and ears, and nose, and most deftly and incessantly does she keep them in motion; like the feelers of some insects which are continually agitated, and which touch every grain of sand in the path, so Laura's arms and hands are continually in play; and when she is walking with a person she not only recognises every thing she passes within touching distance, but by continually touching her companion's hands she ascertains what he is doing. A person walking across a room while she had hold on his left arm, would find it hard to take a pencil out of his waistcoat pocket with his right hand, without her perceiving it.

Her judgment of distances and of relations of place is very accurate; she will rise from her seat, go straight towards a door, put out her hand just at the right time, and grasp the handle with precision.

When she runs against a door which is shut, but which she expected to find open, she does not fret, but rubs her head and laughs, as though she perceived the ludicrous position of a person flat against a door trying to walk through it.

The constant and tireless exercise of her feelers gives her a very accurate knowledge of every thing about the house, so that if a new article, a bundle, bandbox, or even a new book, is laid any where in the apartments which she frequents, it would be but a short time before, in her ceaseless rounds, she would find it, and from something about it she would generally discover to whom it belonged.

She perceives the approach of persons by the undulations of the air striking her face; and she can distinguish the step of those who tread hard, and jar the floor.

At table, if told to be still, she sits and conducts herself with propriety, handles her cup, spoon, and fork, like other children; so that a stranger looking at her would take her for a very pretty child with a green ribbon over her eyes.

But when at liberty to do as she chooses, she is continually feeling of things, and ascertaining their size, shape, density, and use—asking their names and their purposes, going on with insatiable curiosity, step by step, towards knowledge.

Thus doth her active mind, though all silent and darkling within, commune by means of her one sense with things external, and gratify its innate cravings for knowledge by close and ceaseless attention.

Qualities and appearances, unappreciable or unheeded by others, are to her of great significance and value, and by means of these her knowledge of external nature and physical relations will in time become extensive.

If the same success shall attend the cultivation of her moral nature, as has followed that of her intellect and her perceptive faculties, great will be the reward to her, and most interesting will be the results to others.

No. X.—Referred to on p 236.

RESOLUTIONS OF CLASS AT ALBANY.

GEORGE COMBE, ESQ.   ALBANY, *Feb.* 8, 1840.

Dear Sir —At the close of your Course of Lectures in this city, on the 7th instant, the Class was organised by the appointment of Thomas W Olcott, Esq. as chairman, and the Rev. Dr. Bullions as secretary   The objects of the meeting were then stated by the chairman in the following words:—

Ladies and Gentlemen.—We have listened to the exposition of the principles of Phrenology by decidedly the most gifted and distinguished advocate and teacher of that science now living, and the object of the meeting now called is to convey to Mr. Combe, on bidding him farewell, the assurance of the pleasure with which we have attended his class and heard his lectures. The importance of Phrenology as a guide to health and physical education, most of competent judges will freely admit The respected senior trustee of the Institution in which we are now assembled has long been an able and faithful champion of this branch of the subject, and Combe on Physiology has been adopted as a text book in this Academy. If the science has not attained the accuracy of precision in details, yet its general principles are beginning to be acknowledged, and to occupy the attention of the most profound and cultivated minds. The proof of this fact I have in the character of the audience before me.—If gentlemen have any remarks or resolutions to offer, they will now be entertained.

After which, on motion of Rufus W. Peckham, Esq, it was unanimously

Resolved,—That we have listened with deep and increasing interest to the lectures delivered by George Combe, Esq. of Edinburgh on the subject of Phrenology and its application

Resolved,—That we feel gratified. and in the highest degree instructed, by the clear and able manner in which the principles of that science have been explained, and that the facts and numerous illustrations with which Mr Combe has fortified and enforced his principal positions, entitle them, in our view, to great weight and consideration

Resolved,—That the application made by Mr. Combe of the science of Phrenology to the explaining of life's complicated phenomena, and to the unfolding of the great principles upon which the physical education and the intellectual and moral culture of the young should be conducted, invest it with an interest, which, we believe, has not hitherto been properly appreciated, and we hope the day is not distant when every parent in this country shall be familiar with those principles

Resolved,—That in our estimation the American people are greatly indebted to Mr. Combe for his eminently successful efforts in promulgating doctrines so vitally essential to the proper development of the physical and mental powers of man, and the increasing consequences of which can be realised in a manner adequate to their importance only by coming generations.

Resolved,—That a copy of these Resolutions be presented to Mr Combe, and that their publication in the daily papers of this city be requested

It was then, on motion, resolved that Amos Dean, Esq, Dr Hamilton, and Rufus W. Peckham, Esq, be a committee to wait upon Mr. Combe, and to present him with a copy of the above resolutions

We assure you, Sir, that it gives us great pleasure in thus being made the medium of the communication of sentiments so fully accordant with those entertained by each of us; at the same time, it is with much regret we feel that, in performing this grateful office, we must bid you farewell.

With sentiments of the highest respect and consideration, we are, your obedient servants,

AMOS DEAN,
R. W. PECKHAM,
W. A. HAMILTON.

No. XI.—Referred to on p. 276.

Extract from the "American Journal of Science and Arts" for July
1840, edited by Professor Silliman.

RESOLUTIONS OF CLASS AT NEW HAVEN.

At the conclusion of the last lecture, and after Mr. Combe had taken
leave and withdrawn, the audience was called to order by the Hon. Henry
W. Edwards, late Governor of Connecticut.

The Hon. David Daggett, late Chief-Justice of the state, was called to the
chair, when the following resolutions were laid in by Governor Edwards,
seconded by Professor Silliman, and carried by an unanimous vote. We
trust that our readers will agree with us that it is not inappropriate to the
object of a Journal of Science to record them with the remarks by which
they were supported.

*The Observations of Governor Edwards on introducing the Resolutions,
were as follows:—*

We have been listening with great interest and instruction, during a
series of evenings,* to the lectures of Mr. Combe on Phrenology, and his
course is now finished. He has displayed much ability and great research
on this subject, and whatever our opinions may finally be as to the correctness of the views he has presented, I think we shall readily admit, that he
has acquitted himself fairly and fully in what he undertook. For one, I
am ready to declare that he has accomplished all that I had anticipated.
He has performed to my entire satisfaction his part of the engagement. If
there be truth in Phrenology, the sooner we know it the better. The subject is of immense importance, and if we are still in doubt, we have been
furnished with the means of ascertaining the truth.

Mr. Combe is now about to leave us, and an expression of our approbation,
in accordance with what has been done at other places where he has lec-
tured, is, I think, due from us, and will probably be very gratifying to him.
I hold in my hand some resolutions which will be submitted to the meeting,
and will, it is presumed, be cheerfully concurred in by all present   .

RESOLUTIONS.

Resolved,—That we have listened with great interest to the lectures of
Mr. Combe, on the physical, intellectual, and moral powers of man, and that,
without claiming to express an opinion on Phrenology is a science, we
have derived from his skilful analysis both instruction and gratification.

Resolved,—That our best wishes attend Mr. Combe and his lady, for a
safe return to their native land, and a happy reunion with their friends.

Resolved,—That Judge Daggett, Governor Edwards, Professor Silliman,
General Kimberly, and Professor Olmsted, be a committee to present to
Mr. Combe a copy of the above resolutions.

NEW HAVEN, CONN., *March* 15, 1840.

The resolutions were communicated to Mr. Combe with the letter, of
which the following is a copy.—

* The course occupied thirteen evenings, each lecture being two hours
long, with a brief intermission.

TO MR. GEORGE COMBE.

Dear Sir:—In compliance with the request of the gentlemen and ladies who have attended your course of lectures on Phrenology, we have the pleasure of presenting you with a copy of the resolutions adopted by them, and avail ourselves of the occasion to communicate the assurance of our high respect and esteem.

DAVID DAGGETT.
HENRY W. EDWARDS.
BENJAMIN SILLIMAN.
DENNIS KIMBERLY
DENNISON OLMSTED

NEW HAVEN, *March* 15, 1840.

Professor Silliman, in seconding these resolutions, said, Mr. Chairman, I have no claim to be called a phrenologist, for I have not studied the subject sufficiently to form an opinion upon the science *as a whole*, and it is not probable that my engagements will ever permit me to give it a thorough investigation. All I know of it is derived from the courses of lectures which I have heard, and of which this is the fourth; from observation of such facts as have come in my way, from credible attestations of its practical applications published in various works, and from personal communication with some of its cultivators.   *   *   *   It appears to me, Sir, that Phrenology involves no absurdity, nor any antecedent improbability. The very word means the science or knowledge of the mind, which all admit to be a pursuit of the highest dignity and importance, both for this life and the life to come, and the appropriate inquiry of the phrenologist is, whether the mind, with its peculiar powers, affections, and propensities, is manifested by particular organs corresponding with the conformation of the cranium, that defensive armor   *   *   *   by which the brain is protected from external injury.   *   *   *   Are we then expected seriously to assert, that which appears self-evident, that the seat of our mental operations, and of our affections and propensities, is in the brain? My consciousness informs me so, and this is the highest possible evidence to me, although *my* consciousness cannot be evidence to another person.   *   *   *   The residence of the mind being in the brain, it is not absurd or irrational to inquire whether it can be read in the form of the cranium as well as in the expression of the features.   *   *   *   Perhaps we may not be able to follow phrenologists in all their detailed divisions of the position of the faculties, affections, and propensities; but, after making all reasonable allowance for some possible errors in discrimination, and for some suggestions of the imagination, may we not still rely upon their ability to indicate, decidedly, the prevailing faculties and the ruling affections and propensities of far the greater number of individuals, in any assembly, either of pupils or convicts, or of people brought together by accident?—In yielding to our convictions on this subject we should, however, exclude smatterers and pretenders, who, having only a superficial acquaintance with the subject, and perhaps no uncommon acumen in any case, examine heads to flatter self-esteem and gratify cupidity —The subject is liable to abuse, and not all who claim to be phrenologists can be deserving of entire confidence; but is not the same true of many other subjects, and especially of surgery? How large a proportion of surgeons should we be willing to employ in passing a knife among the nerves and arteries of our own bodies, or of those of our dear friends?—We are persuaded, then, that phrenology has its foundation laid in truth, and that its first principles, as regards the great regions of the head, are established upon the same ground as that which sustains all the physical sciences, namely, induction, indicating the correspondence of the phenomena with the theory. * * * This apologetic plea for Phrenology has been thrown in, not because we have made up our minds *to go for the whole*, but because we would strenuously maintain the liberty of free investigation. Philosophical is as sacred as civil and religious liberty, and all three are indispensible to the perfection of man's faculties, to the improvement of his condition, and to the just comprehension of his duties.

No XII.—Referred to on p. 284

PRESENTATION OF A VASE TO MR. COMBE.

The exquisite vase, subscribed for by the class in attendance on Mr. Combe's Phrenological Lectures in this city, was presented to the distinguished writer and lecturer, on Monday evening, 23d March, 1840, at Howard's Hotel, in presence of the subscribers, by a Committee consisting of the following gentlemen:—Mr. E. P. Hurlbut, Rev. T. J. Sawyer, Dr. Foster, Dr. Boardman, Mr. S. W. Dewey, Mr. F. C. Benedict. And as this may be considered the termination of Mr. Combe's lectures in the United States, we present our readers with the following accurate report of the proceedings.

The Chairman of the Committee, Mr. Hurlbut, thus addressed Mr. Combe:—

" Sir.—The members of the class who attended your lectures, delivered in this city during the past year, have instructed us to present you with this vase, which, in their names, we now beg you to accept.

" It bears upon one side three medallic likenesses, exquisitely wrought—one of Gall, to whose great discoveries in nature we are indebted for the true science of mind—one of Spurzheim, who first aided in illustrating and establishing it.—and the other of yourself their first and favorite British disciple.

" This high and just association will ever endure He who founded, and they who first illustrated and advanced the true science of intellectual and moral philosophy, will descend the stream of time together, shedding lustre upon future ages, and living in the grateful memories of generations to come after us.

" Upon this vase are also presented other medallic likenesses,—one of Rush, whose far-seeing eye, penetrating the veil of nature, which Gall afterward lifted, had vision of some of the great truths which he demonstrated,—and the other of Caldwell, who was the first among our countrymen to embrace and defend the doctrines of the great German, with boldness and vigor peculiarly his own.

" We feel a patriotic pride in associating the names of two of our own countrymen with the most distinguished names of Europe connected with mental science.

" You are soon to return to your native land—to your and our fathers' country.

" Your visit here has awakened the interest of thousands in your welfare —of thousands who are not wanting in gratitude for the instruction and

delight which your discourses have afforded them—but who have had no
opportunity to manifest, as we do on this most favored occasion, their high
appreciation of your character and attainments, and the enduring impression
which your visit has made upon their minds. Their and our best wishes
attend you.

"Receive, then, this vase—(the superscription upon which is also graven
upon our hearts), and bear it to your home—a tribute to truth, and to the
champion of truth, and rest assured, that, in our estimation, we could be
called to perform no prouder office, than to render a just tribute of respect
and admiration to the author of 'The Constitution of Man.'"

Mr. Combe received the vase and spoke to the following effect.

"Gentlemen:—Although I cannot correctly say that I am unused to
public speaking, yet, on occasions like the present, words fail me to express
what I feel. I accept of your handsome and generous gift with the highest
gratification. The classical elegance of form, the exquisite workmanship,
and the appropriate devices which it bears, render it a gem of beauty. As
a mere physical object, indeed, its merits in this respect have been appreciated in this city; it has gained the gold medal offered for the encouragement of art, and it will successfully sustain the strictest scrutiny of the distinguished artisans of the country to which I am about to carry it. But it
is as a moral monument of your favorable estimation of my labors among you,
and of the interest which you have taken in the science of mind, that it
possesses to me an inestimable value. To Dr. Gall alone belongs the glory
of having discovered the functions of the brain: Dr. Spurzheim generously
devoted his whole life to the extension, improvement, and diffusion of this
splendid product of Gall's originality and genius; and it is difficult to do
justice to the noble sacrifice which he made to the cause of truth. When
Dr. Spurzheim became the disciple of Gall, no human being defended Phrenology except its author: and he not only stood alone, but encountered the
hostility of civilised Europe, from the emperor to the peasant, a few high
minded individuals only excepted, who were silenced by the hand of power
if they rose superior to the influence of scorn. It is no slender honor to me
that you associate me with such men. Mine has been a flowery path compared with theirs. It is true that, when still a young man, without name,
fortune, high associations, or any external advantages to sustain me against
public disapprobation, I fearlessly risked every prospect which the future
held forth to my ambition, and became the defender of Phrenology when it
had few other friends in the British Isles. Professional ruin was prophesied
as the inevitable consequence of this, as it was then styled, rash and incon-
siderate step. But for the encouragement of the young and ardent worship-
pers of truth, I am enabled to say these auguries never were realised. Many
were the shafts of ridicule that were hurled against me, and bitter the taunts
poured forth by a hostile press; but they never penetrated to my soul, dis-
turbed my peace, or impeded my prosperity. I mention this not in the
spirit of vain glory, but to confirm the young in the assurance, that the path
of truth and independence may be safely trodden even against a world in
arms, if courage and perseverance be added to prudence in the advance.

"I have sojourned among you now for the greater part of two years, and
I am about to leave your country. That I have experienced some incon-
veniences, and encountered several disagreeable incidents during my stay
is only what belongs to the lot of humanity; but these sink into insignifi-
cance when contrasted with the generous cordiality and enlightened sympathy which have been showered upon me by yourselves and your fellow
citizens. I have held converse with many enlightened minds in this country; minds that do honor to human nature; whose philanthropy embraces

not only patriotism, but an all-prevailing interest in the advancement of the human race in knowledge, virtue, religion, and enjoyment in every clime. Many of these admirable men are deeply interested in phrenology. The gifted individual to whom Massachusetts owes an eternal debt of gratitude for his invaluable efforts in improving her educational establishments, has assured me that the new philosophy is a light in his path to which he attaches the highest value. You, sir, have shown, in a late valuable work, that has issued from your pen, that you are penetrated to the core with this last and best of human sciences;* and many who now hear me have expressed similar testimonials to its worth. I return, therefore, highly gratified with much that I have experienced among you, and I shall not need this emblem of your respect to maintain the recollection of such men as I have described, engraven on my affections for ever.

"It is an additional gratification to me to see on this beautiful work of art the heads of two distinguished Americans, Dr. Benjamin Rush, and Dr. Charles Caldwell. The former has made the nearest approach of any modern author to Dr. Gall's discovery, while the latter has manifested great zeal and high talents in its defence. Allow me to add one brief expression of admiration and gratitude to a young countryman of my own, Mr. Michael Morrison from Edinburgh, whose exquisite skill chased these admirable ornaments on your gift. Among his first efforts in the art was a wax model which he executed of my head in Edinburgh. Several years ago he came to this country, was highly esteemed as a man and as an artist, and the embellishment of this vase was almost the last act of his life. Ten days have scarcely elapsed since he was laid in a premature grave It would have delighted me to have addressed to his living ear, the tribute which I now offer to his memory.

"Again, gentlemen, I assure you of my heartfelt gratitude and lasting respect, and with best wishes for your happiness and prosperity, bid you farewell."

The vase is of exquisite workmanship—being of Grecian model, with three medallic likenesses on one side—one of Gall, one of Spurzheim, and one of Combe, with the motto "res non verba quæso," and two medallic likenesses on the other—one of Dr. Benjamin Rush, and one of Dr. Charles Caldwell, with the following inscription;—

Presented
to
George Combe, of Edinburgh,
by the class in attendance upon
his lectures delivered in the
City of New York,
in 1839, on the subject of
Phrenology;
In testimony of their profound respect for the
distinguished Lecturer, and of their
belief in, and admiration of,
the noble science
of which he is the ablest living
teacher and expounder."

* Mr Combe here referred to a work recently published by Mr. Hurlbut, "Civil Office and Political Ethics," the "ethics" of which are admirably adapted for the guidance of the people of the United States in the cause of true patriotism and virtue.

Round the base of the vase are chased the heads of several animals as emblematical of comparative Phrenology; and below them, are engraved the following words, "Mr. James Thomson, manufacturer of this vase, received a gold medal from the American Institute, for its superior workmanship."

No. XIII —Referred to on p. 285.

EXTRACT FROM REPORT OF PHILADELPHIA, WILMINGTON, AND BALTIMORE RAILROAD.

In consequence of the absence of the engineer of the road in Europe, we are unable to give a detailed report of the manner of construction, and amounts of excavation, embankment, and bridging of the road. Some particulars relative to its character may not prove irrelevant; several kinds of rails have been adopted for different sections of the route, in all of which, strength, and consequent permanence, have been made essential requisites. The bridge rail, weighing 40 lb per yard; the T rail, weighing 56 lb. per yard; and the heavy-bar rail, $1\frac{3}{4}$ inches in thickness, by $2\frac{1}{2}$ inches in breadth, weighing 40 lb. per yard, are used throughout the whole, with the exception of a portion of the route between Philadelphia and Wilmington, upon which the heavy plate bar has been laid.

The superstructure of the road consists in longitudinal sills, connected by cross ties of locust, red cedar, or seasoned white oak, and surmounted by longitudinal string pieces of Carolina heart pine, on which is laid the iron rail. Upon the greater part of the road, however, the strength of the iron bar is such as to render unnecessary the use of the longitudinal string pieces, the bar being supported by the cross tie alone.

Between the city of Wilmington and the Susquehanna river, the road-way is graded thirty-five feet in width with superior bridging, all but one being built of the most substantial stone masonry and brick arches, making them secure from risk of fire Upon other portions of the road, the surface width is twenty-five feet, having, throughout nearly the whole length of the line, a surface graded sufficiently wide for two tracks of railway. The whole distance was contracted for and finished, by different contractors, in various quantities of from five to ten miles in extent, and amounts from $10,000 to $60,000. The following are the average rates of prices paid for labor and material.

LABOR.

Excavation, $12\frac{1}{2}$ cents per cubic yard.
Embankment, $12\frac{1}{2}$ do. do.
Rock blasting, 60 do. do.
Culvert masonry, $1 80 per perch, containing 25 cubic feet.
Bridge masonry, $3 per perch, containing 25 cubic feet.
Lattice bridging, $20 per linear foot.
King post bridging, $9 do.
Laying iron rails, $37\frac{1}{2}$ cents per yard.

MATERIAL.

Hemlock sills, $12 per thousand feet.

Locust ties, 67 to 80 cents each.

Yellow pine string pieces, 6 inches by 6 inches, from $18 to $28 per thousand feet.

Stone for bridges, culverts, &c., 70 cents to $2 50 per perch.

Railroad bars, $70 per ton—costs, &c. included

Cast iron chairs, 4½ cents per lb.

Spikes, 9 cents per lb

Land damages, $250 per acre.

Fencing per pannel, $1 to $1 25.

These are the general charges for graduation and materials, collected and averaged from the contracts on file at the Company's office.

No. XIV.—Referred to on p 309.

NOTICE OF THE LAWS RELATIVE TO BANKS IN THE STATE OF NEW YORK.

When Mr. Van Buren was governor of the state of New York, a gentle-man by the name of Forman submitted to his consideration a plan for im-proving the paper currency of this state, which Mr. V. B. slightly recom-mending, placed before the legislature of the state. From this plan sprung a law, passed April 2, 1829, entitled ' an act to create a fund for the benefit of the creditors of certain monied corporations, and for other purposes," commonly called " The Safety Fund Law."

By this law it was provided that every corporation having banking powers, thereafter to be created, or whose charter shall be renewed, should, on or before the 1st of January in every year, pay to the treasurer of this state a sum equal to half of one per cent. of the capital stock of the corpo-ration paid in

This payment is directed to be continued until each bank shall have paid into the treasury three per cent. upon its capital, which is to remain a per-petual fund called " The Bank Fund," and to be appropriated to the pay-ment of such portion of the debts, exclusive of capital stock of any of the said corporations which shall become insolvent, as shall remain unpaid, after applying the property of the insolvent corporation to that purpose.

This fund is invested by the comptroller as a separate fund, and belongs to the banks contributing to it, in proportion to their contributions. The *income* from this fund, after paying the salaries of the bank commissioners, and some other expenses, is paid over to the banks in proportion to their contributions

If this fund gets below three per cent. of the bank capital, as before men-tioned, the banks must contribute and make it up.

Upon the happening of a bank's insolvency, the Court of Chancery directs a receiver to take charge of its effects, and to divide the property of the bank among its creditors; and the receiver is put in funds by the comp-troller out of the " bank fund" to pay off the residue of the debts. If that fund is insufficient, the receiver awaits its being filled up by future contri-butions from " the Safety-Fund Banks."

This law also provides for the appointment of three " bank commission-ers of the state of New York," whose duty it is to visit every four months all the banks subject to this safety fund law, and thoroughly to inspect their affairs—to examine their books, debts, credits, amount of specie on hand, and to ascertain their means of fulfilling their engagements. They may examine any of the officers of the banks, or any other person on oath. And if from their examination, or in any way, it appears that any bank is insolvent, or has violated its charter in any respect, the commissioners immediately apply to the Court of Chancery for an injunction against the bank and its officers, and its affairs are wound up

These commissioners report annually to the legislature. A copy of one of their reports (1837) accompanies this statement.

Under this system it seems between 90 and 100 banks have been created, or had their charters extended within this state There is now a bank in almost every county, and some counties have several

These are called "Safety Fund Banks." They are corporations, and I give a brief summary of the provisions of their charters.

Each bank is created by a legislative act obtained on petition. The act defines the powers of the corporation, limits its existence to some twenty-five or thirty years, locates it, prescribes the amount of its capital stock, subjects it to the safety fund law bank commissioners' investigation, and prescribes the manner in which its capital stock shall be subscribed for, distributed and paid in The stock is apportioned among subscribers for it by commissioners appointed by the act of incorporation. The subscribers pay in the amount of their subscription in specie, or *current bank bills*, and the latter are always employed in payment. These bills are the issues of other safety fund banks, and thus the paper of one bank is the basis of another's issues

These banks, when first incorporated, were authorised to circulate in their own bills twice and a half the amount of their capital actually paid in, but have been recently limited to one and a half that amount. This restriction, however, has been created since the suspension of specie payments in 1837

The explosion just referred to grew out of the inflation of the paper currency by the safety fund banks of this state, and sister institutions of other states.

A country bank in this state having a capital of $200,000 would not have in its vaults in specie over $20,000 or 10 per cent. of the capital, which might not amount to 5 per cent of their circulation.

After the explosion of 1837, came the new system of banking, by an act passed April 18, 1838, entitled "An act to authorise the business of banking "

Under this act institutions called "free banks" have been extensively organised.

I enclose a slip from a newspaper, containing some sound comments upon this new system of banking, from a gentleman of high intelligence in general, and of great experience as a banker *

This " general banking law," as it is called, authorizes the comptroller of this state to have bills for circulation engraved in blank, in the similitude of bank notes of different denominations, which are countersigned, registered, and numbered in his office

These bills can be procured by any person, or association of persons, who will organise as bankers under the law, file their statement and certificate, and pay over to the comptroller stock of the United States, or any of

* The slip referred to, has been printed in the text, p. 309, title " Scarcity of Money."

the States of the Union, which shall be equal to stock of this state producing 5 per cent. per annum, at such rate as he shall approve, not exceeding its par value, or by delivering to him bonds and mortgages upon real estate, bearing at least six per cent. interest.

The mortgages transferred must be upon improved, productive, and unencumbered lands within this State, worth, independent of any buildings thereon, at least double the amount for which they shall be mortgaged.— The person or association assigning the bonds and mortgages, or paying in State stocks to the comptroller, may receive the interest to accrue thereon, unless default shall be made in paying the bills or notes of the banking concern, or unless, in the opinion of the comptroller, the mortgages, stocks, &c so pledged are insufficient to pay the bills or notes.

The banking company, upon thus securing the comptroller, procure the bills, fill them up, and put them in circulation as money.

For fuller details on this subject, see pp. 307–8–9.

No. XV.—Referred to on p 345.

RELIGIOUS DENOMINATIONS IN THE UNITED STATES.

Denominations	Churches or Congregations	Ministers	Members or Communicants	Population
Baptists	6319	4239	452,000	
" Freewill	753	612	33,876	4,300,000
" Seventh Day	42	46	4,503	
" Six-Principle	16	10	2 117	
Catholics	418	478		800,000
Christians	1000	800	150,000	300,000
Congregationalists	1300	1150	160,000	1,400 000
Disciples of Christ (Campbellites)	..	.		
Dutch Reformed	197	192	22,515	450,000
Episcopalians	950	849	..	600,000
Friends	500		..	100,000
German Reformed	600	180	30,000	.
Jews	..	..		15,000
Lutherans	750	267	62,266	540,000
Mennonites	200	.	30,000	..
Methodists	..	3106	606,549	3,000,000
" Protestant		400	50,000	
Moravians or United Brethren	24	33	5,745	12,008
Mormonites	.	.	12,000	12,000
New Jerusalem Church	27	33	.	5,000
Presbyterians	2807	2225	274,084	
" Cumberland	500	450	50,000	
" Associate	183	87	16,000	2,175,000
" Reformed	40	20	3,000	
" Associate Reformed	214	116	12,000	
Shakers	15	45	6,000	6,000
Tunkers	40	40	3,000	30,000
Unitarians	200	174	.	180 000
Universalists	653	317	..	600,000

" The above statements of the number of churches, ministers, and memveral denominations, have been derived chiefly from recent official documents published by the different denominations; but the last column contains rather a vague estimate which has appeared in various publications of the total number of people who are attached to, or show a preference for, the several different religious persuasions."—*American Almanac*, 1841, p. 157.

THE END.

CPSIA information can be obtained
at www.ICGtesting.com
Printed in the USA
BVHW012150060122
625648BV00002B/48